WILD
AMERICA

When Daniel Boone goes by at night

the phantom deer arise

and all lost, wild America

Is burning in their eyes.

STEPHEN VINCENT BENÉT: "Daniel Boone"

WILD AMERICA

The record of a 30,000-mile journey around the
continent by a distinguished naturalist
and his British colleague

by

ROGER TORY PETERSON

and

JAMES FISHER

Illustrated by
ROGER TORY PETERSON

Foreword by
PATRICK O'BRIAN

A Mariner Book
HOUGHTON MIFFLIN COMPANY
Boston   New York

For Guy Emerson

For information about permission to reproduce selections from this book, write to
Permissions, Houghton Mifflin Company, 215 Park Avenue South,
New York, New York 10003.

For information about this and other Houghton Mifflin trade and reference books and multimedia products,
visit The Bookstore at Houghton Mifflin on the World Wide Web at
http://www.hmco.com/trade/.

CIP data is available.
ISBN 0-395-86497-6

Grateful acknowledgment is made for permission to quote from Selected Works of
Stephen Vincent Benét published by Rinehart & Company, copyright 1933, by
Rosemary Carr Benét, and from Essays of a Biologist by Julian Huxley,
published by Alfred A. Knopf, Inc.

Printed in the United States of America
QUM 10 9 8 7 6 5 4 3 2 1

Contents

Foreword

ONE OF THE FEW encouraging things about the present age is the widespread appreciation of birds in so many of their aspects: perfection of flight; beauty of form and plumage very often, and sometimes of song; their infinite variety; their astonishing feats of migration. And there is the pleasure of naming, of distinguishing, and of sharing one's delight.

This delight is raised to a very high degree when a man who loves birds goes abroad and there meets someone of a like mind who can show him new warblers, thrushes, finches, birds of prey. I have had this pleasure in some European countries—bearded and griffon vultures in Spain; the black woodpecker, spoonbills, great white egrets, and the goosander in Austria; flamingos, bitterns great and small, rollers, and bee-eaters in France—but this was nothing to my astonishment in the United States, where almost everything except for the starlings might have stepped from the pages of accidentals.

By extraordinary good luck, my editor and his wife were people who could find their way through the maze of American warblers without a moment's hesitation. Two of our friends were in New York at the time, friends who had climbed the Caucasus to see the snow cock of those parts and who had done their best to find the African peacock. They took me to Jamaica Bay — this was in November — and there I saw my first snow geese, coming in from the far north. The bay also held black duck, hooded mergansers, a sharp-shinned hawk, all equally new, all heartily welcome; but none of them lives so vividly in my memory as those splendid geese. Then some days later we motored up to Plum Island, where I hoped to fulfill one of the ambitions of my life by gazing at a great northern diver. These birds are not unknown in Europe, though none of my friends had ever seen one, but in North America they are so usual that they have no grander name than the common loon. I had great hopes, the more so as the amiable guides, who took us on in their truck, assured us that they had seen a couple that morning, not two hundred yards from the shore. But even as they spoke a vile mist began falling from the sky, and by the time we reached the strand nothing whatsoever could be made out. Horned larks on the way back, snow buntings and even a tree sparrow were little consolation, though my editor did say that there was always the next time, and he was rash enough to promise me a bald eagle.

The next time, the next visit to the States, did indeed produce eagles — two very young ones, black from head to foot, coming back to look at their nest, which had been blown to pieces the night before. It also produced Carolina wrens (we were near Charleston), pelicans, darters, and, to my extreme satisfaction, several anhingas, to say nothing of a green-backed heron steadily beating a large tadpole to death while an alligator glided silently toward a duck, the very picture of rapacious malignance.

Then up and away, across the whole expanse of the enormous country: prairie, wilderness, desert, mountain piled upon mountain — wild America indeed, but from a height of thirty or forty thousand feet rather than by foot or covered wagon. What indomitable fortitude they had, those men and women who first reached the Pacific shore; and what incredible changes the last few generations have seen. Yet there are still some things that are now as they were when the first settlers arrived. Not far north of San Francisco seals still haul out, covered with mud, and bask, yawning from time to time; the magnificent redwoods still reach halfway to heaven; and a dear young woman with a spotting telescope showed me a Bonaparte's gull standing calmly on a sandbank, as his forebears had stood before men ever reached the continent.

It was, I may add, a bird I had sought in vain the length and breadth of the Mediterranean. But what were my few miles and weeks (most of the time devoted to lectures, interviews, and book signings) compared with the heroic three thousand miles and hundred days of the two internationally recognized experts here before you, each stage of their enormous journey guided by local ornithologists? What indeed. It would not be worth mentioning but for the fact that there was one point in common: James Fisher too came to the States for the first time, and he too was received and shown the birds by an immensely knowledgeable American. To be sure, their journey was much more considerable in time and distance, their science much greater; yet since delight is unquantifiable, I like to think that mine was at least comparable to theirs.

But thirty thousand miles is a most prodigious journey: It took them from the northeastern extremity of the States right down by way of Florida and its charming swamps to Mexico and even beyond, into the fantastic wealth of birds south of the border (135 species in five days, sixty of them new even to Peterson). They continued to the Grand Canyon and on to the Pacific, and so to the ultimate northwest, continuing by air to the Pribilof Islands. They saw wild America, the true wild America and its multitudinous birds; they saw it the hard way, often by foot, and their living pages make it the best vicarious traveling imaginable, above all if you enjoy the company of men who possess great knowledge without pedantry, a deep love of their subject, and a most uncommon power of conveying both.

PATRICK O'BRIAN

Acknowledgments

BEFORE AND DURING our travels around the perimeter of Wild America we were helped, directly or indirectly, by a host of people. We are particularly indebted to Guy Emerson for his kindness and stimulus; he would have gone with us had his time allowed. For thirteen years he had held the record for the greatest number of birds seen by an observer in one year north of the Mexican border. Wistfully he watched us break this record. Senator Thomas Desmond was also greatly interested in our venture and gave us much encouragement, for he wants to see the completion of our Field Guide to the Sea Birds of the World.

To our wives, Angus Fisher and Barbara Peterson, we are deeply in debt; they not only spent long weeks getting us ready for an expedition they could not join, but also had the task of typing at least half a million words before the manuscript was boiled down to a book.

We wish to thank the following noncommercial organizations,

institutions, and government services for making available to us their personnel, boats, and other facilities during parts of our journey: the National Audubon Society, the National Park Service, the U.S. Coast Guard, the U.S. Fish and Wildlife Service, the Institute of Marine Science (Aransas Pass, Texas), the Scripps Institute of Oceanography, and the State of Louisiana Department of Wildlife and Fisheries.

For helping plan our trip, acting as our guides, checking over the manuscript, or for other assistance we express our gratitude to the following (many of whom appear in the pages of this book): Paul Adams, Robert Porter Allen, John H. Baker, Glidden Baldwin, Dan Beard, Jr., Belle Benchley, Mr. and Mrs. Stephen Briggs, Charles Brookfield, Susan and Paul Brooks, C. D. Brown, Harold Bryant, Margaret and Eddie Chalif, Glen Chandler, Edward Châtelaine, Roland Clement, Boughton Cobb, William Collins, Carlotta and John Connelly, Annette and William Cottrell, Betty and Chester Coulter, Mrs. A. G. Davenport, Irby Davis, Albert Day, John De Weese, Mr. and Mrs. William Drury, Sr., William Drury, Jr., Philip DuMont, Garrett Eddy, Joseph Ewan, W. J. Fitzpatrick, Luther Goldman, Mary Van Grimes, Sam Grimes, Ludlow Griscom, Gordon Gunter, Connie Hagar, Syd Heckler, Harry Higman, James Hoffmann, Ruth Hopson, Thomas Horne, Lorna and Carl Hubbs, M. L. Kelso, Karl Kenyon, Peter Koch, Eugene Kridler, Oliver La Farge, Roland F. Lee, Sigrid Lee, George Lowery, Sr., George Lowery, Jr., C. Russell Mason, Bona Mae and Donald McHenry, Mrs. Cosey McSparron, Mr. and Mrs. Jack Merritt, Charles Mohr, Joseph Moore, Stanley Mulaik, Grace and Robert Cushman Murphy, Robert Newman, Edward O'Neill, Wilford Olsen, Clarence Olson, Henry Fairfield Osborne, Jack Paniyak, Charlie Peterson, Matt Peterson, Sydney Peyton, Bob Reeve, Harry Schafer, Jr., Nick Schexnayder, Alexander Sprunt, Jr., Herbert Stoddard, Arthur Stupka, Ben Thompson, Seton H. Thompson, Jr., J. Thorpe, Raleigh Trevelyan, Leslie Tuck, Lewis Wayne Walker, Harry Walters, Frank Watson, Ford Wilke, and Abbie Lou and Laidlaw Williams.

In the editing and production of the American edition of this book our debt is great to Paul Brooks, Lovell Thompson, Austin Olney, Benjamin Tilghman, Morton Baker, Helen Phillips, and the many other members of the Houghton Mifflin staff who so skillfully handled the manuscript and illustrations.

R.T.P. and J.F.

WILD
AMERICA

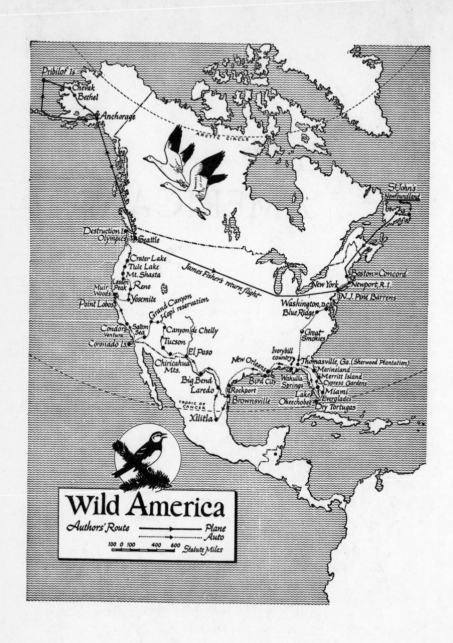

Pribilof Is.
Chevak
Bethel
Anchorage

ARCTIC CIRCLE

St.John's
Newfoundland

Destruction I.
Olympics Seattle

Crater Lake
Tule Lake
Mt. Shasta
Lassen
Peak Reno
Muir
Woods Yosemite
Point Lobos

James Fisher's return flight

Boston Concord
New York
Newport, R.I.
N.J. Pine Barrens

Grand Canyon
Hopi reservation

Condors
Ventura
Coronado Is.

Salton
Sea
Canyon de Chelly
Tucson

El Paso

Chiricahua
Mts.

Big Bend
Laredo
Rockport
Brownsville

TROPIC OF
CANCER

Xilitla

New Orleans
Bird City
Wakulla
Springs
Lake
Okeechobee

Washington, D.C.
Blue Ridge

Great
Smokies

Ivorybill
country

Thomasville, Ga. (Sherwood Plantation)
Marineland
Merritt Island
Cypress Gardens
Miami
Everglades
Dry Tortugas

Wild America

Authors' Route ————————→ Plane
                  ....→ Auto
    100 0 100   400   600 *Statute Miles*

Prologue

THAT AUTUMN DAY, as I walked across St. James's Park, I was so preoccupied that the moorhens, blackbirds, and wood pigeons went almost unnoticed. My pace quickened; a plan was forming. When James Fisher came to London the following morning I would tell him of it.

I had come to love England during my prolonged stay—the more because the average Briton, even if he lives in the heart of London, has a passionate curiosity about the outdoors and wild things. The programs of the BBC and the space given by the press reflect this trait. I had acquired friends who seemed as completely devoted to the study of the natural world—the real world—as I am. One of these obsessives was James Fisher.

Our first meeting was in the summer of 1950 on the Island of Gotland in the Baltic Sea. We were hastily introduced to each other in a busload of ornithologists which was about to leave from the downtown square of the ancient Hanseatic town of Visby. Our destination was Stora Karlsö, the oldest Swedish seabird sanctuary.

That was the first of many field trips which we were to make together in Europe, to places as wild and remote as Swedish Lapland, Narvik Fjord in Norway, the highlands and islands of Scotland, the Swiss Alps, and even that bird paradise on the Mediterranean, the Camargue. There were also, of course, many excursions in England on James Fisher's home territory. James, a leading authority on Gilbert White, drove us one Sunday to Selborne, where we climbed the zigzag trail into the historic old beech hanger. It was there that White discovered that the wood warbler, willow warbler, and chiff-chaff were really three different birds, even though they looked so very much alike. On an April day, when the yellow wagtails were arriving, we visited Peter Scott's goose grounds on the Severn. There the great waterfowl artist proudly showed us the newborn Hawaiian geese and the trumpeter swans of Her Majesty the Queen. The following July we even attempted to reach fabulous St. Kilda, the sea island where a million puffins breed, but the sloop chartered for the voyage failed us midway across the Hebridean sea. During a gale the engine sputtered out, forcing us to hoist sail and maneuver back to the lee shore of a coastal loch.

So much had I seen of wild Europe, and especially of wild Britain in the company of my colleague, and so much had I learned through his tutelage about the geology, the green mantle of plants, the birds and other animals, and particularly the interwoven history of human occupation, that I had a growing desire to reciprocate, to show him my own continent. As author of the monograph on *The Fulmar* and co-author (with Ronald Lockley) of the volume on *Sea-Birds* in the New Naturalist Series, James Fisher was already well informed about the seabird colonies on the North American side of the Atlantic (most pelagic species are common to both sides). But a large percentage of the other wild creatures would be new to him.

"If you come to America," I suggested, "I will meet you in New-foundland and conduct you around the continent. We will go as far as the Yukon Delta and the Pribilofs—by way of Mexico—and you will see a more complete cross section of wild America than any other Englishman, and all but a few North Americans, have ever seen."

Most visitors to America see only the cities. They are shown

New York with its skyscrapers, Detroit with its acres and acres of cars in the parking lots outside the General Motors plant—these and other evidences of modern materialism. Few are aware of another side of the continent as expressed in National Parks, National Nature Monuments, Fish and Wildlife Refuges, Audubon Sanctuaries, and other endeavors that fall under the category of "nature conservancy."

My offer, I must confess, was not entirely devoid of self-interest. All of us enjoy showing things to others. I had seen all forty-eight states; mine were the accustomed eyes—James Fisher's would be fresh eyes. I would see America again through his eyes.

He became the willing victim of my plan. The following April (1953) he boarded one of the big silver air transports operated by BOAC and his odyssey began. During the fourteen weeks—exactly 100 days—when he was away from home, he covered 30,000 miles and on his return could truly say he had seen "Wild America." So could I.

This book, a record of our journey, is woven together from our combined notes. After introducing each chapter, establishing the continuity and background, I usually turn the narrative over to James Fisher, who quotes directly from portions of his journal under the dateline.

ROGER TORY PETERSON

1

Atlantic Gateway

A PLANE droned in the predawn sky. James Fisher would be on
North American soil in a matter of minutes. My own plane had
arrived several hours earlier at this "halfway house of the Atlantic"
as Gander is sometimes called by passengers from New York. To
many transatlantic sky travelers, Newfoundland, Canada's newest
province, means simply a cup of coffee on the run while the big
plane refuels before taking off across the water.

Stray wisps of fog were beginning to blow in; a plane should have
no trouble landing, however. From overhead came the incisive lisps
of unseen fox sparrows, the first migrants of the season. These large
rusty-tailed sparrows had made their nocturnal way across the Gulf
of St. Lawrence and the width of Newfoundland, a distance of at
least 300 miles, to this spot, their natal home, without benefit of
complicated instrument panels. They seemed to be attracted by the
airport lights. But where was the plane? Where had it gone? The

guard at the gate informed me that the aircraft from London had decided not to chance it. It might not have been able to take off again in another twenty minutes; the fog was closing in fast. So the plane had continued on to the fog-free airport at Stephenville on the west coast of the island, nearly 300 miles distant.

What a bore! Few places on earth can be as dreary as Gander on a foggy day. The airfield, an appalling area of runways, sprawls over a bleak featureless landscape. Nothing to see; nothing to do except sit about in the terminal and watch the other earthbound travelers. Nevertheless, this barn of a building is truly one of the crossroads of the world. Nearly as many people as live in all Newfoundland stop briefly each year at this one spot in the province. Looking about me I was struck with the human diversity: a group of young Frenchmen; a crew of Hindustani seamen in turbans (what they were doing at a Newfoundland air terminal is anyone's guess); a Slavic-looking woman in a shawl; a New York debutante; and a group of middle-aged Oklahomans with Stetsons and loud neckties. This was the gateway to and from the continent.

Newfoundland was the logical place, I reflected, to introduce James to North America. This island province with its moors and sea cliffs strongly suggests parts of Scotland and Ireland. So do the people—and the birds. More than half—nearly three-fifths—of the birds of Newfoundland are found on both sides of the Atlantic. For example, nearly every species of hawk and owl is also found in northern Europe, and the seabirds are almost identical. The impact would be lessened by starting in Newfoundland. From here we would proceed to New England, where many Britons seem to find a comforting reflection of the mother country. Later, after six weeks of gradual acclimatization I would introduce James to the vivid contrasts of Texas and Mexico.

The following afternoon an eastbound Dakota was due from Stephenville. James would certainly be on it. But the fog was as thick as ever. Periodically, when the mist turned into fine cold rain, visibility would improve. By noon the runways were clear but the ceiling was very low. The hours dragged on. The attendant at the desk told me to be patient. I waited outside; when the plane finally did arrive I could hear the roar of its motor as it rushed over the field but could not see it in the driving mist. The drone of the engines became fainter, then increased in volume as the aircraft made a wide swing and returned for another try. The low clouds parted overhead and for a brief instant I glimpsed the silver skyship before it was again swallowed up in the void. The motor died away in the west; the pilot had wisely decided not to try to slip under the low overcast.

When I spoke to James over the phone at Stephenville his first words were: "This is bloody awful." I reminded him of our difficulties in Scotland the year before when we were immobilized by weather for a week. Newfoundland enjoys west coast Scottish weather—North Atlantic weather. We had allowed extra days for just such an emergency. But I had promised to give a lecture in St. John's on the 13th; that date was inflexible. It would be risky to wait for better flying weather, so I told James I would take the train—the interminably slow narrow gauge train—which makes the journey to St. John's twice weekly. He was to get there when he could.

When I arrived late the next afternoon James was there ahead of me, on the first flight that had been able to land at Torbay Airport at St. John's for nearly three weeks.

I fired a barrage of questions: "Have you had a chance to look around?" I asked. "What was your first North American bird?" James had already started his journal.

April 11

The last I saw of our Kingdom out of the airplane window yesterday was the Firth of Clyde and that great knob of granite in the middle of it, Ailsa Craig, with its white mist of gannets wheeling around their rocky nesting places in the evening light.

My first sight of the New World, at daybreak this morning, was a brown-and-spruce landscape, a mosaic of brown bog, silver water, little rivers, great dark green stretches of spruce forest with brown, irregular, open patches between. Through parted clouds, more shining water, and snow patches, and an interminability of spruces, like Sweden. Then came a calm coast. It seemed almost beachless and tideless; peninsulas, lagoons, at last a little beach. And below, gleaming white with black wing-ends, flew my first New World bird.

This is where you came in, I said to myself, for my last bird in Scotland had been the gannet, and here it was, my first in Newfoundland. With it were familiar herring gulls—yes, and greater black-backs.

Transatlantic travel is now reduced to a quick succession of unromantic waiting rooms, with polite female voices echoing through loud-speakers, all of which (the loud-speakers, I mean) are permanently off adjustment. The Atlantic passage itself is a period of coffee, shiny magazines, coffee, conversation with neighbors, coffee, meals in elaborate cardboard boxes, coffee, sleep, and coffee.

My ticket was marked Gander; but here we were off Newfoundland's southwest coast circling round a lot of military-looking aircraft parked on a great slab of concrete by the sea. When we got out of the Constellation we found we were in a U.S. air base, Stephenville. We were shepherded quickly indoors to a vast waiting room heated to some phenomenal temperature, full of refrigerated slot machines packed with Coca-Cola; and so unusual is it for anyone to desire to go specifically to Gander, that I had some difficulty in preventing my aircraft from taking me on to Boston.

There was nothing else to do but work. I had the galley proofs of *Sea-Birds* with me, a hangover from my office (I had cleared my desk into my briefcase), so into these I inserted my personal New World gannet record, and spent an hour or two with them. Nobody was allowed out of the passenger hall; and the only alternative to bird watching was word botching.

Stephenville is a real boom town; everything is brash and new. That evening, after an abortive attempt to reach Gander on a Trans-Canada Dakota, I was let out of the airport to an hotel which the airway company had found for me; the taxi rolled through yards of concrete buildings and dusty roads; the houses had false fronts, and the cars mouth-organ faces. Every house and fence round town—in the suburbs—was of wood, with wooden duckboards across the mud. I took an evening walk away from the town, where spruce woods ran down to a beach of glacier-carried worn round stones the size of ostrich eggs, sedimentary, conglomerate, perhaps granite—where had they come from?

Almost at once I thought I heard a blackbird and went to look for it. Then there was the usual chuckle and the typical excited alarm note; but a rather disappointing song, like a halfhearted song thrush, told me what I really knew, that this was not a blackbird but the famous American robin. It was very big, with a chestnut breast, slate back, and white round its eyes. That April everybody was still singing the song about the "poor little robin, walking, walking to Missouri," but there wasn't anything poor or miserable about this bouncing, exhibitionistic, assertive, agreeable, arresting thrush. It was twice the size of our little robin redbreast; as big as a fieldfare, it seemed, yet awfully like our English blackbird in many of its voices. It did not flick its tail, though. My first New World songbird was thus, most appropriately, a robin.

April 12

The weather cleared early and our Dakota took off. Most of the leg to Gander was cloudless, and by the bank of a lake in the glaciated landscape I saw a cow moose (in northern Europe it would be called an elk). This was paper country; Grand Falls with the Bowater mills (which makes paper for the London *Times*) passed below us. The interior was intensively lumbered. Many lakes had a boom of end-to-end logs across a corner, which impounded a flock of floating logs awaiting transportation. These gave a lived-in impression to the continuous tree-scape. Some parts were clear-felled; other great stretches, greener and fresher than their surroundings, showed where self-sown regrowth had reclaimed old cleared areas. The whole landscape of dark old spruce, greener new spruce, and open brown barrens still had patches of snow. The higher ponds were still frozen, the middle ones had unmelted ice across one end; and the lower ones, blue and wind ruffled, were as empty-looking as holes in the ground.

Like many another airfield in northern North America, Gander shows all the contrast between the modern and the primeval. The international airport communicates with the towns along the coast only by the narrow gauge railway and by air, though a highway linking east and west Newfoundland will soon pass through it. Round the airport, spruce forest rolls as far as a high-flying observer can see, much of it virgin, for it has not yet been worth while to thrust into *every* valley for lumber. Between the stretches of forest are irregular open patches of red sphagnum bog and countless lakes and ponds. The landscape more closely resembles that of Sweden than any other part of Europe I have seen. Everywhere is evidence of the complete glaciation of the country in the Ice Age—a rubbed and polished landscape.

We were only ten minutes at Gander before flying on, in the first passenger aircraft bound for St. John's in three weeks. As we flew close to crazily dissected and indented coastline in the worsening weather, I caught sight of a few grounded icebergs. April was early for these to have arrived on the Newfoundland coast. One or two were really big and castellated. Against the dull sky one of them caught a lonely ray of sunlight and for an instant twinkled blue-white.

So far the impact of the New World had been unexpected—but unexpected in the unexpected way. I found myself all along seeking the differences and finding the similarities. What a wonderful queer lonely empty but somehow *familiar* place Newfoundland was from the air.

There was quite a crowd to meet the aircraft at Torbay, St. John's airport, but no Roger; however, very soon a charming smile introduced itself as Leslie Tuck, the Dominion Wildlife Officer. Leslie, a Newfoundlander born and bred, is the first to occupy this post, created after the recent federation of Newfoundland in Canada. The most able field naturalist in the province, Leslie had me birding in five minutes. Outside the airport he translated a somewhat plaintive sound (of willow-warbler tone but not pattern) to me as the voice of the dominant passerine of Newfoundland's scrub and spruce, the newly arrived fox sparrow, a streaked bird with a bright rusty tail. Soon we saw a green woodpecker, except that it was brown with a white rump instead of the bright green of ours; it was the flicker, one of the many replacement species I was to see on this side of the Atlantic. Quickly in the same little wood we picked up the tiny golden-crowned kinglet, so like the Old World goldcrest, indeed somewhere between our goldcrest and firecrest.

On our way to town in Leslie's Chevrolet we found, among the shanty outskirts, horned larks chasing each other on a muddy lot. The horned lark, the only true lark native to North America (where there are many races), is a handsome bird, with yellow and black on its head. In western Europe, where it is perhaps rarer than anywhere else in the temperate Northern Hemisphere, we call it the shore lark. In England it is a regular visitor only on the east coast.

When we got to the hotel, we found that Roger had not yet arrived. He came later, on the afternoon overflow train.

April 13

In a clearing in the spruce forest, where a little snow still lay against fallen logs, we met the black-capped and brown-capped chickadees. The former, black-bibbed as well as black-capped, looks very much like the willow tit; in fact it is supposed to be a race of the same species. Roger doubts this and so do I, because it has a piping note which sounds nothing like our own bird. It was the brown-capped chickadee which sounded rather like our willow tit.

Chickadee

Where there are little bands of tits (pardon me—chickadees) there are usually woodpeckers. We soon saw a hairy woodpecker, the counterpart to our great spotted woodpecker. Overhead flew siskins, a much duller species than our siskin of the Scottish woods.

Before Roger's lecture in the evening Leslie took us to tea with the Lieutenant-Governor of the Province of Newfoundland, Sir Leonard Outerbridge, an experienced naturalist and sportsman keenly interested in the conservation of Newfoundland's wildlife resources. We discussed Newfoundland's "partridge" and its preservation as the country's only game bird (apart from its high-ground cousin, the rock ptarmigan). The "partridge" is not, of course, a partridge, though no Newfoundlander calls it anything else; it is the willow grouse, or willow ptarmigan, *Lagopus lagopus,* which is found at scrub-line all round northern Europe, Asia, and North America, except in Britain, where it is replaced by the red grouse (simply, a race of the willow grouse which does not have white wings or go white in winter). In Newfoundland the willow grouse have been decreasing on the Avalon Peninsula—a decrease quite independent of the normal cyclic fluctuations. Newfoundland hunters have to state their last year's bag when they buy their new licenses. Do those who have killed many declare them all? Do those who have killed none boast of some? How is the new Wildlife Service to obtain dependable information? Although there is now a lively co-operation between the Dominion (federal) wildlife office and the provincial game wardens, it will be some time before game management,* as a science with its system of food crops and refuges, comes to Newfoundland.

* Newfoundland has had game laws since 1845, and they are now excellent.

Owing to its isolation since emergence from the last Ice Age, Newfoundland has what must be described as an impoverished fauna. Only 227 of the 790 bird species known in North America have been recorded in Newfoundland, and only 121 have been found nesting there. Newfoundland lacks mammals too. The moose has been very successfully introduced from the Canadian mainland (six or seven animals, about fifty years ago) and now numbers at least 30,000. Many would recommend that the ruffed grouse and the spruce grouse be also introduced. These fine game birds inhabit in continental Canada the same spruce and birch wood zones that dominate Newfoundland, and are not in that province simply because they never crossed the barrier of water after the Ice Age; they never "found" Newfoundland. They would certainly do well, far better than the black game (from Britain), ring-neck and golden pheasants (from the Orient), and bob-white quail (from the U.S.), which have all been tried, unsuccessfully.

Roger's evening lecture packed the hall; it was a great success. Mrs. Gosling, the energetic president of the recently formed Natural History Society, made a charming speech of introduction, and later, on behalf of the Society, presented Roger with a caribou head carved from a walrus tusk by one of the Grenfell Eskimos. They seemed to regard the occasion as a sort of home-coming for Roger, because it was he who painted the color plates for *The Birds of Newfoundland*. The chief game warden, Harry Walters, brought in some of the originals and put them on display. Wherever one goes, from one remote end to another of our two great Unions, this interest in natural history is growing, developing, hungrily seeking inspiration. Our hosts in St. John's were as enthusiastic as they were kind.

April 14

This morning, in Leslie Tuck's car, we began our long trek to St. Bride's on the Avalon Peninsula. From there we shall go tomorrow to the great gannet colony at Cape St. Mary.

In the mosaic of woodland and ponds we picked up some new members of the spruce-bird community, the red crossbill, white-winged crossbill, and pine grosbeak. All these are also Old World birds. But the fluffy gray Canada jay was not; and instead of the mallard, the pools in the forest were occupied by the peculiarly New World black duck, or "black mallard." Newfoundland is one of the few parts of the northern world from which the mallard is absent.

At one place in the woods Roger, through a drizzle of rain, heard the brown creeper, another conspecies, only racially different from the tree creeper I had seen pottering around my English garden the day before I left. Over the trees were ravens—they too were the same species as those of Europe; but the American crows were different.

By the sea, almost all the birds were species I knew well on British shores: red-breasted merganser, eider, herring gull, great black-back, great northern diver (loon), black guillemot, and purple sandpiper.

Perhaps the most vivid impression of the whole long day in the spruce woods was a reminiscence of home, a voice as familiar to me in my own English garden as on the cliffs of St. Kilda and the remote Shetland Islands. I heard this voice in many places along the roadside wood edge. I heard it in the rain, and in the sun. Memory is a bad servant when it is charged with finding subtle differences in bird song; but I thought that the wren, which in North America they call the winter wren, sang more clearly and musically in Newfoundland, though perhaps not with so much punch as the explosive little bird of Britain.

JAMES, as the opening pages of his journal reveal, was "seeking the differences and finding the similarities"—particularly in the birds. I was rather amused because at home he had always seemed scornful of mere bird listing—or "tally hunting," as he called it. That was boys' play, he said; he was interested in the more scientific aspects of bird watching—such things as population dynamics, geographic distribution and ecology. But, secretly, the truth of it is that he had run out of "new" birds in England. Here he was, plunged into a new avifauna, experiencing something that took him back twenty years or more, to the period when he was getting "life" birds on almost every field trip. I noticed that he was even more diligent than I in keeping his score up to date on the little white check-lists that I had furnished. Every time he got a new bird he shouted "Tally ho." And, for the first week, every time we saw another robin he burst forth with the opening bars of "poor little robin."

Actually, out of the 46 species which we listed during our week's stay in Newfoundland, only 17, a little over a third, were new to him. But many of his old friends went by new names on this side of the Atlantic. Common guillemots were common murres, divers were loons, tits were chickadees, two-barred crossbills were white-winged crossbills, tree creepers were brown creepers, wrens were winter wrens, long-tailed ducks were old-squaws, goosanders were mergansers, shore larks were horned larks, willow grouse were willow ptarmigan—and so on. Just to be polite—and knowledgeable—I called out the birds by their British names while James used the American names. It was most confusing at times; but we kept this up for a hundred days.

It occurred to me that we might as well do things up brown and try for a record. Guy Emerson, a New York banker who always arranged his business trips so that he would catch the spring migration of warblers in Texas, the shorebirds in California, and the ducks in Utah, had, in 1939, run up a grand total of 497 species (no subspecies included). For thirteen years this record stood unchallenged as the greatest number of species seen by an observer in a single year in North America, north of the Mexican border. Although our expedition around the perimeter of the continent was not to be solely a bird trip (we were interested in everything that walked, hopped, swam, or flew, and the plants and rocks too), nevertheless, we had the ideal chance to top Emerson's score.

Although Newfoundland was only a modest start we would, in the next few weeks, be breasting the full tide of the advancing stream of spring migration.

Winter Wren

2

Sea Cliffs of Cape St. Mary

*W*E ARRIVED at St. Bride's as it was getting dark. Kerosene lamps were being lit in the homes that outlined the cove, and a smell of fish hung about the wharves.

The day had been dank and cheerless, drizzling half the time. Although Newfoundland is noted for its fog and rain, this section of the Avalon Peninsula, jutting into the sea, gets far more than its share. I thought of the dogwood and redbud that was now in bloom around my home in Maryland. Here the vernal calendar had been put back a month—at least. Wet and shivering, we found the house we were looking for on the far side of the little town. Entering the wooden gate we were greeted by Mr. and Mrs. Thomas Conway, whose hospitality soon made us forget the bad weather.

The reason for our long trek over narrow roads through the spruce forest to the southern end of the Avalon Peninsula was to visit the gannet colony at Cape St. Mary. James is a world authority

on the gannet. His first love is the fulmar, that pearly gull-like relative of the albatross, but I suspect the gannet is his second. He plans to write a monograph on it soon, with his friend John Barlee. In 1939, with H. G. Vevers, he made a world census of the gannets; they and their correspondents visited nineteen out of twenty-two gannet colonies in existence. Of the 167,000 gannets breeding in the world at that time 109,000 were in Great Britain and Ireland. The New World came off a poor second with only 28,000 birds in six colonies (three in the Gulf of St. Lawrence and three off the shores of Newfoundland). Ten years later, in 1949, they repeated the census, finding twenty-nine colonies and about 200,000 birds. Gannets are on the increase.

The most spectacular New World colony, the one at Bonaventure Island off the Gaspé, is visited by scores of bird students every year. It has become a profitable thing for the innkeeper on the island to cater to—and even advertise to—an unending succession of summer gannet watchers. Kodachrome movies of this colony have been seen by hundreds of thousands of people in the Audubon Screen Tour audiences throughout the United States and Canada. On the other hand, the colony at Cape St. Mary sometimes goes for several years unvisited by any of the field-glass fraternity.

One of the main objectives of our Grand Tour of Wild America was to visit the nesting colonies of as many species of North American seabirds as possible. We had planned to collaborate on a field guide to the seabirds of the world, following the formula of my other Field Guides. Therefore I wanted James to see those seabirds which are not found on his side of the Atlantic—and particularly, the wealth of seabirds in the North Pacific.

But gannets are gannets. Those on the coast of Scotland are identical with those in Newfoundland. However, James wanted to see at least *one* New World gannetry. The one at Cape St. Mary was not very well documented even though its history goes back to about 1880. That is not old as gannetries go. The one on the Bird Rocks in the Gulf of St. Lawrence was recorded by Jacques Cartier in 1534. Several of the British colonies have histories that go back even farther than that, and James is quite sure that some have, in fact, been occupied for thousands of years. These are birds of ancient design; the gannet tribe goes back in the fossil record forty million years, at least.

After dreaming fitfully of gannets that night at the Conways' I was awakened by James, who reported that the weather was improving, the fog had gone.

April 15

This morning it looked rather better. I had a hard time getting Roger out of bed; it was about 9 A.M. when we started off for Cape St. Mary.

On the tip of the Cape there is a lighthouse, but this is served by sea, which this morning was too rough for small boats. To go overland from the village of St. Bride's to the lighthouse means ten miles out and ten miles back through a particularly sticky bog. Fortunately, we had a guide, Paddy Conway of St. Bride's, and he had a pack pony, and the pony carried our gear. At first the track was distinguished by deep mud ruts and telephone poles. Every now and then it went under water and we skirted round. After a bit we diverged toward the coast through a spruce bog in which fox sparrows were plaintively singing, reminding me very much of the Coigeach of Ross in the Highlands, with stunted spruce instead of heather. A juniper was growing prostrate, shaped by the winds, and there was much crowberry, *Empetrum nigrum,* and everywhere in the oozy sphagnum bogs was a new and unfamiliar plant, the plant of

Newfoundland's old coins, the pitcher plant. Roger picked one to
show me. It is said to be carnivorous. Its leaves, shaped like slender
purplish pitchers, are usually half filled with water; the lip of the
pitcher is covered with stiff downward-pointing hairs which make it
impossible for any trapped insect to climb out.

We reached the sea bluffs and dry ground, to find, in rough water,
under a bold 400-foot headland some hundreds of harlequin ducks.
These fantastically patterned ducks, which the Newfoundlanders call
"Lords and Ladies," had not yet departed for their breeding grounds
on the white-water rivers of Labrador. Long-tailed ducks (or old-
squaws) constantly flew past in little parties, and there were some
red-breasted mergansers. There were many eiders, the males black
with white backs, and a biggish flock of solid black ducks with
yellow noses. The last proved to be the American race of the
common scoter (which has much more yellow on its bill than our
European form).

It was a slow journey. After about seven miles we descended to
a westerly cove where there were two houses, two men repairing
a fence, and a prodigious smell of drying fish. The fish racks were
flat slatted shelves of split wood, giving good circulation of air; there
were also drying houses for fish. Here our guide borrowed a cart.
We crossed the river by a little slung bridge, while the horse took
the cart through a ford. The rest of the track to the lighthouse was
almost a "road," with dry footing. Tired, we ate lunch, reclining in
a bed of prostrate matted spruce, while the sun came out fleetingly.
Progressively the weather got better, so that by the time we had
crossed an upland barren of juniper and crowberry and sighted the
cart (which had gone ahead), it was full sun. Paddy was talking to

two lighthouse keepers. As we approached the lighthouse (we had first seen its top about five miles away) we also heard, carried on the wind, the noise I associate with the finest remote Atlantic rocks, the noise of Eldey and St. Kilda, of the Bass and Mýkines: the thrilling rattling of gannets, and the *taterat,* the angry sound of kittiwakes. The dear noises of the seabird colony, the great gannet noise. Only the fulmar was lacking.

By now the day had become really fine, though windy, and tired though we were from our ten-mile hike (it seemed like twenty) we all made haste to the noisy cliff. Round a cape east of the lighthouse the gannet rock suddenly appeared—just as I had remembered it from the photographs. We were on the top of a sloping 400-foot cliff; we went down this a bit to a vantage point out of the wind with one of the light keepers, another Conway (who had been in the British navy during the war). While Roger set up his cine camera, I counted the occupied gannet sites visible on the west side of their nesting rock.

Between us and the gannet rock was a great rock-bound cove with very steep slabby sides; the broader ledges were covered with guillemots, which looked rather like rows of erect white-breasted penguins, but mainly it was a kittiwakery, perhaps one of the greatest in the Atlantic New World, where there are not many. There were about 3000 occupied kittiwake sites here. Periodically, the birds would panic and swirl past the cliff face like a blizzard of snow. The locals call these small gulls *tickle-ace,* or something like that.

Circumventing the noisy kittiwake slab we finally reached the gannets, whose great stack (350 feet) is connected with the 400-foot mainland cliff only by a low impassable ridge.

What a wonderful show they put on for us! Thousands of birds, with a wingspread of six feet, covered the top and sides of the stack. Gleaming white with a golden wash on the backs of their heads and jet-black wing-ends, they were at the peak of nuptial beauty. Our glasses showed a bright green stripe along the top of each toe— clocks on their black socks. Paired birds faced each other, bowed, and lifting their heads high, crossed their bills. A constant succession of newcomers came in from the sea and made their awkward land-ings against the capricious wind; they back-pedaled with their wings, threw their big feet forward, and trusted to luck. Others, tails depressed, took off from the slope with a curious retching groan, losing altitude at first as they pitched into space, before leveling off. Some joined those who were diving from a height, headfirst, like slender arrowheads into the deep blue water beyond the surf. But most of their fishing was probably done far from the home rock; gannets commonly fish fifty, or sometimes a hundred miles from their colonies. They must spend up to six hours on the wing on these ration runs, for they cruise at about forty miles an hour.

I estimated occupied sites on the top; and worked around and down to cover the east side of the colony. It seemed clear that, unlike most British colonies, the gannetry at Cape St. Mary was not fully tenanted in mid-April, and that the number of its occupied nests does not become stabilized until May. Our count, and estimate, gave 3476 occupied sites. This included about 13 sites occupied by birds on the rather inaccessible mainland ledges to the east of the stack. In 1939 Oliver Davies and R. D. Keynes, the last gannet counters to visit this place, had estimated 4394 occupied sites in the fullness of the season. Roger tells me that there are still many gannets passing northeastward along the New England coast in mid-April.

The attachment of the gannets to their nest sites at the time of our visit was not great. Some of them, even though separated from us by a hundred feet or more, would leave their nests entirely, although they had already built them up with much fresh grass. There were many fresh nests quite unattended. Had egg-laying been near, few would have taken the chance of losing nest material or even nest sites to their neighbors.

It was about four o'clock, with long shadows, before we gave much attention to the guillemots on the kittiwake slab. Although guillemots (which in North America are called murres) are abundant off Canadian shores, most Americans do not have the opportunity to see them as readily as we do on the rocky shores of Britain.

For many years our knowledge of the guillemots of Newfoundland had been confused. The island is within the range of both the species, the common guillemot and the Brünnich's (which is an exceptionally rare visitor to Britain). At first it was thought that all the guillemots of Newfoundland were Brünnich's. But Peters and Burleigh (1951) state that all the breeding birds are common guillemots, and the Brünnich's, although abundant in winter, are "not known to nest in Newfoundland." Recently, however, Leslie Tuck has discovered a minority of Brünnich's guillemots breeding in

two colonies off the east coast of Newfoundland. If we had not taken Roger's new 30× Bausch and Lomb telescope with us, the situation at Cape St. Mary would have remained uncertain, for it was only when we put the powerful glass on the broad gray slab that we could detect among the crowded birds some which had shorter bills with a white mark at the base. Taking ledge by ledge I called out numbers while Roger jotted them down. A little over 10 per cent (actually 11.4) were Brünnich's guillemots, a substantial and hitherto unrecorded minority.

Another investigation we were able to carry out with the powerful glass was a count of the relative number of "bridled" birds in the population of common guillemots. North Americans usually refer to these individuals as the "ringed" phase. The bridle, spectacle, or ring—call it what you will—consists of a white ring round the eye with a white line running back from it. H. N. Southern, who meticulously examined the east Atlantic situation, discovered that the proportion of bridled guillemots mounts steadily from under 1 per cent in the southern parts of the bird's range to 50 per cent in south

Iceland and Bear Island. No such investigation has been made, however, on the west Atlantic population to see if there is a similar gradation, except that recently Dr. Harrison Lewis found that 17.7 per cent of the guillemots in the sanctuaries along the north (Labrador) shore of the Gulf of St. Lawrence were bridled. The interesting thing about our sample at this Newfoundland colony is that we got the same result—actually, 17.3 per cent.

We left the kittiwake slab when the light became too weak for photography and tracked to the lighthouse where Keeper Conway's pretty wife gave us a fine cup of tea. As there was only another hour of daylight we were offered beds, very kindly and quite seriously; but we said we really must push off (just as well in view of the next day's weather).

We got caught by night before we returned the cart to the cove. From there Paddy and the horse and a borrowed flashlight guided us back to St. Bride's. It was a tedious journey, though the way across gullies and bogs, often without any track at all, was found unerringly by Paddy and his horse (we were not sure which). A crescent moon descended into the sea before we were half way; it was quiet and still. There were faint shafts of aurora borealis, and the snipe were out, chippering and winnowing, much to Leslie's delight, as he counts these birds each spring.

Roger had bad luck earlier in the day when filming on a steep slope; he strained a muscle on the climb up. This played up seriously on the long way back and slowed him up a lot. He was very cheerful and good about it, but I knew he was in pain, particularly when we had to make the descent into each steep ravine which lay across our path and the equally steep climb out on the other side.

The route from the cove to within two miles of St. Bride's was really trackless; it was interesting how the necessity for concentration in the dark brought back unexpected memories of the outward journey through this very complicated terrain, including steppingstones in the river which we had to cross. Roger, with his limping leg, slipped and went into the icy water "by mistake on purpose" (to cool his wound?)—and had to change into a borrowed pair of heavy stockings. He said his leg felt better after that.

Paddy, I believe, thought once or twice that we'd never get there, though he was very skillful and patient. He knew the country perfectly. We at last picked up the telephone poles of the last two miles and splashed home—through puddles now, not round them. As we neared St. Bride's our footfalls on the stony roadway awakened people, who came out of the houses with flashlights and shone them at the strange cavalcade of horse, guide, and mud-spattered bird watchers. It was half past midnight; we were dog tired. Fourteen hours on the march—but what a day!

JAMES was as reluctant as I to quit the comfort of his bed the following morning. We woke about 10 A.M. finding ourselves very stiff and out of training; it was blowing and snowy. Had we stayed at the lighthouse we would have had a far worse passage home, even with daylight, than on the quiet dark night.

It was a foul ride in the Chevy back to St. John's, though bravely we stopped now and then for a look at the sea. James added another bird to his lengthening list of oceanic acquaintances, the double-crested cormorant—an early arrival in these waters.

The softly falling flakes of snow had turned the spruce forest into a Christmas tree landscape. While we were crossing an open stretch of barrens, bleak in its white mantle, two willow ptarmigan flew across the road, alighted and walked about in the snow. But instead of their winter camouflage suits of white these two birds already had their spring plumage—brown with white wings—so they were very visible. I had, oddly enough, never seen this species, the commonest of the three ptarmigan, in North America (although I had seen it in Sweden—and we were to see many more in Alaska). These little sub-arctic chickens that grow feathery snowshoes for winter travel are circumpolar.

Although we had two or three more days in Newfoundland our trek to the gannetry marked the high point of our brief stay. It was still much too early for the wood warblers (a purely New World family), which enliven northern spruce forests from May to September. Not even the relatively early rusty blackbirds had arrived. We would meet these summer residents of Newfoundland en route.

But we seemed fated to have as much trouble getting out of this sea-girt province as we had when we came in. This time, when our plane was due to arrive, the weather at Gander, instead of being too bad, was too good. The aircraft, boosted by a following wind (east and southeast), still had plenty of fuel and had flown on without stopping to pick us up. However, we got space on a local flight to Halifax, Nova Scotia, where we would at least be able to find some way of getting to Boston.

That evening, James wrote in his diary: "Today I set foot for the first time in my life on the continental New World. Tomorrow it will be the fabulous United States of America. Roger seemed to be making all too little of this business, until I remembered that he belonged there."

Kittiwake

3

The Rude Bridge

By the rude bridge that arched the flood,
Their flag to April's breeze unfurled,
Here once the embattled farmers stood,
And fired the shot heard round the world.

RALPH WALDO EMERSON

THE UNITED STATES border, under our aircraft's wings, came imperceptibly. At one moment the spruce trees were growing in New Brunswick, at another, in Maine. They looked just the same spruce trees. Roads zigzagged like pale threads through the complicated maze of evergreen woods and lakes; here and there were scattered farms and, at crossroads, small towns. For a long time we were too far inland to see the coast, and when the sea came up again, we had crossed New Hampshire and were in the State of Massachusetts.

Boston began to come up with the sea, and various never-before-seen objects were identified from the air by James, including a clover-leaf crossing, a baseball field, and Boston's only skyscraper. He failed at a drive-in motion picture theater, which had to be carefully explained to him. Our little plane load had Boston's seaside airport to itself that Sunday morning.

April 19

The U.S. Customs passed me through very quickly, but Roger, with his big collection of movie apparatus, was asked a lot of questions. Beyond the barrier beckoned Bill and Annette Cottrell, who were to be our hosts in Boston, or rather Cambridge—my first hosts in the United States. Bill is a librarian at Harvard University.

We plunged at once into a brief tour of colonial Boston, most beautifully driven by Annette.* Because it was Sunday, we were able to do all the proper sights in a very short time, from the city center, the old New England administrative buildings, offices, houses, churches, and the squares to the great university in Cambridge. It was eighteenth-century more purely and consistently than I had expected, and with no self-consciousness whatever, so natural, so like home: more like home than any of my Anglo-Bostonian friends had warned me. Not surprisingly, Bill's study at Cambridge, Massachusetts, bore a remarkable resemblance to one I knew in Cambridge, Cambs. Annette's kitchen was like an English kitchen, until I looked out of the window and saw at the feeding tray the little North American siskin that we'd been hearing so often in the Newfoundland forests. These pine siskins, so much duller in color than our own pretty siskins, were having a big year in the eastern states, one of their "invasions." A little later, out of the same window, I saw two other birds which were quite new to me—the bronzed grackle, a glossy, iridescent bird, and the blue jay that Audubon made so much of in his often reproduced plate. These were very colorful birds to have wild in the garden of a university town—would we rival them in England, I wondered? Perhaps our little varied gang of tits, and in particular, the brightness of the blue tit, might make up for our

---

* American female drivers, I discovered then and subsequently, are better than British, on the average.

not having the blue jay. But how right Audubon was to put his maximum drive and energy into that plate!

The New England countryside near Boston was inundated this mid-April by the flooding of the Concord River. The flood waters were receding but still covered much of the low land. The landscape was leafless but budding; New England was on the verge of spring. In spite of the real differences in plant and animal life, the physiognomy of the countryside so closely resembled a spring flood in Northamptonshire, Hampshire, or Somerset that I had (metaphorically) to pinch myself. Massachusetts is as well wooded as the Weald of Sussex and Kent, but there was just one puzzle which worried me for some hours—one element was missing. It was not till the late afternoon that I got it—rookeries. There were no rookeries. There was no big common social bird, no busy noisy rooks at black nest blobs in the naked April treetops.

Round the flooded fields and tree-walled riversides, I was quickly introduced to three New World blackbirds—the meadowlark (not a lark), the red-wing, black with bright scarlet epaulettes, and the cowbird, which, like our European cuckoo, is a brood parasite, and lays in the nests of other species. There was also a subtle little flycatcher, the phoebe, which said, indeed, a quiet *phoebe*—a bird which Audubon himself studied closely and was very fond of. Most exciting of all were the wood ducks, whose drakes have the most handsome, formal-looking garments of any duck in the world.

In midafternoon Susie and Paul Brooks welcomed us in their lovely, children-echoing farmhouse in the township of Lincoln; a farm in a rolling mixture of paddock, park, pond, and wood. Paul Brooks is our publisher, a devoted naturalist, traveler, and camper of long experience. Augmented by the Brookses, we piled into the station wagons and went off birding again. It soon became clear to me, outnumbered by a galaxy of distinguished American hosts, that the enthusiasm of my guides was not entirely reserved for the birds. It is true that our party dallied with, and the ignorant Englishman was introduced to, such novelties as the pied-billed grebe, which is the counterpart of our dabchick, the great blue heron, a counterpart of our common heron, but six inches taller, and to the ring-necked duck, counterpart of our tufted duck. We also met a beautiful small hovering falcon, closely resembling our kestrel, which the Americans (no doubt humorously) alluded to as a sparrow hawk. We met the killdeer, which fills the farmland niche of our lapwing, and the mourning dove, which takes the place of our turtle-dove. The newly arrived swallows were hawking everywhere over the water, and we encountered chipping sparrows and field sparrows, which are truly buntings of a sort.

But all this ornithology seemed to be taken as a matter of course by the North Americans. It became gradually clear to me that I was really being shown something else besides birds. This turned out to be the American Revolution. The trouble about visiting Concord on April 19 with amiable and intelligent Americans was that six of the rebels at once tried to tell me about the shot heard round the world on April 19, 1775. Concord's quiet colonial wooden houses glinted in the April sun through April trees; by its square green stood its towered and spired colonial church; a house nearby even had a glass-framed bullet hole. How the wooden house blesses the wooded landscape!

We crossed the rude bridge that arched the flood and found that, no doubt by careful arrangement with the management, a flag was (indeed) to April's breeze unfurled. In the bare trees along the river-bank was a busy flock of rusty blackbirds. Making noises like rusty hinges creaking, they rustled through the upper branches of some

American elms and poplars at the place where once embattled farmers stood and the American Revolution was born. To me the place where it began will always now be mixed with the sound of rusty blackbirds. Were they on passage there on April 19, 1775?*

Three or four miles down the road we came to Walden Pond. To North Americans, Henry Thoreau occupies a place similar to that of W. H. Hudson in England, that of a naturalist-philosopher. His life and thoughts were not very similar to those of Gilbert White, but like Selborne, his Walden has become a place of pilgrimage. To me Walden Pond was an anticlimax; the climax of the day was the bridge over the Concord River and the wooden colonial houses. It is true that Walden Pond had no tins and picnic mess (perhaps it would, later in the summer); but it looked like many an acid pond in Surrey's greensand heath. At Selborne the little curate comes back for every pilgrim; but Thoreau seems to have left Walden. Perhaps he will come back again to the quiet pond, where he watched and wondered—one day. Or are there too many people, too many cars on the road? The woods are still there, and the same animals and plants—most of them, anyway—but he would no longer find the seclusion he treasured.

Ludlow Griscom, the great New England ornithologist, has shown in his *Birds of Concord* that the area of my first day's birding is almost certainly the most continuously and consistently bird-watched area in the New World. Some notes of Thoreau's go back to 1832; and since 1868, when William Brewster began to visit Concord, the published and unpublished detail gathered has been amazing. Brewster collected so many skins and facts, and analyzed them with such painstaking and complex methods, that most of his work was unpublished when he died. Fortunately Griscom has been able to analyze it at Harvard; and the links between Brewster (who died in 1919) and the present are so strong that today we have "eight decades of matchlessly complete data," as Griscom puts it. There are few areas of England, save perhaps London and Oxford, where there has been such continuity of observation. What is the most well-watched, well-recorded bird place in Britain? The London parks? The Norfolk

---

* Perhaps not; it was an exceptionally hot and early season, and the migrants may have gone on. The apples were in bloom on April 19, 1775, and the soldiers marching to Concord were overcome by heat prostration (Ludlow Griscom, *The Birds of Concord*, Cambridge, Mass., 1949).

Broads? Or perhaps some remote island like Scotland's St. Kilda, whose very remoteness has made it a mecca for bird pilgrims?

What a day: Concord, Walden, Lincoln, Lexington, Cambridge; with a lovely New England dinner party at the Paul Brookses' to end with. Roger and I fell asleep quite late that night over Bill Cottrell's bird books.

IT WAS FITTING that James's first day in the United States should be spent in the Concord Valley. For not only is that part of Massachusetts the cradle of United States history, but also of American ornithology —although Philadelphia could make equal claims, because the Declaration of Independence was signed in the city of brotherly love and ornithologists Wilson and Audubon once lived there.

It was only a few blocks away from the Cottrells' house—on Brattle Street—that William Brewster and Henry Henshaw met on Monday nights, years ago, to read Audubon aloud and to talk birds. That was in 1871, only twenty years after the death of Audubon. Others soon joined in the informal seminars, and after two years, the Nuttall Ornithological Club, named after an early Cambridge ornithologist, was formed. This, the oldest bird club in America, still holds its meetings in Cambridge. The American Ornithologists' Union sprang bilaterally from the Nuttall Club and, in turn, a committee of the A.O.U. in 1884 sparked the Audubon movement. Today the National Audubon Society (which is the counterpart of England's Royal Society for the Protection of Birds), several state Audubon Societies, and hundreds of local Audubon groups are the most potent force in wildlife conservation in America outside the federal government.

Of all the state societies, the Massachusetts Audubon Society is by far the most influential, with a current membership of 7000, not counting their junior members in the schools. As I have written in *Birds Over America*:

> Bird watching became a respectable pursuit in New England long before it was countenanced elsewhere . . . As frontiers dissolved and communities weathered, the center of ornithological interest moved westward, until now we find the more progressive work (ecological studies, behavior studies and the

*like) being turned out in such states as Ohio, Michigan, Wis-
consin and California . . . In large cities like Cleveland, St. Louis
and Detroit, bird clubs that numbered scarcely 100 members
a decade ago now have more than 1000. As an "Audubon
Screen Tour" lecturer, I have been astonished at the size of the
audiences that filled the halls—1200 in Omaha, 1600 in Kansas
City.*

More than 200 cities are now on the Screen Tour circuit and the
yearly audiences are estimated at 750,000.

But Massachusetts still boasts more bird watchers per square mile
than any other state, and probably produces more experts. The man
most responsible for this is the redoubtable Ludlow Griscom, who
has been called the "virtuoso of field identification." The rank and
file of bird spotters around Boston feel they have arrived when they
are finally invited to go on a field trip with him. It was on the morning of our second day in Cambridge that the great man came round
to the Cottrells' to "take us out" as described in James's journal.

April 20

It was a cold and windy day. Everybody sorted themselves out in
different cars, clutching the latest Bausch and Lomb prismatic telescopes—which appear to be the badge of the higher U.S. ornithological brass. We sped north along U.S. Highway 1, aiming toward
Newburyport, at the mouth of the Merrimack River.

Newburyport, a complex, old New England maritime town, reminded me much of King's Lynn in North Norfolk (one of the
oldest ports in England). Like Lynn, Newburyport has seen busier
days; like it, its sea approaches run through great estuarine washes;
and like it, it has inherited fine architecture from an earlier era of
success. The estuary had green boggy banks, and to the east stretched
broad goose marshes, salt swards with hundreds of Canada geese,
quietly grazing. On the water were many ducks, mostly blacks. Among
them was a small one, compact, and neat; a study in black and white,
with a great white head patch like a woman's wind scarf—my first
buffle-head, a fine drake, on its migrant way to Canada's northwest.

Also tarrying here before leaving for the Northwest was a fluttering flock of about a hundred small dainty gulls, whose heads were bearing the first feathers of their dark hoods of summer—Bonaparte's gulls. Among these summer gulls of northern muskeg, Ludlow Griscom spotted an outlander—an immature European black-headed gull. Although the dark-hooded gulls are generally, throughout the world, inland or coastal species, and by no means birds of the open ocean, Bonaparte's gull has been wind-drifted across the Atlantic to the British Isles at least ten times; and the black-headed gull of Europe has been borne many scores of times in the other direction. At least four black-heads carrying rings have been recovered in the New World. For at least fifteen years, without missing a season, at least one and perhaps as many as three have made their headquarters at the end of the large sewer pipe that dumps its waste into the Merrimack here at Newburyport.

Only the more hardy members of our party braved the cold wind for long outside the shelter of the cars, and eventually, by common consent, we moved toward the coast through great stretches of sea marsh which lay between us and the outer dunes. At the Plum Island Coast Guard Station, just inside the breakwater, were three pale

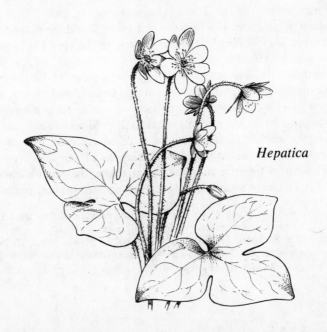

Hepatica

Iceland gulls floating, gliding, and settling, now on the sands, now on the breakwater. They were immature, light speckly birds on passage to the coast of Greenland—the only place in the world where this bird nests. There is no good record of its ever having nested in the country after which it is named. Actually, it is probably not a distinct species, but a light-colored "white-winged" race of the herring gull.

We could not stay long with these Arctic migrants, but were quickly whisked off through the dignified little port town of Ipswich, with its houses of retired sea captains rising in tiers on the hill, each house with its captain's walk on the roof. We soon reached the Ipswich River Wildlife Sanctuary, a new wildlife sanctuary of the Massachusetts Audubon Society. Russell Mason, the director of the Society, greeted us warmly and I had my first demonstration of the amount of interest in nature study in North America; Griscom, Peterson, and Fisher were the victims, over lunch, of a genial ambush by some hundreds of Audubonites who had been tipped off via the grapevine that we would be stopping by.* Sandwiches and microphones were thrust into our hands; a tape machine recorded, for (we were told) Station WGBH, words of greeting, and all that kind of thing. "What, Mr. Fisher, are your first impressions of America?" Was I to say big, or terrific or cold (it was, rather); or, "Your police are wonderful" (so far, I hadn't seen any)—or, what should I say? I talked a bit about my first taste of New World birds, and of the organization of birding in England where, in the year 1953, one bird book was published a week.

Ludlow Griscom and Roger took their turns at the mike, and while the tape was still flowing, I dodged the crowd to see my first evening grosbeaks, noble counterparts of our European hawfinches. On a garden tree sat a lovely male, dull gold with black and white wings, the world's most intensively watched grosbeak that day. Like a bright gold ornament, a goldfinch showed in the same tree, and I was able to ponder, at short binocular range, the relative charms of this brilliant yellow and black creature and its subtler, more varie-

---

*There was one practical result of our visit. Because of the unprecedented invasion of people, the limited comfort facilities at the Sanctuary were sorely taxed, and necessitated a shuttle service by bus to Newburyport. At the next board meeting of the Massachusetts Audubon Society it was voted that six new lavatories should be installed.

gated, European counterpart.

The flooded New England landscape through which we passed on our way home was very moving; the paucity of agriculture, compared with my ineradicable mental picture of England, gave a curious feeling of space. We paused by some agreeable flooded woodland near Middleton, and here I met my first Parulids—the wood warblers of the New World, members of a family that dominates the summer woodlands of the North as does the Sylviid family in the Old World. Roger identified for me two species, the myrtle warbler, bluish with a yellow rump, and the yellow palm warbler, with a rusty cap and a bobbing tail. He said that these two are always the first to arrive on their passage to places north; in another two weeks wood warblers of twenty to thirty species would swarm through the leafing woodlands.

That evening we attended a meeting of the oldest bird club in America. The Nuttall Ornithological Club meets in the Biological Laboratories at Harvard University, and I have seldom enjoyed a scientific evening more. I found myself somewhat pitchforked into a dissertation on the fulmar ("You needn't read *all* 496 pages of your book," said Roger). My discourse was certainly not purely ornithological, for I remember telling the story of the first reference to the word "fulmar" in any form of literature.* Paul Brooks told me afterwards that it was all he remembered of my fulmar talk, but then he is not only a naturalist but a literary man.

Like the best old, traditional scientific societies, the Nuttall Club cultivates an atmosphere of after-dinner freedom. Like the Royal Society's Club or the Zoological Society's Club, or the British Ornithologists' Club in England, it has put formalities in their place—in the closet, with the gowns and mortarboards.

It is at informal conversational meetings that we all sharpen our powers of thought. (In England much of this conversation takes place over tea. Those two directors of fieldwork units at Oxford, David

---

* I quote this in *The Fulmar* (pp. 79–80), from the Icelandic saga of Hallfredh Ottarsson (A.D. 963–1000). Hallfredh, somewhat of a rascal, met an old love of his, Kolfinna, when she came with her women and cattle to her husband's upland summer farm. What happened there the saga is somewhat equivocal about; but to the injury to Kolfinna's aged, sour husband (who was down at the home farm), Hallfredh (who was a poet) added an insult in satirical word play. "Thrammar til hvílu," he said of the old man, "svá sem sílafullur fúlmár svimmi á báru trödh"; which may be translated, "He trudges to his bed like a fulmar full of seafood swimming in a pen of waves."

Lack of the Edward Grey Institute of Field Ornithology and Charles
Elton of the Bureau of Animal Population, encourage all their teams
to break their work at teatime, and stick their necks out in controversial talk. Many university zoology courses have teatime seminars
at which the students, and not their teachers, are encouraged to do
the talking.) Almost as vivid as memories of days in the field are
memories of hours of talk: tea with Peter Scott at the New Grounds
in Gloucestershire; dinner at the Cottrells'; midnight at London's
Savile Club, when the conversation begins to warm up by the fire;
even breakfast—breakfast with the Petersons especially, for Roger,
the obsessive, always wants to talk about birds. I have seen him many
times, at an International Ornithological Congress—where the talk
ranges wide—assume a faraway look when the conversation drifts
away from ornithology, only to take it up, at the exact sentence where
he left off, when it comes back. When I'm driving, Roger nearly
always starts a difficult subject, like bird navigation or subspeciation,
when I'm threading my way through the stickiest London traffic, or
through the business center of some complicated town.

Roger talked of birds at breakfast next morning, all right. In the
Cottrells' back yard was his new, shiny green Ford Country Sedan,
seventeen feet long (half as big again as an average British car), and
in his mind were plans for the next twenty thousand miles.

THE NORTHEAST can hardly be called *wild* America, but tucked
away here and there are small remnants of wilderness that have
withstood three centuries of ever-expanding civilization. Our round-
about journey from Boston to New York in the new station wagon
continued to be a mixture of the historical and the ornithological.
When we stopped at Plymouth to look at the venerable rock where
the Pilgrims stepped ashore, we saw our first laughing gulls, dark-
mantled and dark-headed. They were probably more numerous in
Massachusetts in 1620 when the Pilgrim fathers landed.

A long run through the empty pine barrens, where few birds and
fewer people live, brought us to New Bedford, where we called at
the famous whaling museum to see relics of days of wooden sperm
whalers and Moby Dick. There were many mementos of ships of the

past and their masters, and a magnificent half-scale model of a New Bedford whaler. James and I had often talked of sailing on a modern whaler to the Antarctic—if our wives would let us.

Roland Clement, of the Rhode Island Audubon Society, met us at the museum to make certain that in our brief transit of the smallest state we should see at least a few good birds. Two dickcissels, hundreds of miles east of their normal range and which should have wintered in Mexico, had spent the winter at a feeding tray with whitethroats and purple finches. The male was just coming into good plumage, with yellow throat and black gorget. Dickcissels and other wind-drifted strays from the West are now becoming almost commonplace at New England feeding stations. But birds of this sort, exciting rarities to the easterner, mean less to the visitor from abroad to whom almost any bird at a feeding shelf—even a cardinal, blue jay, or junco —is new.

The state bird of Rhode Island is (of all things!) the Rhode Island red chicken, but a far better choice would have been the osprey. These spectacular black and white "fish hawks" had just returned from the South and we saw several of their huge nests, including one on a cartwheel on a pole. Many bird lovers (if we may use that term —just this once) erect these osprey poles, and Robert Cushman Murphy, whom we visited the next day on Long Island, had a new one at the bottom of his garden, with nothing on it yet but hopes. The hopes were good ones, for along this part of the coast the osprey is a common, everyday bird, a creature—like Europe's stork—protected by public opinion.

In Britain, a hundred years have passed since the osprey was a familiar nesting-bird; even then it was found only in the Scottish Highlands, although in earlier times it nested more widely. The Highland lochs became its last refuge, and here it was systematically exterminated by collectors, notably the great hunter Charles St. John. I remember a discussion James and I once had over tea with Lord Hurcomb in Sweden: Couldn't Swedish osprey eggs be transported to Scotland? There, on the shore of some likely loch, they could be hatched and hand-reared. If there is anything to "imprinting"—the theory that young birds are conditioned by their surroundings in their first hours of life—the osprey might become re-established in the British Isles.

At the old Puritan town of Newport, where we were joined by

William Drury, Jr., even birds like ospreys could hardly compete for our attention with certain impressive human artifacts—the controversial "Newport Tower," for example, a plain empty shell which stands in Touro Park. Although romantic antiquarians have advanced the theory that the circular stone tower was built by Norse explorers to Vinland (supposedly in 1353), most scholars now reject the idea. They assert that it is in reality a watchtower built by the English as recently as 1640. James, a Norseman at heart, wanted to believe in the tower, but he bowed to the verdict of the experts.

When the tower was built—whether in 1640 or three centuries earlier—the peninsulas and islands of Narragansett Bay must have been as wild a stretch of coast as existed anywhere—the site of clamorous colonies of terns and other seabirds, the tarrying place of migrating waders, including the Eskimo curlew, probably now extinct. But the Narragansett headlands, situated at the break between the rock coast and the sand coast—with a mixture of both—became very valuable real estate when the Four Hundred, those very successful hybrids of American enterprise and European aristocracy, chose Newport for their fashionable residences. Their Golden Age mansions are strung along the peninsula to the southwest of the city. Newport changed from a town where New England puritanism ran deep to a resort of fashion—and dollars. Standing in their own grounds, each with its arrangement of lawn, border, arboretum, drive, avenue, vista, are the homes of Count von Reventlow, of Countess Lâzló Széchényi, of Adams, Bogart, Cushman, Douglas, Fahnestock, Firestone, Hutton, Loew, Mesta, Sherman, Vanderbilt, Van Rensselaer. As we drove around Ocean Drive and gaped at the mansions James commented that "the tradesmen must polish their vans before they come out here."

Dozens of cruisers and destroyers rode at anchor in the bay, which is large enough to hold all the fleets of the world without crowding. Because of the numerous protected harbors where pods of boats may be safely deployed, the deep waters of Narragansett have become a home base for a substantial part of the Atlantic fleet of the U.S. Navy. When Bill Drury pointed with pride to one of the big warships, exclaiming, "There's one of our battle wagons now—going upstream," James couldn't resist letting go with another of his Fisherisms, "Oh—so they really *can* go upstream!"

Because of the navy, the posh country estates, and the bustling towns of Newport and Jamestown, little privacy has been left the seabirds that formerly nested among the rocks and islands. The waders—in smaller numbers than in the old days—still stop briefly in their passage and a few terns, including the beautiful roseate tern, continue to nest on one or two small islets. Most of the other summer birds have fled elsewhere. But in winter the dunes, the sheltered blue waters, and the islands, partially deserted by people, come into their own.* The unique winter visitor to the Narragansett country is the large European cormorant, which, on this side of the Atlantic, makes its main winter headquarters here, on the rocks of the lower bay. We saw two or three sitting upright on a large buoy, their black wings unfurled to the breeze, when we crossed the Jamestown Bridge, headed for New York.

* The largest "Christmas Bird Count" ever made north of Cape May, N.J., was scored at Newport on December 27, 1953—131 species. A total of 7384 observers throughout the U.S. and Canada took part in the 1953 Christmas Counts organized by the National Audubon Society. All birds on each count must be seen in a single day (by any number of observers) within a 15-mile circle.

Evening Grosbeak

4

Wild Trails for the Millions

THE NOISELESS CHAMBER which had whisked us 102 floors above the level of the street came to a stop and we stepped out onto a circular observation platform. From our Olympian vantage point on the Empire State Building, 1250 feet above New York's sidewalks, we looked down upon a glittering bespangled landscape—or, rather, manscape. Even the tallest of the other great skyscrapers—the Chrysler Building and Rockefeller Center—were below the level of our eyrie, here on the tallest building on earth. Electric lights were being switched on almost simultaneously in hundreds of offices, in this twilight hour, as charwomen came in to clean up, while in other hundreds of offices, lights were being turned out, giving a winking, twinkling effect to the great city. Far below sparkled long jewel-like strings of street lamps (150,000 of them illuminate the pavements of New York), and neon lights, sodium lights, mazda lights, blinked red, yellow, and white. The brightest channel of light which extended northward until it was lost near the hazy horizon was Fifth Avenue. To the west, where two ribbons of light crossed, a bright glary patch marked Times Square. Taxis moved like tiny beetles along the floor of the sterile man-made canyons. Their impatient hooting and tooting mingled faintly with the sounds of the river boats on the dark Hudson, the far shore of which was illuminated by large neon signs. There is a breath-taking beauty about the big city from the air—particularly at night.

Certainly no area in all North America is as completely urbanized, as completely synthetic, as this. And yet, divorced as it is from the wilderness, wild America is to be found here in strong distilled form —in the museum, at the zoo, the botanical gardens, and at the National Audubon Society. In fact, only a few blocks north of us, Cinerama was bringing wild America to wildest Broadway. James and I attended the show that evening and had a three-dimensional preview of parts of our journey—Cypress Gardens, the Oregon Coast, Crater Lake, Golden Gate Bridge, the Grand Canyon, and other spots which we were soon to visit. We agreed that Cinerama is far more convincing than the other 3-D effects the motion picture industry has developed. You really do get some of the sensation of being there. And now, even those who cannot afford to travel *can* travel through this new medium. How exciting the gannets of Bonaventure would be in Cinerama—or the oystercatchers at high tide on Hilbre Island at the edge of the Irish Sea!

There are some who maintain that to understand wilderness values you must also know the metropolis. Our friend Guy Emerson, who

lives in a brownstone house in Greenwich Village but spends half his time away from New York, adheres to this view and so does Joseph Wood Krutch, who explains his point so logically in *The Best of Two Worlds*. It is certainly true that many of the best naturalists and biologists have lived at least for a while in large cities such as New York and London. Even John James Audubon, who symbolizes the wildlife conservation movement in America, lived for a few years in New York City (there is an Audubon Avenue, an Audubon Theatre, and an Audubon telephone exchange). The city is full of Auduboniana. If you peer through the iron gate of the little cemetery on 155th Street, off upper Broadway, you will see the runic cross which marks his grave. Most of his originals—not original prints, but the watercolors from which the engravings were made—can be viewed at the New-York Historical Society. Many of the old engraved copper plates, from which the prints were struck, line one of the upper hallways in the American Museum—and prints themselves are to be seen almost any day in the windows of the Kennedy Galleries. If you wish to see an unbroken set of Audubon—the gracious librarian at the National Audubon Society will show you one.

James is a vice-chairman of the Royal Society for the Protection of Birds, which is the British counterpart of the National Audubon Society. I wanted him to see what they were doing up there on Fifth Avenue. The Society now has a more spacious building than the one in which my office was located before the war. We visited the library, which is the finest library on birds in New York, and the educational department, where leaflets and pictures are sent to a third of a million Junior Audubon members in the schools each year. We stopped in at many of the other offices and cubbyholes, where various things were going on, and gained the impression that the Society is growing rapidly in size and influence, keeping pace with the increasing conservation needs of the country.

The American Museum of Natural History, across the park from Audubon House, is a fabulous monument to man's curiosity about the world he lives in. Some would call it a mausoleum, because 800,000 bird skins, the results of more than a century of collecting, lie neatly labeled in insect-proof trays. In other long cabinet-lined halls are stored 3,450,000 insects, 150,000 mammal skins; 150,000 amphibians and reptiles and countless thousands of mineralogical specimens. These are only a part of the vast treasure, estimated at

11,000,000 specimens, filed away in the massive cluster of buildings on Central Park West. John Q. Public is hardly aware of the wealth of study material on the upper floors of the museum, and perhaps cares less; what interests him are the fifty-eight exhibit halls open to him.

Here, if he chooses, he may see a replica of an African waterhole, complete with giraffes, or a glass model of a one-celled protozoa; or a reconstruction of an extinct moa; a drop of water magnified (in a glass model) one million times; one of the world's largest meteorites, brought back from the Arctic by Admiral Peary; a herd of African elephants; a corn goddess sculptured in stone by the Aztecs; shrunken heads from South America; dinosaur eggs 60 million years old; fragile moths and butterflies; the largest crystal topaz in the world and other famous gems; or bird habitat groups by the dozen.

Or if he wishes to expand his vision beyond this terrestrial sphere, he may step into the museum's Hayden Planetarium. Here a complex piece of projection apparatus, a weird-looking instrument some twelve feet long, with a large globe at each end, is installed in a hemispherical dome, 75 feet in diameter. It can either turn on an axis parallel to the polar axis of the earth and transmit the images of stars and planets across the darkened dome exactly as they travel across the night sky—or after certain adjustments are made, the heavens can be viewed as from other points on the earth's surface; or time may be pushed backward or forward—back 5000 years when Alpha Draconus was the North Star, or ahead 12,000 years when Vega will mark the north pole of the heavens. The Hayden Planetarium, attended by half a million people each year, was the fourth of seven planetariums now in operation in the United States.

When James and I climbed the stone steps at the east entrance of the museum and walked into the stately Theodore Roosevelt Memorial Hall, with its walls of cream-colored marble, we encountered groups of school children being herded about by their science teachers. There are days when the museum is flooded with children, thousands of them. They must make up a good percentage of the total of 2,250,000 visitors who are clocked annually at the museum gates. On the other end of the spectrum of attendance are the scientists from all over the world who find in this great institution a workshop and clearing house of ideas. Most of their work goes on in the laboratories, study collections and lecture halls on the upper floors.

When we stepped out of the elevator on the fourth floor we found ourselves surrounded by a swarm of earnest-looking people, mostly men, who wore rectangular white name tags on their lapels. They were ichthyologists and herpetologists—the "ichs and herps"—who were holding their annual three-day convention.

Between our appointments with curators, we took time out to look at a new hall in the making, a series of exhibits of North American forests. Unfortunately, Dick Pough, curator of conservation, who is the guiding spirit behind this new project, was not on hand to explain things to us; he had just gone off to Arizona to assemble material for a saguaro group. The Great Smoky display, a replica of an actual group of primeval hardwoods, was already finished down to the last synthetic dogwood blossom and trillium. We would visit this very spot in North Carolina in a week. The Olympic rain forest exhibit was nearing completion. It cost a small fortune to create ($40,000, we were told), and Francis Lee Jaques, who designed it, really outdid himself. He managed to get more atmosphere into it than pervades any other habitat group I have ever seen in any museum. Great boles of Douglas fir and Sitka spruce, too large to get through the doors, had been brought into the museum in sections (or rather, in slabs with the bark attached) and later reassembled. It was a stroke of genius on Jaques' part to put a large mirror on the ceiling where the sawed-off tree trunks meet it, so that one has the illusion that the trunks continue on up.

Certainly these dioramas, a deceptive amalgamation of painted background and carefully reproduced plant and animal material, which draws upon the skills of a team of artists, taxidermists, carpenters, metalworkers, masons, electricians, and other *préparateurs,* have reached their highest development here. The day of a hundred stuffed creatures in one long case is gone. To the late Frank Chapman, the famous ornithologist, is given the credit for devising the first habitat groups half a century ago. But these had one weak point; placards can contain only so much information and many people do not bother to read them. Now an ingenious device known as the Guide-a-Phone has been installed. Each visitor is furnished with earphones and a small receiving set worn over the shoulder. When he enters an exhibit hall his set picks up a twenty-minute lecture (which is continuously broadcast) which tells him what route to take in the hall, explains each exhibit and sounds a bell when it is time to move on to the next exhibit. Now the technicians are toying with the idea of a selector on the Guide-a-Phone whereby one can tune in on a general lecture, a children's lecture, or an advanced lecture.

In this great museum the exhibits of various sorts, 2300 in all, occupy 23 of the museum's 40 acres. The officials of the institution will proudly tell you that it takes 125 men to keep clean the more than 1,000,000 square feet of floor and two men just to replace the 31,000 light bulbs. Simply to walk through the whole museum without stopping would require ten hours.

Here Gotham's millions of residents, insulated from much of the natural world by their sterile environment of steel and concrete, can yet learn more about the creatures with which they share this planet than can many who live in the wildest of wild places.

Lord Grey of Fallodon once remarked it was well worth a trip across the Atlantic just to spend a few hours at the American Museum of Natural History. These were James Fisher's sentiments, too. One recently completed hall—The Hall of Pacific Bird Life—held him spellbound, for here were eighteen habitat groups, mostly of his beloved seabirds. One display showed the ship followers, the albatrosses and petrels; another the guano islands of Peru. There were replicas of scenes and birds of the Galápagos, of Laysan, Papua, the Solomons, the Australian Great Barrier Reef, and islands in the Bering Sea.

A museum-haunting Jules Verne could live his life entirely in New York and yet write knowingly about the far ends of the earth. But the real naturalist prefers the outdoors; and he makes the most of what he has near home. Many a top botanist and entomologist has made his first collections around the city edge. Birds, of course, have an immediate appeal because they are blessed with wings. If a lad in the Bronx cannot travel to the northern tundra, he may yet see a rough-legged hawk at Clason Point on the East River. Or if he cannot go to the West Indies to see sooty terns, there is always a chance that a hurricane may strand one at Gravesend Bay in Brooklyn, only a subway fare away—or, after a nor'easter, a dovekie from Greenland may be found on the beach at Coney Island. Some of the best naturalists I know were reared in crowded New York City—Joseph Hickey, for example, now a professor of wildlife management, who as a boy climbed into the treetops near his Bronx home, the better to see the migrating warblers.

The little pockets of wildness in New York City are going, one by one, as they are in London and in every metropolis. In this mobile age everything within fifty or a hundred miles of most large cities is undergoing change. When James and I drove south along the New Jersey coast, I was shocked to see how things had altered since the war's end. The sandy coast, the dunes, and the estuaries are now one continuous line of flimsy beach dwellings, bathhouses, billboards, and hot dog stands. Even Barnegat and Brigantine, wild beaches that resounded to the calls of plovers and curlew when I knew them, are now almost completely built up. Only one stretch of pristine seashore remains—Island Beach—ten miles of barrier island, acquired just in the nick of time by the State of New Jersey. Here the clean sweep of the beach and the dunes with their unique plant associations, holly, hudsonia, and marsh flowers, make the cluttered settlements seem incredible, like sores spreading over the land.

5

City in the Woods

THE CHESAPEAKE BAY BRIDGE, four and a half miles long, rose to its crest against a Peter Scott evening sky and dropped in a long sweeping curve toward the distant dark woodlands. Fifty miles of rural and suburban Maryland lay between us and my home, where Barbara would be waiting. From the roadsides, ditchsides, pondsides came a chorus that had begun tuning up, somewhat tentatively, in the afternoon and was now swelling to its nighttime climax, a chorus that had started in New England and was to accompany us until we reached the Gulf of Mexico—the music of the frogs and toads.

James had met his first spring peepers in a pond behind the Drurys' house in Rhode Island, four nights ago. After dinner that evening we had walked across the damp fields toward the clear plaintive birdlike peeping until the myriad voices almost shouted at us from the dark pool and then fell silent. To easterners this nostalgic sound more than any other—more than that of any bird—is the

true voice of spring. It is a voice of resurrection: "Spring is come!"
Everyone knows the voice and is glad, but few have ever seen the
tiny inch-long singer. Tonight, with the peepers, there were multi-
tudes of cricket frogs rasping out their strident notes, and here and
there a green frog gave its single croak, like the plucking of a loose
string on some instrument. But James found it hard to believe that
the peepers were, in reality, frogs and he seemed even more dubious
when I told him that the long pure trill that purred on a high pitch
from some of the ponds was also made by a batrachian, the American
toad. It sounded, he thought, like a blend of bird-trill and insect-trill.
At one roadside stop we heard both it and the song of a brother
gnome, Fowler's toad, a more nasal trill that started with a *w* sound
—*waaaaaaaaaaa*.

These sounds that pipe and trill from a hundred throats on evenings
in spring are love songs of the swamp. They are ancient music, for
the frogs sang their songs ages before the birds did; they were here
first. The amphibians were the first class of backboned animals to
climb out of primordial seas onto the land. The ardent males puff
out their throats like bubble gum, and bleat, trill, peep, click, quack,
or croak, depending on their kind. This orchestration of frogs and
toads is one of the outstanding things about spring nights in eastern
North America. True, one can hear frogs in Europe too—I have
heard as many as four kinds on still nights in the Camargue reed
beds in southern France. But in England there is only one native
frog, and two toads. Now two Continental frogs are invading the
south of England and one of them, the marsh frog, is accused of
giving the British ones a rough time of it.

This evening was windless—perfect for night sounds. Once we
heard the squeaking of flying squirrels, nearly overlooked among the
more frequent, almost supersonic squeaks of pipistrelle bats coursing

overhead in the darkness. A whip-poor-will chanted from the dry oak woodlands, beating out its name rhythmically, endlessly. Certainly, no other bird pronounces its own name more distinctly—or monotonously. I started to count (trying for John Burroughs' old record of 1088 *whip-poor-will* calls in succession without a breather) but had only got up to thirty when a car coming down the road cut the sequence short with an emphatic *Whip!*

How much sound there is at night around the nation's capital—and how oblivious is the average Washingtonian to it! His ears, attuned to motor cars and traffic seldom detect the music of nature —the voices of birds, frogs, or of insects—or the whispering of wind in the leaves. How often, at an outdoor barbecue, or when having drinks on the terrace after some Washington dinner party, have I heard, above the buzz of conversation, night herons quawking overhead on their way from Rock Creek Park to the Potomac, or the distant hooting of barred owls or the rasping snore of barn owls. Barn owls, symbols of wisdom, have lived in the northeast tower of the old Smithsonian building continuously for nearly ninety years. Over downtown roof-gardens the "peenting" of cruising nighthawks can often be heard above the hum of traffic, and in one suburban area, I have even listened to the moon-larking of that long-nosed recluse, the woodcock. The season opens in early spring with the aerial singing of the woodcock and the chorus of frogs, gives way by midsummer to the nocturnal stridulation of katydids and crickets, and ends in autumn with the lisps and chips of unseen birds hurrying southward on the cool northwest winds.

When James and I pulled into the driveway at Glen Echo on this warm April evening the barred owls were whooping it up down in the swamp by the canal.

April 26

More than any other large city in the world, Washington is a city of woods and parks; fingers of the wilderness penetrate nearly to its heart. Roger's home lies just outside the District of Columbia, on the slopes above the towpath of George Washington's Chesapeake and Ohio Canal, separated only by woodland from the Potomac River.

The house was once the slave quarters of a larger neighbor, and hides in the wood edge, so that the spring flush of advancing warblers can be heard from indoors, and an opossum comes at night to the feeder. The drawing room has a big picture window framing an ingenious indoor garden and many living plants which creep about, so that nature seems continuous inside and out. Barbara said that the little striped ground squirrels (chipmunks) once burrowed under the baseboard of the house and into the indoor garden, to be followed a week or so later by a rodent-hunting pilot blacksnake that came in through their tunnel and made itself at home among the ferns. Much as she likes wildlife this was too much: flying squirrels could enter the open windows at night if they wanted to, and could even spend the day sleeping in the folds of the curtains—but snakes must go!

The excitement this day, Sunday, was a luncheon picnic of the ancient Washington Biologists' Field Club. Every year, when the shad fish run into Chesapeake Bay and up the Potomac, this eclectic body has an open-air shadbake (and in the autumn, an oyster roast), on its treasured islet in the river, Plummer's Island—one of the most intensively botanized, zoologized, ecologized wild islands in the world, I suppose. Roger and I walked along a narrow path through riverside woodland densely carpeted with blue phlox until we reached an arm of the fast muddy river where a captive rowboat awaited us. By means of ropes and pulleys we pulled ourselves over to Plummer's Island, and scrambling up the wooded hill to the hut at its top, we found it already stiff with prominent biologists. There were mammalogists, botanists, ornithologists, herpetologists, entomologists; many were federal employees, associated with the Smithsonian Institution, the Fish and Wildlife Service, the National Parks, and the National Herbarium. The dedicated men assembled here represented the core of the hundreds of wildlife technicians, biologists, and conservationists whose job it is to keep wild America wild.

It was very difficult to meet, at the same time, life-birds such as Clarence Cottam and the red-bellied woodpecker, John Aldrich and the American redstart, Howard Zahniser and the parula warbler, let alone those already on my tally, like Alexander Wetmore and the downy woodpecker, Frederick C. Lincoln and the black and white warbler. It was a delightful and informal occasion, upon which I found a kind sympathy from those with whom I was conversing, for my more-than-occasional "Oh, just a minute," or "Do you mind?"

or "Roger, is that a—?" The novelties came so quickly for me. Delicately sailing across the canal, folding up wings and legs into sudden immobility by the bank, came the little green heron; soaring over the riverwood, the black vulture; lurching boldly through the new leaf and laughing loud, the pileated woodpecker. The yellow-bellied sapsucker at last was no longer just a name. And how big the crested flycatcher; how spotty the wood thrush; how tame the Carolina chickadee; how tiny the blue-gray gnatcatcher.

We sat, we talked, and we raised our field—or beer—glasses from time to time. Deft professional hands turned the fillets of shad over the grill, while a pretty remarkable selection of the finest biological thinkers of the U.S. queued up with cardboard plates like hungry schoolboys. I, mindful as I was of the honor of my invitation to this exclusive club, felt like a fourth-former who, asked to tea with the sixth-form fagmasters at the end of the term, finds them human after all. And most human of humans, if he does not mind my saying so, was a past president of the International Ornithological Congress and President of the American Ornithologists' Union and Secretary of the Smithsonian Institution, Alexander Wetmore. He had a ticket in his pocket for the morrow, for Barro Colorado Island, that incredible oasis of tropical bird life in Panama; and could scarcely disguise his excitement at the prospect of some interesting birding on his old stamping ground.

ON THE DAY of the picnic the woodlands along the Potomac were like flower gardens. The new green leaves of the trees had expanded sufficiently to block some of the sunlight, therefore many of the early flowers of the forest floor—the trailing arbutus, hepatica, spring beauty, trout lily, and bloodroot—were already past. But the paths and grassy glades were showy with beds of woodland phlox, their large pale lavender-blue blossoms clustered at the top of foot-tall stems. Violets looked up shyly; there were at least three species of blue ones, a creamy white one, and a yellow one. North America, with nearly eighty species, is abundantly blessed with violets. Wild geraniums added their purplish-pink to the floral color scheme, and the golden ragwort a touch of strong yellow. The flower that seemed to intrigue James most was the Jack-in-the-pulpit, which he recognized as a sort of arum. He examined the tubular greenish "pulpits" with their striped canopies and commented, "A wizard plant!"

When Europeans come to America they quickly notice one thing about the flowers: a large percentage of those growing along the roadside are plants that they already know, adventive plants which have come from Europe. A roadside is a roadside the world over. A farm is a farm—and a vacant city lot is much the same in Brooklyn as in Liverpool. Plants which through the centuries have become reconciled to disturbed soils in the Old World find no difficulty establishing a beachhead here. Their seeds arrive as stowaways on cargo boats; they hitchhike inland along the railroad tracks and highways; some have been deliberately introduced. Hundreds of species—no one knows exactly how many, because new ones are constantly being noticed—are now part of the American flora. The list is long: dandelion, black mustard, spearmint, peppermint, forget-me-not, mullein, field daisy, several clovers, several hawkweeds, several buttercups, bouncing Bet, white campion, butter-and-eggs, burdock, chicory, Queen Anne's lace, yarrow, teasel, tansy, and many, many others. On the outskirts of New York City, entry port for millions of human immigrants, 40 per cent of the flora is of Old World origin.

The woodland flowers, on the other hand, are mostly new to Europeans. The genus may be familiar, but the species is not. However, along the woodland edges this day there were several flowers that were old friends to James Fisher. The garlic-mustard (hedge garlic) with its heart-shaped leaves and clusters of small white blos-

Jack-in-the-Pulpit

soms would be in bloom now near his home in Northampton, England. And Sweet Cicely, too, or something rather like it. These familiars were growing not only in the low "flood forests" along the Potomac, but also in Rock Creek Park, which we visited late in the afternoon.

The National Zoological Park, located midway along the length of Rock Creek Park, the long wooded ravine that probes deep into the city, acts as a sort of decoy to wildlife. Some years ago night herons, flying over Rock Creek, discovered the great flying cage where ornamental wading birds are kept. Stimulated by the nesting activities of their captive brethren they built their own twiggy nests on branches of the trees overhanging the enclosure. Basically, they were one colony, separated only by wire: inside were the tame birds, outside were the wild ones. The growing heronry splattered the sidewalks below with excrement. When park officials cut off some of the overhanging branches most of the herons (but not all) started another colony on a wooded slope nearby. This Rock Creek Park heronry has expanded a great deal since the day, more than twenty years ago, when Bill Mann, the zoo's director, first showed it to me. Now, there must be at least 400 nests among the high tops of the maples and oaks. James and I tried to count, but we soon decided that the time to make an accurate census is a bit earlier in the season, before the new leaves are out.

Nearby, over the flying cage of the birds of prey, sat a half-dozen wild black vultures, hungrily eying the chunks of raw red meat which the captive birds were wolfing. These six unemployed vultures were all that remained of the winter roost; the others were nesting now—in rock ledges and in hollow logs up and down the Potomac Valley. In winter I have seen as many as 100 black vultures roosting above the flying cages and fully 300 turkey vultures in the woods nearby. The aggressive black vultures keep their red-headed relatives in their place; there is almost complete segregation. On the roof of one of the nearby apartment buildings on Connecticut Avenue the turkey vultures often warm their toes on the ventilators—lending a touch to the Washington scene reminiscent of one that London once knew in medieval times when kites and ravens scavenged London's streets. (We are not implying anything about the District of Columbia's department of sanitation.)

Two things set Washington apart from other American cities—its gracious municipal architecture and its trees. The original plan of the French designer, L'Enfant, envisaged a stately city, reflecting the eighteenth-century Age of Reason. The fine buildings would be set off by broad vistas, accentuated by avenues of trees. In the ensuing years, natural woodland parks were set aside to insure breathing spaces for the growing city. But today there are certain city planners who seem to have forgotten this ideal of beauty and repose.

One Sunday several winters ago, when crossing the Connecticut Avenue bridge, one of the high bridges over Rock Creek, my companion, a news photographer from Texas remarked: "Look at all that land going to waste down there—all that valuable real estate."

I suggested that natural or "inspirational" values were important too—in fact, beyond price; but his only response was a blank stare.

Although many men—far too many—have this blind spot, Washington has always known leaders with vision. More than one president have paraphrased the thought that "men will not take as elevated a view of the national destiny working in the basement of a warehouse as they will on the heights of an Acropolis." * If the environment is drab or shabby the thinking and impulses of statesmanship are likely to become shabby.

John Quincy Adams, speaking of Rock Creek Park, said that after a round of trying official duties as President, he would seek relaxation in "this romantic glen, listening to the singing of a thousand birds . . ." Theodore Roosevelt recalled with pleasure that when he was chief executive he often took long walks, "perhaps down Rock Creek, which was then as wild as a stream in the White Mountains." Even foreign diplomats have sung the praises of Rock Creek. Viscount Bryce, the British Ambassador, exclaimed: "What city in the world is there where a man . . . can within a quarter of an hour and on his own feet get in a beautiful rocky glen such as you would find in the woods of Maine or Scotland?"

And yet this park which has served almost as a place of worship for statesmen is threatened with a new express highway. There has also been much recent talk of building one the length of the Chesapeake and Ohio Canal, the historic old canal which was conceived by George Washington and later built for the purpose of opening up the lands beyond the Appalachian mountains to settlement and trade.

* *Washington—City in the Woods.* Published by the Audubon Society of the District of Columbia, 1954.

When a Washington newspaper ran editorials advocating the construction of a modern parkway along the canal the defenders of wilderness rose up in defense. Most powerful spokesman was Justice William O. Douglas of the Supreme Court of the United States, who challenged the writers of the editorials to walk the length of the canal with him so that they might see for themselves the wisdom of keeping the historic waterway with its picturesque lock houses as an unspoiled area.

The newsmen accepted the challenge. Starting at Cumberland, Maryland, on a cold gray morning, the last day of winter, they stepped briskly away from an old stone lock house toward Washington, 189 miles away. Close on their heels followed thirty-four other woods-walkers of every hue and stripe—bird watchers, photographers, conservationists, reporters, a radio broadcaster (who made tape recordings of birds and other sounds along the way), and also two stray dogs. When the motley collection of hikers approached Washington eight days later (some had dropped out) they were

greeted by groups all along the path. Canoeists in the canal carried signs such as: LESS CARS—MORE CANOES. A Park Service sight-seeing barge drawn by two mules met the foot-weary travelers, who swarmed aboard, and the last five miles into the city became a tri-umphal procession—suggestive of Cleopatra's retinue on the Nile. While the good Justice sat in state on the poop of the barge with a twig of wistaria in his hand, crowds ran along the banks and waved from overhead bridges. Observers noted that somewhere along the line Douglas had got his chin into some poison ivy, but he was jubi-lant, for he had seemingly won his point: during the long hike the newsmen—in spite of their blisters—agreed that at least parts of the canal, the towpath, and its wild border of woodlands, should be preserved against the intrusion of highways. Let us hope that Doug-las' effort proves not to have been a quixotic one.

Washington is a very satisfying city for the naturalist—if he does not mind the humid, almost tropical, summer climate. Here the facili-ties for those of his guild are second to none: wild country almost at the city's door; vast study collections in the Smithsonian and the Na-tional Herbarium; stacks of reference books—some almost priceless —at the Library of Congress; experts by the dozen, all willing to help, in the offices and laboratories of the Fish and Wildlife Service, the National Park Service, the National Forest Service, and the Na-tional Museum. Here, influential conservation organizations such as the National Wildlife Federation, the Nature Conservancy, the National Parks Association, the Wildlife Management Institute, and the Wilderness Society have their headquarters, as do magazines such as *The National Geographic Magazine, Nature Magazine, American Forests Magazine,* and *The Living Wilderness.* Of the local natural history societies, the Audubon Society of the District of Columbia, is by far the largest, with 1200 members. It publishes *The Atlantic Naturalist* and is, perhaps, the most effective local Audubon group in the country.

If we had only one more full day, I said to James, we could run out to Patuxent, the research center of the Fish and Wildlife Service, and see the bird-banding setup.* James told me to forget that word

---

* More than 7,000,000 North American birds have been banded (or ringed); 500,000 are added yearly. The little aluminum leg-bracelets carry numbers which are duly recorded on punch cards and kept on file at Patuxent, near Laurel, Maryland.

if. We just couldn't do everything. There was a visa we must get for him at the Mexican embassy, some shopping to do, and some more packing.

James, the expert, directed the packing of the station wagon. Into it went our duffle bags, field clothes, sleeping bags, a bird blind, cooking equipment, a tape recorder, photographic gear, and even a portable refrigerator, in which we stored our film. We took so many books and maps that the car, now quite full up, was almost a traveling library. After strapping the big parabolic reflector (for the sound equipment) to the roof we were ready to go, ready for the next twenty thousand miles.

As we pulled out of the driveway a high wiry *zi-zi-zi-zi-zi-zi-zi* on one pitch sounded in the big oaks overhead. The first blackpoll warbler had arrived; spring migration was already nearing its climax.

Dutchman's Breeches

6

Down the Blue Ridge

$\mathcal{U}$NLIKE EDWIN WAY TEALE, who in 1947 accompanied spring northward,* we were going southward, meeting it head on. But one does not meet spring at any precise point except on the calendar; it is a progressive series of events. Each migrant bird arrives at approximately its appointed time; each flower comes into bloom at its proper place in the floral procession. And spring is a fluid thing, influenced by altitude as well as by latitude. It flows not only northward, but upward, first into the valleys, then slowly up the slopes of the hills and the mountains.

For nearly a fortnight, ever since our departure from Newfoundland, we had been breasting the tide, but this morning, the 29th of April, we temporarily reversed the process. Before us rose the Blue Ridge, the first great natural wall on the Virginia plain as one pro-

* *North with the Spring* (New York, 1951).

ceeds westward from the city of Washington, eighty miles away. As
we climbed the motor road in second gear each switchback brought
an almost perceptible change in the aspect of the forest which clothed
the mountain flanks. The showy white bracts of the dogwood that
were in full glory in the valleys and the garish pink blossoms of the
redbud that were already past their peak near my home were here just
coming into bloom. A few hundred feet higher they were still in bud.
The progress of spring had been shoved back at least three weeks by
the time we reached Skyline Drive, the lofty parkway which traces
its course for ninety-six miles along the crests of the Blue Ridge at
an average altitude of 3000 feet. Our journey along its serpentine
length on this late April morning was a demonstration of vertical
magic. Repeatedly we went in and out of spring. When our road
dipped into valleys between the mountains we were plunged into the
lush green fairyland of spring at flood tide; climbing out again we
soon found ourselves in a more austere landscape, the landscape of
late March or early April. In one or two spots where the road attained
an elevation of nearly 4000 feet the aspect was quite Canadian, som-
ber with the dark spires of red spruce. Here the deciduous trees, the
birches, oaks, and maples, were naked, still devoid of leaves.

Where the road followed the very spine of the ridge, breath-
taking panoramas dropped away on either side. We stopped at the
overlooks—lay-bys, James called them—where from the western rim
we could look out over the lush farmlands of the Shenandoah Valley.
Through our binoculars the red barns and white farmhouses far below
seemed like toys in a terrain model landscape. Beyond, in West Virginia, were other mountain ridges and behind these still others, each
one bluer and hazier with the distance. As mountains go, the Appalachians may seem rather disappointing to those who are seeking the
dynamic grandeur of the Alps or the Rockies. They are ancient
mountains, among the oldest on earth, whose parent rocks were first
raised up more than 500 million years ago. During the Paleozoic, in
the heyday of ancient Appalachia, the peaks may well have exceeded
the massive heights of the Alps or the Rockies. Over the ages they
were planed down by weather and erosion and from time to time
were partially lifted again by the folding of the earth's crust. The result
is what we see today, green mountains with softer more feminine contours than those of younger more vigorous ranges. As Henry Sharp,
the geologist, puts it: "The venerable finished beauty of these moun-

tains tells a story beside which that of the Alps is like the raw rough-
ness of a new-quarried block compared to a finished statue."

When the Shenandoah National Park, which embraces Skyline
Drive, was established by an Act of Congress in 1935, some purists
were critical. They claimed that the area did not measure up to
National Park standards. It was mostly second-growth woodland, they
said; there was relatively little primeval forest within its 300 square
miles—just a few pockets of hemlock and some very old oaks that
had escaped the axe. The lumbermen, only a few decades before, had
come and gone and most of the wildlife had been exterminated by the
hill people. The National Park Service answered the critics by pointing out that the East could not possibly compete with the West; there
are very few samples of the primeval remaining. If the East is to have
wilderness it must restore it. The second growth, now thirty, forty, or
fifty years old, which clothes the Shenandoahs, will, while our sons
are alive, become trees eighty, ninety, or one hundred years old. Our
grandsons may see a forest approaching its climax.

There are already signs of returning wildlife. As we passed Old
Rag, a rocky outcrop to our left, two ravens played at gymnastics
on the updrafts; later we stopped to look at one of these big ebony
birds which sat, unafraid, less than a hundred feet from us in a dead
tree. The raven, which had all but disappeared in most parts of the
eastern mountains, is now returning. A pileated woodpecker, big as a
crow, with a flaming red crest, flew across the highway and was later
heard calling far down the mountain slope. This is another bird that
has made a return—a very remarkable comeback. Forty years ago
some ornithologists predicted it would go the way of the ivory-billed
woodpecker.

A few bears roam the Blue Ridge; they are increasing. But even
though the cutover forests are growing up again we shall never again
in the eastern highlands know the Wild America that Daniel Boone
saw. Two centuries have seen the complete extermination of the timber wolf, the mountain lion, the eastern bison and the eastern elk.
The sinewy backwoodsman was a dead shot and he knew no game
laws. It is doubtful, even if there were such laws, whether the wolf or
the mountain lion would have been spared. The way of life of the
wolf conflicts too much with the interests of man. However, a few
mountain lions, even in this modern era, would not be a bad idea.
The deer coverts of Pennsylvania and West Virginia, overpopulated

in many places with half-starved and runty stock, would benefit by a certain amount of predatory selection.

On a tree trunk beside a path near the road we saw a white blaze. Farther along the path where it crossed an open bald was a cairn of rocks. These were markers to guide hikers along the Appalachian Trail. This Olympian pathway which paralleled our route and occasionally crossed it has its northern anchor on the bleak summit of Mount Katahdin in Maine, not far from the Canadian border. It wanders tortuously in a generally southwestward direction, climbing the highest peaks along the way, until it ends at Mount Oglethorpe, Georgia, a distance of 2050 miles. Although half the population of the United States lives only a few hours from one part of the trail or another, it traverses wild country—high country—nearly the whole way, descending only to cross water gaps or farm country between the ranges. Although numerous hikers are to be met with on some sections of the Appalachian Trail, only one man, Earl V. Shaffer, has ever walked the entire distance in one continuous hike. Starting at Mount Oglethorpe in Georgia on April 4, 1948, he averaged 17 miles a day, cooked his meals (mostly cornbread) in a pan, slept out (sometimes in fire towers), and reached Katahdin four months later. He wore the same pair of boots the whole way, but they were almost in tatters at the end.

Although thousands of hikers avail themselves of the trails and campsites of Shenandoah it will always be primarily a park for the motorist—much more so than any of the other National Parks. The week-end visitation from nearby cities is enormous. During 1953 more than 2,000,000 people passed through the tollgates.

When the Indians prophesied that the invading whites would become "as numerous as the leaves of the trees" they foresaw the future clearly. But even civilized man needs the esthetic stimulation which the wilderness alone can provide. Some of us would even die spiritually if we could not withdraw occasionally from crowded contact with our fellowman. On the other hand, many men have become so conditioned to the complexity of city life that they regard the sky merely as something which they see at the end of the street. They appear to have a mistrust—almost a fear—of the natural world. We see such people even on Skyline Drive, but they stay in their cars and keep the radio going full blast.

Late in the morning we dropped off the ridge at Rockfish Gap, where we stopped at a small country store for cokes. Before getting back into the car we spotted our first Baltimore oriole, a bright orange flame in a large elm. There were yellow warblers about, too, and other farm-country birds that we had not seen on the mountain-top. For two or three hours we sped southward through the great Appalachian Valley which lies just west of the Blue Ridge, and then, hot and sweaty with the unaccustomed summer heat, we sought the cool mountains again.

Another great highway, the Blue Ridge Parkway, takes up where the Skyline Drive leaves off. In beautifully engineered grades and curves it winds southward along the ridge for more than 400 miles and finally deposits the motorist near the foot of the Great Smokies, where Appalachia attains its climax.

At the edge of an open slope matted with the sere dry sedge of last year we noticed a half-dozen large dead trees, naked and bleached. These were chestnuts, victims of the chestnut blight, an Asiatic fungus, which was first noticed near New York City in 1904. Sweeping inland and southward the plague killed off nearly every chestnut tree in its path, from Canada to the Gulf. No greater catastrophe has ever befallen a tree in our times. These snags before us on the skyline had probably been dead for thirty years or more; their stout trunks and twisted weather-polished limbs are practically indestructible. Springing from the roots of two or three of the old tree skeletons were suckers of new growth. Shoots such as these often raise hopes that the chestnut might make a comeback; but usually the saplings wither and die about the time the first nuts are produced.

Dogwood

Wistfully I thought of the happy days long ago when I went with my father in the autumn to gather chestnuts. My own boys will never have that experience.

But what, one might ask, is one tree more or less in a region which has such a profusion of species? Probably nowhere else in the world is there a richer, more diverse deciduous forest than that which clothes the rounded contours of the southern Appalachians. The number of native trees in Great Smoky National Park alone is greater than that of all Europe. Europe lists 85 native species; the Smokies, 131.

What is the story behind these figures? Most of our trees and shrubs assumed their present form ages ago—some millions of years ago, in fact. The Arctic was warmer then and the continents were joined in the far North. The modern forest which was then evolving was circumpolar; plants slowly extended their domain from Europe and Asia across to North America while others, of American origin, traveled in the other direction. There was a great mingling of influences. The Arctic was near the center of this circumpolar forest. Then came the "Big Ice." Slowly it spread out from the pole; ice thousands of feet thick blotted out the center of the great forest. Some species of plants undoubtedly perished, others "migrated" southward. The mountain ranges of Europe—the Alps, Pyrenees, and Carpathians—extending from east to west, formed walls which blocked retreat. The hard-pressed plants survived the changing climate as long as they could. We cannot even guess how many species disappeared. Europe again has a green mantle of trees, but today it is made up of relatively few species if one does not include those numerous exotics which have been so widely planted.

The North American mountain ranges extend from North to South; there were no latitudinal walls to bar retreat. Many of the trees survived the Ice Age in the great reservoir of plant life which had its center in the South not far from the Smokies—roughly around Chattanooga, Tennessee. At the end of the long period of cold some of the hardier trees migrated northward again by way of the valleys and the lowlands. Others climbed the mountains until they were isolated on the summits; that is why there are "Canadian" trees such as the red spruce in the Carolinas.

In Asia, as in North America, there were no serious barriers to obstruct. That explains why the tall stately tulip trees (*Liriodendron*)

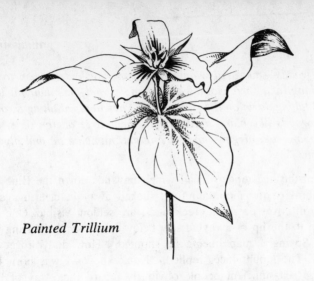

Painted Trillium

which we had been admiring in the valleys are not found in Europe only 3500 miles away, but are to be seen—or at least trees very similar—9000 miles away across the broad Pacific. A botanist from Appalachia would feel quite at home in parts of China or Japan. He would find not only trees very similar to those he already knew, but also such "American" spring flowers as those we were seeing this very day—Jack-in-the-pulpit, skunk cabbage, mandrake, trailing arbutus, trilliums, Dutchman's breeches, dwarf ginseng, and many, many others.

In fact, there is a human connection between the ginseng of eastern North America and the ginseng of China. The *jen-shen,* or root of life, a member of the English ivy family, was regarded for centuries by the Chinese as a cure-all: it supposedly could prolong life, was valued as an aphrodisiac, and could remedy every known human disorder. In due time the rapidly multiplying Chinese had uprooted it from every corner of their overcrowded land. When (in 1715) ginseng was discovered in North America, the herbalists of the Flowery Kingdom, anxious to have it, offered high prices. Both the Cherokees and the mountain folk ranged widely over the hills in their assiduous search for the precious "sang." A mountaineer once described to Donald Culross Peattie a group of "sang diggers":

They was the most terrifying people I ever see. I was over in the balsams near the pink beds, when I see them coming through

*the woods—men and women with eyes that didn't seem to see
nothing, and their clothes all in tatters, and their hair all lank
and falling down on their shoulders. They humped along through
the woods like b'ars, muttering to themselves all the time, and
stooping, and digging, and cursing and humping on and digging
again.*

From the fine modern road which unwinds down the Blue Ridge
the cabins of the mountain folk, tucked away in clearings on the
slopes, in coves or along creek beds, are seldom visible. One hiker,
coming to the lip of a ravine saw below him a small clearing and a
cabin. Spying a man hoeing he shouted, "How do you get down
there?" The mountaineer replied, "Don't know—I was born here."

These self-sufficient people obviously regard their way of life as
the normal one; those from the outside are the "quare" ones.
Descendants, for the most part, of Scotch-Irish or English Presby-
terians, they found in these unsettled mountains the fulfillment of
their longing for complete freedom—at times it was scarcely more
than freedom to starve—but freedom. Here there were no tax
collectors, no recruiting agents. Even to this day they have nursed
a disdain for certain forms of authority. In some parts of the southern
highlands it is not wise for the wandering bird watcher to investigate
a thin blue curl of smoke rising from the woods. Because of his
binoculars and suspicious actions he might be mistaken for a revenue
officer—a "revenooer"—whose dangerous mission it is to ferret out
illicit stills. But the motor car and the radio, bringing contact from
the outside are rapidly changing the hill people. Soon their "Eliza-
bethian" dialect and ballads will fade away and the only hillbillies
left will be those phonies on commercial radio and television. It
is one of the purposes of the two National Parks of the southern
highlands—Shenandoah and Great Smoky—to preserve some of
the old log cabins and split-rail fences, mills, and other examples
of this rapidly fading bit of Americana.

During the afternoon, mile after mile of the Blue Ridge rolled
smoothly from under our wheels. It seemed regrettable that we could
not linger in each azalea-covered glade, but we had an appointment
to keep in the Great Smokies. We were almost lulled by the ever
changing panorama—deep woodlands of hemlock and rhododendron,
high meadows, balds, and the occasional rustic cabin with its little
plot of tilled land. No ugly billboards; no advertisements advising

us to try some new wonder medicine; no posters urging us to vote for some local candidate who had been defeated in last year's elections. Nor did we pass through a town—not one. However, we realized that we must be thinking of getting back to civilization soon, unless we planned to bed down in the back of the station wagon. In another hour it would be dark. Presently at a bend in the road there was a signpost. It read:

ASHEVILLE — 132 MILES.

"Where in this world," commented James, "could one drive so far—actually hundreds of miles—without passing through a single town or village, even a small one?"

A month later this highway would be buzzing with cars, but we were ahead of the tourist season. That is undoubtedly why we saw so many mammals that night before our headlights. In the late afternoon we had seen a woodchuck, as our eastern marmot is called, sitting upright at the mouth of its burrow. Woodchucks are not nocturnal but possums are; we saw a dead possum lying on the roadbed where it had been run over the night before. This marsupial, slow-moving and rather stupid, is probably killed by cars more often than any other mammal, except perhaps the skunk. Several times our noses informed us where a skunk had met its end under the fast-moving wheels of some previous car; the strong odor of this black and white "wood pussy" persists in the area for several days.

Our headlights, probing the ribbon of concrete ahead, frequently picked up the eyeshine of mammals. We strained our eyes to see the creatures before they plunged into the dark thickets to the side. Once pale yellow-green eyes turned out to be those of a vagrant house cat. And there was a hound dog, seemingly lost. I caught a glimpse of a possum and we saw a raccoon before it ambled into the darkness. We learned on this, and subsequent nights, that the key to mammal identification at night on the road was their tails; we almost always had rear views. The skunk's tail was a furry plume, held aloft; the possum had a naked ratlike tail, and that of the raccoon was bushy with black rings. When a fox broke into a run before the car and raced us down the road, we could not be quite sure at first whether it was a red fox or a gray. The yellow glare of the headlights seemed to bleach out the color to an indeterminate hue. I said, "Gray." James replied, "Yes, gray—no!—red." I acceded that it was a red until we got close enough to see the black on the tip of its bushy tail. It was indeed a gray fox; the red fox has a white tip to its tail. Within the space of an hour we saw one red fox and two grays.

I do not recall ever having had a more successful night spotting mammals in the headlights. We watched for owls too but did not see any. It must have been after 10 P.M. when we stopped at a grove on a ridge to listen for *Bubo,* the horned owl. The moon was out; it was a night for the owls to be talking. As we stood there, ears extended, a curious rush of wind could be heard, first on the distant mountain slope, then closer. Sudden gusts swayed the tops of the trees; wisps of haze crossed the moon. A storm was building up somewhere. There was no use listening further for owls.

At midnight when we had our coffee at Canton just west of Asheville before going to bed, we learned that disastrous tornadoes had swept through Tennessee and other neighboring states. We were on the edge of the storm belt.

7

On Top of Old Smoky

$\mathcal{T}$HE NOISES of the morning were drowned by wind and rain; our Smoky Mountain view was obscured by a bluster of wet mountain weather. James took the wheel; slowly we climbed the winding grade through the Cherokee Indian Reservation while the southeasterly gale slatted the car's windows. Murky skies blotted the top of old Smoky; our rising trail led into a mist through channels of rain-shiny fields and woods. New fat streams poured down the hillsides.

Round a windy corner, soon after we crossed the southern boundary of the park, we caught sight of a white-breasted bird a bit larger than a pigeon standing on a long heap of road gravel. James put foot to the brakes and we quickly jumped out to get a close look. It was a gull; its black head and dark mantle identified it as a laughing gull. Was it injured? Apparently not; reluctantly, the tired bird flew up and slanted across the now dying wind out of view. But what was it doing here, 3000 feet up in the mountains on North

Carolina's State Highway 107? The answer was—doing something that no laughing gull had ever been seen to do before; resting in the Great Smokies. When, a few hours later, we saw Arthur Stupka, chief park naturalist, he confirmed that our bird was a "first record" for the Park. Like many such "firsts" it was almost certainly a wind-drifted stray. It had been caught in the Atlantic gale that had been raging, and was blown—or rather, carried, like a swimmer in a too strong current—from some part of the coast between Florida and the Carolinas, where this strictly coastal species lives. To the lost bird, 300 miles from salt water, the heap of gravel by the roadside must have seemed the nearest thing to a sea beach it could find in the forest. Our travel year of 1953 was a year of storms and gales, with cyclones and lesser winds developing in the Caribbean much earlier in the season than usual and petering out at varying distances inland. These storms bore their pathetic wads of exhausted seabirds, to run out of fuel and ground, as our tired laughing gull did, at queer out-of-the-way places.

The wind died down by midmorning; the rest of the day was showery and sometimes we were enveloped in cloud. Everywhere, whenever the intermittent sun broke through to light the dripping trees, we caught the flash of some male warbler, but more often we heard their sibilant songs. It rained rain—and wood warblers, to confuse, utterly, James's Old World-tuned eyes and ears.

April 30

Warblers, warblers, everywhere, nor any time to think. "A Hundred Miles of Warblers" was the title of Edwin Way Teale's moving chapter in his *North with the Spring*. Ludlow Griscom had counseled him: "Be near Asheville, North Carolina, the third week in April and you will see the warblers pour across the mountains." It is now a week later than Griscom's deadline but the great rush of these punctual jewels of the trees is still on. We are in the thick of it; we have been in their migration stream for the last four or five days, all the way from New Jersey to the Smokies. During this time we have seen and heard no less than twenty-seven of the thirty-five species that use the Appalachian route in spring.

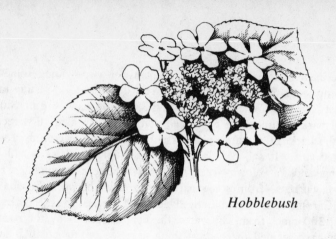

Hobblebush

The Parulidae [the wood warblers, or New World warblers] are a family of songbirds that is probably ancient, and evolved in tropical *North* America. For in the Tertiary period—the last sixty or sixty-five million years—North America was cut off from South America by sea-gaps in Central America, which persisted, in one place or another, until perhaps two million years ago. In the southern part of this disconnected continent large areas were for millions of years quite tropical (as parts of southern Mexico and Central America still are today) and Ernst Mayr and others consider that several New World families of birds evolved there, among them the New World "vultures," turkeys, limpkins, trogons, mockers and thrashers, wrens, vireos, and wood warblers. The wood-warbler family is the largest of these groups, with over a hundred species, of which about half cross the Mexican border into the United States and Canada. Certainly the Parulidae have had a great success, though the Sylviidae [Old World warblers]—their counterpart, on a separate and even more ancient branch of the tree of bird life—have almost three times as many living species. The New World "warblers" have much brighter coloration, on the whole, than those of the Old World; at least the males do, for they have sex differences. Their songs have not the variety, and gentle lilting poetry, of the Old World family, but capture the listener's ear with trills, zips, buzzes, and hissing jumbles.

Roger, with his magic ear and skillful eye, picks the warblers out of cover before I have time to start wondering what they are. "Take your word for it, old boy," I have sometimes to say when I tick off a new one in my list—making a mental note to get a clear view of it for my diary. How often I fail and the little birds make their cheerful noises! Few of them really warble; their sounds buzz and tinkle, slurr and twitter, stutter and trill. Regular, irregular, explosive, lazy, soft, wiry, their voices make me a confused catalogue, with *bee* and *buzz* and *bz; char, chee, churr; errr; me, miss; orrr; sar, see sir, switch; teach, tea, tew, ti, tiz, teet, to, tory, tsee, tseet, tweet; up; way, wee, weet, which, wi, wont, woods; you; zee, zh, zhee, zi, zip, zit, zray, zree, zur.* All the way from New Jersey we were pursued by the voices of these little birds. They beat through the hum of the car, even the moan of the wind. We heard them whenever we stopped in a leafy place, or by scrub or swamp.

In the leafy woodlands, every day, we met parula warblers, high in the dripping canopy, buzzing up their little trill (which ascends the scale and whips off at the end with a snap). This was one song I *did* learn, and one warbler I learned by sight quickly enough, too, with its blue back, double white-barred wings, and its dark-banded yellow breast. *Zeeeeeeeee-up* the parulas cheerfully buzzed, in all weathers. Some were territorial singers already established, others were en route to more northern woodlands where they would swing their nests in the festoons of usnea moss.

Another warbler I soon learned, by sight more than song, was the black and white warbler with its longitudinal zebra stripes. This we saw often, for though it was a bird of the big-leaf deciduous woods it kept low, sometimes creeping about trunks and low branches. It flitted about on frequent flycatching forays, and called a tinny thin tune: *see   see* —often repeated. Roger regarded this an easy one, *see   see* but I heard many such tunes (I thought). I confused it with a double-note song of the American redstart—and also that of another warbler, the black-throated green, that was "warbling" (I suppose that's it) its way to evergreen woods in places north. All these New World warblers seem to sing on passage more than our European Sylviids. Roger said I had no business to confuse the dreamy *zee   zee* of the black-throated green with anything else, but *zoo   zoo zoo* he had yet to discover my vast capacity for confusion. He has had time to learn his wood warblers by degrees—and when I told him to try starting among two dozen of them, from scratch, he smiled and then changed the subject.

Black-throated Green Warbler

There was a lot of overlap in habitat between these everyday warblers of our journey. Little bands of half a dozen species were quite usual. No doubt many of those on passage hunted in any sort of foliage that produced insect food. The pretty, startlingly pretty, cock redstarts, flashing bright orange on tail-sides and wings, seemed everywhere; but once afoot in the Smoky forests I began to see that they were really birds not of the big trees, but of the secondary woods and wood edges. Less easy to place in a habitat were the myrtles. Like many of the black-throated greens, they were passengers, bound for the northern pine-and-spruce woods, and like them, were refueling on their long journey anywhere from the top of an 80-foot buckeye to roadside bushes or farmside appleblossoms. Only once did I hear a snatch of song from a myrtle warbler on the Blue Ridge, a wandering, under-breath little mumble, but often a loud single *check* gave it away, usually before a sight of its yellow rump flash.

Another everyday warbler was the prairie; this yellow little bird wagged its tail and sang from the dry hillsides and slashings, where scrub recolonized the clearings. Roger said that it sounded "like a mouse with a toothache," but to me its ascending chromatic *zee-zee-zee-zee*—a plaintive and pretty song—somehow fitted the scene and landscape as does the willow warbler's song at home in Europe, and whenever I heard it I thought of our familiar little Sylviid's lilt (quite different though this is), floating from the common above Selborne's beech-hanger or from the edge of an old English oak-wood, or an upland birch stand in the Highlands.

The hooded warblers had perhaps the finest song I heard from a wood warbler. They were brightly whistling *sweeten the   tea   o* from the undergrowth; the yellow, olive-backed males looked as if they had pulled black Balaklava helmets too far down on their breasts, to stretch a great gap through which their yellow faces peered. Two other birds of the undergrowth and the wet forest floor were the oven-bird and Louisiana water-thrush, biggish flat-footed warblers which were more like small thrushes, specially adapted for leading nightingale-lives, walking and leaf-turning on the ground. "A voice in the woods," wrote Roger in his *Field Guide to the Birds* of the oven-bird, and a voice it remained to me, for I never got a good enough view of it or its cousin the Louisiana water-thrush to distinguish their field marks, clear though these may be. Every day we heard both; from streamside a high slurred whistle, thrice repeated as a preliminary to an under-breath warbling, a breezy, descending jumble of sound, the song of the Louisiana water-thrush; and from the floor of the deciduous woodland *teach, teach,* or *teacher, teacher,* the chant of the oven-bird. Our great tit in Europe cries *teacher,* too, but not like this, not in this bold crescendo. Roger pointed out that the oven-birds that said *teacher* were probably passengers, bound for the North, while the *teach* birds were locals, already at home, and singing in their Carolina accents. The oven-bird is one of the many that have local dialects.

Hopping low in the vegetation by the streamside, often in full view, flashing its black domino or "raccoon mask" was the yellow-throat, singing its fast clear *wichity, fidgety, fetchety-fetch.* The Kentucky warbler, olive-backed and yellow-breasted, with black cheeks trailing off as black side whiskers was a bird I saw only once, but several times heard calling to Roger from low growth at the edges of wet woodlands and bogs—*tory-tory-tory-tory.* Roger called back, once or twice.

On our way south, yesterday, we also picked up the yellow, the black-throated blue, the cerulean, and the Blackburnian warblers and the yellow-breasted chat. None of these had I seen before, nor the golden-winged, blue-winged, Tennessee, magnolia, yellow-throated, bay-breasted, and Canada warblers, which we added today in Great Smoky. Considering that we found the last seven in about an hour near the Park headquarters, where we hit our biggest "wave" of migrating warblers, I must be forgiven for being confused. I still am confused.

Even the warblers themselves get confused—at least the golden-

winged and blue-winged do. I still have to look up which of the
two says *bee-bz-bz-bz* and which says *beeee-bzzzz*. "Both species
occasionally sing the song of the other," murmured Roger casually
(afterwards I checked his *Field Guide* and found R.T.P. was quoting
from it—he must use it a lot).

There is little time to take notes on this part of our journey.
Many of the notes I did jot down make no sense at all when I try
to sort them out. What would have happened to my notebook had
we been watching the fall migration, I pale to think! The parulids,
like the "sparrows" and the New World flycatchers, are maddening
to the novice and need five years', not five days', experience and
practice. In the fall when many of them lose their distinctive breeding dress, there are a couple of dozen yellow, buff, olive, and gray
little birds to choose from, all neatly arranged and ticketed by Roger
in his plates, "Confusing Fall Warblers." Immature forms are even
more confusing, and one kinglet and at least two vireos can make
confusion worse confounded. The result is a morass of uncertainty.

JAMES's bewilderment with the New World warblers was not a patch
on my own confusion when I first crossed the Atlantic and tried to
make order out of the warblers of the Old World. It was my verdict
that they *all* looked like Tennessee warblers in fall plumage—plain
little olive-green, olive-brown, or olive-gray jobs. Our warblers, at
least in the spring, had distinctively patterned males. But in due
time, by fitting voice, habitat, and appearance together like the pieces
of a jigsaw puzzle, even the modest Sylviids sorted themselves out.

A far bigger task than learning the two-dozen warblers in the
Smokies, I am convinced, is to sort out its 130 indigenous trees—
let alone the 1300 flowering plants. For it is the staggering variety
of its flora that sets the Smokies apart from all other National Parks.
Here are the last remnants of the great primeval hardwood forest,
and this, in addition to the fact that here are the highest peaks in the
East—sixteen topping 6000 feet—determined its destiny as a national
recreation area. Authorized by Congress in 1926, there were no
federally owned lands with which to start the park. The states of
North Carolina and Tennessee acquired the land piece by piece,

using state funds and donations which were matched dollar for dollar by that great conservationist, John D. Rockefeller, Jr. In 1940 the park was formally dedicated and presented to the people of the nation.

Great Smoky Mountains National Park, covering more than half a million acres, is 40 per cent virgin, the largest block of primeval woodlands left in eastern North America—may it ever remain axeless. Some sections seem all but pathless, although 653 miles of footpaths and bridle trails have been created for that minority of the 2,000,000 yearly visitors who, having a drop or two of Daniel Boone's blood in their veins, would leave the highway and the main camping grounds.

These woods-walkers need not fear the lurking Indian as the first mountain settlers did, although 3000 Cherokees still live in the hills, mostly in the Reservation just outside the Park boundaries. They are descendants of those fiercely liberty-loving Cherokees who in 1838–39 hid deep in the Smokies while General Winfield Scott herded their less spirited brethren westward over the "Trail of Tears." Today, some of the Oklahoma Cherokees, like the Osages, ride about in Cadillacs, for oil was found on their unpromising land, but the eastern branch of the tribe, as a distinct unit, still preserves the traditions of their once powerful nation.

To climb the Smokies—or any high mountain range—is a lesson in vertical distribution, a forceful sermon on the relation of living things to altitude. We repeated this experience several times during our brief sojourn. From the gentle Tennessee meadows, with their early flowers, bright at their edges with white dogwood and shad, we climbed nearly five thousand feet back into North Carolina. Gradually spring fell behind us, and the leafy canopy shrank from full broad green to yellow bud. We left the stately tulip trees behind and then the mountain magnolias, their big blossoms waxy white against the dark hemlocks; and eventually the lovely silverbells. It was too early for the flame azaleas, although we saw their first blossoms down in Gatlinburg. In another two or three weeks the mountainsides would be afire with their orange-yellow and flame-orange blossoms. Later, the purple rhododendrons would put on their spectacular show—a display that could be equalled only in the Himalayas.

When we reached Newfound Gap, the highest point on the transmountain highway, we were among the spruce and fir. Yellow birch and aspen were barely out of bud. Here where the Appalachian Trail crossed the highroad we were in the Canadian Zone, in country almost precisely like that where the trail starts on the flanks of Mount Katahdin eighteen hundred miles by trail to the northeast.

From Newfound Gap a spur in the road leads to Forney Ridge, under Clingman's Dome, the highest point (6311 feet) of the highest highway in the eastern states. Here the clouds closed in upon us, to open up again and disclose a breathtaking panorama of evergreen-clothed peaks. On a mossy spot beside the road shoulder stood a ruffed grouse—the king of North American game birds. It remained motionless for a moment, then exploded with a roar, flashing its broad rufous, black-banded tail as it whirred into the dripping spruces.

We looked for bears, and although this stretch of road is the place where I had found them before, we saw none. Nor did we see any when we returned again after dark. We spotted a deer in the probing beam of our headlights, once or twice we saw a fox—but no bears. It is when the summer traffic starts that the bears patrol this high stretch of road, begging the tourists for food. Since the Park was established, the bears have thrived; so much so that several families of them have become "panhandlers"—beggars—and in their own interests the public has been forbidden to feed, touch, tease or molest them. It is the Park Service's view that wild animals should remain wild. But not even a panhandler could we find this night, nor did we hear a saw-whet owl, that tiny owl of the boreal woods, among the sprucelands of the tops. We stopped and listened, stopped and listened; I whistled and tooted in my best saw-whet accents—but no reply. We retreated to Gatlinburg having heard little but the wind.

Tomorrow, we decided, we would forsake the car and get the feel of the forest loam under our feet.

May 1

April rained itself out in the small hours of the first of May and the morning sun, shining down from a blue sky, sparkled in thousands of raindrop lenses. Quickly the forest dried as we drove up the middle prong of the Pigeon River, swollen with rain from the Tennessee slopes of those great wooded hills, Le Conte and Chapman. Led by Arthur Stupka and his wife and the Glidden Baldwins, who are authorities on the big trees of the Smokies, we left the cars near the meeting of two streams which had cut down to staircases of smooth, pebble-worn rock, all overhung by the forest hemlocks, and giant shiny-leaved rhododendrons. It was a steamy valley, cushioned with moss and full of the good smell of rotting wood. To our north rose Greenbrier Pinnacle, to our south all 6430 feet of Mount Chapman. As we took the trail up the Ramsay Prong the valley closed in, and the forest grew bigger, and wilder. I began to feel that I was walking in one of those dreams, down interminable corridors, between infinitely high pillars—those dreams in which proportions inexorably change.

"The first thing I've got to do," said Alice to herself, as she wandered about in the wood, "is to grow to my right size again . . ."

But I never grew to my right size again, in all the time we spent in the great stand of trees in the valley of the Ramsay Prong. The bushes were trees, and the trees were emperors; even the shadbushes seemed forty feet high. Near the beginning of the trail a tulip tree towered higher than any tree I had even seen in Britain; and from then on big trees of at least six kinds thrust up from the tangled forest floor for about a hundred feet, or more. The forest track wound under them, through dense undergrowth; rhododendrons of enormous size formed dark jungles through which our uphill trail became a leafy tunnel. Every now and then we paused like dwarfs at the foot of some great bole: a Canada hemlock—the big *Tsuga canadensis*—eight feet or more across at the roots and five at man height; a tremendous silverbell; a pair of yellow buckeyes, each nearly a hundred feet high; vast smooth-trunked beeches; the biggest maple tree I had ever seen, a sugar maple; and a seventy-foot wild pincherry, the grandfather of all cherry trees, whose top was lost in the green canopy and whose lowest branch, a great horizontal arm, must have been forty feet above us. At one point our path took us between two forest giants, buckeyes I believe they were, the same two trees that we had seen only a week before in the Great Smoky diorama in the American Museum. But wait a minute, I said to myself; how can one have his cake and eat it too? This was indeed, an Alice-in-Wonderland forest. Roger told me that although this was the identical spot shown in the Museum exhibit, the scene was recreated from tree trunks felled outside the Park.

The spring woodland flowers were already past their peak. They were at their best just at bud-bursting time before the expanding green leaves cut off the light from the forest floor. But everywhere in the cool glades trilliums lifted their creamy white blossoms; not the big white ones we had seen along the Blue Ridge, but *alba,* the whitish form of the red trillium. These showy three-petaled, three-leaved flowers which belong to the lily family have their headquarters here; several rare kinds are found in the Park.

Glidden Baldwin stopped in a grassy place to pull up a green shoot. "Here," he offered, "try this."

It was a sort of leek or wild onion. It tasted like strong garlic.

"That's a ramp," he said. "The mountaineers sometimes have

ramp parties. They all get together on a spring Sunday and eat ramps and drink beer."

It sounded very cozy. We didn't have any beer with us but we all sampled the ramps. I daresay one could be quite self-sustaining in these genial hills if he knew the wild vegetables, greens, fruits, and herbs.

The Smokies are not only the eastern headquarters of North America's trees and flowers, but also of newts and salamanders. Under the first wet fallen branch we lifted we found Jordan's red-cheeked salamander, an amphibian known nowhere else in the world than in the Great Smoky National Park. Here there are about thirty species of salamanders, far more than in any other area in the world, for it was here that the Plethodont salamanders had their origin; the only family of vertebrates to arise in these ancient hills. We never found another Jordan's, but dusky salamanders were everywhere, wiggling away whenever we tipped over a loose stone or moved a mossy log.

These wonderful woods were not as full of sound as one might expect. It is axiomatic that in a mature forest birds are fewer than in secondary growth or along the woodland edges. Here in the heart of the grand forest we heard less song than we had heard along the highway or around the well-manicured Park headquarters. We heard, of course, the flute-like notes of the wood thrush, and blue jays called occasionally. The only woodpecker we heard was the big pileated. Black-throated green warblers lisped dreamily from the hemlocks and Blackburnian warblers sang their high wiry notes. I thought the Blackburnian with its flaming orange throat one of the most striking small birds I had ever seen. A lazy gravel voice was the most frequent bird song this morning. It belonged to the neat-looking black-throated blue warbler which lives in the rhododendron thickets.

There were other sounds too: a sharp rattle like a wooden ratchet-rattle, and a ubiquitous *chuck*. I looked hard for these birds, and Roger let me hunt for them for a mile or two before slyly telling me they were mammals. The first I soon saw, the red squirrel of the evergreen forest, which reaches its most southerly limit here. It is a very different creature from our tufted-eared European red squirrel, much more yellow-red; and one I saw well had a dark line along its sides. The woodsmen call them "boomers." They assert that they are so fast that "if lightning strikes the top of a tree where a boomer is, the boomer can beat it down to the ground." The *chuck*-ing came from chipmunks. I could never spot one of these little striped ground squirrels before it spotted me (I saw plenty later); but their bird-like noise was everywhere among the rocks and gnarled trunks.

Round a corner of the trail we found bear spoor—but no bears. Several of the trees were nicked and scraped with claw marks. The mountain folk insist that bruin makes these signs, while he stands erect, to advertise to other bears how big and tough he is. Stupka did not think much of this theory, but confessed he had no better one to offer. Perhaps bears just like to fool around.

We picnicked by the Ramsay Cascade, basking in an opening where the leaf-roof parted to let the sun illuminate a waterfall pouring down steep rock steps. On a flat slab, watersmooth from the winter flows, we ate our sandwiches, and looked back downstream through the fantastic forest through which we had climbed.

The lumbermen never got up the Ramsay Prong. Thirty years ago they were very near; all through the Appalachian chain, in the sheltered valleys, the stands of large deciduous timber fell before them. Their clearance was something quite different from the work of the old mountain farmers, axeing their little farm fields from the timbered slopes. But the National Park movement—and the Depression—halted them, before they had cut roads and dragways and railroad arms to the last of the giants. In our valley was the finest mixed stand of trees in the eastern United States.

Leaving the great forest was like coming out of a dream; not a sinister dream, for there is nothing terrifying in the grandeur of Great Smoky's deciduous woodland. It is just big beyond belief, and benign in its bigness. I thought it was the most beautiful forest I had ever seen.

That evening at the Stupkas' new ranch house, overlooking a broad green vista of hills and mountains, we watched the evening shadows creep up the slopes. From the window we could see a nest box on a tree, and as we looked a little eye appeared at the entrance hole, and then two eyes. Then they disappeared. Then they appeared again, and after them came a little furry animal; at least the front half of one. But the flying squirrel was shy; it went back into its box again, and no doubt waited until it was fully dark to glide and climb, glide and climb about its own little Tennessee hunting ground. Brown bats flitted about, too, as we watched, and a whip-poor-will struck up its chant as the round pale moon slowly rose over the Great Smokies.

8

Deep South

*H*EAT LIGHTNING lit up the evening sky with its intermittent flashings. Only a few miles to our left lay the Okefinokee Swamp, seven hundred square miles of trackless wilderness, in the heart of which flows the Suwannee River. We had come far this day, cleaving Georgia almost full length from top to bottom.

The easily eroded soil of Georgia seemed unbelievably red to James. He intended to stop and scoop up some for Selina, his eleven-year-old daughter who was collecting samples of earth, but the heat was beginning to make us apathetic. By noon the high mountains had dropped far behind. The hills became gentle and rolling; some had farms, others were cloaked in a dark mantle of pines. But it was not until dusk that we noticed the country had completely flattened out. Instead of the Piedmont with its loblollies and other comparatively short-needled pines, we were in the land of the long-leaved pine, with needles twelve to fifteen inches long, and live oaks, squat broad trees festooned with streamers of Spanish moss. And there were groves of pecan trees; roadside stands advertised the confectionery specialty of the region—pecan pralines. Somewhere today we had left the last robin behind; we stepped up our consumption of Coca-Cola—we were, indeed, in the Deep South.

The heat lightning, aftermath of storms that had preceded us, silhouetted the pines and the banners of Spanish moss, like stage settings for a mystery play. Stimulated by the brimming rain pools beside the road and out on the flats, every frog for miles around was tuning up. Above the hum of the motor we could hear the rasping, clicking sound of countless cricket frogs, the music of swamp chorus frogs, the sheeplike *baaa* of the narrow-mouthed frog, the short rolling purr of tree toads, and, of course, the deep bass *jug-o'-*

Horned Owl

rum of the bullfrog. There were others I could not be quite so sure of, although I have no excuse not to know them since I own Arthur Allen and Paul Kellogg's album of frog recordings, "Voices of the Night." One surprising sound, I think, was made by the barking frog, while a grunting note was probably the alligator frog. Pulling to the road shoulder and cutting off the motor we could hear hundreds of pygmy cricket frogs, like a myriad of tiny tinkling sleighbells, and oak toads, which sounded for all the world like the earnest peeping of tiny baby chicks. But the familiar voice of the spring peeper was absent. There are twenty species of toads and frogs in this part of Georgia. "How wonderful," commented James, not for the first time, "to have a batrachian chorus like this." I told him he did not have to live with it.

It was late when we arrived at Sherwood Plantation near Thomasville, to be met by Herbert Stoddard. Before turning in we walked down the road to hear one more selection by the assembled frog orchestra. Each musician trilled, peeped, grunted, or croaked according to the manner of his kind. This was cosmic music. And as we walked back to the house yet another voice was added to the chorus; the big goatsucker of the southern low country slowly repeated its name—*chuck-will's-widow*.

May 3

Herbert Stoddard woke us before it was light; Roger and I could have used about four more hours sleep. The new day was quite windless and at first overcast. When the sun came out, the temperature quickly reached ninety degrees (it didn't have to go far) and stayed above ninety in the shade until dark. It was the hottest day I had known for many years, and the dawn chorus at Thomasville of all the frogs in south Georgia, just like the night chorus of the day before, provided an accompaniment to the heat. My first day in truly subtropical climate was a day of adventure and new experience; and the frog chorus served as overture and curtain raiser.

The red dirt road that we took ran through a very open kind of pine forest. There were big trees some distance apart and very little undergrowth. Many of the trees were slashed with chevrons, below which hung little tin buckets; they were being bled for the spring harvest of turpentine. Herbert told us that this open style of forest was a consequence of burning to improve the pasture, and that it was bound to prevent regeneration in the long run. However, it's an ill wind that blows nobody any good; and pinewoods like this, with a predominance of large timber and plenty of space between, is just what the rare red-cockaded woodpecker prefers. Throughout the warmer southeastern states, in those commercial forests where there is an enlightened policy of leaving a good sprinkling of large timber, the red-cockaded woodpecker has survived. In many other sections it is going. The nest is always excavated in a pine with a rotten heart after a hole has been driven through the solid wood. The carpenter uses the same hole every year or at least the same tree, starting a new hole when no gum flows from the enlargement of the old one. Herbert knew where a pair of red-cockaded woodpeckers had their nest in a swampy stretch of woods. We approached through the saw-grass and saw palmettos to the foot of the tree and scratched the bark with a stick. A buzzing like that of angry bees told us that the young were still at home. Withdrawing a bit, we saw the male sweep in and brace himself at the nest hole; he had white cheeks, a zebra back, and an almost invisible red cockade above each ear.

Here in southern Georgia, roses, the favorite flowers, bloomed in every garden, climbed every wall and, in town, brightened the public square, even climbed the lamp posts. Mockingbirds sang from the magnolias and barefoot brown-skinned children walked idly along the dusty roads. Gracious plantation houses with tall white columns, which cotton built, seemed to look back sadly to days before "the war between the states." It was just as I had always pictured the Old South.

As we motored southward across the Florida border, the country became flat again, but it was covered so continuously with pinewoods that it was not until we reached Apalachee Bay that we saw it was coastal country. Suddenly we emerged from the pineland into a tropical-looking landscape with pools, palmettos, and a jungle of low green vegetation, from which receded an arm of dead-calm water bordered with tidal mud. It was my first view of the Gulf of Mexico.

Sixty-four thousand acres—exactly 100 square miles—of this varied coastal terrain are embraced in the St. Marks National Wildlife Refuge, created by the Fish and Wildlife Service for the birds

that use the Mississippi Flyway. The most important winter visitors
that enjoy the hospitality of St. Marks—the hordes of black ducks and
pintails—had gone, but a few hundred gadwalls, shovelers, baldpates,
green- and blue-winged teals, wood ducks, and lesser scaup were still
on the ponds. Only the wood duck would stay to nest; the others,
already late for their nuptial appointments, would soon leave for the
prairie heartland, far to the north.

The waders—the sandpipers and plovers—leave later than the
ducks, so many of these visitors to St. Marks had not yet gone. Roger
says that the peak of their spring migration is nearly a month later
in the northern U.S. than it is in England. I was introduced to Wilson's plover, a large heavy-billed edition of the ringed plover, and
to a big "shank," the willet, which flashed spectacularly patterned
black and white wings when it flew. There were two new "stints," the
least and semipalmated sandpipers, also the white-rumped sandpiper,
the stilt sandpiper, and the dowitcher. And there were others, including several kinds that we have in England, the ringed plover, turnstone, sanderling, knot (some were in high red-breasted plumage),
and Hudsonian curlew, which we in Europe call whimbrel. At one
time I had under observation half a dozen birds I'd never seen before
in my life, including two seabirds—the Forster's tern and the royal
tern. But I had to force myself from these fascinating novelties to
look at the first wild alligators of my life, floating still as logs on the
surface of a lagoon.

The Refuge, since it was taken over, has been greatly improved
for the benefit of birds. Surrounded by a canal, it has a new drainage
system and about a tenth of it has been converted from salt water to
fresh. A rather surprising (to me) colonist of the new dykes and road-
banks, was the prickly pear cactus *Opuntia,* in full flower with showy,
waxy yellow blossoms, and there were many yucca bushes with their
clusters of white bells. These gave a xeric, almost desert-like, touch
to an otherwise watery landscape.

Sitting about on the moss-draped snags with their wings half spread,
cormorant fashion, were darters (anhingas, water turkeys, or snake-
birds—call them what you will). We watched one swim about almost
completely submerged except for its extremely thin head and neck;
it looked for all the world like a swimming snake. This world-wide
tropical species, a cousin of the cormorant, a seabird—at least by its
natural order—has a primarily fresh-water distribution. Once only

has Roger ever seen one within sight of the salt.

Here were other decorative marsh birds—the handsome white American egret, with a yellow bill; the smaller snowy egret with bright yellow feet; the delicate and subtly colored Louisiana heron, dark with a white belly; the all-dark little blue heron and the least bittern. Aside from the ospreys, whose bulky nests we could see in dead trees on the skyline, the red-shouldered hawk (rather like our buzzard) was the only bird of prey this day. Big, brash, noisy, and striking, the boat-tailed grackle was everywhere; this large glossy black bird was the most typical voice of the Gulf Coast.

By the time the day was out, we had seen (and without trying to see how many we could see) no less than 125 different species of birds. A rather significant fact was that only 21—roughly one-sixth— were Old World species. In Newfoundland the majority of birds were like those in the Old World, but as we moved southward the unique character of the true American avifauna began to assert itself. It is difficult to write of a day in which new impressions crowded upon me so fast.

Just north of the St. Marks refuge is Wakulla Springs, the largest and deepest fresh-water spring in the world. When we arrived (after lunching on soft-shelled crabs), queues of tourists were waiting for the glass-bottomed boats to do the tour—a short run on the river and half a dozen turns around the drowned circular cavern of limestone, 185 feet deep. Here, before our eyes, where half a million gallons of water per minute gushed forth, the river is born. The near-overhead sun illuminated circling shoals of fat blue catfish and long thin garfish in the incredibly clear blue-green water. Unsullied by silt, every streamer of deep green waterweed, every fish, every turtle was plainly visible even in the deepest pools. Negro boatmen were telling the oft

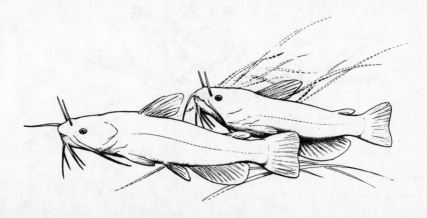

told story in rich, slow, Uncle Remus voices. In the territory of one catfish there was a sunken pole lying across the uneven bottom, and the catfish had formed an attachment to this pole, regularly executing a little swimming dance, a performance which took it under and over the pole several times. Our boatman, who knew this performance well, relied on the law of averages. "Henry," he exhorted, "jump ober de stick"—"Henry, per-fawm fo' de folks"—"Henry!" After ten minutes of this Henry finally swam over the stick.

The short ride down the river was most beautiful. We passed directly under several osprey nests with their owners sitting quite unafraid above us. A little warbler, the prothonotary, golden and blue, darted in and out of the dark cypresses. We passed a partly submerged log which two gorgeous wood ducks were sharing with several big turtles with hieroglyphic markings. We saw several kinds of turtles in the clear water; Roger decided that some were Blanding's turtles but that most of them were sliders.

As Roger and I pottered about the bank with our photographic gear, the southern voices of the boatmen drifted toward us: "Dat am de limpkin, de rarest bird in all America." "Dat am de eagle" (referring to the osprey). "De folks come fum miles aroun' to see dis 'ere limpkin and dis 'ere eagle." Which was true.

In the live oak trees near the car was a gray squirrel; the Florida race is, I should judge, half the weight of the gray squirrel of the northern states, the race so successfully introduced in Britain. I saw a bright green chameleon, or *Anolis,* which jumped from a palmetto frond to the trunk; pausing, it inflated its throat-fan, which turned a bright carmine red.

Roger was indefatigable. He was soon up to his waist in the river, his movie tripod at its fullest extent, his hat rammed on the back of his head in the blazing sun, determinedly stalking a family of limpkins. I must say I did not expect to see one of the rarer birds of America, the curious anomalous rail-crane, the limpkin, teaching its young to eat giant snails in the shallows less than a hundred yards from a noisy uninhibited amusement park. It is interesting to think that those limpkins are protected largely because Wakulla is a showplace. Often we find that places designed primarily for public entertainment and amusement can also be effective sanctuaries for nature.

AT THIS POINT James deserted me. He had been getting more of the sun than he should. His arms were stiff and peeling. Suffering a little from heat shock, as the thermometer climbed to ninety-five, he was glad to sit around in the shade, drinking cokes and watching the gray squirrel. But I just couldn't miss the opportunity to film the limpkins. Although the Negro boatman's claim was far from true that the limpkin is "de rarest bird in all America," it is by no means common. Although there are a fair number in the 'Glades and especially around Lake Okeechobee, there are not nearly as many of these strange marsh birds as there were formerly. Florida "crackers" still comment on the excellent flavor of roast limpkin and even though these gangly bittern-sized birds are now protected by law some of them undoubtedly find their way to the oven. Here at the spring the limpkins have absolute security and have become so conspicuous that no tourist leaves without seeing at least one. There are about twenty-five pairs along two miles of river. Everywhere the groves of cypress and the blue gardens of pickerelweed and hyacinths echoed to the loud wails of these "crying birds"— *kr-r-r-eow . . . k-r-r-r-eow!* In high spirits, the boys on the swimming pier upstream would wail back; another limpkin would join in and soon the chorus would increase to half a dozen earsplitting voices.

It was to this vocal accompaniment this hot Sunday afternoon that I photographed a family of six birds, which stood about very decoratively at the base of an old buttressed cypress. The young birds were almost exactly like their parents, olive-brown, liberally sprinkled with white spots, but their bills were shorter. The cypress "knees," which emerged above the water, were studded with clusters of pale translucent pink eggs. These pink pearls were the eggs of the green snail, *Pomacea,* the main food item of the limpkin. There seemed to be a tremendous quantity of these large snails; whenever one of the birds wanted one, it would simply wade into the water, probe about with its long, slightly decurved bill, and emerge with the dripping mollusk. Wedging the shell firmly among the cypress roots it would work at it with the tweezer-like tip of its bill until the door of the shell, the operculum, was torn away and the soft animal extracted.

One of the adult limpkins swam a few feet (the first time I had ever seen a limpkin swim) to a shallow bar. Soon one of the young birds swam out to join it. I would have thought that a young bird so completely grown would do its own foraging; but no, when its parent pulled a large snail from the water it rushed in, seized it greedily—and swallowed it whole!

As I stood waist-deep in the clear water—it stays at a constant 70°–72° F.—I wondered if this could have been the fabled Fountain of Youth for which Ponce de León was searching. Instead of eternal youth, the conquistador found death, when an Indian arrow struck him.

On our way back to nearby Georgia in the evening (I was going to write "cool of the evening," but it wasn't any cooler) we saw nighthawks diving and booming over the town of Tallahassee. They have become town birds in much of the East now, nesting on the flat gravel roofs of buildings. It was in one of Herbert Stoddard's open pine forests, next morning, that we again saw the nighthawks perform. The European counterpart, the nightjar, with which James was very familiar, is similar in size, but is strictly nocturnal. It declares ownership of its territory by perching motionless on a post and producing a continuous churring sound. But the nighthawk, or bull-bat of America, marks its territory high in the air with its conspicuous display flight. The male cruises erratically about in the sky, climbs a bit, then folds its wings and dives headlong toward the earth, checking itself by an upward swoop in which the air buzzes through its primaries so violently as to make a zooming noise. Here in the clearings of the pine forest we were watching nighthawks in an ancestral habitat—where they had lived and laid their two eggs before they discovered the roofs of cities. In fact this was a most unusual stand of yellow pine, a mature forest that looked exactly as did nearly all yellow pine forests throughout the South before the coming of the settlers. Stoddard, who as a tree consultant was instructed by the landowner to maintain this forest in its present state by harvesting only the trees which were dying, showed us certain ground plants —a dwarf oak, a dwarf chinkapin, and a wiry grass—which he said were indicators of the mature yellow pine forest. "You do not get these until the timber is one hundred years old," he said.

In addition to these tracts of timber which he manages for others, Stoddard has his own woodlands. Cleared areas and fire lanes are planted with lespedeza and other food plants for wild turkeys and quail. Stoddard, whose monograph *The Bob-white Quail* is the classic work on the South's favorite game bird, is no less an authority on turkeys. Hundreds roam the great estates in this part of Georgia, but so wary are they that only the sharpest eyed will get even a glimpse of one before it slips away. Our eyes must not have been sharp enough that morning. A blind had been baited with corn; we approached with circumspection, but drew a blank. The birds had fed and gone. Later, however, a hen turkey dashed across the road and traveled a hundred yards before it faded into the trees.

We drove past a grove of tung nut trees which Stoddard was growing experimentally and we skirted a lovely still pond in a forest glade, where wild magnolia trees, *Magnolia grandiflora,* were in bloom, their great waxy white blossoms set in clusters of deep glossy green leaves. The pond had been created by beavers; when we examined the dam they had built, Stoddard commented: "They are the best wildlife engineers of the lot. I couldn't possibly make a more effective dam if I spent hundreds. They know exactly where to put things and how to control the water level."

By the time we took leave of the able naturalist who had been our host for the last two days, we had become deeply impressed by a rare demonstration of what private landowners can do in practical conservation. Here we had witnessed a perfect blend of enlightened forestry, farming, wildlife management—and gracious living. James commented that here, around Thomasville, he sensed "an unusual feeling of security."

Yes, security; that's the word for it, I thought, as we drove away from Sherwood Plantation.

9

Wildlife Cheesecake

$\mathcal{F}$LORIDA IS the land of cheesecake—the publicity man's term for gilding the lily (or peeling the onion). To publicize the Sunshine State's semitropical charms to winter-weary northerners, curvaceous maidens are pictured with hibiscus blossoms in their hair. They are photographed in billowy colonial gowns beneath cypress trees and magnolias, in more abbreviated garb on water skis, and even swimming in pools among ten thousand floating oranges or grapefruit—*ad nauseam.**

Florida has its natural history cheesecake too. Wakulla Springs, Silver Springs, and the other commercialized springs that gush from north Florida's underground limestone caves are truly beautiful and impressive spots, but even they have their sideshow aspects—especially those "trained" catfish which the guides point out as we cruise in the glass-bottom boats.

---

* I suppose so—have not reached nausea yet.—J.F.

Some of Florida's tourist exhibits, such as the show at Marineland, we must admit, are very well presented. This scientifically designed oceanarium nestles among the dunes on the outer beach eighteen miles south of St. Augustine, the oldest city in the United States. Five million gallons of sea water daily are pumped through two huge tanks which are connected by a flume. Two hundred glass portholes, lining corridors at two levels, serve as windows for those who would see what goes on in this kaleidoscopic world of sunlight, shadow, and blue-green water.

In the larger tank, 100 feet long, 40 feet wide, and 18 feet deep, there is no segregation. All the creatures live together as they do in the open sea. Huge loggerhead turtles, big as washtubs, glide past the observation windows, bulky 400-pound jewfish momentarily blot out the view as they swim by; giant whip-tailed rays slowly flap as if on batlike wings. Moray eels thrust their snakelike heads from rocky grottoes; schools of brightly colored parrotfish and angelfish flash among the sea fans and corals. Dominating all are several huge tiger sharks, 10 or 12 feet long, which lurk about the barnacle-incrusted timbers of a sunken ship.

James and I arrived just in time for the last daily feeding of the porpoises. These playful cetaceans, confined to the smaller, 75-foot tank, are the main attraction at Marineland. An attendant in a sailor's middy walks out on the feeding platform with a bucket of defrosted blue runners and rings a bell which summons a dozen large grinning heads to the surface of the water. In expectation, these fun-loving mammals jostle each other while the attendant dips into the bucket for a tidbit. Striking a dramatic pose, with one leg thrown back, expressly for the benefit of the many shutter-bugs lining the rail, he

holds the fish aloft. A porpoise erupts from the water in a ten- or
twelve-foot vertical leap and deftly takes the fish while the cameras
click. Like any other Florida tourist, James could not resist this bit
of acrobatic cheesecake and soon exposed two rolls of film. That
evening he wrote the following in his diary.

May 4

Marine Studios (Marineland) must be one of the most remarkable
aquaria in the world; its tanks, continually refreshed by sea water
from the neighboring ocean, contain an extraordinarily dramatic collection of fish. One of them even has a living coral reef, with many
species of beautiful coral fish in it. The management, conscious of
the demands of the public, sends a member of their staff in a diving
suit into the big tanks periodically, to entertain the sharks and dolphins (and, of course, the visitors).

The dolphins of Marine Studios (they call them porpoises) belong
to two species. The bottle-nosed dolphin is an inshore species common along the Atlantic coast of the United States. The length of
adults is usually from nine to twelve feet, and it is perhaps the commonest American dolphin. The Studios have also a small long-beaked
gray dolphin with many small white spots on its back; this long-
snouted animal, known as the spotted dolphin, is a rather rare offshore species. Both sorts were swimming blithely together in the big
tank at the Studios. The bottle-nose even breeds in captivity here;
first- and second-year young were darting happily about, very much
more active and playful than their parents. I do not think there is
any other establishment in the world where dolphins breed in captivity. At feeding time these tame dolphins give the most incredible exhibition of aquatic gymnastics. Undoubtedly Marine Studios, through
its successful venture in public entertainment, has been able to finance
a great deal of research into the natural history of the sea.

May 5

This morning we drove into Daytona Beach along the Atlantic
sands where so many speed records have been tried and made. It is
certainly one of the finest sand beaches in the world—very broad,

white, and hard—miles of it, with little bands of sanderlings and turnstones pottering at the water's edge. An incredible place, Daytona. There must have been four miles of beach hotels with the same tables, the same umbrellas, the same verandas, the same half-lived-in look. Indeed, the winter season was over and many of the hotels did not look lived in at all. Not far from here, though nobody knows exactly where, is the point where Ponce de León, the Spaniard, was in 1515 the first European (apart from the Norsemen) to set foot on the mainland of North America. It must have been somewhere near Cape Canaveral where the coastal bar and lagoon systems broaden out.

After a detour of thirty miles on the back roads of Merritt Island, we picked up a rare sparrow with a curious fizzing song, the dusky seaside sparrow, *Ammospiza nigrescens*. It is confined absolutely to Florida, to the marshes at the northern end of the Indian River, that great lagoon which runs along the east coast of the state where it helps form the inland waterway. The type locality of this dingy blackish little sparrow is Merritt Island itself, and it can only have a population of a few hundred individuals. There is another very rare species, a greenish bird, the Cape Sable seaside sparrow,

Ammospiza mirabilis, which even Roger has never been able to find. In several days we will be within a few miles of it. This species probably numbers only a few score individuals, now believed to be confined to marshes south of the Tamiami Trail near Ochopee. It was the last new species of bird described from the United States (in 1919). Actually, we are sure that these eccentric sparrows, the dusky and Cape Sable, are no more than very well marked geographical races of the ordinary seaside sparrow, *A. maritima,* because they do not overlap the ranges of any of the races of this species which lives locally in salt marshes all the way from Massachusetts to Florida and Texas. Roger believes that hurricanes in times past could account for the numerous well-separated forms of this rather sedentary bird by having wiped out great sections of the population as well as their environment.

Leaving the coast we crossed the wide reaches of the St. Johns River marshes to the charming inland town of Orlando, where Roger had been stationed at the air base during the war. Here was the first noticeably high ground we had met in Florida, and increasingly, as we turned south again, block upon block of citrus trees—oranges, lemons, and grapefruit—thousands of acres of orderly groves. Nestled in these hills are the famous Cypress Gardens, which have been transformed by an enterprising promoter into the kind of tourist spot that only Florida could contrive. We knew what we were in for, since we had seen something of Cypress Gardens in three dimensions and glorious technicolor on Cinerama in New York. We arrived in good time for lunch before the two o'clock show. The great thing at Cypress Gardens is to be in charge of a speed or movie camera, or at least to have one slung around your neck. If you are thus equipped, the obliging management shoves you onto a special grandstand jutting into the lake and even goes so far as to provide you with a helpful character with an exposure meter who gives a running commentary on the light intensity and a very accurate (as it proved) prescription for the optical stops. The object of all this nonsense with the cameras of course is to photograph the aquashow.

Small fast motorboats began hurrying about the lake, and shortly one more purposeful than the others appeared towing five young ladies in bathing dresses and ballet skirts, on water skis. These all waved very charmingly. We were too busy with our cameras to wave back. The motorboat went round again. The next time past the girls in perfect unison stood on one leg and again waved charmingly at the photographers. After that the real stuff began. A girl came by at breakneck speed on one water ski, doing all sorts of turns and swerves; then a young man with a girl on his shoulders; then three daredevil young men who skied up and jumped over an inclined platform. The climax came when a young Mexican appeared skiing behind a motorboat not on a pair of water skis but on his flat feet! After the show was over the girls all posed for the photographers again on land. Roger and I went off to the Gardens.

A winding path led along the edges of the groves of cypress, which stood knee-deep in water, and then took us back into jungle-like gardens planted with palms and exotic borders of perennials and annuals. We'd lost the robin, but tufted titmouse, Carolina wren, mockingbird, thrasher, and cardinal were singing—all typical birds of southern gardens. Hidden in the thickets, a white-eyed vireo sang *chip-o-the-white-oak!* The only warblers were the successful little parula warbler and the yellow-throated warbler, both of which nest in the pendent streamers of Spanish moss.

But the most extraordinary thing about Cypress Gardens was the butterflies, especially the swallowtails. These were quite astonishing to one accustomed to Britain with its one rare swallowtail species.*

* *Papilio machaon,* which is also found in North America west of Hudson Bay.

Zebra Swallowtails

Here were no less than eight swallowtails: a black one with yellow spots, *Papilio polyxenes* (the black); a large brown one with a band of yellow spots, *cresphontes* (the giant); one striped yellow and black, *glaucus* (the tiger); a black one with blue clouding, *troilus* (the spicebush); another blackish one, *palamedes* (the palamedes); a striped white one with very long tails, *marcellus* (the zebra); a deep glossy green species, *philenor* (the pipe vine); and a black "tailless swallowtail" *polydamas* (the polydamas). Roger had never seen this last butterfly before. It was almost extinct between 1920 and 1933 but has made a good recovery. We were very lucky with our swallowtails, for perhaps only in May in Florida could so many have been seen at the same time.

While we had been watching the butterflies, the girls who earlier had been doing clever stunts in the water had quickly changed into blue, green, and crimson crinoline dresses and were reclining in the gardens on grassy banks.

JAMES WAS HAVING a real eyeful of America's fabulous winter play-ground this fine May day. I had a difficult time dragging him away from Cypress Gardens—and the butterflies—but I wanted him to see a nearby bird sanctuary which might be classified by some as pure "cheesecake." On Florida's highest hill (Iron Mountain, 304 feet), overlooking thousands of acres of orderly orange groves at Lake Wales, is the Bok Tower, an ornate 250-foot carillon tower mirrored in a reflecting pool. The top of the tower, the highest point above sea level in Florida, falls one foot short of the 555-foot Washington Monument in Washington, D.C. The Bok sanctuary, actually a human sanctuary, at first attempted to be a bird sanctuary as well. Flamingos were brought in to grace the reflecting pool. Few of the visitors saw anything incongruous about flamingos under moss-hung pines and palmettos. The flamingos undoubtedly did, but their clipped pinions prevented them from seeking the broad sea horizons and shallow mangrove flats which they prefer. There are the same songbirds in the Bok sanctuary that one would find in any Florida country garden, but the story is told that the management once tried to improve the situation by introducing fifteen or twenty nightingales from Europe.

The nightingales sang their rich bursts throughout the groves until late June, when they abruptly stopped, as nightingales do. Meanwhile the local mockingbirds, not to be outdone, had picked up the music of the aliens. For the rest of the summer the mockers acted as substitutes, chanting in the best nightingale accents.

Florida abounds in jungle gardens, rare-bird farms, monkey jungles, reptile institutes, tropical arboretums, and Seminole Indian villages all competing for the tourists' attention. To the average visitor from the North these exhibits represent "Wild Florida." But many of them are as artificial in their way as Miami Beach with its preposterous "tropical modern" hotels.

Perhaps the number one exhibit in this category is the flamingo flock at Hialeah Race Track near Miami. A large wing-clipped colony lives on an island in the artificial lake which is surrounded by the oval track, progeny of a few birds brought in some years ago from Andros in the Bahamas. During the first seven years of their captivity they raised no young; now that their diet has been corrected they nest each year, the bright rose-red has returned to their faded plumage, and the colony has grown to more than 500 birds. At the beginning of the racing season a "flamingo derby" is staged. The birds are herded en masse onto the track for a mad dash around the course.

Many tourists see only these show places. But if they would only abandon the crowded highways and drive down the long lonely roads which cross the Kissimmee Prairie, the Big Cypress, or the " 'Glades" —as James and I did—they would really see Florida. Between these slender threads of roadway are great blocks of wilderness, hundreds, even thousands of square miles in extent, wild areas seldom entered except by the occasional cowboy, trapper, or Seminole.

Few people realize just what vast expanses of south Florida are now devoted to cattle. As we sped south along the straight road to Okeechobee we left the citrus groves behind and finally the pines. We were on the vast Kissimmee Prairie, an endless sea of grass stretching from horizon to horizon. Only an occasional clump of palmettos in the distance betrayed that we were in Florida. On entering the prairie country I warned James to look out for owls on fence posts, and sure enough, not far from Okeechobee, in the middle of a dry cattle range, a little knob on top of a post came alive and looked like something, and the something, when we stopped, proved to be a burrowing owl. It was undoubtedly nesting in the dry bank along the roadside. Although these owls in the West often use prairie-dog burrows, in Florida they must excavate their own. The little long-legged owl was quite tame and allowed us to come within a few yards before it made off in a sweeping, undulating flight to another post.

It was immediately after we saw the owl that we spotted the sandhill cranes. Two great gray birds with periscope necks and red foreheads stalked through the sawgrass in the warm evening light. They bugled harshly, took wing as if to retreat but settled again into the marsh. The next time we saw this stately species was in Alaska—thousands of miles away.

Angelfish

10

World Invader — The Cattle Egret

THE NIGHT CLERK at the Southland Hotel in Okeechobee glanced at our signatures and looked up.

"Glen Chandler has been expecting you," he said. "If you want me to, I'll ring him up; he should be home."

In a moment I was speaking to Chandler, the Audubon warden. He seemed excited.

"What are the chances of seeing cattle egrets?" I inquired.

"I have good news," he replied. "Today Sam Grimes and I were out at Kings Bar and we found a nest. Sam says it's the first cattle egret's nest for North America!"

A prediction I had made the year before had come true.

The cattle egret, or buff-backed heron, is an Old World heron with an affinity for cows. It is a familiar sight to travelers in Africa and the warmer parts of Asia, but is local in Europe, confined to a few colonies in southern Spain and Portugal. Dancing attendance upon the herds of cattle (or, in the tropics, water buffalo), it catches the grasshoppers disturbed by the grazing beasts; occasionally it may pick off a parasite.

In April, 1952, Guy Mountfort and I, gathering data for our *Field Guide to the Birds of Britain and Europe,* had traveled from London to Spain to make the acquaintance of this beautiful heron and other Spanish specialties. South of Seville, on the road toward Gibraltar, we saw our first cattle egrets in the company of a magnificent black bull that was perhaps destined for the arena in Seville or Jerez. But there was no antagonism here. The birds walked inches from the beast's nose as he grazed. Perhaps the *toro* sensed the symbiotic relationship existing between himself and his white attendants. I contrasted this amiable tableau in the meadow to the grim encounter—man against the beast—that I had witnessed at the Plaza de Toros in Madrid.

For as long as anyone can remember cattle egrets have nested on the edge of the vast Marismas, which are formed by the delta of the Guadalquivir River. To travel there requires complicated preparations. Our host, Mauricio González (who was later to translate our *Field Guide* into Spanish) assembled a caravan of a dozen horses and mules and half a dozen horsemen and *guardas* for the 18-mile trek across the Sahara-like dunes and pine woods. Our destination was the Coto Doñana where Abel Chapman studied birds a half century before. There Mountfort and I lived in the fabulous hunting lodge—the *palacio;* my room was that of the Marqués del Torero, while nearby were the quarters formerly used by King Alfonso. The *pajarera,* three or four miles from the *palacio,* occupied several wide-spreading cork oaks, the same ancient trees in which Abel Chapman found the colony. We estimated the total number of birds to exceed 4000, more than half of which were cattle egrets. The exact location of the colony could be pinpointed by the long ribbons of flying egrets trading to and from their distant feeding grounds.

The cattle egrets, standing on their twiggy nests, were still at the peak of nuptial beauty with buffish plumes on their backs and breasts. Their bills were suffused with red and their legs and eyes were a garish puce-pink. Later in the season the red flush would leave the yellow bill and the legs; they would lose their buffish plumes and become quite white.

On returning to the United States after my Spanish adventure, I learned of a most astonishing event. Cattle egrets, the first ever recorded in North America, had just been reported from three different states.

The presence of these Old World birds had been known in South America for about twenty years. Just how they made the jump across the Atlantic and exactly when no one seems to know. About the year 1930 they appeared in British Guiana where they found their ideal niche—herds of Brahman cattle complete with Hindustani herdsmen—exactly as in India, where the species is abundant. To use the words of the ornithologist F. Haverschmidt, who has lived several years in the Guianas: "The unhappy feeling remains that a wonderful event has occurred about which we know very little."

Could they be descendants of birds which had escaped from some zoo, perhaps the one at Georgetown? There is no evidence that they are. Did someone deliberately introduce them from abroad? There would have been some record of the project. Or did the first ones come as stowaways on a cattle boat? The most likely theory is that they were wind borne. The distance across the Atlantic is much less between the bulge of Africa and northern South America than at other points. Cattle egrets have frequently been reported at St. Helena, in the South Atlantic. Such vagrants assisted by strong winds could conceivably cover the distance before they were completely exhausted. Other birds must have reached our shores in such a manner in centuries past; the glossy ibis, for example.

In twenty years, the original South American flock of cattle egrets increased to thousands and spread to Surinam, Venezuela, and Colombia. A correspondent in Georgetown wrote me that part of the reason for their explosive spread was because they raised two broods each year, in contrast to the little blue heron's one. Haverschmidt on May 28, 1953, counted 1112 birds roosting in the bushes along the river at Nieuw Nickerie.

William Drury, Jr., of Cambridge, Massachusetts, had seen the cattle egret at Aruba, in the Netherlands West Indies when he was in the U.S. Navy. But the bird was far from his thoughts when he started out, on the morning of April 23, to make a check of the spring migrants in the Sudbury Valley at Wayland, Massachusetts. His companions were Allan Morgan and Richard Stackpole. They stopped at Mrs. Francis Erwin's farm to look over Heard's Pond. Almost at once Morgan found a dark heron-like bird with a decurved bill, which they identified through the telescope as a glossy ibis. This was certainly enough to highlight one day, because it was the first record of a glossy ibis in the Sudbury Valley in 102 years. As they started to leave, Morgan noticed a white bird fly in and alight among a herd of heifers. Their first reaction was that it was a snowy egret, a remarkably early spring record, but the binoculars showed that it was no such bird. Drury, scarcely crediting his eyes, correctly identified it.

Rushing to the nearest telephone, they called Ludlow Griscom, urging him to come quickly to corroborate the find. Griscom advised them to take no chances. "Do not wait," he said. "Collect the bird." Scientific ornithological tradition demands that the first record of a new species for a region be substantiated by a specimen. This was a "first" for the continent.

Morgan possessed a federal collecting permit, but the bird in typical leechlike fashion stayed so close to the cattle that there was real danger of shooting a heifer instead of the heron. Two shots

were fired but the bird did not lose a feather. Alarmed by these unfriendly actions, it flew quickly away over the orchard and toward the next farm. There a herd of black Angus would act as decoys, it was thought, but after a brief reconnaissance, neither herd nor heron could be located. It was still rather early in the morning—about 6 A.M. The frustrated ornithologists aroused a sleeping friend who owned a small plane; with this air support they soon located the missing bird. By shouting instructions through the open door of the low-circling plane to a jeep below the observers directed the ground party to their quarry. After several attempts, first using the jeep as a blind, then a tractor, the bird was shot. The cattle egret was officially added to the North American list and the specimen was placed in the Museum of Comparative Zoölogy at Harvard University.

Naturally, the first reaction was that it was probably an escape from some nearby zoo. A quick check revealed no clues. Then came astounding news from New Jersey. Two days after the Massachusetts affair, a cattle egret was discovered on a farm at Cape May. Later, a second bird appeared. Bird watchers, by the hundreds, from Philadelphia, Washington, New York, and even farther, poured in by car and by train to see these two distinguished visitors, which remained for months. Fortunately, the owner of the farm, Michael McPherson, was very interested in the birds and allowed no harm to come to them.

Then, on the first of June, Louis Stimson, touring the northwest shore of Lake Okeechobee in Florida with his wife, discovered *ten* cattle egrets, in two groups of four and six!

In July I returned to London to complete work on the European field guide. One afternoon, just outside the publisher's office, whom should I meet but Richard Borden of camera-gun fame, with whom I had worked at the National Audubon Society and the National Wildlife Federation. He invited me to his hotel for a cool drink and, full of gossip, I told him the news of the cattle egrets. I amused him by implying that I had perhaps disturbed the birds so much in Spain that they had hopped the ocean. I predicted, in all seriousness, that someday they would nest in the United States. "Dick," I advised, "if you ever see a small egret walking around the feet of cows, look twice at it."

"That reminds me," Borden replied. "I photographed some snowies with cows in Florida this spring."

I suggested he look carefully again at his film. He did, and discovered to his delight that he had unknowingly photographed cattle egrets, not snowies!

Borden's movies were taken on March 12, 1952. But there is evidence that there may have been cattle egrets in Florida even before that. Willard Dilley of Homestead, Florida, saw a cattle egret at Clewiston in May, 1948, but did not report it because he assumed that it had escaped from captivity.

There were other sight records during 1952, indicating a fantastic invasion. One even turned up near Chicago. Inasmuch as there was a whole flock around Lake Okeechobee, it seemed inevitable that they should nest. Late in the year they disappeared, to reappear in the spring. Where had they gone? Back to South America? The far-ranging movements of cattle egrets in other parts of the world have always puzzled migration students.

Before James and I left Newfoundland, Leslie Tuck had asked whether we would care to see the skin of an egret in his office. The bird had come aboard a trawler on the Grand Banks, 200 miles from St. John's, sometime between October 24 and 29, 1952. Tuck assumed it to be an American egret, but when he drew the specimen from the tray, I felt that something was wrong. The bird had a yellow bill and black legs; that added up to American egret if one tried to run it down in the eastern *Field Guide*—but it was much too small. Was it a cattle egret? There was just a touch of buffish on the crown —but those blackish legs, how to explain them? Every cattle egret I had seen in Spain had reddish or yellowish legs. I did not know at the time that juveniles could have blackish legs. At my suggestion the bird was sent to the museum at Ottawa for checking. My suspicions were confirmed. It was indeed a cattle egret, the first record for Canada.

When James and I, continuing our odyssey, arrived at the Southland Hotel in Okeechobee, Florida, on the night of May 6 and heard the news, I was elated. Things had come full cycle. James commented that a grand tour such as ours was bound to turn up at least one or two "firsts."

We were tired from our long drive through the Kissimmee Prairie, so we decided to turn in early. Our room was oppressively hot; not a breeze stirred although all the windows were open. James was obviously embarrassed by the heat, but he was eagerly looking forward to the morning. The cattle egret would be new for him.

May 6

Glen Chandler, the energetic Audubon warden, was at the hotel before we had the sleep out of our eyes. Roger and I waited for the neighborhood drygoods store to open its doors so that we could get some protective head covering. We wound up with tropical helmets and would have looked like intrepid explorers except for the flamboyant Florida shirts we had bought.

No sooner were we on the road following Glen's car south of town when Roger shouted, "Stop!" In an open prairie landscape cut off by a ditch there was a herd of cattle and with them fourteen white birds—egrets; about the size of snowy egrets. We put the telescope on them; snowies will sometimes consort with cattle, but these were cattle egrets all right, with pinkish or yellowish bills. Roger did a fine bit of stalking with his movie camera and I stalked the stalker and got a Leica shot or two of him photographing the cattle egrets before the nervous birds flew away.

Our objective was a large mixed heron and ibis rookery on Kings Bar out in the lake where, only yesterday, Grimes and Chandler had actually found a cattle egret's nest, the first in the United States. As we drove along we passed marshy ponds and rain pools. In one of these were four Florida mottled ducks, really the local replacement of the black duck—or mallard—depending on your point of view. In another rain pool at the edge of a field there was a new surprise, a big flock of handsome white and black storklike birds. They were wood ibises, which are not true ibises at all, but storks of a group that is widespread in the more tropical parts of the New World. These great white birds, their naked dark heads down, busily sweeping for food, imprinted themselves on my memory more than anything else I saw on this memorable day. They were accompanied by another fantastic bird I'd never seen before. Like knives, or perhaps scissors, a flock of black skimmers sliced the water-surface of the pond from end to end, charging in a loose formation almost between the legs of the wood ibises. With their extraordinary lower mandibles, a third longer than the upper ones, and held almost at right angles to their necks, the skimmers were colorful, irresistible, unforgettable. Nobody quite knows the real function of the elongated lower beak of this aberrant tern, the skimmer. Roger assured me we would see many more black skimmers; but this first introduction to a graceful band, with vermilion beaks and poised and beautiful flight, contrasting so vividly with the long-legged wood ibises, gave me great pleasure. Roger said he had never before seen a skimmer away from salt water. To see a flock feeding on a rain pool in a farmer's field was unheard of.

At the fish camp where the gasoline boat was docked, we discovered that we had forgotten to bring lunch. We were able to pick up several bottles of soft drinks however, and three small packages of crackers. Loading the small boat with our camera equipment and the hide, we gave the outboard a whirl and sped down the winding water of the Kissimmee to the vast, almost horizonless lake. Distorted by mirage Kings Bar lay three miles offshore. We had some trouble landing, as there is no solid ground anywhere. Ibises erupted from the willows in great flocks, glossy and white ibises together. This one island must harbor almost the entire U.S. population of the eastern glossy ibis (which as far as I can see is identical with the birds I saw in Italy). What herons there were on Okeechobee! The rookery was an incredible place. I'd seen mixed rookeries before, but never before had I had to wade through a tropical lake to see one. Chandler went ahead, keeping alert for poisonous water moccasins. Wriggling through the bushes in two feet of water is quite a feat, especially when the surface is covered with an interlocked blanket of water hyacinths—gorgeous, almost orchid-like plants which float on the surface, supporting their showy clusters of lavender flowers with balloon-shaped bladders.

We followed the jungle-like trail which Chandler had hacked with his machete through the willows and buttonwoods the day before. Birds boiled up from the bushes by thousands: Louisiana herons, snowy egrets, American egrets, little blues, even one or two yellow-crowned night herons, anhingas, and white ibises, and glossies of course. We came to a little clearing; Chandler hesitated a moment, then pointed with his machete to a platform of sticks.

"I think that's it," he said. "There was just one egg yesterday, now there are two."

Roger put up his hide. Chandler and I left him there while we explored the other end of the island.

To INTERRUPT James's account, this is what happened while they were gone.

I did not use the wooden platform that Sam Grimes had placed about fifteen feet from the nest. Intending to disturb the birds as little as possible by using a longer lens, I erected my burlap hiding place in shallow water about thirty feet away. Grimes had determined that this was the nest, Chandler said, when from a distance he had seen two cattle egrets copulating beside it. However, after he had put up his blind they did not return, but sat in the tall bushes above, where he photographed them. Fearing to keep them off too long he decided, after an hour, to abandon his efforts.

Less than fifteen minutes after my companions had gone, the herons and ibises settled in the dense thickets on all sides. Coarse croaks were counterpoint to the bubbling *wulla-wulla-wulla* of the snowies and the rasping of the chicks. A Louisiana heron went to its own nest five or six feet from the twiggy platform on which my six-inch lens was focused. Then through the coarse fabric I saw a white bird swing in and walk deliberately down the branch to the two blue eggs. This was it! I pushed the button and ran off about ten feet of film. Eagerly I peeped through a slit in the blind to confirm the identification. My heart dropped. The bird had black legs and bright yellow feet. The owner of the nest was a snowy!

I had no doubt that the cattle egrets were nesting nearby; at least two flew back and forth overhead among the disturbed snowies when James and Chandler returned. Unfortunately, to determine just which nest was theirs would have required more time than was at our command. The sky was threatening, black clouds were piling up to the west. We had to leave fast.

Sam Grimes, hearing the news, returned three weeks later. On May 30, he discovered three more nests of the cattle egret and photographed the birds. He reported that the nest I photographed was indeed that of a snowy. The cattle egret's nest which had been about five feet away had apparently fallen from its support before our arrival. There, in the water, he found the flimsy remnants.

During the summer of 1953 the cattle egrets returned to McPherson's farm at Cape May. This time there were six. Virginia and Maryland were added to the list of states where the species had been seen. Later in the year, on November 21, Stimson counted 152 cattle egrets on the south side of Lake Okeechobee. This was a far greater number than was hitherto believed to exist in Florida. Either they had enjoyed phenomenal nesting success or had been augmented by others from South America. Several birds showed up at Key West, but these may have been new birds arriving, not birds departing.

At about the time that Queen Elizabeth paid her royal visit to Bermuda, three adventurous cattle egrets also arrived at that outpost of Empire. The distance from the Florida mainland is about 1000 miles. One bird stayed about and came to an ignoble end late in the winter, when it was found drowned in a rain barrel.

Since then, things have been snowballing. In May, 1954, Grimes and Stoddard discovered a colony of 300 nests on Kraemer Island, and Sprunt estimated that 2000 birds were then in the state. Surely some were still moving in from South America. In August Mrs. William Keeling wrote me that she had just seen 20 cattle egrets among the other herons at Eagle Lake, Texas. And so the invaded territory expands. I predict that the bird will do extremely well on the coastal prairies of Texas. The semi-arid, veld-like terrain, oak mottes, thicket-lined rivers (for nesting) and hybrid Brahman livestock are made to order for the cattle egret. So is much of the Rio Grande Valley as far up as New Mexico. If the bird ever reaches California it should do well throughout the central valleys. But somehow I would not expect it to breed in the northeastern states, nor in the upper Midwest, even though there are plenty of cows.

Biologists are buzzing with conjecture about this "population explosion" which seems to be world-wide. The cattle egret was a new bird for Australia in 1948, when Herbert Deignan discovered hundreds in Northern Territory. They have spread widely in Africa, too. This successful species has now established beach-heads on every continent—except Antarctica, where there are no cows.

What effect will the newcomer have on the native American herons? Will it compete? Is it a good or bad acquisition? Naturally, after experiences with imports such as the house sparrow and starling, we view exotics with a jaundiced eye. This is the first example, in our time at least, of an Old World bird invading the continental New World without our assistance (although the fieldfare colonized Greenland in 1937). It apparently got here on its own two wings and the wind. But the environment it found—pastures and cattle—was man-created, introduced from the Old World to the New. The bird is merely completing the picture. Its food habits, with accent on insects, are in the main different from those of other herons. Although it shares the same heronries with snowies and ibises, there is no basic conflict. All seem to benefit. Predators (crows, raccoons, and other egg eaters) make fewer inroads, relatively, if the colonies are large.

The cattle egret, beautiful and beneficial, is a fine addition to the American avifauna. The day might well come when it will be as familiar to many Americans as the starling or ring-necked pheasant.

11

Kites over the Sawgrass

OKEECHOBEE means in Seminole "Big Water." Any word in the Seminole Indian language ending in double *e* denotes water: *Kissimmee,* winding water; *Pahayokee,* grassy water; *wampee,* a water plant (pickerelweed); *hatchee,* river.

Lake Okeechobee, with an average depth of only five or six feet, sprawls over an area of 700 square miles. Although the highway completely encircles it, for great stretches the lake itself is hidden from the motorists' view by a 20-foot dyke built to prevent a repetition of the disasters of 1926 and 1928. Thirty-six hundred people lost their lives when hurricanes of incredible violence pushed the waters of the lake over the settlements on the southeast and west shores. In the little town of Moore Haven, 1500 people drowned. It is said that these two storms were among the principal causes of the collapse of the "Florida Boom" of the twenties.

There is a vast loneliness about the big water; its featureless horizons suggest the ocean or the Great Plains, domed over by 180 degrees of unobstructed sky. It lies between two blank spots on the map of Florida, two great areas almost devoid of towns and roads. To the south lie the Everglades, which it once nourished with its overflow; to the north the Kissimmee Prairie, through which we had driven on the endlessly straight road. Ecologically the Kissimmee Prairie is like a displaced part of the American west. Cowboys, booted and spurred, peered at us from under their broad-brimmed Stetsons. And the sandhill cranes and burrowing owls almost gave the illusion that we were in Montana or Wyoming. However, the grass is much longer and coarser.

At Clewiston, on the south side of the lake where the Caloosahatchee breaches the dyke and carries off the overflow, we again went out onto the lake. Once within the great earth wall we were completely cut off from civilization. No cottages dotted the shore. Flat marshes, cane patches, and lotus beds extended great distances out into the lake until open water shimmered to the empty horizon. It was in the hope of seeing America's fourth-rarest bird (or is it third?) that we had again ventured out on the big water. I had hoped we might use the airboat, which employs an airplane propeller and wind for its speedy propulsion over the shallow water of the marshes, instead of an outboard motor, which frequently stalls in the mud and becomes tangled in the waterweeds. This "machine of the devil" as an English friend described it, was first developed at the Bear River Refuge in Utah to facilitate the gathering of ducks afflicted with botulism. I wanted James to have a ride in one, but it was being repaired.

May 7

Roger had promised me a ride in an airboat, but we had to hire an outboard instead. The young man at the engine knew where to find us one of the rarest birds of the United States, the Everglade kite.

The giant snail, *Pomacea caliginosa,* is the staple diet of two birds which could not live in Florida without it—the limpkin and the Everglade kite (or snail kite). It is a huge snail; we found many of its thin discarded shells among the reeds, and on the stems, like clusters of small pearls, were its pinkish-white eggs. It was the other snail bird, the limpkin, that put us on to our first Everglade kites. One of these extraordinary birds—a kind of compromise between a crane and a water rail—was shrieking, yelping, and caterwauling around a patch of reeds. Apparently they are more vocal just before a storm; thunderheads were threatening in the west. We got to the place where the bird was crying by charging blindly through the marsh. Every now and then our boatman would jump out into the water up to his waist, free the propeller, and give us fifty yards of push into clear water. No sooner had we spotted the noisy limpkin than we saw our first Everglade kite in the distance. The big dark bird sailed lazily along at reed height, then dropped into the reeds and disappeared. We quickly saw another and later a third. We maneuvered slowly to get within binocular distance of the first bird, which had come into view again, perched among the tops of the reeds. These birds can climb about in the reeds like any bittern and in their own way have as much agility in their unusual medium as the

limpkin. Our snail kite had found its snail; holding on to a cluster of reeds with one foot and grasping the snail in the other, it carefully picked the animal bit by bit out of its shell by means of its curious slender hooked beak.

The Everglade kite is much wider-winged than any of the other three American kites, more like a harrier, but without the typical action of the harrier. In the air, of course, it has no maneuvering to do, for it is not looking for prey more mobile than snails. This explains, of course, the calm quartering of the reeds by the birds— that slow, low, steady flight, head down, watching the marsh like a black tern. Occasionally they hover on beating wings like an osprey or large kestrel and drop out of sight into the reeds. I do not think they paid much attention to our boat, but I am sure the airboat would have frightened them (Roger says not). One of the birds was certainly a female or a first-year male, rather streaked and not unlike a female harrier. Another was an adult male, quite black except for the white at the base of the tail which both sexes have; at close range bright red legs and bare red skin around its face gave it a most attractive touch of color.

JAMES, with his private passion for seabirds, his diary hinted, was more impressed on this day by the flock of black skimmers which sat on a sandy spit in the lake and dodged his efforts at photography. And for a quarter of an hour he wasted time trying to photograph a very tame least tern that kept returning to a stake marking a boat channel.

I emphasized to him that relatively few American ornithologists have seen the Everglade kite—although our young boatman practically guarantees success to his bird-watching customers. There are probably no more than twenty-five pairs remaining in the United States today—perhaps all of them in this limited area. This puts the species about on a par with the California condor for Number 3 place among rare North American birds; it is anyone's guess which of the two is the rarer. Actually the condor would be the greater loss because it represents a full species, whereas the kite is a local subspecies of a bird that ranges from southern Mexico to the Argentine.

Fifteen years ago Marvin Chandler, the first Audubon warden at Lake Okeechobee, showed me several kite nests in the big glossy-ibis colony, and I had great sport stalking perched birds with my Leica. By wading on my knees, only my head above the tepid water, I could get close enough for some fine shots with the six-inch lens. These I used later in designing a poster which implored duck hunters not to shoot these harmless Raptores. They were distributed by the National Audubon Society and displayed at all fish camps and gun clubs around the lake. Our boatman still had a small supply which he put up wherever he thought they would do the most good.

It is the trigger-happy duck hunter who is the greatest threat to the few remaining kites; they look like any other hawks to him. The unscrupulous egg collector is the next menace, although there are not many active oölogists left in the United States. They are not the problem that they still seem to be in England.*

As late as 1920 there were probably hundreds of Everglade kites still left in Florida. But today the last ones have gone from the St. Johns River and they are no longer found in the Everglades; so the name "snail kite" is now the more appropriate. Marsh drainage did much of the damage. Even temporary drainage eliminates the *Pomacea* snails on which the birds depend. Fortunately, Okeechobee is undrainable; but *raising* the water would be just as bad.

All four North American kites are now far rarer than they were formerly. This afternoon we had seen the rarest of the four, and before the day was out we were also to see the most beautiful one, as James recounts in his diary.

IN THE LITTLE TOWN of Clewiston, with its stately avenues of royal palms and neat houses, we were looking for a bird of exceptional rarity, the smooth-billed ani. An extraordinary, swallow-shaped, graceful hawk came wheeling over us. It had staring white underparts and wing-linings, black wing-ends, black tail-streamers, and

---

* James might contradict this—we ran into three during our North American journey!

when it turned and swung over the casuarina trees, it was black on the upper parts. Its tail was much longer and more deeply forked than that of any other kite. This, the swallow-tailed kite, is common only in the lower Everglades and in a few other swamps in the South. Although it once roamed as far north as Minnesota, Roger tells me we are not likely to see it again after we leave Florida.

It was Jack Merritt of Clewiston who finally showed us the anis. We could not find the little flock at first; we drove up and down the streets looking at every garden, finally to discover them in a field at the edge of town. These close cousins of the cuckoo were quite black and slender, long-tailed, short-winged, and with enormous high-ridged bills; they seemed very loose-jointed. There is another species, the groove-billed ani, which lives in Texas, but with this exception there is nothing else like the bird—although, flying in the distance, it might be mistaken for a grackle. We watched the flock, as the evening fell at Clewiston, assembling at their roosting tree. Until the nineteen-thirties the smooth-billed ani was a vagrant to the United States, but in 1937 a flock, perhaps hurricane-borne from the West Indies, arrived at Miami Beach, where they roosted in an immense clump of bamboo. Since then the bird has bred at more than one place in Florida, though the only regular colony is that at Clewiston; the townspeople are very proud of this ornithological distinction. The birds, as is their custom, nest communally. All the females of the flock lay their eggs in a large nest in more than one

layer, with leaves in between. It is probable that the heat and fermentation of the leaves aid in the incubation of the eggs.

While we were watching the anis go to bed, nighthawks hawked for dragonflies over the rooftops and vacant lots of the town. So did a dozen gull-billed terns. It was a bizarre setting for terns. But anything seemed possible in this strange part of Florida. And somehow it was difficult to be overwhelmingly surprised by the snail kites and the anis, incredibly rare though they were. By now the incredibly rare was becoming almost commonplace.

12

The 'Glades

*N*O WHITE MAN, even to this day, has ever traveled the full length of the Everglades in one continuous journey. The 'Glades really begin at Lake Okeechobee, a hundred miles from the southern tip of Florida. The whole of the southern end of the great peninsula which constitutes the Sunshine State is one vast wilderness of marshes, swamps, sawgrass, and water. The Everglades proper is, in truth, a river of grass, a broad shallow slow-sloping river choked with sawgrass through which the water, swelled by rains, flows, or rather oozes, for a hundred miles until it merges imperceptibly with the tidewater of the Gulf of Mexico. If we accept the concept of a river it is certainly the widest river on earth—fifty, sixty, even seventy

miles across. The Indians called it *Pa-hay-okee*—"grassy water."
The following description is largely from James's notebooks.

THIS SEA of sawgrass, sodden and waterlogged in summer, drying
in winter, is a fantastic plain of slough and swamp. Between sixty
and sixty-five inches of rainfall on south Florida in the course of a
year—mostly in spring and summer—are caught by this sponge of
low vegetation, the Everglades, and flow slowly, southward, through
it; flow visibly only when the water runs high after the rains. Over
a third of the Everglades is neither water nor land but something
between the two. Here and there are higher spots, dry all the year
round, which are dominated by cabbage palms, or even the rare wild
royal palm, growing in the rich black soil of plant decay which the
Calusa Indians used to cultivate and which the Seminoles still do.

Below the sawgrass is the muck; the sticky basis of the great slow
bog-river; and below the muck a sedimentary oölitic limestone. Like
all such limestones that water comes in contact with, it is dissolved
partly away. Here and there are islands where the limestone comes
to the surface; most of them run north and south as the dissolving
stream gently flows past them, and upon these "hammocks," or
Indian island gardens, grow West Indian trees in jungly tangles:
Caribbean pine, gumbo limbo, blolly, paradise tree, mastic, royal
palm, cabbage palm. Underneath there is often a tangle of saw
palmetto, and the sinister strangler fig grows on, grows over, envelops,
and finally suffocates its host trees.

To the east, along the coast, the busy towns—Palm Beach, Fort
Lauderdale, Miami, Coral Gables, Homestead—all stand on a ridge
of limestone that is comparatively high, as much as twenty-five feet
above sea level. But the average height of the Everglades above sea
level is not much more than eight feet; and within the last century
there has been considerable lowering because of rash experiments in
clearing and burning, which have resulted in the oxidization and
denudation of the muck, the sticky black Everglades soil. To man,
the Everglades has been a continuous challenge. He has involved
himself in drainage schemes far more costly than he ever dreamed,
many of which have been disastrous failures. Land won from the

sloughs and swamps, and densely peopled with fruit growers and catch-crop market gardeners, has been drowned more than once, with heavy loss of life, when violent hurricanes pushed the rising water over it. To drive roads through the Everglades men have had to blast right through the muck down to the limestone bedrock and build on that, which is why the great west road out of Miami across the Everglades, the Tamiami Trail, was fifty years building, and why there is a block about the size of Devonshire (one of the biggest English counties) in which there are no main roads at all. Nothing but the Okaloacoochee Slough, the Big Cypress Swamp, the largest of the Seminole Indian reservations, the ruins of Sam Jones town, and seventy miles of rather abortive canal from Miami to Okeechobee.

The Everglades National Park embraces nearly a million and a quarter acres—more than half of that part of Florida which lies south of the Tamiami Trail. It is one of the largest National Parks and the newest, pledged to the nation in 1947.

The mangroves occupy the entire southwest half of the park, growing wherever the water is salt—all over the islets or keys in Florida Bay, round the entire coast and round the multitudinous creek and

White Ibis

river mouths. Fingers of mangrove forest poke up all the rivers until with the last of the tidal salt water the growth is only of hedge thickness. Beyond this, the "rivers" continue into the sawgrass interior, winding, joining chains of lakes, joining and rejoining each other, forming a maze which to the traveler is an inextricable confusion of rock, mud, plants, and water. Some Everglades water tracts, too higgledy-piggledy and choked with vegetation to be called rivers, and yet with a system and flow of their own, are called sloughs. The big Taylor Slough is crossed at its upper end by the highway into the Park; and it was here we made our first stop on hot—desperately hot—sunny May 8. We pulled up at a parking place: a signpost read ANHINGA TRAIL, and an elevated board walk, 200 feet long, invited us, cameras and all, into the middle of the slough.

One of the most gratifying results of the creation of national parks and nature reserves in the United States of America is the tameness of the indigenous wild animals; a phenomenon which dates back into the last century with the early years of Yellowstone. It is true that in many other parts of the world protected wild life has become ridiculously tame; in Gloucestershire, England, wild mallard, pintail, shoveller come to Peter Scott's hand to be fed; and many ducks winter in the London parks, on petting terms with the visitors. But only in North America, so far, has it been possible to combine the national park (where man is encouraged) with the nature reserve (from which, at least in the old days, man was supposed to be kept away). Here, on Anhinga Trail, under our feet which clattered over the board walk, floated sleepy alligators. Quietly on its huge yellow feet a purple gallinule bobbed and jerked about the water-lily leaves, and stepped, like a proud chicken, a few feet below us. I hurriedly set up my Leica with the 12-inch Kilfitt lens. Roger said that this particular purple gallinule is the most photographed bird in the whole state of Florida; it is now appearing in the kodachrome films of six different Audubon Screen Tour lecturers!

On a bush overhanging the slough sat a water turkey, the trail's own anhinga, turning its head from side to side to watch the visitors. There were a few egrets—both snowy and American egrets. And like a ghost, among the sedges at the slough edge, stood a really rare bird, the great white heron of America.* At first we had ignored

---

* In the view of Ernst Mayr and others, the great white heron is probably a local color-phase of the great blue heron.

it; we thought it was just another American egret until we noticed its pale legs. It was only twenty yards away; fifty years before, A. C. Bent in Florida Bay could not get within two or three hundred yards of one! Roger's movie started on all lenses (except the Kilfitt, which I had).

The history of the Florida herons, of the desperate straits to which they were reduced by the plume hunters at the turn of the century, has often been related. The great white heron suffered with the others. But it does not seem ever to have been brought *very* near extinction by humans; indeed, nature has probably been harder on it than man. Its breeding has always been confined to the mangrove zone of Florida—to Florida Bay and the chain of Florida Keys, in which the special Great White Heron National Wildlife Refuge was established in 1938. At that time the bird had been decimated by the hurricane of 1935, which also took such a toll of human life in the Keys. Just after this catastrophe, Alexander Sprunt, Jr., of the National Audubon Society in an aerial survey could find only 146 birds in nine-tenths of their range. But so remarkable are the powers of recovery of herons that seven years later, Earle Greene of the Fish and Wildlife Service found that the great white herons had bounced back to between 1500 and 1800 birds.

We must have stayed a couple of hours with our tame great white heron of Anhinga Trail. All was quiet, except for a continual stream of human visitors chattering away on the board walk; the anhinga never left its post. The alligators floated, and a huge one, which we had not seen before, swam up, very, very slowly; we heard another growl in the distance. Under the sunning, lazy body of the smallish alligator, many slender garfish nosed about with rippling fins.

At the ranger station we were introduced to several of the young men who acted as Park rangers. The tourist season here was just about over; one of the rangers, who asked Roger to autograph his *Field Guide,* was leaving in a day or two for Glacier National Park in Montana, where he would take up summer duties.

The ranger station was at the edge of a dry hammock with a specially fine group of (natural) royal palms, twisted sausage-red gumbo limbos, and strangler figs. Upon the tamarinds and on the smooth gray cement-like trunks of the royal palms were pretty tree snails—*Liguus*—with colorfully banded shells. Some had already gone into aestivation, the operculum sealed tight for the summer. These beautiful snails are rigidly protected in the park. Many hammocks have their own special variants of the "lig" color patterns, and collectors in the past have been known to clean out entire populations. Behind the remnants of a once substantial inn which had been torn down, was a bed of bright red flowers, alive with butterflies, mostly swallowtails and big pale cloudless sulphurs.

This hammock is now known as Paradise Key; it was formerly Florida's Royal Palm State Park. Here we encountered a really West Indian bird, which breeds no farther north than south Florida, the black-whiskered vireo, a plain little greenish bird with a black whisker mark. We heard it singing a rhythmical, penetrating song in the hammock, and heard it again later when we reached the mangroves. This bird was a reminder (if it was needed at a temperature of well over 90° F.) that Florida, though north of the Tropic of Cancer, is truly tropical. Another reminder was a large slim butterfly, black with yellow bands, the Zebra, *Heliconius charitonius*. It had the most curious delicate flight—it does not beat so much as quiver its wings, and with a shivering delicacy picks its way very slickly through undertangle of the most jungly complication. Although the Zebra occasionally reaches South Carolina, it is truly a tropical species of a tropical family, of which the famous Amazon naturalist Bates wrote: "This elegant shape, showy colors, and slow, sailing mode of flight, makes them very attractive objects, and their numbers are so great that they form quite a feature in the physiognomy of the forest, compensating for the scarcity of flowers."

Just so was the situation in the Everglades hammocks. There were no flowers to speak of—except butterflies. But up the trees among the airplants were a few pale but interesting-looking orchids.* As of flowers, so there was a lack of warblers; indeed, apart from the black-whiskered vireo and the ubiquitous white-eyed vireo, the only songbirds in the hammock were mockingbird, prairie warbler, and cardinal. There were red-wings and grackles about the slough, but on the whole, the Everglades were singularly lacking in small birds.

We took on about half a gallon of root beer and coke with a salt pill to balance up and pushed on southwest, farther into the Everglades. After about sixteen miles of good unsurfaced road with a verge

* There are 84 varieties of orchids in this area: 25 epiphytic, 50 terrestrial, and 9 humus. Some have blossoms no larger than the head of a pin, others a profusion of showy blossoms on stems four to six feet long.

Heliconius

on one side alive with dragonflies, through a landscape of sawgrass and low cypress islands, we found ourselves among the mangroves. In the narrow belt where the mangroves began we saw towering over the other vegetation a few extremely slender palms of a new, rather rare species, the Paurotis palm.

Here near the southernmost point of the continent, we took a side road to Snake Bight, a bay just east of the mangrove key named after Guy Bradley, the Audubon warden who was murdered by the plume hunter Walter Smith in 1905, and who is buried at Cape Sable. There was the usual string of brown pelicans in the distance. Among the several species of herons scattered over the glistening, eye-hurting tidal flats was a new one, a curious bird quite unlike the others, dancing and bowing on the sands. This was the rare reddish egret, catching little fish. There are keys in Florida Bay where this bird, once almost lost, now nests; it is making a comeback.

We ate our sandwiches, and drove back to the main road and on toward Cape Sable, a broad peninsula joined to the mainland by a narrow isthmus. On the north side of this isthmus at its narrowest point stands the Coot Bay ranger's station, fitted out with a gasoline depot and a fleet of motor and outboard craft. It was in the finest of these boats, belonging to Park Superintendent Daniel Beard himself, that our friend and guide Joseph Moore, the Park biologist, took us deep into the glades where mangroves grow to 50 feet on some of the wooded keys. Moore navigated unerringly across the bight of Coot Bay and through narrow dark passages arched over with mangroves. Herons flew overhead and a great pack of white ibis scattered on our approach.

These Everglade rivers in their salt mangrove sections are the last real refuge in the United States of the manatee, one of the few surviving representatives of the *Sirenia,* spatula-tailed cleft-faced, vegetable-eating aquatic mammals. The usual evidence of a manatee, or sea cow, is a disturbance or "boil" of water. We didn't even see this, but we got to the East River rookery, and spent a good two hours photographing the nesting birds before the late afternoon sun dropped behind the clouds. Here nested countless wood ibises, white ibises, snowy egrets, little blue herons, American egrets, and Louisiana herons. The main island looked like an overloaded Christmas tree, as if someone had tried to make snow out of candle wax. All over the mangroves was a frosting of white birds, parents standing on guard, parents bending over flat dirty nests, and, on top of the trees, gatherings of unemployed-looking wood ibises. As we got nearer they took off with a great balancing and tilting of wings, bowing and bill-clattering all the time.

I WOULD LIKE to continue where James left off in his description of the East River rookery. This was the third time I had visited a large nesting concentration in the 'Glades. Here, twelve years before, I had spent a day slapping mosquitoes in my burlap blind in the midst of a great nesting of white ibises, estimated to exceed 100,000. Long snaky ribbons of these white birds with red faces, and long curved red bills, twisted out of the sky, broke ranks, and fluttered like snowflakes into the mangroves. That was a bit later in the season; they were only beginning to get their nesting under way at East River this year, but there were certainly hundreds, perhaps thousands present, mostly around the edges of the mixed colony. The wood ibises had nested much earlier; their young were already quite grown and would soon be flying. They looked very much like their parents, white with the outer half of the wing black and with a naked gray head.

The sun was beginning to play hide and seek among the great cumulus clouds that were rising out of the west. Soon there would be no sun at all for photography; so we worked fast, Joe Moore easing the boat close to the most photogenic groups of balancing and teetering "flintheads" while James and I fired away. I used the 16 mm. Bell & Howell and the 4-inch lens on the camera gun. Ordinarily I prefer to work from a tripod, but in a moving boat it is impossible; then the camera gun with its Nydar gunsight is the answer.

With the diminishing light the mosquitoes were getting pretty bad
—or I should say, intolerable. I was reminded of my visit in 1937
to the wood ibis colony in remote Cuthbert Lake—nine miles to the
southwest as the ibis flies. In those days, I hauled a ponderous
4 x 5 Graflex about with me. When focusing on the birds, it took
all my will power to keep both hands on the camera; clouds of
mosquitoes swarmed over my unprotected arms, particularly just
above my elbows, where I had been sunburned a week before, and
where I had become badly burned again on the tender new skin.
The little brown vampires settled by the hundreds while I was im-
potent to brush them off. To this day I carry a reminder of that
ordeal in a heavy band of freckles on each arm—produced, I suppose, by some alchemy of the poisons of sun and mosquitoes.

While we were at the rookery a swallow-tailed kite soared over,
its tail acting as a sensitive rudder; earlier we had seen two or three
at the Coot Bay ranger station. This graceful raptor is perhaps commoner here than at any other place on the continent.

But we had to start back quickly—while there was still daylight

enough to light our way. Threading through the tall mangroves of East River we were soon on the open choppy water of Whitewater Bay where our speedy boat skipped and pounded into the fresh breeze. We were deluged with salt spray, but the cameras, stowed forward, were safe. Turning our bow toward the wall of dark mangroves, we entered the tea-colored channel which would take us back to our mooring at Coot Bay. This channel had been recently dredged by the Park Service; but Moore showed us the site of an ancient canal dug by the Tekesta Indians in pre-Columbian times, perhaps about the year 1200. Centuries of silt had filled it in, but its straight course could still be traced through the vegetation. He also pointed out, growing on the higher ground beside it, a modest tree whose name—manchineel—is enough to send a shiver through those who have had experience with it. Rain, dripping from its leaves, raises huge blisters; eating its fruit brings agonizing death. Calusas and Seminoles, it is said, lured their enemies to take shelter under its branches during rainstorms, and, using its leaves, poisoned springs where their enemies came to drink. Recently a biologist at the University of Miami, doubtful of its lethal properties—or at least believing them exaggerated—brought specimens to his laboratory for analysis. He wore heavy rubber gloves; even with this protection, one of his arms swelled up and became temporarily paralyzed. He later discovered a tiny pinhole in the glove.

No mangrove forest in the world can compare with this one we had been passing through. Usually low-growing elsewhere, the trees attain a height of 50 feet around Whitewater Bay and over 80 feet near the mouth of Shark River, a few miles to the northwest. There were three species of mangroves growing along the canal. The red mangrove is the most familiar, supported by an impenetrable labyrinth of stiltlike roots on which clusters of coon oysters can be seen clinging when the tide is out. The black mangrove does not have stilts but sends pneumatophores up through the mud like a carpet of thin fingers, suggesting those beds of nails on which Hindu fakirs lie. The third species, the white mangrove, lacks these distinctions, and in that way is identified. These glossy-leaved trees, with their elevated root systems and pneumatophores, catch the silt, hold it, consolidate it, and slowly, steadily build the land.

A million years have done little to change the life of a pool in the mangrove swamp. "If you don't believe it," writes Bob Allen, "crawl with crocodile and terrapin through the slime and watch the lowly gastropod leave his smooth track beside yours. A million years have not changed them. Stay out there at night, and you will hear, as I have, the noiseless murmur of the Pleistocene."

We looked for crocodiles on the banks of the canal; in January I had seen one here. The American "croc" is a rather rare animal, which lives in the salt water among the mangroves in this lonely part of Florida. The alligator, more widespread, is a fresh-water saurian with a wider snout and darker color.

As we crept through the tunnels of mangroves at our boat's slowest speed, we were prepared to see almost anything in the deepening twilight—even the extinct Florida rhinoceros. We were nearly eaten alive by mosquitoes when we docked, in spite of the smelly lotions we had rubbed on ourselves. They were tiny mosquitoes, but stung like fire when they made contact. We could hardly get into the Ford station wagon fast enough.

On the long road back (it was twenty-seven miles to Park headquarters) we caught sight of four or five raccoons, hunting for crayfish along the ditches. Caught in the glare of our headlights they shambled into the shadows like high-rumped miniature bears. We saw no bobcats; they are abroad at night, but once near Coot Bay I saw one of these long-legged cats walking down the road in broad daylight.

We stopped briefly at Anhinga Trail; an alligator bellowed in the distance, but all was silent again when we walked out on the wooden pier. Sweeping the pool with our flashlight we could spot the alligators motionless on the still water. Lining up the beam with our eyes we caught their bright red, rather sinister eyeshine. A silent show of fireflies, flashing intermittently in the blackness, accompanied us back to the car while a chuck-will's-widow chanted softly in the distance. It was late when we got back to neon-lighted Miami.

13

America's Coral Islands

$\mathcal{F}$ROM THE Everglades to Miami Beach—from the sublime to the incredible. Hotel after hotel, all with their rows of well-tanned, well-heeled visitors from New York sitting in rocking chairs, hoping to be seen by other well-tanned, well-heeled visitors from New York. James wrote in his diary:

> Can there be any other community so large and at the same time so unequivocally devoted to pure recreation and entertainment? The fashionable seaside places of Brighton, Worthing, Torquay seem puny and amateurish compared with Miami Beach. Was there ever such conspicuous consumption, so many luxury hotels, row upon row, between boulevard and beach, each with its crescent approach? The place was a riot of parthenonian, byzantine, banker's gothic, broker's perpendicular, glasshouse,

gashouse, bauhaus, bathhouse, and madhouse. We wondered how often the tenantry moved from one of these expensive curiosities to another.

But the city of Miami itself, just across Biscayne Bay, is a fairly normal American city, with its many little businesses, factories, offices, churches, restaurants, motion picture theaters, and houses. It was in a residential area in the northwest part of town that we had intelligence of a rarity even more esoteric than the cattle egret or the ani; a tropical bird new to the United States, the spot-breasted oriole, *Icterus pectoralis.* This bright orange and black oriole is not a vagrant from the nearby West Indies, as one might suppose, but belongs to Central America. No one knows how it arrived in Miami, where it was first discovered in August, 1949. During the summer of 1953 five nests were found in different parts of the city. Exotic butterflies have in the past established breeding stations around Miami, but they could easily have come in as larvae or pupae on shipments of tropical plants. But how would a bird from Central America gain a foothold? We had the oriole's address—street, block, and house number —so, with an hour to kill while a tire was being repaired, we set forth. We could not find the bird at first, but after tactful inquiry at a couple of houses we spotted the male in a grove of banana trees across a canal. Our binoculars revealed the ragged breast spots that distinguish it from the black-throated oriole, *Icterus gularis,* which lives in Mexico. In fact, when the birds were first discovered they were thought to be that species, until a local cat collected a specimen for science.

Our destination this day was Key West—a drive of 155 miles down the Overseas Highway—and tomorrow, the Tortugas. James had always wanted to see the Florida Keys, that long line of islands strung like beads into the Gulf of Mexico.

Just after crossing the bridge onto Key Largo, we stopped at a mangrove-bordered lagoon where a crocodile was known to live. Several years before, its mate had been wantonly shot from the road by a passing motorist. We could not find the old bull croc; but when we met Bob Allen, an hour later, he assured us it still had its head-quarters in the lagoon. "It wanders quite a bit in the summer," he said.

It was a great relief to reach Bob Allen's comfortable dwelling. This was the only house in the small town of Tavernier not destroyed by the hurricane of Labor Day, 1935, so Bob had bought it, confident in its ability to withstand any blow the Caribbean could muster. Bob showed us the secret of getting creative work done in this enervating climate—an air-conditioning unit that he had installed. The cool air was as refreshing as a mint julep; for a week we had endured tropical temperatures. James said he began to see the point of air conditioning, not as a support of an advertisers' race in the glossy weeklies, but as a method by which a new vitality would permeate the hot and humid South.

When we stepped outside again the hot air met us like the blast from a furnace. Overhead, hanging on narrow motionless wings against the billowing trade-wind cumuli, were a dozen man-o'-war birds, their scissor-like tail-streamers trailing. We were to see many more of these aeronauts from the West Indies in the next two or three days.

Bob (who was to join us on our expedition to the Tortugas) took the wheel. The afternoon was getting on; we still had a hundred miles or more to Key West; but it was fast road. During the hurricane of 1935 forty miles of the overseas railway were swept away and no attempt was made to rebuild it. Instead, parts of the railbed and some of the railway bridges have been taken over by the highway.

It was too dark to look for key deer when we crossed the bridge onto Big Pine Key. The attendant at the toll station informed us that twenty minutes earlier two of these tiny deer had crossed the road. Unlike the upper Keys, which are covered with West Indian hardwoods, Big Pine is clothed in Caribbean pine and is the last stronghold of this dwarf race of the white-tailed deer. Whereas a big white-tailed buck in New England might tip the scales at 300 pounds, a buck key deer weighs only 50 pounds. For many years these "toy" deer held their own against the fugitive Calusas and the early Spaniards; it was the more recent settlers of the Keys, the "Conchs," and the Cubans who nearly wiped them out. Running them with dogs, even setting fire to the smaller Keys, they forced the little deer into the water, where they were shot from boats or finished off with hand axes. By 1950, probably not more than 40 survived. They had complete legal protection; a warden was assigned to watch over them, but in less than a year eight were killed by cars on the causeway.

From this low point, the population doubled in two years to about 70. None was killed by a speeding car for more than a year. This improvement had been brought about by carefully picking up the cigarette butts tossed from passing cars, for it was the little animals' craving for tobacco that had lured them to their death.

When we reached Key West, night life at this busy naval base was in full swing. Trying not to run down any of the young sailors who were having an evening on the town, we picked our way to the waterfront, where Stephen Briggs awaited us with his motor yachts *Ungava*

and *Tayto*. After leaving the station wagon at the Ford garage for a checkup we bedded down on the *Ungava* in preparation for departure at dawn.

The throbbing of the engines awakened us at 5 A.M. Through sleepy eyes we saw Key West with its Bahamian frame houses receding from us. The jade-green shallows in which several distant great white herons were wading soon gave way to bluer, deeper water. It would be a six-hour journey to Fort Jefferson in the Dry Tortugas— the most isolated and least visited spot in the eastern United States. James was as enthralled by his introduction to flying fish as I had been twelve years before, when I made my first boat journey to this remote atoll.

May 10–12

The seventy miles from Key West to the anchorage in the Tortugas went fast in the *Ungava,* in a close burning heat. Steve Briggs and his wife and Bob Allen—Floridians—simply looked brown and genial and enjoyed it. Roger and I enjoyed the company, the scenery, the birds, and the fishes, but not the heat. Both of us were reaching the stage where we had few layers of skin to lose, and it was a moot point whether the pressure of a shirt or the sun was more irritating. But we soon forgot the heat in the contemplation of a succession of flying fish processions under our bows. I found my first flying fishes more amusing, prettier, and more powerful then I had expected; they zipped magically out of the water, glided an incredible distance; indeed before they entered the water again, there seemed to be a hesitant moment in which they appeared not to obey the laws of gravity—and when they did touch the water by momentarily dipping their tails, they seemed to get a boost for a second short distance. All the way, as we passed other Keys (mangrove-covered Man and Woman, Boca Grande, and the Marquesas in the distance), these silvery flying fish fanned out from our bow. As our boat bore down upon them they flew races with each other, skittered, glided on, and plunged in with a final unequivocal dip beneath the surface of the tropical sea.

The sun was nearing the zenith when the Tortugas appeared on

the shimmering horizon, first the tall light which stands guard on Loggerhead Key, then the low massive fort on Garden Key. Close to the fort was another smaller key over which hovered a dusky smudge that grew larger, then smaller, constantly changing shape. Our glasses showed that this nebulous coronet was composed of myriad birds, thick as swarming bees around a hive—the famous sooty terns of Bush Key.

Four hundred and forty years before our visit Ponce de León, the discoverer of Florida, sighted this same swarm of birds. He called the islands "the turtles," and Las Tortugas they have been ever since; waterless islands where the sea turtles lay their eggs; the only coral islands in the United States. The Tortugas are one coral atoll, mostly submerged; at present the atoll breaks surface in seven different places (formerly ten), of which the three largest are Loggerhead Key, Bush Key, and Garden Key.

Garden Key, where we dropped anchor, is almost wholly occupied by one of the most extraordinary human artifacts in the New World, the slave-built, brick-built, hexagon-built Fort Jefferson, with its endless wall, fifty feet high and eight feet thick, and the sites for 450 guns in its three stories and miles of galleries. This fort was started in 1846, primarily to guard the sea approaches to the Gulf of Mexico against the threat of British expansion; and for thirty years the work of building went on. By the time it was nearing completion (at the cost, it is said, of a dollar for every one of its 42,000,000 bricks) the fort was defensively obsolete. It never fired a gun in anger, and the British never came, except as tourists! Subsequently it was used as a prison, as a coaling station, as a wireless

station; now it has become a picturesque ruin, since 1935, a National Monument.

The Fort Jefferson National Monument, which embraces the whole archipelago is, through its very inaccessibility, a perfect sanctuary for the tropical seabirds that breed in thousands on the coral sands of Bush Key. For nobody can visit the Dry Tortugas unless he be self-supporting, with his own vessel, or with a vessel or seaplane he has chartered. There is a fine anchorage in the lagoon of the atoll, where the clear blue-green water laps the landing wharves of Garden Key. There the barracudas twitch slowly under the bows of anchored ships, and yellowtails, parrotfish, angelfish, and other tropical fish of coral colors dart about the incrusted pilings of old hurricane-wrecked quays.

It was here at the landing that we were greeted by John De Weese, the resident superintendent. We crossed the medieval-looking drawbridge across the wide moat where sharks once were kept, and followed our guide through the long dark galleries with their cannon emplacements and up the spiral stone staircases from level to level. It was here, in this Bastille of the Gulf, that Dr. Samuel Mudd was wrongly imprisoned as an accomplice when he set the broken leg of Booth, President Lincoln's assassin, and here he redeemed himself by saving the lives of many men when an epidemic of yellow fever swept the fort. In the hexagonal parade ground within the fort

grow graceful coconut palms and dates. Past residents had also planted tamarind, Jamaica dogwood, and gumbo limbo—there is good shelter here for little migratory birds. There are days, De Weese told us—particularly in April and in September—when the scattered trees in the enclosure and even the lawns swarm with tired passerine birds resting from their journey to or from Cuba or Yucatán. Although it was now nearly mid-May we spotted a few late migrant warblers, mostly females—magnolia, Cape May (new to me), black-throated blue, bay-breasted, blackpoll, and redstart. They crept about the tops of the trees and we could watch them perfectly from the galleries above. There was a fine group of swallows hawking over the fortress walls—bank, rough-winged, barn, and cliff swallows. We also spotted a yellow-billed cuckoo and three hawks—marsh, pigeon, and sharp-shinned. De Weese showed us a barn owl sheltering in a hole in the ruined officers' quarters.

Tropical seas bathe the Dry Tortugas, even though they are over 80 miles north of the Tropic of Cancer, for the water heated by the Caribbean's tropical sun circulates their way; everything about them is

tropical—their coral, their shells, their fish, their bay cedars, coconut palms, cacti, moon-vines, and sea beans. But the most convincing sign of their utter tropicality is their seabirds, two of which, the sooty tern (black-backed with white underparts), and the noddy (smoky brown with a whitish cap), nest nowhere else in the United States. Two others, the brown booby and the blue-faced booby, wanderers from the West Indies, are seen here every year, but nowhere else in the United States.

During the heat of the day many of the unemployed noddies come across from Bush Key to sit on the ruined quay near the fort. We waded knee-deep through the limpid water (watching out for barracudas), to the rusted girders on which the birds sat; we could reach up slowly and touch some of them before they took wing.

When we rowed the dinghy across the channel to Bush Key later in the afternoon, a dark noisy cloud of sooties boiled up and squawked deafeningly at us, but soon they settled. They were very tame; it was not long before we could pick our way through their crowded ranks to the noddies on the bay cedars beyond without creating too much fuss. For hours we sat on the beach watching the sooties squabbling over the tiny territories round the scrapes which pass as nests. Bodies flexed, wings held out and slightly opened, necks arched, they squawked and crowed at each other. They bowed, like book ends opposing each other, touched bills, flared up in emotion, suddenly to break off and preen; they fiddled with their egg, billing it into a more comfortable position against the incubation patch. Some nibbled and struck at our intruding fingers, without rising from their egg.

The noddies nest mostly in the bay cedar, but also on *Opuntia* (prickly pear) cactus in the interior of Bush Key. Some of the nests, on the edges of bushes, overhung those of sooty terns below. They were loose and untidy and made of seaweed and little sticks; in some were lumps of shell. Some were dense and deep, built on the surviving structures of previous seasons. Not all appeared to have eggs (they lay single eggs normally, like most other tropical terns). In 1907 that pioneer student of terns, Professor J. B. Watson, found the first eggs on May 4; most were laid between the 11th and 16th of May. The season seemed to be about the same with us in 1953.

John James Audubon saw these tropical birds in 1832. He stayed in Key West that summer, and visited the Tortugas on the U.S.

Revenue Cutter *Marion;* having already published over a hundred plates of his immortal *Birds of America* he was now famous, and privileged to voyage in government ships. In Audubon's year there was clearly a ternery of immense size on the Tortugas. The first lieutenant of the *Marion* told him "both species were on their respective breeding grounds by millions"! We expect he took this with a pinch of salt. Indeed, these are the most populous terns of the tropical seas; on some islands in the Indian Ocean there *are* sooty colonies of over a million nests! But it is difficult to guess, from Audubon's account, just what numbers he found. Certainly in his time there were many more noddies than there are today. Bird Key, where Audubon found the big sooty colony, no longer exists. It started to sink in 1928 and disappeared entirely during the big hurricane of 1938. Since then the birds have used Bush Key, closer to the fort.

"At Bird Key," wrote Audubon, "we found a party of Spanish eggers from Havana. They had already laid in a cargo of about eight tons of the eggs of this [sooty] tern and the noddy. On asking them how many they supposed they had, they answered that they never counted them, even while selling them, but disposed of them at seventy-five cents per gallon; and that one turn to market sometimes produced upwards of two hundred dollars, while it took only a week to sail backwards and forwards and collect their cargo." A sooty tern's egg, Roger tells me, weighs thirty grams, or about fifteen eggs to the pound. Eight tons would come to nearly a quarter of a million eggs! If Audubon's figure was true, and the eggs had all come from the Tortugas (and none from the Bahamas and Cuba), then there must have been, since then, a spectacular decline in the only tropical tern population of the United States. No doubt this was primarily the work of the eggers. Uncontrolled, these people can undo a large population of social birds in a very few years. The turn of the century, with commercial persecution, was a terrible time for Florida's birds. Anyway in 1903, the first year for which we have any reliable information about the size of the ternery, there were only about 7000 sooties' nests and 200 noddies'. But slowly the sooty tern population climbed back, in the first quarter of the century, to 9000 or 10,000 nests. When the National Park Service took over in 1935, there were 15,000 nests; by 1937, 50,000. During the forties the number ran between 32,135 and 54,500, culminating in 95,438 in 1950, as censused by Willard Dilley.*

Several times during our three days at this tropical atoll Stephen Briggs put us ashore on Bush Key for sessions with the birds. At the suggestion of De Weese, we confined our operations to the morning and the late afternoon when the sands were somewhat cooler than they were at midday. Our time was mostly devoted to watching, counting, photographing, even sound-recording. Clearly there was room on Bush Key, and on its neighbor Long Key, and their connecting spit, for the nests of even more sooties; the Tortugas were by no means full up, and it seemed quite possible that if the islands had been of about the same area in 1832, they could have supported enough terns to produce the eight tons of eggs that Audubon mentioned!

All over the beach, and among the sooty terns, were little holes in the firmer parts of the sand. A casual human invader of the sands

* In 1953 we were on the islands from the 10th to 12th of May (at the same season as Audubon, who was there from May 9 to 11, 1832). My own estimate of the number of occupied nests—80,000—was not far off. A census based on sample plot counts which was made two weeks later by the Park Service came up with a figure of 84,569 sooty nests.

The noddies had 421 nests. In the present century they have been supposed to have had 2000 nests in some years and as few as 70 in others, but most often they ran between 400 and 500.

Man-o'-War Birds

sees no more than quick gray movements at these holes—unrecognized shapes scuttling in. But if he waits quietly, sits to watch, *Ocypode albicans,* the ghost crab, comes out. This pallid wraith is the beachcomber of the Tortugas. In 1917 Paul Bartsch found that these crabs ate the eggs and probably killed the young of the least terns on Long Key. Certainly the quick scuttling crabs that rustle and click about the sands scavenge lost sooty tern eggs at the edge of the colony, though even the bigger of these crabs do not seem to try to put the sooties off their eggs as they did the least terns. These queer ghost crabs appeared to be the principal scavengers, except for some important birds. There were a few ring-billed and laughing gulls hanging about, and we saw a herring gull or two on our first day, but the real opportunists* were the man-o'-war birds. The magnificent frigate birds (we can call them that) numbered about eighty, and made their headquarters in a row of tallish bay cedars at the edge of the noddy colony. There were always a dozen or more hanging in the wind over the colony and another half dozen perched like great marine vultures on the channel posts. They were ideal subjects for the camera gun. Roger found it no trick to hold them in the Nydar gunsight while he ran off film at 64 frames per second, which is the slow-motion speed. These long-billed, buoyant birds, with their seven-foot wingspread and long tail-streamers, are the most masterly soarers of all the seabirds; only the petrels and albatrosses can outdo them as sailplanes—and these do not soar and hang on the wind as continuously and skillfully. Dr. Frank Chapman once said that the man-o'-wars "perch on the air above their homes."

Man-o'-wars have never bred in Florida, but every summer a few thousands haunt the southwest coast, the Keys, and the Tortugas; their nearest nesting places are in the Bahamas and Cuba. At the Dry Tortugas they lead their normal lives, never deliberately landing on the water (they quickly get waterlogged), but catching surface life, usually fish, with fast skillful dives and swoops. When the

---

* I am tempted to point out that the "real opportunist" was James. Steve Briggs had loaned me an adapter ring which made it possible for me to use my 12-inch Kilfitt lens on the Cine-Special. But whenever I switched momentarily to the camera gun and the Bell & Howell with the 4-inch lens for flight shots James appropriated the Kilfitt and fastened it to his Leica. We agreed to take turns with this very desirable lens, but just whose turn it was often became a moot point during the remainder of our trip.—R.T.P.

young terns hatch, the number of man-o'-wars goes up, for they apparently scavenge sickly, weak, and foolish young birds.

Between Garden Key and Loggerhead Light, four miles distant, are several large floating buoys. As we approached one of these in the *Tayto,* we saw sitting on it two large white birds. They were blue-faced boobies. Roger was astonished, because it was on this very same buoy, twelve years before, that he had photographed two blue-faced boobies—the first time, in fact, that these West Indian wanderers had ever been photographed in the waters of the United States. This time it was my turn to photograph them. When the boat, its motor cut off, drifted toward them, they bowed gravely in unison and waited until we were not fifteen feet away before they reluc-tantly abandoned their perch. On the wing they looked like small gannets but with more black in their wings. Perhaps they were the same two birds Roger photographed in 1941. Apparently they must be pretty faithful to their buoy; the fishermen say they are always there.

WE SPENT our last evening on the *Tayto* eating delicious yellowtails which James and Steve Briggs had caught, and listening to the never ceasing clamor of the colony. Individual voices were lost among the thousands of others, but occasionally a bird flew directly over the boat, clearly enunciating its *wide-a-wake*. The curtain of the night dropped almost with a thud, as it does in these southern latitudes, and long after the red glow faded, a steady procession of home-coming birds continued to stream in from the Gulf. Aiming the strong beam of the ship's spotlight into the air we could pick up their white breasts. Turning the beam downward into the still water near us we became aware of other, more silent seafarers, huge fish —barracuda and tuna—idling back and forth, attracted by the hull of our boat or perhaps by its lights.

When we last saw Fort Jefferson late the next morning it had a little crown of man-o'-war birds suspended above one of its towers, where air currents, deflected upward against the walls, had lifted them. But we did not see another sooty tern all the way back to Key West. Although, as Dr. Robert Cushman Murphy points out, these conspicuous black and white terns probably fly hundreds of miles every day and cannot rest upon the water, away from their populous colonies they seem to be swallowed up in the immensity of the ocean.

14

Ivory-Bill Quest

"In Britain," James said, "you couldn't drive six hundred miles in one direction without going over the edge." Yet at the end of this one day's driving, from the outskirts of Miami to northern Florida, that is what our meter registered. We had started at dawn, but even with this early getaway we had little time to do anything except look at the landscape. But what an interesting landscape it was, one that changed markedly half a dozen times—from mangrove coast to glades to cypress swamp to prairie and then to endless pine forest. In this single day we had a pretty complete view of the face of Florida.

The Tamiami Trail, the long ribbon of concrete that runs straight west across the tip of Florida spans the entire width of the 'Glades —a distance of 40 miles (to "Forty-mile Bend") before it changes direction. On its right flank is the equally straight Tamiami Canal, a fine place for birds but a snare for the incautious. Years ago, two bird-watching schoolteachers whom I knew skidded their car into the canal and were drowned. When I was learning to drive it was predicted that I would probably come to a similar end; therefore I have always been a bit defensive on this score and nothing short of an ivory-billed woodpecker flying across the highway would cause me to avert my gaze more than momentarily.* Some years ago Allan Cruickshank did see a bird fly over the very road which we took that morning from the Tamiami into the Big Cypress, a bird which to this day he swears was not a pileated woodpecker but an ivory-bill. Ivory-bills were constantly in the backs of our minds; indeed the long fast run was necessary if we were to keep our tryst with Herbert Stoddard, who had promised to go with us on the morrow to search the Chipola for these giant woodpeckers. James wanted to stop at one of the Seminole villages along the canal, but I dissuaded him. These were "tourist Indians" I explained, not bona fide Seminole settlements; to see the real thing we would have to go by dugout far back into the swamp.

As we sped westward across the open glades the waving seas of sawgrass stretched to the horizon. It was not until we approached the far side of the great "river of grass" that the flat monotony was broken by islands of small cypress, which looked as though they were dwarfed by the winds. Actually their anemic stature, only a few feet high, was because the bed of limestone on which they grew was covered only by a very thin layer of muck. When I was here in January they were dead looking, devoid of their needles, like discarded Christmas trees; they are the only trees in south Florida to stand bare in winter. But now these "deciduous evergreens" were pale green with the new growth of spring. With each mile they gradually became larger, but it was not until we reached the heart of the "Big Cypress," the great wooded swamp on the west side of the sedgy Everglades, that we saw cypress of any size. Even here only a few trees along the strands attain the ponderous proportions of those which one occasionally sees along the edges of certain southern rivers—giants with buttressed bases ten or twelve feet in diameter. Eight hundred years is said to be the maximum age for a bald cypress, but one ancient tree in Seminole County, Florida, is believed to have been there before the time of Christ. The spreading buttresses

* Hm, hm.—J.F.

of the bigger trees give them firm anchorage in the muck, and the erect "knees" sent up from the root system supposedly allow the roots to "breathe" in times of high water, for these forests are periodically flushed by floods.

Every cypress hammock was studded with airplants that from a distance, reminded James of rooks' nests in the spinneys at home. They sprouted from the delicate branches in large dark tufts like clumps of witches' broom or mistletoe. These were really aerial pineapples of a sort—bromeliads. Their stiff, pointed, pineapple-like leaves hold water at their enlarged bases—which become a trap for insects, dead cypress needles and dust. From such atmospheric debris these strange growths draw their sustenance. Tongues of flame, several inches long, crowned many of the plants; these were the scarlet bracts which enclosed the spikes of bluish flowers, now unfolding.

As cypress gradually gave way to pine at the prairie's edge, the airplants gave way to Spanish moss. These gray banners which hung from every tree, and occasionally even from the telegraph wires, are neither Spanish nor a moss. Like the airplant, Spanish moss belongs to the pineapple family; in fact, it even belongs to the same genus as the airplant, *Tillandsia*. When Linnaeus coined the name, he was under the impression that these plants, living an arboreal, almost aerial existence, abhorred water. Therefore he named them after a Swedish student, Tilland, who became so seasick on the water that he once chose to walk more than 1000 miles around the Gulf of Bothnia rather than cross it in a boat. Actually Spanish moss likes humidity and nowhere is it thicker than in the river valleys. To some, the thick gray beards that festoon the dark avenues of live oaks in southern towns, or wave gently from the cypress snags and from the pines, are depressing, but most of us react differently to *Tillandsia*—to our eyes it imparts a grace, a quiet beauty to the southern landscape. Without it, certainly, the South would lose its most distinctive trademark. It is not a dead thing, as it might at first appear. Pull off a few strands. They have a fuzzy, velvety feel. Look closely. A soft coat of dead cells covers a greenish living center. At the bases of the threadlike leaves are tiny yellowish flowers; it obviously can reproduce. But the roots are hardly more than attachments; they do not penetrate the wood. Spanish moss does not kill the tree on which it grows, but takes its nourishment from the air—how else would it survive when suspended from telegraph wires?

Nowhere are there finer displays of *Tillandsia*—more luxurious moss-scapes—than in some of the small towns we passed through. Squat live oaks, broader than they were tall, arched over the streets and formed a closed canopy from which the moss hung in ragged banners. In contrast to these cool shady tunnels there were also sunny avenues lined with stately royal palms whose pillar-like trunks had the deceptive appearance of having a smooth coat of cement. We had seen a few wild royal palms in two or three of the hammocks in the 'Glades, but where did all these town palms come from? We inquired about this and were assured that the long rows of royal palms we had seen in Miami and in other south Florida cities were not pinched from Florida's limited stock of wild trees but came from Cuba or else were grown in nurseries. They grow fast; the very tall trees in Clewiston, we were told, were not much more than twenty years old.

Seventy-five species of palms—perhaps more—grow in Florida. But most of them are exotics; palms from India grow alongside palms from south China, the Canary Islands, or Brazil. The cabbage palmetto, *Sabal,* is the common native species, the one that forms islands of plume-topped trees in swampy pockets and gives such a tropical look to the landscape, while the saw palmetto, also a *Sabal,* grows in scrubby form on sandier soil, under the pines.

All afternoon we drove through almost endless pine forests. At first they had been rather open and parklike; each picturesque tree stretched its virile arms, uncrowded by its neighbors. But now, as we progressed northward, the stands became denser. Herbert Stoddard had told us that when the Spaniards first penetrated the Southeast they entered what may have been the largest "pure type" forest in North America, if not the world; a belt of long-leaf pine which occupied the well-drained lands of the coastal plains for 1500 miles, from southeast Virginia to east Texas, interrupted only by narrow bands of hardwoods along the rivers. Even today, the towns and the roads are but minor interruptions in a monotony of pines.

In contrast to the sameness of the pine-scape, the rivers which we crossed were like botanical gardens. White spider lilies raised their pallid blooms at the edges of dark bogs, and once in an open spot we saw the golden trumpets of a carnivorous plant related to the pitcher plant. Every stream, every water-filled ditch, was choked with water hyacinths, their orchid-like blossoms forming masses of lavender bloom on the sluggish water. Buoyed up by bladders at the bases of their bright green leaves they slowly drifted on the current, like miniature floating gardens. No one will deny that this alien from Brazil is beautiful, but its beauty is almost the kiss of death to a southern stream. It soon crowds out the native aquatic plants. This would be forgivable if birds and other wild creatures found it edible, but they do not, although cows will often wade up to their bellies to eat it. First introduced into Louisiana in 1884, this pest—which seems to divide, subdivide and multiply like the amoeba—quickly spread over thousands of acres of inland waters. One Floridian tossed some plants from her fish pool into the St. Johns River: within ten years, they had multiplied some millions of times, had traveled many miles and completely choked the broad river in places. Since then, staggering amounts—millions of dollars—have been appropriated to keep the St. Johns and other hyacinth-infested waters navigable.

James and I took turns at the wheel; every one hundred miles we changed over and while one of us drove the other dozed. The afternoon was oppressively still and hot; Coca-Cola stops became a habit. We crossed the Suwannee, the river made immortal by Stephen Foster; and we crossed the Steinhatchee, the Aucilla, the Ochlockonee. The northwestern flank of the Florida peninsula, we agreed, was certainly one of the least settled parts of the state, and except for the Everglades, perhaps the wildest. How could anyone be sure there were no ivory-bills in some of these woodlands?

When we were reunited with Herbert Stoddard at the inn at Blountstown that evening, he said he could not promise that we would see an ivory-bill; we had a chance, but one day was too short a time. But if we could spend a month exploring the swamps of the Chipola and the Apalachicola, he was confident he could show us this almost mythical bird—the rarest bird in the world.

May 14

Before dawn, an all-night restaurant in Blountstown saw a posse of ivory-bill searchers among the bacon and eggs. It was hot and humid and the frogs were in full chorus. I was still rubbing what little sleep I had had out of my eyes, but Herbert Stoddard was already buzzing with anticipation and activity, while Roger was eating absent-mindedly and talking busily to George Lowery, Sr., Parker Grant, and Leon Neel, Herbert Stoddard's assistant. We motored to a farm near Chipola Park just as dawn was breaking, where we met our guide, M. L. Kelso, who spends much of his time collecting reptiles for Ross Allen, the dealer.

Herbert unlashed his canoe from his car's roof, Kelso found us a couple of outboard dinghies, and we quietly took the water of the Chipola River, a broad, slow tributary of the Apalachicola. At once we were in a wonderland of water and trees. The Chipola's flow was scarcely noticeable, as we motored, paddled, drifted among the maze. Was it lake or river, were its cypresses growing on land or water? We glided downstream, talking in whispers. The morning mist waved and snaked over the water, whose unruffled surface merged with it like a fogged photograph, so that a hundred yards from our boats water, trees, and sky resembled a Chinese painting. Spanish moss hung down from the branches of the tall cypresses, into the rising mist. Invisible birds sang in the mist, and the only sight of life was the rippling, widening, quickly dying splashes of all sorts of turtles—half a dozen kinds at least—slipping, sometimes with little plops, into the swamp-river water, from half submerged snags or cypress-knees. Kelso knew all the different turtles halfway across the river. "There goes a chicken turtle," he would announce, or "that's a slider." Once, swimming sinuously with a sideways sweep, a water snake crossed between our boats, and dodged our clumsy efforts to catch it.

The stage directors for a set such as that we were now floating upon, would call for music—suspense music. Music for "dawn in the enchanted forest." Monotonous, repetitive music. Just such music was provided by an orchestra, an orchestra somewhat smaller than that we had become lately accustomed to; but an orchestra of frogs, toads, and birds, whose little voices mingled and shrilled, rose and fell. Again and again came the quick, stuttered phrases of the red-eyed vireo, or the yellow-throated vireo, the one almost hypnotic in the endlessness of its repetition, the other more musical, less inevitable. Parula warblers filled glass after glass in a trickle-up of buzzing water; and, on one note, in a steady metronomic monotone, came from cypress, water-tupelo, oak, the *weeting* of the prothonotary warbler, the "golden bird of the wooded swamps," as Roger has called it. Not often enough—but now and then—we caught a glimpse of the cock, a study in orange and blue-gray. Never did we see or hear so many prothonotaries as on this day in the water-wood.

As the sun soared quickly—too quickly—the voices of other birds joined the overture—mocker, Carolina wren, cardinal, summer tanager. Rough-winged swallows and purple martins appeared, with the morning hatch of insects; and it was not long before the sun had sucked away the mist, and warmed the air enough to bring to wing the soaring birds of prey. Turkey vulture, red-shouldered and broad-winged hawks, osprey, all crossed the treetops above us. Once we saw a buoyant falcon-shaped bird, with a black tail and whitish head, the rare Mississippi kite. It planed, glided, dived, as if the air was its playground, which it was.

We drifted, with motors cut off and paddles across our knees, listening intently for the nasal tooting of the ivory-bill. Flicker, pileated, red-bellied, hairy, downy woodpeckers we heard, or saw, but no ivory-bills. When James T. Tanner investigated the Chipola-Apalachicola swamp in June, 1939, he "estimated from the size of the forest and the locations of the reports of ivory-bills, that there probably were two pairs or four individuals in the lower part of the swamp." But he himself never found one there. It was not until 1950 that any were actually seen—Whitney Eastman found them. The tract was immediately closed to all shooting; and Mr. Kelso was appointed warden.

James Tanner, in his study of the birds in the Singer Tract of Louisiana, found that ivory-bills were late risers—not out of their roost holes until long after the songbirds had begun to sing and the other woodpeckers had begun calling. We reached the last-known ivory-bills' roost-hole just when the bird, or birds (if any) could have been expected to come out, climb to the treetop, preen, stretch, peck wood, and call, before their first morning flight. These morning flights, Tanner found, are usually pretty noisy. *Kient-kient-kient,* the birds cry, loudly and frequently as they forage. This tooting call is unmistakable, and quite unlike the loud stuttering laugh that the other big crested woodpecker—the pileated—utters. If the roost-hole had been in use, we would undoubtedly have heard the bird.

No sound. The last Florida ivory-bill—perhaps the last ivory-bill in the world—had gone from its last known roosting place. It was an oval hole, about 4 by 5 inches, in a large cypress, about 40 feet up. The cypress stood by itself in a pondlike diverticulum of the Chipola, a lakelet bordered by other big cypresses, with dark festoons of Spanish moss. It was nearly two years since anybody had seen this hole in use. We turned away and landed nearby in the primeval tupelo and oak forest, stumbling ashore over fallen logs and pushing our way through underbrush. Roger discovered a coral snake as it crept from under a log. Kelso, in his element here, seized the brightly banded red, yellow, and black reptile in his bare hands. An experienced snake catcher, he has perfected the quick confident grasp on the neck. This was not a false coral snake; its nose was black. It was the deadly true coral.

Our ivory-bill hunt had turned into a herpetological expedition. On a low swamp island where the ground had been rooted up by a band of half-wild razorback hogs we found several salamanders and the remnants of turtle eggs unearthed by raccoons. As we were examining one of the turtle nests a very large snake slithered away, but could not escape Kelso's quick grasp. Kelso held the writhing reptile aloft for us to see—a rare beautiful creature, *Lampropeltis getulis goini,* a race of the king snake described only four years previously, entirely restricted to the Apalachicola and Chipola valleys. Back at the farm he showed us other recent captures, which he kept alive in drums until the day Ross Allen made the rounds. Mrs. Kelso, standing at the kitchen door, wanted her husband to give up his snake catching. Sooner or later, she said, "he'd get bit." He was inclined to agree with her; so far he had been lucky.

I WAS NOT ABLE in the course of our long journey to show James a rattlesnake—although I saw several (including a tremendous one) in October when I retraced our route through the Everglades. The coral snake, in fact, is even more deadly than the rattler, because its venom works on the nerve centers, not the bloodstream. Had one of us been bitten by the one we caught, our snake kit and little rubber suction cup would not have helped much.

How relatively safe, James thought, how benign, is England, with only one poisonous creature, the adder, and no plant more discom-

forting than the nettle. In America there seem to be so many hostile things in the woods and swamps and deserts: deadly snakes—copperhead, cottonmouth, and coral snake, and rattlers of at least a dozen sorts; the gila monster, a venomous lizard nearly two feet long; spiders—tarantulas and black widow—that are occasionally fatal; venomous scorpions; ticks that may carry spotted fever; mosquitoes that transmit malaria; plants with toxic properties—poison ivy, poison sumac, and the dreaded manchineel. And of course, such extremely uncomfortable plants as cholla cactus, such unfriendly animals as barracuda and grizzly bears, not to mention skunks and porcupines. But we seldom worry about these things—only herpetologists and those who really ask for it get into serious trouble. Ross Allen has been bitten seven times by rattlers; the last three times almost fatally. But the average person is less likely to be killed by a venomous snake than he is to be struck dead by lightning. Even so, one watches his step in ivory-bill country.

We had not found our quarry this day; perhaps we did not have enough faith. But I count myself lucky to be one of the small company of living naturalists who has actually seen the ivory-bill. That was in 1941 when I saw the last two females in the Singer Tract. They did not look as much like pileateds as I had expected; with long recurved crests of blackest jet, and gleaming white bills, they seemed unreal birds—downright archaic. It was easy to track them, for as soon as they landed after a flight, they betrayed their location by their curious tooting notes. When they flew, they pitched off on a straight line, like ducks, their wings making a wooden sound. After we had followed them for nearly an hour they made a long flight and we could not find them again. A single bird was seen in the neighborhood as late as 1946.

At the time of our visit to the Chipola no ivory-bill had been seen there for many months and the sanctuary had been discontinued. We wondered, as we took a parting look at its last known haunt, whether the ivory-bill had finally joined the spectral company of the great auk, the Carolina paroquet, and the passenger pigeon.

15

Flying Gardens of Avery Island

NEW ORLEANS, offspring of the tawny Mississippi, is only 110 winding miles upstream from the greenish water of the Gulf of Mexico. Few Americans ever see the "father of waters" below this point where it crosses the broad coastal marshes to the bewildering maze of the delta. The Louisiana State Game Commission had offered to fly us down there in one of their patrol planes; we would observe a white ibis colony from the air and, if weather permitted, we would land at one of the mud-lumps in the Gulf where pelicans and royal terns nest. But when we reached the airport low pregnant rainclouds appeared from the southeast; bad weather was in the making. We took off anyway for a short flight over Lake Pontchartrain; it soon proved too gusty to proceed to "Ibisia" on the far shore, so we swung back over the sprawling city, crossing and recrossing the meanders of the great river where ocean-going vessels rode at anchor. Visibility to the southeast was shut out by gray mist and low scudding clouds.

It would be too risky to attempt anything today; regretfully we returned to the airport.

Bob Newman was to join us here in Louisiana and ride with us to Mexico. We would need his sharp eyes and his expert knowledge of Mexican birds when we crossed the border. But we learned from George Lowery that Bob was out in the Gulf on the *Atlantis,* the marine research boat; he had been out there for more than a month making observations on trans-Gulf migration. However, when the boat docked at Galveston to take on supplies, we would make connections.

No one visits New Orleans—at least, no one should—without taking dinner at Antoine's, Arnaud's, or one of the other world-famous restaurants in the French Quarter. For this city, a descendent province of Mediterranean peoples, makes a specialty of gustatory pleasures. We did not choose to be different. Except for bird watching, what greater pleasure is there than eating? After our oysters Rockefeller and fine wines at Antoine's, we strolled back to the waterfront plaza where the car was parked, to find that in our absence someone had tried to break in. He must have been interrupted, perhaps by our return; a window had been jimmied and cracked, but nothing had been taken.

Turning our backs on New Orleans the next morning, we crossed the Huey Long Bridge and set our course westward. Flat featureless marshes stretched before us league after league to the horizon and beyond. Far out on these seemingly endless marshes was Avery Island, a low wooded hill which I had once seen from the air while assisting in a January goose count. I had heard a lot about this place and so had James; Julian Huxley had counseled him not to miss it.

Many years ago when John Marsh took over a large area of unpromising-looking swampland under a grant from the King of Spain, he discovered that he had acquired a bit of Eden. He and his descendants, the Averys and the McIlhennys, who established their home on what is now known as Avery Island, found that they could be almost entirely self-sustaining there. The rich soils of their island paradise would grow oranges, avocados—in fact, almost anything. The live-oak woodlands were populated with wild turkeys and rabbits. They could vary their diet with bear steaks or venison if they chose, or they might roast a possum with a sweet potato in its mouth. Ducks and geese by the hundreds of thousands swarmed in the surrounding marshes during the colder months. Nor was there any lack of seafood; terrapins for delicious soups, shrimp by the bucketful in the bayous, and redfish in the nearby Gulf.

The name McIlhenny became known throughout the land because of the Tabasco sauce which is produced here ("New Iberia" on the label). When deposits of salt were found under the island, the salt mines competed with the Tabasco sauce as a source of income for the fortunate owners. Inasmuch as the island was a "salt dome" it was inevitable that oil should be found too (on the day of our arrival one of the wells was on fire, sending up great clouds of dense black smoke). At times, as many as 1700 people, blacks and whites, have been employed at Avery Island. The little kingdom of which the late E. A. McIlhenny was the supreme ruler, might almost have been described as feudal. The vast marshes insulated his domain from the outside world almost as effectively as the fortified walls of a medieval city.

Edward Avery McIlhenny was a naturalist. To develop his Garden of Eden he planted thickets of rhododendrons, groves of bamboo, lotus beds. But his unique achievement was the creation of "Bird City."

In his youth McIlhenny had been witness to the slaughter of plume birds in the South. During this period, a frequent guest at his family's estate was an English gentleman who had once been Lord Mayor of London and had spent many years in India. He told of a rajah who in the seventeenth century had built a park on the outskirts of Juraspore. This potentate created ponds, planted them with ornamental aquatics and shrubs, and built bamboo enclosures. In these great flying cages he put herons, ibises, and other birds which accepted their captivity gracefully and nested much as they would in the wild. When the rajah passed from this world, the enclosures slowly fell to pieces but the birds stayed on. Even though the cages were gone, they returned year after year to the neglected gardens to rear their families.

"Why not try this experiment in Louisiana?" suggested the Englishman. The few remaining egrets desperately needed protection. Young McIlhenny thought often about the flying gardens of Juraspore. Could they be duplicated at Avery Island? It was worth a try. In a protected spot was a small pond where willows and buttonwoods grew. This could be developed.

In 1892 the visionary young man built a small dam. The pond became a small lake. Over the water he erected a flying cage, a simple open framework fifty feet square enclosed by wire poultry netting. Then he spent days combing the swamps for the elusive egrets. This was no easy task, for all the large nesting colonies of earlier years had been destroyed. He finally located two nests, each with four young, which he put into the deep pockets of his hunting coat. Returning home, he housed them in two wire-covered boxes until they were ready for the freedom of the flying cage. Each morning he went out to the bayous with a casting net and brought back a bucketful of shrimp and killifish, which he carefully fed by hand to the scrawny babies. It took hours each day, but all eight young egrets survived. Fearlessly they followed their benefactor about; he often took them outdoors, and when they learned to fly, they even perched on his horse. In November, the doors of the big cage were left constantly open; the birds were free to come and go. Even when the structure was torn down in the hope that it would induce them to migrate, they returned to the site to roost, but when the first sharp frosts came, they departed.

The following March six snowy egrets returned to the platform of the old flying cage. Two pairs nested and when they left in November, the little colony had grown to thirteen birds. The following spring all thirteen returned; five nests were built and twenty-one young birds were successfully reared.

By 1905 the colony had grown to 1000 pairs; by the end of 1908 there were 10,000 birds. Bird Town was rapidly becoming Bird City. Additional dams increased the water area to 35 acres. The maintenance of the heronry became a major operation. McIlhenny's men built long platforms above the water to accommodate the prolific birds; by 1911 there were 32 of these platforms. Each day the men went into the woods to gather twigs, which they broke into convenient lengths, and piled them into a waiting truck. A truckload of twigs a day—25 to 30 truckloads in a season—were deposited in little heaps on the platforms or along the shore for the use of the home-building herons.

In 1912 Bird City reached its zenith. By running strings twenty-five feet apart and counting the nests between, six men working a full day arrived at a total of 22,204 nests. At the end of the summer, including both adults and their young, there must have been over 100,000 inhabitants in this Ardean metropolis.

Since 1912 there have not been as many. The banning of the plume traffic took the pressure off the egrets and many of them could then nest unmolested in other colonies. But thousands of snowies and hundreds of other herons remain at Bird City. Even though Edward McIlhenny is now gone, his family still keeps the

nesting platforms in repair and instructs the men to put the piles of twigs by the roadside. Avery Island is now a showplace, a demonstration of what A. C. Bent calls "one of the most remarkable and successful experiments in conservation of which we have any record."

It was 150 miles from the Mississippi to Avery Island, yet we were still among the bayous and delta flats of North America's largest river. We turned off the main highway at the town of New Iberia, where on the map a secondary road was marked "Bird Sanctuary and Jungle Gardens." Following its straight course for several miles across the fresh green marshes, which were in constant motion this windy day, we arrived at a tollgate where a small tribute is exacted from all those who would enter this kingdom in miniature.

May 17

"Bird City" was an amazing sight. When we drew up by the side of the lake nearly every waterside stand of trees appeared to be covered with flowers—most of them snowy white (and American-egret white), some subtly tricolored. The latter were the purplish-dark, russet-breasted, white-bellied Louisiana herons. And besides this border of heron flowers, more heron flowers—all white—crowded three long platforms that rested on stilts in the middle of the lake. McIlhenny had not only sown the borders of his avian garden with wild herons, but had planted them in beds!

Roger and I lugged our photographic gear round to a thoughtfully provided observation platform, like an elevated wooden pulpit, at the lakeside. I exposed yards of film and Roger, using his cine, ran off hundreds of feet. All the herons were breeding and most of them had young. In the rookery there was continuous, excited movement, a croaking, chattering, clattering movement of squawking adults and frog-voiced nestlings. Returning snowy and American egrets were greeted by their mates with a noisy unfolding of wings and plumes, heads raised among a cascade of erected feathers. Neighbor sparred with neighbor, expertly avoiding each other's vicious jabs.

Though it was long past honeymoon time, I saw a pair of Louisiana herons entwine their necks, and was reminded of a moving passage in the works of Julian Huxley, who with his writings (and with his

friendship) has so much inspired my own interest in birds. Here is
his account of the honeymoon of the Louisiana herons at their yet
eggless nest site at Avery Island:

> *For three or four days both members of the pair are always
> on the chosen spot, save for the necessary visits which they
> alternately pay to the distant feeding ground. When both are
> there, they will spend hours at a time sitting quite still, just
> touching one another. Generally the hen sits on a lower branch,
> resting her head against the cock bird's flanks; they look for all
> the world like one of those inarticulate but happy couples upon
> a bench in the park in spring. Now and again, however, this
> passivity of sentiment gives place to wild excitement. Upon some
> unascertainable cause the two birds raise their necks and wings,
> and, with loud cries, intertwine their necks. This is so remark-
> able a sight that the first time I witnessed it I did not fully credit
> it, and only after it had happened before my eyes on three or
> four separate occasions was I forced to admit it as a regular
> occurrence in their lives. The long necks are so flexible that
> they can and do make a complete single turn round each other
> —a real true-lovers'-knot! This once accomplished, each bird
> then—most wonderful of all—runs its beak quickly and amo-
> rously through the just raised aigrettes of the other, again and
> again, nibbling and clappering them from base to tip. Of this I
> can only say that it seemed to bring such a pitch of emotion
> that I could have wished to be a Heron that I might experi-
> ence it. This over, they would untwist their necks and subside
> once more into their usual quieter sentimentality.**

Forty years ago, when Louisiana herons were commoner at Avery
Island than the snowies (it is rather the other way round, now),
Julian Huxley made these observations on their courtship. Some of
his conclusions were far in advance of their time and have become
foundation stones of our present understanding of bird behavior. But
Huxley's pioneer work was distinguished not only by the scientific
importance of its conclusions, but also by the felicity with which his
observations were described.

At the time of our visit most of the Louisianas were busy with
their young, and performing another ceremony that Julian Huxley had

* *Essays of a Biologist* (London, 1928), pp. 110–11.

described—the greeting-display at nest-relief. We could tell that the mate was coming, not by searching the crowded air, but—like Huxley —by watching the spouse occupying the nest, which rose, erected wings and plumes and squawked. The arriving bird pitched down and did the same; both burst into excited crying, bowed to each other, exploded their plumage to its filmy feathery crisis, changed places on the nest, and, having done so, performed the greeting ceremony again—and again and again. During the encores after the changing of places, the free bird offered the other twigs—bits of nest material, accentuating by this the ceremonial nature of the performance, for the time was long past when the twigs could have been of any use. Useful, of course, was the ritual (twigs and all), for thus is the bond of marriage cemented, and the pair refreshed with mutual love.

The American egrets and snowies also did these things. They were crowded more closely than the Louisianas, so that we could see their nest-relief more often; at any time among the fantastic assembly we could pick a snowy's nest where it was happening. All the time the young implored their parents for food, stimulated no doubt into begging activity by the rough and jumble (not quite tumble) of the greeting-dances.

Under the platforms a floating log quietly, slowly began to drift; but there was no current, no stream. With this movement it became no longer a shapeless log, but a log with a ridged back, regularly broken into a succession of nodules, and turret-eyes, and a long flat

snout. Big alligators live in this lake, and wait for the young egrets that stray, fall, or totter off the platforms; occasionally (we were told) they give the stilts a nudge to encourage them. They do not make any difference to the success of the colony, and are, in fact, protected here. Indeed, they are effective natural scavengers. A young heron that falls from the nest is doomed anyway; its parents (whose limited mentality reacts more strongly to location than anything else) will not go down to feed it, and it would die a lingering death of starvation if the 'gators were not on hand. From a tidy lawn by the lakeside, we watched a large one floating, still, among the lily pads; and, as we watched, a baby alligator, not much more than a foot long, climbed on to its back, and then another and another. Roger filmed this pleasant domestic scene. Probably the alligator was a big female; we felt that the big bull we heard once or twice, roaring across the pond, would have made a quick meal of the small ones.

Water-turkeys—*Anhinga*—had nests in the trees among the herons and sat about like slender snaky cormorants, their black and silver wings half spread. Florida gallinules (moorhens) and resplendent purple gallinules were about too, adding their touch of color to the bird gardens of Avery. What a place! We saw all the herons we could have seen, except the American bittern, nine species out of ten.

NICK SHEXNAYDER, the warden of the nearby 40,000-acre Rainey Sanctuary of the National Audubon Society, who joined us at Avery Island, informed us that the storms of the previous fortnight had destroyed almost all of the nests in the other heronries in the district. Only here, in this protected spot, sheltered from the winds, had the egrets and other colonial birds succeeded in raising any young.

Before leaving this bit of paradise, we stopped at the Averys' gracious mansion among the live oaks for a round of cool mint juleps. There we made the acquaintance of young Ned McIlhenny, who seems to have inherited his grandfather's deep interest in ornithology. We left, assured that the flying gardens of Avery would not be neglected, even though their creator, like the Rajah of Juraspore, is no longer there to keep his eye on things.

16

Lydia Ann

LEAVING BEHIND the man-created bird city of Avery Island, we drove westward down shady avenues of live oaks hung with gray banners of Spanish moss. Beyond lay a vast expanse of flooded marshes and rice fields. The names Boudreau, Broussard, and Le Blanc appeared again and again on mailboxes and storefronts. This was Evangeline's country, the home of Acadians—"Cajuns"— descendants of early French settlers exiled from Nova Scotia.

Ever since our entry into the Pelican State foul weather had threatened. Now rain squalls off the Gulf succeeded one another. At Lake Charles we were informed that there had not been a day without rain for nearly a month. Fields were flooded from horizon to horizon. We drove one stretch of seventeen miles of country road, with water lapping at the floorboards of the car and only the tops of fence posts to guide us. Little companies of northbound black terns crisscrossed the watery highway as though this were their normal habitat. I was reminded of a time when I had driven under similar conditions in Florida with fish swimming down the road before the car! Actually these were extreme flood conditions, even for Louisiana. A day or two later all travel, including transportation by train, became impossible through the area. Towns were cut off for a week.

Next morning when we crossed the Sabine River into Texas the newspapers reported tornadoes in nearby areas. A twister hit Waco, a city nearly the size of James's home city of Northampton, and leveled a swath five blocks wide and five miles long, leaving 113 dead and 500 injured. The great storm that devastated coastal England and Holland four months earlier was still fresh in James's mind. What must it be like to live in a country which can expect such storms nearly every year—both sea storms and land storms? I assured him that no one area received the brunt of successive storms; but I admitted that Texans and others who live in the flat country between the Gulf and the Great Lakes have the uneasy distinction of being more likely to be killed by tornadoes than the residents of any other part of the world. This region is one of nature's great battlegrounds, where cold dry air masses from the north and warm humid air from the south often collide.

There was no word at Galveston from Bob Newman. We learned that instead of making its scheduled landing, the *Atlantis* had changed course and was plowing southward through the heavy seas toward Yucatán. Bob was stuck out there in the Gulf unless the Coast Guard could be prevailed upon to take him off. It began to look as though we would not have a guide in Mexico.

The sky at Galveston had an ominous look, dull and gray. A flock of eighty cedar waxwings talked in muted lisps from the telegraph wires in one of the suburbs. By noon the sky had become so dark that we had to switch on the parking lights and soon the headlights. Our road took us directly toward that part of the flat horizon where the sullen sky was blackest. Then the storm broke. It was one of those persistent, seemingly endless downpours that accompany a cyclonic storm. The rain pelted the windshield in long, near-horizontal sheets, making it almost impossible to see the road. Other drivers pulled off to the side to wait out the tempest; but we crawled ahead. I fully expected to see the limbs of trees hurtling through the air if the wind velocity increased the least bit more. It was the most violent rainstorm I have ever tried to drive in short of an actual hurricane, but I allowed James to believe that this was not unusual for Texas. In fact, he was ready to believe almost anything about Texas.

Fortunately, we were not in the path of the vortex, and as we drove southwestward, we left the rains behind. The coastline made a gradual bend toward due south and there was a definite break in the climate. The countryside was visibly more arid; mesquite, catclaw, and other prickly western plants dominated the prairie-like landscape. We began to notice western birds that rarely cross the hundredth meridian, that arbitrary and invisible line which, to the biologist, separates East from West. We ticked off Bullock's oriole, orange with large white patches on its wings; soon we were to see the hooded oriole, a slim bright flame that makes its home in the palms lining the streets of south Texas towns, and the little Inca dove, another town bird.

America, James had found by this time, was a land of distances. This fact of distance has led to the development of two distinctly American adjuncts to automobile travel, the diner and the motel. The original diners, which I remember vividly, were discarded railroad cars that enterprising short-order cooks had remodeled into small roadside restaurants with a long counter and a row of high stools for the customers. Today the diner has all but forgotten its origins. New diners are built to look vaguely like railroad cars, but are far more spacious. Some are almost palatial, gaudily trimmed with chromium and mirrors.

James thought the motels were an extremely good idea. These airconditioned units, built in a long row around a central court, are an outgrowth of the small roadside tourist cabins that sprang into being a generation ago when the American public, nomadic at heart, took to the highroad in an ever increasing number of cars. The cabins still compete with the flossier motels for the motorist's patronage, but little by little, the more luxurious accommodations are taking over.

No one interested in birds passes through the coastal town of Rockport, Texas, without stopping at the Rockport cottages to pay respects to Connie Hagar. Perhaps no one in America can claim as consistent a record of bird observation in a single area as can this little ninety-three-pound bird of a woman. Now in her late sixties, Connie has missed scarcely a morning with the birds since the day nearly twenty years ago when the Hagars established residence in Rockport. On an earlier visit she was so entranced by the number of birds she saw that she gently broached to her husband the idea of returning there to live. Jack Hagar, not keen on birds, but a very indulgent husband, said it was agreeable to him, but he must have something to do, so he bought the tourist cottages.

The calm water of the bay, only two hundred yards away, is virtually in the Hagars' front yard. Godwits, curlews, stilts, and other waders parade along the sandy beach, as do herons of several species. But it is not the water birds that make Rockport unique. This gently curving stretch of coast is a jamming-up place, in spring, for countless songbirds traveling northward out of Mexico. Winds from the north—"northers"—pin the small migrants down along the edge of the Gulf. In late April when conditions are right, the groves of live oak, yaupon, and sweetbay in the Hagars' back yard often swarm with warblers of fifteen or twenty species. Hundreds of birds drift in and out of the tight-twigged, wind-sculptured trees.

One spring morning Jack Hagar rushed in and insisted, "Come quick, you have a blue lawn." Rushing out, Connie found the ground solid blue with bluebirds, almost completely obscuring the grass.

On another occasion indigo buntings were so numerous that a visiting New Englander commented "thick as blueberries on the bush."

Rockport citizens, curious at first about the little woman with binoculars who talked about "getting" her birds, now know her well. They see her every morning making the rounds, accompanied by her wire-haired terrier Patch, who, she says, is allowed to bark at boys on bicycles but not at birds. Everyone tries to help by reporting what they have seen. One day a neighbor telephoned, "Come over—my yard is full of little injured birds—their breasts are stained with blood." They were rose-breasted grosbeaks!

The fame of Rockport has spread. It has become such a mecca for migration students that the cottages are always booked solid for the entire month of April. Reservations must be made weeks in advance. Guy Emerson has not missed an April at Rockport for about eighteen years. When James and I pulled into the Hagar driveway the main part of the spring flight was concluded. It was the third week of May and most of the field-glass fraternity had departed too, all except an old friend, C. D. Brown—"Brownie"—of New Jersey, who makes this pilgrimage every spring. Two weeks earlier a group, including Mrs. Hagar and himself, had piled up the all-time record for the number of birds seen by a single party in a single day in the U.S., a grand total of 204 species between dawn and dark. My own best day's list, made years ago in New Jersey, stands at 172.

During the three hours of daylight still available to us, we lingered around the Hagar bailiwick. At the bay's edge, an incredibly lovely roseate spoonbill, shell-pink with blood-red "drip" on its shoulders, swung its long spatulate bill from side to side in the shallows. A few Canada-bound warblers, bay-breasts, Blackburnians, and magnolias, mostly females, flitted among the live oaks. Most of the other songbirds we saw were local residents.

It was dark before we bade goodbye to the Hagars and drove the last few miles to the Institute of Marine Sciences at Port Aransas, where the director, Dr. Gordon Gunter, found us beds for the night. On the morrow he would take us to Lydia Ann Island, one of the many sanctuaries which the National Audubon Society guards along the Gulf Coast.

May 19

Roger and I had two breakfasts—one in our own quarters when we got up at six, and another with Thorpe, the Audubon warden, and Hildebrand, a marine biologist, in the laboratory across the way. Dr. Gunter urged an early start in the sturdy fishing boat belonging to the Institute, so that we might reach Lydia Ann with a couple of hours in hand before the heat became intolerable. By eight o'clock there was already a heat haze and shimmer. We motored north into the Laguna Madre. A big tanker in ballast glided slowly in from the Gulf through the Aransas Pass. North along the inland waterway a tug pushed its low-laden oil barge, their shapes wriggling in the heat waves. The lowness of the countryside and its busy gulls, terns, and waders reminded me a bit of the coast off Suffolk south of Aldeburgh; with barges instead of pleasure yachts and a landscape of derricks and refineries instead of medieval churches and tree-skirted villages. Not far away, to the north (we had passed within a few miles of it yesterday), lay the Aransas National Wildlife Refuge, a "super refuge" of more than 50,000 acres, perhaps the most famous place for waterfowl in Texas, and the winter home of the last flock of whooping cranes in the world.*

Consistently, wherever we touched the lagooned coast, ever since we came into Florida, we had been reminded of North America's great riches in members of the heron family. Almost before Lydia Ann Island was in sight we could see five species in the air—great blue heron, American egret, snowy egret, reddish egret, and Louisiana heron. Our new friend of yesterday, the roseate spoonbill, was about again, looking as if it had been invented specially for the illustrated bird books of the nineteenth century. The black vulture, as well as the turkey vulture, was still with us, lazily gliding on the thermals.

Probing in the shallows, trotting on the sands, nervously shifting from place to place in small flocks were numerous waders, indicating that much of their spring passage was still to go. And here were avocets, whickering and zipping, lots of them, with their upcurved bills, but, unlike our European avocets, they had pinkish heads and necks. Here too were resident waders—Wilson's plover, black-necked stilt (very like the European stilt), and noisy, brash willets, flashing their black and white wings. Twice we saw the Cuban snowy plover, which in England would be called the Kentish plover. When are we going to adopt some sensible common names and drop these silly, geographical ones?

Of the migrants still on passage, we saw many of the old familiars—black-bellied plover, ruddy turnstone, both the yellow-legs, pectoral and white-rumped sandpipers, dunlin, semipalmated sandpiper, and sanderling. Perhaps the semipalmated sandpiper was the commonest of that group of little sandpipers, which in England are called "stints" and in America "peep." There were a few whimbrels—Hudsonian whimbrels—and with them a quite extraordinary caricature of a whimbrel or curlew, a bird with a thin decurved beak literally twice as long as the whimbrel's (seven inches!), a study in buff and cinnamon, and the owner of a real curlew voice—*curlee, curlee*. This rare and wonderful bird, the long-billed curlew, is a bird of the prairie heartland of America. Driven to the west by the spread of man and his farming, its principal refuge is now more in the Canadian prairie belt than that of the United States. On passage it is much rarer on the eastern seaboard than it used to be. If we

---

* Twenty-one individuals in 1953.

had been making our trip a century ago, we would certainly have
found this bird in Florida, but Roger had told me not to expect it
before Texas and, as usual, he was right.

As we approached Lydia Ann, the long low island began to look
really exciting. Now we saw that there was a large mixed colony
of reddish egrets and Louisiana herons. They appeared to be feeding
young in scattered nests in a noisy association, a true colony, along
the rather dry bank of a muddy inlet. Some hundreds of yards farther
were three clamorous colonies of royal terns, a few hundred pairs.
A minority of Sandwich terns, somewhat smaller with slender yellow-
tipped black bills, were nesting among the royals. Close beside them
were a few small groups of laughing gulls.

How we got ashore with our photographic gear intact I do not
know; it was certainly more by luck than good management, for
never in my rich experience of mud (or experience of rich mud, if
you like) have I met anything as glutinous, adhesive, and thoroughly
stinking as the mud into which we stepped from the deck of the
boat. There was nowhere we could get ashore on Lydia Ann without
first stepping into tepid waist-deep water and running this mud
gantlet; often I felt I was going to leave my feet behind.

Two weeks earlier storms had shoved high water from the Gulf
into the lagoon and drowned out fully half the nests on the island.
The young reddish egrets on the higher ground at the south end of

the island had survived but the royal terns were making a second try.* In full view, we stalked to within long-lens distance of these big orange-billed terns without causing them to leave their nests. Some of them had white foreheads. I thought that these were immature breeders, but Roger tells me that unlike the Caspian tern, which retains its solid black cap until nesting is completed, the royal tern begins to get the white forehead of autumn plumage soon after its egg is laid—or even before. I had previously encountered (with Roger) the Caspian tern on its breeding grounds in Sweden, and knew the rasping, almost gannet-like alarm note which the greatest of all the terns utters. The bold royal terns, which are almost as big as Caspians, had more baritone voices; where the Caspian growls, the royal quacks. And instead of laying two or three eggs, it usually lays only one, so close to those of its neighbors that the sitting birds are almost cheek to jowl. Several times, as we watched, the colony flared up, as terns do, in a blizzard of wings, to return a few minutes later like falling snowflakes.

Our kind hosts sweated it out on the boat moored offshore while Roger and I sweated with our optical machinery. The heron colony, like the tern colony, showed sanctuary tameness. The birds allowed us to use our long lenses on them without leaving their charges.

Scarcely a generation ago that extraordinary species, the reddish egret, seemed to be completely gone from the United States until the National Audubon Society discovered a colony in Texas and immediately gave it warden protection. Today there are several thriv-

* Some years when repeated storms wipe out successive nestings there is no reproduction. In 1953, the birds of Lydia Ann recovered their early losses.

ing colonies on the Texas coast, all under Audubon guardianship.

Many herons have plumes on back, neck, breast, and crest, which they erect for the purpose of intimidating rivals and trespassers, but in no other heron that I have seen is the display propensity so intensely developed as in the reddish egret. Its plumes stand out "like the quills of a porcupine," as A. C. Bent puts it. Gray-blue on its back, pinkish brown elsewhere, it has a flesh-colored, black-tipped bill, which, in display, it points upward. Curving its neck gracefully, strutting and bowing, it utters at the same time a curious sound which is something between a chirp and a boom. When it is feeding in the shallows the quickest way to pick it out from the other herons is by its actions, a mad erratic ballet. Roger wrote in his eastern *Field Guide:* "It lurches about and often acts quite drunk."

The reddish egret has two color phases. But instead of denoting age as in the little blue heron (the young are white, adults blue), the dichromatism of the reddish egret bears no relation to age or sex. There is some regional difference, however. In the West Indies 9 out of 10 individuals are white; but in Texas this white phase is a small minority—perhaps 1 in 100, according to Bob Allen. It was particularly interesting and amusing to us that one of the young birds in a nest which we studied and photographed, and which had two normal reddish parents, was a white one. One reddish adult at a nearby nest had several snow-white feathers in its wings.

We waded or, rather, staggered through the mud back to the boat again, grateful for another wonderful heron day. By now we had seen every one of the thirteen heron species known in North America with the exception, oddly enough, of the American bittern, and had photographed most of them.

THE CAR was like an oven when we unlocked the doors; it had been standing under the merciless Texas sun through the heat of the day. Taking leave of our friends, Gunter, Thorpe, and Hildebrand, we sped off down the six-mile causeway toward the mainland. Halfway across the engine sputtered and died; we had forgotten to watch the fuel gauge. While James sweltered in the stalled car, I legged it back to Port Aransas and came back with a two-gallon can of gasoline. We would have to be more careful. It wouldn't do to run out of gas in the wide-open spaces ahead.

Avocets

17

Wilderness Lost

"BETTER FILL UP your tank before you leave Kingsville," we were advised. "It's seventy-two miles before you'll get another chance."

Dead straight, mile after mile after mile—until we had to force ourselves not to doze momentarily at the wheel—the highway thrust through the heart of the fabulous King Ranch. This cattle empire of the Klebergs, nearly a million acres of prairie, is the largest ranch in the nation. It is so vast that the state of Rhode Island could be fitted into it with 400 square miles to spare—or the combined counties of Cambridgeshire and Northamptonshire in England. The fast ribbon of concrete that unrolled before us was almost deserted of traffic except for an occasional truckload of vaqueros returning to their evening camps. Most of the cowboys who tend the herds are Mexicans whose families have been employed by the King-Kleberg family for generations. Out on the tawny plains we could see herds of the unique cattle—the Santa Gertrudis—developed by this ranch;

a heat-resistant, tick-resistant breed, selectively crossed from Indian Brahmans and beef-giving Herefords.

But how dry everything looked! There had not been a rain of any consequence in weeks. In this kind of country the balance of moisture is so delicate that the desert soon takes over if the rains do not come. Here on the King Ranch, where thousands of acres of mesquite have in recent decades replaced the grass, they are now using huge bulldozers to root out the invading brush so that the grass may wave again. In Texas, it is a constant struggle between man, the climate, and the good earth.

The landscape still looked parched—more parched than it should have been—when we left the monotonous cow country and entered "the Valley." A severe cold snap three winters before had killed about 85 per cent of the citrus groves and in their stead were great fields of cotton.

This part of Texas, the southern tip, is a country of blazing heat and vivid contrasts. Zoologically, it is largely Mexican. Geographically, it is desert, a desert irrigated from the great border river, the Rio Grande, that rather untamable, unpredictable river, nearly dry one year, in flood the next. Agriculturally, the lower valley is a country of recent, rapid, far-reaching changes, which have swept away the jungle-vegetation of the old cutoffs and oxbows of the Rio Grande— the resacas—and cleared thousands of acres of mesquite scrub; and put in their place broad highways, shiny new neon-lit towns, great citrus groves, and cotton fields—and in places, weary, barren stretches of lost topsoil.

Because of these sudden changes, the pressure on wildlife has been great in this corner of the United States—as great as anywhere. These wild borderlands that once knew the jaguar and the ocelot have been reduced to one small pocket of wilderness, the Santa Ana tract, less than 2000 acres between Alamo and a loop of the Rio Grande. Saved from the axe and the inevitable bulldozer, just in time, it is the only bit of the old natural Rio Grande forest left. This relatively small refuge and the Laguna Atascosa Refuge, created on 40,000 acres of desert prairie, are the only two pieces salvaged (from the wildlife point of view) and are now administered by the Fish and Wildlife Service. But in this unique area where, zoologically, East meets West and Mexico spills across the border, it is still possible to see more birds in a day than in any other spot in the U.S.

(with the probable exception of Rockport, Texas). Here James had the biggest Big Day of his life.

May 20

Birds-birds-birds! Luther Goldman and Roger showed me more birds today than I have ever seen in one day before. Luther, who manages two wildlife refuges, is one of the best field men I have ever encountered. He seems to have inherited the genius of his father, who was the great collector of the birds of Mexico.

As completely civilized as the Brownsville-Harlingen region is, it is surprising how many birds can be found tucked away in the little groves along the river, around the resacas, on the farms, in the gardens—even in town. In a town park we saw a big derby flycatcher, the same striped-headed, rusty-tailed bird that Hudson wrote about and called "Kiskadee" in his *Birds of La Plata*. We found its bulky nest in an acacia tree. It was a reminder (if one needed a reminder in this blazing heat) that tropical America nearly touches the tip of Texas.

We parked our cars near a citrus grove and walked along the field edges to a biggish stand of mesquite, huisache, and mimosa not far from the Rio Grande. A trail tunneled through the brush under ebony-trees, and here and there the darkness was split by open clearings, in which the birds were busy. They were rather silent in the morning's heat, which had climbed to somewhere near that of human blood. Roger and I swallowed salt tablets, mopped our brows, eased our helmets, and burrowed into the shade. We were surprised to see a number of late north-going songbirds, including a Connecticut warbler and a yellow-bellied flycatcher, Canada-bound migrants that we had missed up to now. These rather obscure birds of northern spruce bog and muskeg seemed queerly out of place among the spectacular southern species—summer tanager in rose-red; cardinal in deeper red; painted bunting in violet, red, and green. There were four flamboyant orioles: orchard, rusty and black; Audubon's, yellow and black; Bullock's, with its deep bright orange extending over its face; and the hooded, with an even brighter orange extending over its head. A chattering rattle in the brush turned into an incredible combination of purple-blue head, black face, and green and yellow body. This was the Valley's most arresting bird, the green jay. It really looks green!

A tiny blurred flash of light shone for an instant, and then brought itself momentarily into focus on a bush-head, long enough to show pink-red bill and metallic green throat, the buff-bellied hummingbird. While I was watching this jewel, Roger diverted my attention to a group of groove-billed anis flying over a clearing. These black cuckoos, with their long tails and tired-looking flight, had deeper bills than the smooth-billed anis we had seen in Florida—they almost had parrot faces.

With admiration I watched Roger sort out the four tyrant fly-catchers that were hawking round the scrub. The flycatchers are the most difficult of all the New World birds to identify—especially in Mexico (Blake in his *Birds of Mexico* lists over 60 species!)—and many of them (particularly in the bugbear genera of *Myiarchus* and *Empidonax*) can be distinguished in the field *only* by their habitat and voice.

Roger spotted a screech owl squinting at us from a tree cavity; and for a fleeting moment I saw a dark shape on the forest floor, shrinking into cover; it looked like a young turkey. It was a chacha-laca, a Mexican game bird—one of the guans—which reaches the United States in these woodlands of the lower Valley.

Here along the lower Rio Grande, a large group of Mexican species —two dozen at least—spill over into the United States. Everywhere in the huisache forest there were pigeons—half a dozen sorts—big, dark red-billed pigeons, tiny sparrow-sized ground doves with their russet wing flash; pretty scaly-backed Inca doves; soft-spoken, plain-looking white-fronted doves; mourning doves, of course; and most numerous of all, white-winged doves. The white-wings were cooing in cockerel-accents from almost every tree, for there had been a shortage of nesting places ever since the cold snap of January, 1951. Formerly they nested throughout the vast stretches of mesquite, but when the mesquite was bulldozed out they were forced to shift to citrus groves, Now, with the replacement of the cold-killed citrus trees by cotton fields, they were facing a critical shortage of nesting sites.

East of Harlingen we were headed for the Laguna Atascosa National Wildlife Refuge, Luther Goldman's pride and joy. For it was he who had done most of the planning and bossed the construction work—the building of roads, dykes, and dams that had converted thousands of acres of sterile, worthless coastal flats into one of the most important refuges for wintering waterfowl in North America. The heat had reduced me to indifference, and I dozed away, to be rudely awakened by Roger whenever a new bird appeared. The prairie became salt-desert, with mesquite and thorn-scrub along little ridges, embracing wide flats of grassland with flowering yuccas standing at intervals and much low cactus. One cactus, an *Opuntia* (I think), which Roger called beaver-tail cactus, was especially prevalent wherever we went. Jack rabbits, like European hares but even longer of ear, bounced through the brush.

Luther made us turn off the main road into a stretch of scrub that looked just like the pictures of the African thorn veld in the movies. I was so overwhelmed with novelty by then that a lion or a giraffe or a herd of antelope would scarcely have been beyond belief. But our quarry, it turned out, was a little bird of dazzling brightness, the vermilion flycatcher. Oddly enough, I heard the cock vermilion before I saw it; a pinging tinkling, in short snatches. It seemed ventriloquial. Puzzled, I looked up and found that the sky was its song station. Larklike, it sang its song on the way up, in a crescendo, suddenly burst to a stop, and swooped to a perch on a mesquite bush. Its tail, wings, and back were nearly black, but the rest of it was a red so bright as to surprise me—and I had thought myself incapable of further surprise.

But there were many surprises. "Road-runner," called Roger, and there it was, running over the prairie, swerving round a bush with one rounded wing thrust out for balance, dashing across a gap with the speed of a sprinting man. With a flick of its long, slim tail, it disappeared completely into a patch of scrub. We would see this ground cuckoo, this killer of snakes and lizards, many times again in the southwestern deserts, but first sights are those we remember.

When we reached the broad lagoon, around which the refuge is centered, we were clocking new birds faster than one a minute. What a wonderful place! Six kinds of herons waded in the shallows; there were five kinds of terns, and eight species of ducks, most of which should have departed for their nesting grounds in the prairies far to the north; and there were twenty species of waders. Here on the coast of Texas, many of the waders were still at the flood tide of their

migration, whereas the spring movement of songbirds had almost
ended.

Far out on the great shallow lagoon, where the shimmering heat
waves formed wriggling mirages, was a big flock of white pelicans,
sitting quietly, like yachts at anchor drying their sails. These were
probably off-duty birds from the colonies in the Laguna Madre, their
only outpost on the Atlantic Coast. The white pelican's main breeding distribution is inland, on large lakes in the western half of the
United States and Canada. The nearest colony to the one in Texas
is 1200 miles west at Salton Sea in California. These big white birds,
far larger than the brown pelicans we had been seeing almost daily
for the last two weeks, have a wingspan of nine feet, almost that of
a condor.

There is probably no other spot in the United States where as many
rare hawks can be found. Swainson's, the hawk of the western plains,
was here and also Harris's, a very dark *Buteo,* nearly black, with
rufous "trousers" and a black and white tail. Luther took us across
the brushy flats, our wheels throwing a cloud of dust, straight to a
tall isolated yucca, in whose top was a large nest. Here a pair of
white-tailed hawks were successfully raising a pair of well-fledged
young. The parent birds, wide-winged and short-tailed, wheeled high
overhead. In the past, egg collectors had done much damage to these
rare birds. We did not find the white-tailed kite (it is now very rare
in Texas) but we did finally see a caracara. From a fence post flew
this "Mexican eagle," handsome with its black crest, red face, and
boldly patterned wings and tail. We would see many more in Mexico.

How important to have refuges like this, I thought, as we turned
our backs on the coastal country and drove inland. How very important is the work of the U.S. Fish and Wildlife Service and the
Texas Game and Fish Commission, and also that of the Soil Conservation Service. What was Texas like, I wondered, four centuries
ago, when Coronado's men came up from Mexico to explore the
Great Plains. Since then—particularly during the last century—man
has farmed, grazed, drained his way through the vulnerable Texas
soil. Prairie has given way to mesquite brush, and brush to barrens.
In places, deserts are on the march.

It is many miles from the Laguna Atascosa on the coast to the
Santa Ana Refuge, upriver, and we had to hurry, for sunset comes
early in the far south. Except at the Dry Tortugas, I had never been

so far south in my life. We reached the tract, the last remaining primeval stand of red elms in the Valley, while the long rays of the late afternoon sun still filtered through the curtains of Spanish moss. The moss-draped elms dominated the woodland, but there were many ashes and some enormous, ancient, twisted, gnarled, crooked ebonies; and much hackberry. At a corner of the woodland we suddenly found ourselves actually on the bank of the Rio Grande. It was not very grand, at that moment; just a trickle of chocolate water in the slender middle of a wide bed that looked as if it had been dry for a million years.* On the opposite bank, in Mexico, motor pumps sucked what they could onto the fields.

We could hear the clatter of another pump close at hand on our

* Later in the season the Rio Grande dried up altogether in lower Texas, and flowed only near its source! Just one year later, on the other hand—in July, 1954—the river went mad in the worst flood in its history. The first hurricane of the season, Alice, did negligible damage along the coast, but when she spun inland "evil Alice" loosed the rains on Texas; as much as 22 inches fell in places (one inch can mean a flash flood). A wall of water, cresting at 62 feet, rushed down the Rio Grande, sweeping away at least one town and also the International Bridge at Laredo (it was 20 feet over the bridge) before it was stopped by the new Falcon Dam, 75 miles below Laredo. When the waters subsided, 153 people had been drowned and 15,000 were homeless.

Black-bellied Tree Duck

side of the river, somewhere within the forest itself. We parked the car, and, led by Luther, carefully approached a small pond, half hidden by the trees, a pond kept level in dry seasons by pumping. In spite of our caution, a group of ducks sprang into the air from behind a screen of willows and fled with strange whistling cries. They returned and circled—fourteen birds—and we got another fine view of them, trailing long legs behind their tails; they had red bills and broad white wing patches. Thirty years ago, the black-bellied tree duck had quite disappeared from the resacas of south Texas, its only U.S. breeding place; but under the protection of the refuges, it has come back over the border.

When the refuge was created, the rare red-billed pigeon soon flocked in, for it had no protection on the Mexican side of the Valley and woodlands were disappearing fast on the American side. We heard its moaning *who-who-wooooooo* many times in the mossy elm wood.

Orioles were everywhere—hooded orioles, mostly—and their nests must have been hidden in the Spanish moss. Luther showed us a hanging nest that had been built the year before by a rose-throated becard, a rare visitor from Mexico that had only recently attempted to nest on the U.S. side of the border. Although there was no sign of a bird in 1953, the old nest, about twenty feet from the ground, was almost intact, hanging from a slender branch of an ash, I believe it was. It was a ball (or vertical ellipsoid), about a foot deep, of twined stems (they looked like vine stems) holding together a construction that appeared to be made of lichens, at least outside. The entrance was quite low down—in the bottom half of the ball.

As the sun began to set, and the long gold shafts no longer slanted through the wood, the chachalacas began to call. They are very noisy at dusk and at dawn, but difficult to see. Once in the twilight, when a rustle and a movement stirred in the brush, we thought that we had discovered one, but the dense catbriars insured its getaway. It probably was not a chachalaca, but that armor-plated mammal, the armadillo, which roams the woods after dark.

It was quite dark when we started back through the Santa Ana forest, through rides among the moss-hung trees. We flicked the head-lights on. At once they caught a queer brown bird, crouching in the middle of the ride; caught first broad white wing-flashes and white tail patches as it plopped down in the dust and turned its gold-red eyes upon us. We stopped the car and watched.

"Pauraque," said Roger. "Merrill's pauraque—it's a goatsucker; a sort of Mexican whip-poor-will."

It was displaying, as some goatsuckers do, by crouching and groveling and jumping. Mothlike, another bird flew in, and sat a few feet away. The pair faced each other and suddenly bounced up into the air in a flutter and flash of wings, subsided and crouched and groveled, fluttered up again. We met half a dozen pairs in the forest trails, and once three together. When we switched off the engine, we heard a hoarse whistling cry, which Roger has written *pur-weeeeeer* and others have written *ko-wheeeeeew* and *go-weeer*. "They say everything but *pau-ra-que*," said Roger. He imitated their hoarse whistles and they flew closer. We could have caught them in a butterfly net.

These queer birds, birds of the hot night, leaping like mad moths in the light-beams, brought our Big Day to an end. Luther Goldman and Roger had shown me 132 species of birds—more birds than I had ever seen in one day before in my life. (My best day's list in Europe—made one day in central France—was 97). And never before had I seen so many new ones in a single day: 38 were "life" birds.

Statistically, about one-fourth of the birds we saw this day—35 species—were birds still on their passage North; nearly one-fourth—

Tarantula

29 or 30 species—were Mexican birds that spill over into southeast Texas. Less than one-seventh—18 species—were birds that also belong to the Old World.

NOT ONLY did the birds reflect our proximity to Mexico this day, but also the flowers, the butterflies (although we saw relatively few), and the big hairy tarantulas that we picked up in the car lights on the road as we left the Santa Ana. Certainly the towns of San Benito, Harlingen, and Brownsville—their people, their stucco patio-type houses, their rows of palm trees—have a strong Mexican flavor.

After a dinner of hot Mexican food, we returned to our cool air-conditioned motel in San Benito to find a message from Bob Newman. The ship's cook on the *Atlantis* had fallen desperately ill; he had to be taken off by a Coast Guard cutter and was being rushed to the mainland. Bob would be coming in on the same boat—about midnight—at Port Isabel. That was not much of a run in the car, but when we hunted up the Coast Guard dock we found that plans had again gone awry. The captain had changed course for Galveston, where there were more adequate hospital facilities.

Would we ever make contact with Newman? We decided to stay over one more day, and then if he had not come, we would go on without him.

But next evening Bob came in on the bus from Galveston. We could relax; we would now have a guide and interpreter to take us by the hand when we crossed the border.

18

South of the Border

Somewhere, somewhen I've seen
But where or when I'll never know
Parrots of shrilly green
With crests of shriller scarlet flying
Out of black cedars as the sun was dying
Against cold peaks of snow.

W. W. GIBSON, "The Parrots"

SOMEWHERE, many miles south of the border, I woke from a doze. We had stopped at a bridge where road menders were working. Just then, cutting across my consciousness came the raucous cries of parakeets in the trees along the river. It was precisely at that moment that I fully realized for the first time that we were really in Mexico.

The Rio Grande—the mighty Rio Grande—had been a disappointment to James. The Apalachicola and other unheard of rivers had proved to be great torrents compared to the brown trickle we crossed at Brownsville. The river had never carried less water within human memory, and the wetbacks, the migrant Mexican laborers who often swam the stream and slipped past the border patrols, were this year known as drybacks. We had no trouble with the customs at the border, although James nearly gummed things up by telling one of the officials that the parabolic reflector, which we carried on the roof, was a flying saucer.

We tried a hotel restaurant in the border town of Matamoros before going on. We were now in the land where American travelers avoid green salads and drink Mexican beer instead of water. But the food here was good. Getting back into the oven-hot car, we headed southward on a two-lane highway where our driving skill was put to the test by innumerable pits and potholes in the concrete. The Mexican side of the valley was desperately dry—even more parched than it had been in Texas—and James saw, for the first time, how bad man-made soil erosion could be. When we passed one small farm settlement where not a green thing survived and where the powdery brown soil whirled away in dust devils, he admitted the sight was terrifying.

We had unconsciously begun to look for new and exciting Mexican birds as soon as we crossed the Rio Grande. Birds of course do not recognize political boundaries and the birds on the Mexican side of the valley are the same as those in Texas; there are no new ones for the first fifty miles. The Mexican crow, a tiny crow with a bass voice, is usually the first. Bob Newman predicted that the next would be the brown jay, but we looked for it in vain that afternoon.

Somewhere along the way James discovered that his binoculars were missing. If he left them at the restaurant in Matamoros, they were probably pinched by now. At Victoria that evening, after an hour's struggle with the Mexican telephone system, he finally telegraphed Luther Goldman to ask him if he would cross the International Bridge and hunt up the restaurant. We could not remember the name of the hotel, so James telegraphed its field characters; it was on the edge of town, and had a most extraordinary table in the lobby, a masterpiece of oak supported by four carved nude figures. If the glasses were there, Luther was to post them to General Delivery at Laredo.

While James was trying to make contact with Brownsville, Bob and I joined the strollers in the city square. In traditional Mexican fashion all the young men walked in clockwise direction around the plaza, giving the eye to the young ladies who walked arm in arm past them in counterclockwise direction. Our eyes were less on the glamorous señoritas than on the clamorous great-tailed grackles that swarmed to the trees in the center of the square, where they would roost for the night. Thousands of large glossy black birds screeched, whistled, and clucked in earsplitting discord. The incredible bedlam that actually drowned out the sounds of the traffic and of the strollers continued long after the sun had gone down. These screeching assemblages of roosting grackles in the town squares are typical of many towns in Tamaulipas.

It never did cool off during the night. And in the morning, as the sun climbed, it became hot, incredibly hot. Even Bob, the hardened Mexican traveler, admitted it was a heat wave. And it was dry. The brown land we were traversing was not exactly desert, but technically "mesquite grassland," only there was no grass; goats had grazed it all away. The scrubby trees, bare and dead looking, were waiting for the summer rains.

At noonday the sun was as near overhead as we could tell by eye (and skin); a few miles south of Ciudad Victoria we had crossed the Tropic of Cancer and for the first time in James's life—or in mine—we were in the tropics. We were in the Torrid Zone, which my old school geography books had pictured as a broad geographic belt populated with anteaters, monkeys, parrots, and other incredible creatures. We could expect parrots, anyway. And we soon encountered them in the tree margins along the rivers, noisy flocks of green parakeets and red-crowned parrots, the noisy heralds of the threshold of the tropics. Often we heard the raucous *heeo, cra-cra-cra!* of red-crowned parrots in the river woods, but seldom we saw them until they flew, for they seemed to sit quite motionless for long spells, invisible among the leaves. But we often saw their little parties flying high overhead, tiny specks in the sky, more audible than visible. Roaming the treetops was another *Amazona* parrot, the yellow-headed. How fast these parrots flew! They streaked from one stand of trees to another, flying high, usually in twos, side by side, shouting in their discordant parrot voices. The river jungle sounded like a zoo, with these various parrots, the chachalaca, and pigeons of three or four sorts—all noisy birds—and looked like a zoo too, with its bright-colored finches, flycatchers, and orioles.

Once when we stopped by the roadside, James and Bob struck off into the dry bush to see if they could find a chachalaca that was calling loudly. Stopping in the shade to dry the sweat off their backs, they heard an eerie scream. James wrote in his journal:

> *Three times it sounded, a mammal's scream. We quietly advanced into the thicket after this queer voice. Overhead a roadside hawk sailed on a thermal, while a white-necked raven made a desultory attempt to mob it. I had binoculars at the ready (I had borrowed a gigantic pair of Bob's). The scream came again. Then round a bush I stepped into a clearing, just as a dog gray fox stepped into it from the other side. We stood watching each other for a moment, and presently the bold animal padded forward right into the middle of the clearing, turned its head to lead my eyes to another gray fox (its mate?) at the clearing's edge, turned to face me again and screamed once more. Unhurried, calm, it then walked off, paused at the edge of the clearing, screamed again and disappeared.*

To tell of all the birds we saw during our first two days in Mexico, birds new to James and new to me, but old stuff to Bob, would read like a partial check-list of the birds of Tamaulipas. But if I were to name the one bird that impressed me most, it would be the potoo. Bob had a list of bird specimens—mostly skeletons—needed by his department at the University of Louisiana. The potoo was on this list.

"Is there any chance of seeing one?" I asked.

Bob said he knew a place down on the Tampico road just over the line in San Luis Potosí, where he had found them in other years. But it was night work. This *Nyctibius*—a distant relative of the goatsuckers—is like a huge whip-poor-will, except that it sits bolt upright, mimicking a dead stub. Once George Sutton, climbing a slope in southern Tamaulipas, grasped at a stump for support, only to have the whole top of it fly off and away.

At a hardware store in Valles we purchased two headlamps, the sort that miners and speleologists use. These we strapped to our heads, and the batteries to our belts. While James took the wheel, Bob watched one side of the road, I scouted the other. Pauraques, our friends of the Santa Ana, were out in force this still warm night. We heard them calling *go-weer!* from the scrub and we saw their baleful eyeshine, and also the cold yellow-green eyeshine of night-hawks on the road shoulder. Once, when we stopped we heard a new voice, *chip-willow,* which Bob said was the Salvin's whip-poor-will.

We had almost given up the potoo, when two huge orange eyes, like reflectors, on the top of a tall roadside snag returned the glare of our headlights. We jammed on the brakes and concentrated our flashlights and head torches on the glowing orbs; they were the largest eyes I had ever seen in a night bird. Round and moonlike they seemed, like jack-o'-lantern eyes or the eyes of a Halloween owl. The bird, almost as big as a barn owl, sat upright on the tip of the dead stub, like a continuation of it. A tree with eyes. Suddenly the dead tree's head detached itself and the eyes disappeared in a silent flutter of mottled wings and tail. The potoo was hunting, snapping moths from the air. Returning to the stub it turned its glowing eyes upon us again. We watched it for twenty minutes and heard no sound, save the snap of its gin-trap of a beak. Finally Bob said he would have to shoot. One shot was all that was necessary; the big bird dropped to the foot of the tree without a sound. We were able to examine it in the flesh, its great eyes, now dim, and its immense veined pink throat, cavernous enough to swallow small birds. There was little room in its wide froglike head for anything but eyes and gape. We stroked its soft plumage and pondered its extraordinary adaptations as a concealed insect trap.

Bob was almost in tears; he does not like to collect. "I wouldn't mind so much, if it had been an ordinary bird," he said, "but it put on such a good show for us."

That night, before he turned in, Bob made up the specimen and suspended the carcass inside the hood of the car so that the heat of the engine would complete the job. It was the skeleton the museum wanted.

"Where, in Mexico," I had inquired, "should one go if he wishes to see the greatest variety of Mexican birds—the best cross section— in the shortest time?"

"Xilitla," was the invariable answer. L. Irby Davis and his group on a Christmas Count of December, 1950, listed 230 species in a single day within a fifteen-mile circle centered at Xilitla, in the lime-stone mountains of San Luis Potosí; this was the largest count ever made in a single day on the North American continent.

So, Xilitla was our goal. There, in a journey of only a few miles, we made the transition from lowland river bottom to high cloud forest. But let James tell about it.

May 24–25

This morning we entered a region of limestone mountains, through a string of villages along the Pan American Highway, native villages that despite their inhabitants, their poverty and their thatched adobe houses had this in common with the native villages of the United States—Coca-Cola and gas pumps. Cokes, by now, were to us as important as gas, fluid that we could not do without. In Mexico, safe water is more widespread than it was, and it is no longer necessary to clean your teeth in soda pop in the bigger towns. But away from modern plumbing in Mexico a coke is just about the only drink; and all three of us were losing moisture steadily and fast, taking our daily salt tablets to counteract the effects of dehydration. And for some reason, we could get our official expedition drink at less than New York prices; we bought it at three cents a bottle from Mexican Indians in Xilitla cooled in boxes of damp earth or wet rags. In Texas we had paid a dime!*

Forty miles south of Valles we dropped down into the valley of the Rio Axtla, pausing to take on gas in the long straggling village of Huichihuayan, where crowds of Mexicans were lounging and idly talking. This village was unmistakably Aztecan with many women in traditional headdress and bare feet. One Indian woman in a pretty striped dress stepped from an open shop as we passed, carrying, as all Indian women do, by habit, her load on her head—a tiny can of condensed milk!

---

* This book, I hasten to add, is not sponsored by the Coca-Cola company.

"Coca-Cola!" exclaimed Raymond Postgate (one of the world's experts on wine) at dinner at London's Savile Club when I got back. "Coca-Cola—my dear chap, my *dear* chap!"

"Try running on a continuous water-debt and salt-debt, in a Mexican cloud forest," I replied, "with the temperature over that of blood, humidity dangerously high, and stream water unsafe to drink. You'll think again. You'll think Coca-Cola more precious than this fancy vintage we're enjoying now."

(opposite) Cloud Forest, Xilitla

About three miles beyond the town we turned onto a gravel road which led toward the river. Tropical deciduous forest this was, though nearly all secondary forest, for the Indians have cleared strips and blocks and cultivated them for centuries. L. Irby Davis, who knows this area well, writes: "It is impossible to say that there is any 'virgin' forest in any part of it." But there were broad stands of big trees, with new, man-planted undergrowth below—coffee bushes, living, as they have to live, in the shade. We passed great mangoes, dark banyans, and spreading sycamores, and under a welcome canopy of shade reached the car ferry over the Rio Axtla. Bob knew the ferryman and had no qualms about leaving the car in his care while we plunged into the forest along the right bank of the river.

The forest was not continuous. Great patches of bamboo bordered part of the river, and inland behind the border of trees and bamboo the rather steeply rolling country was cleared for maize crops. We negotiated ditches and natural hedges and scrambled hard through forest, field, and scrub. One big patch of woodland was nearly dark under the high sun, so close was its canopy, so dense its great standards, so thick its epiphytes and airplants. Its roof was so light-obscuring that there was little undergrowth—mostly ferns and fallen trunks.

It was no bird or exotic mammal that made me realize one of my boyhood dreams of the dark tropical forests of the Americas—dreams inspired by the journeys of Bates and Wallace. It was a six-inch butterfly, flapping slowly through the dark wood path, a butterfly of the bluest, purplest metallic sheen when caught in a rare sun ray, of the deepest black in the shadows. I tried to hat it; as well try to catch a bird, for it jinked up to the canopy in a twinkling and was gone. Another soon came, and others. The forest-ride was their beat; at intervals never great, one after another came drifting along. "The first sight of the great blue *Morphos* flapping slowly along in the forest roads," wrote Wallace, "can never be forgotten by anyone with a feeling of admiration for the new and beautiful in nature." "When it comes sailing along," wrote Bates of one *Morpho* species, "it occasionally flaps its wings, and then the blue surface flashes in the sunlight, so that it is visible a quarter of a mile off." Air travelers, flying over Central America sometimes see their heliograph-like flashes over the roof of the jungle.

Roger, who never visits a new spot without collecting a butterfly, stumbled about the stumps and logs in fruitless chases. I just watched him, and the *Morphos* eluding him, and thought of the school library at Eton, and the specimens in the school museum that I had once arranged, and even tried to paint pictures of. "One day I'll see you," I had said to myself, or rather, to those dead specimens so far from their home.

Roger seemed even more enthralled by the butterflies than by the birds. The *Morphos* escaped from him—except for one frayed specimen—but he easily captured the other kinds. Whenever he netted a new one he would rush up to show it. One handsome swallowtail had yellow markings; another was all black punctuated by a row of bright red submarginal spots. Then there was a marbled whitish butterfly that clicked as it flew and assumed an upside-down position when it landed on a tree trunk. Of smaller kinds there were any number, some of which Roger papered in three-cornered envelopes made from sheets torn from his notebook.

The Axtla River was low, weedy, and warm. I swam in it a little, for fun, and to pick up a mangrove swallow that Bob had shot that had fallen in the middle of the slow stream. It was one of the birds on his list.

A green kingfisher sped by, flashing a novel beauty; but novelty was now our daily bread. A pair of rose-throated becards had their big baglike nest in the sycamore on the bank opposite. Orioles were in the big sycamore too—the Altamira black-throated oriole—and tanagers; the yellow-winged tanager, purple-blue with bright yellow wing flashes; and a tiny purple-blue gem with yellow underparts—Bonaparte's euphonia. Bob, the expert, called out "black-headed saltator" and "blue-black grassquit" and "boat-billed flycatcher" and "Giraud's flycatcher." I became almost dizzy trying to sort them all out. We met about 50 bird species in this river forest in three hot hours. Overhead was a new swift, the white-collared swift, operating downriver from its home in the 5000-foot mountains. We were only about 300 feet above the sea at the Rio Axtla, and before the day was over we would climb at least half as far as those swifts.

Back through the dark wood of the *Morpho* butterflies we went, through the cornfields and bamboo-brakes; Roger brandishing, still vainly, his net; Bob totting up his notebook; Fisher feeling the rising heat. The car, which we had locked, was a furnace. We ran it onto the little ferryboat, where Roger turned his attention to a swarm of orange heliconian butterflies—"Julias," he called them—which were sunning themselves on the hot iron railing. We crossed the Axtla, following its right bank for a while before the road started its long, tortuous climb into the mountains.

Bob discovered that he had lost his wallet. This was serious. Not because of the money; there were keys, permits, and other things. "You know," he said, "it must have been where I shot the mangrove swallow."

At this point we were opposite the *Morphos'* dark forest strip. I decided to have a try for the wallet; perhaps I could find it. I stripped on the riverbank, swam across, landed on a slab of limestone, and padded up and down the water's edge under shouted directions from Bob. Roger chased butterflies. I looked for twenty minutes, but no luck. As I stumbled back along the bank to a diving place an Indian came out of the trees and looked at me with a gentle smile. Did he wonder, I thought, whether the mad Americans made a habit of running naked about the forest? I dismissed the possibility of his recognizing the mad English; the mad Americans and the mad English are much the same in the skin anyway, and under it or over it, for that matter.

As the road turned away from the river toward the mountains the scenery rapidly became wilder and steeper. In some of the little side valleys there was a trickle of water and the deciduous forest began to march down the slopes. Around a series of hairpin bends we entered a real jungle, the finest bit of jungle we were to see in Mexico—giant trees, madly twined creepers, thick underbrush. The place was called Y Griega.

These tall forest giants that stood above us and below us on the steep slopes looked like primeval trees, but even here we could see planted coffee trees growing in the shade. Lianas hung loosely from high branches like heavy cables. There were strange jungle plants with large shiny leaves; one of them looked like the decorative *Monstera* so popular in florist shops. *Morphos* jinked across the road, while Roger worked himself toward a state of collapse in their pursuit. Pervading all was a ghostly sound, the sad hollow *oo-whooooooo* of white-fronted doves, a sound that, to Roger, became the voice of this forest.

But it was not easy to spot things in this verdant jungle. We got a fleeting glimpse of a couple of Prevost's caciques, black oriole-like birds with long conical yellow bills. From time to time we heard strange noises to which we could assign no name.

"Listen," said Bob, when a sad querulous piping note sounded to our left. "Tinamou—rufescent tinamou." There was little hope of seeing this primitive henlike bird that skulked in the brush.

Another loud puzzling call, made by some large ground bird, came from the dark shrubbery above the bend of the road. Abandoning his butterfly hunt, Roger stalked the insistent calls and put up four crested guans, large chachalaca-like birds that erupted across the road and scaled down into the ravine.

I had always imagined that my first experience of a dense tropical forest would be by the banks of some slow, low equatorial river. The woodlands by the Axtla could hardly be called dense; here in central Mexico we had to travel *uphill* to reach the densest tropical jungle. I never expected to drive uphill, fortified by Coca-Cola, to see it

As we climbed farther up the mountain the country closed in, became a muddle of canyons and gorges with eroded limestone blocks and buttes. The road wound through cuttings and edged along minor precipices. The valleys were choked, and the buttes were crowned, with dense woody vegetation. We stopped by a widening of the road where a limestone wall overhung a dark cave.

"Bats," said Bob. "We'll need our headlamps."

The cave, which we entered down rocky steps, ran, narrowing, a hundred feet or more into the mountain, then broadened into a chamber, with a few tumbled blocks on the irregular water-smoothed floor. The end of the vault sloped steeply up to a spiral chimney, lit faintly from above through a narrow natural window. We heard a whispering sound, the whirring of bat wings, and when we shone our torches up, little awakened bats took off from the cave roof, whirled around, and settled upside down again from some tiny foothold in the ceiling.

"Some of these caves have vampires," said Bob, the word "vampire" echoing from the Gothic walls of our grotto, "but I don't know about this one. I don't see any pools of blood on the floor."

Roger and I poked around; we didn't see any either.

"I wouldn't swear these bats are not vampires," said Bob. "They look a bit small, but vampires are not large bats."

Bob went for his gun, and I hastily retreated, wishing to be elsewhere when the roof came down. I stood outside while Bob stalked his quarry.

BANG-abang-awang-wang-ang-ng-g. Good shot, Newman, I said to myself, and looked around to see if the cave was still there. *BANG-abang-wang-dang-bang.* "Good shot, sir."

A minute's aftermath of silence. I lit my way into the cave again where Roger was standing. I was calculating the possibilities of ricochets and wondering where we had parked the first-aid kit when I discovered Bob groveling on his hands and knees in a corner.

"You all right, old boy?" I said (in a tone of voice that Roger afterwards identified as that of a taxi driver with a drunk).

Bob said, "Uh," and the cave answered Uh, in a groaning sort of voice; he collapsed at full length and rolled into a trough of the cave floor, his flashlamp clutched in one hand.

"Roger, come here quick—Bob's bought it," I snapped.

"Don't bother, Roger," said Bob, "one of them's over here somewhere—but I've *not* caught it; can't find the little so-and-so at all. Shine your lamp this way, James."

Until he reads this, Bob Newman will never know that I was just about to ask Roger how we could most quickly communicate with his next-of-kin.

We never did find the fallen bat, and could not say whether it was a vampire or not. Probably not, for there had recently been a campaign against vampires in this part of Mexico because they carry rabies. On the floor of the cave, we noticed evidence of a bonfire which had been set, probably, to exterminate the bats.

A few miles farther up the road we rounded a bend and the valley suddenly widened. Below us a side canyon was green with forest and white-gray with limestone exposures, and from it came a sound we had not heard for many days, the hiss of running water. And on the hill flank opposite, 2000 feet from sea level, sprawled a stone village, with wooden tiles and thatch, Xilitla.

Xilitla is a primitive village, an Indian village, a poor but happy village. Bob had friends there, and called on one of them for the key of the Methodist mission; the kind missionaries, who were away, had arranged to lend us their house. We found a lock-up for the car, and humped our gear to the mission house along a narrow flagged mule track. Exhausted, we dropped hotly into comfortable chairs, and drank tall glassfuls of cool spring water straight from the tap; Bob assured us it was safe. The house was set a little above the Indian houses all around, with a pretty view, looking out over the huge gently waving leaves of a banana grove, to the forest valley and the steep wooded mountainsides beyond.

The forest of Xilitla and its mountain massif, the Cerro San Antonio, is a typical rain- and cloud-forest. Its rainfall, which falls mostly in late summer and autumn, is said to be a hundred inches a year. Such rainfall, falling on limestone hills, erodes by dissolution as well as by force, and the whole country is a mass, not only of ravines, buttes, canyons, and arêtes, but also of caves and sinks. In some of the caves the roof had fallen; here the tropical forest grows over great gashes and to the edge of quarry-like precipices. Such a cave is the great amphitheater of the Cueva Saltire, which Bob Newman described as "resembling the shell on the stage of the Hollywood Bowl." We had seen its dark opening in the distance, from the road.

We dragged ourselves outdoors again, enduring the lash of the heat, and found our way to the Cueva Saltire, a mile below the town. We scrambled through a natural tank trap of shattered limestone boulders to reach the mouth of the spectacular cave; in a sense, it was all mouth. An enormous semicircular cliff, undercut and overhanging, half enclosed us. Towering a hundred feet or more above us, it plunged the same distance below our vantage point, until its foot was lost to sight beyond the convexity of the steep slope on which we sat. What we were sitting on was, in fact, the apex of a great pile of boulder talus that was quite clearly once the cave's roof. It had collapsed and its ruins lay sloping against one wall of the cave.

The Cueva Saltire was the noisiest cave I have ever been in, for shrieking at the tops of their voices were at least two dozen green parakeets, which had their nest sites in cracks and niches high on the overhanging wall. Back and forth they flew across the dark abyss, the green of their plumage as shrill as their screams. At the focus of the great reflecting wall which acted as a parabola our own voices were sometimes drowned out by the excited parakeets.

"Look," Bob shouted. He nudged me and had to shout again, "Look—motmots!"

In a clump of bushes a pair of big green birds, blue-crowned and tinged a bit with reddish, were bobbing and flirting their tails. Little

objects followed them as they flew, like butterflies attached by string, and it was some time before my memory of the days when I worked at the London zoo reminded me: of course—their terminal rackets. For motmots have their middle tail feathers prolonged to twice the length of the others. Beyond the rest of the tail these feathers run as bare shafts almost to the tip, where they end in broad rackets like inverted shields. These rackets were the satellites that were following the blue-crowned motmots about as they fussed in the bushes, quietly hooting (we had to await a lull in the parakeet chorus to hear it) a double hoopoe-ish note. One bird carried food in its bill; a nest must have been nearby.

We left these birds of the shadows after some time and stumbled out into the sunlight, to catch the rest of the day. A canyon wren sang its willow-warbler-like cascade somewhere in the rockfall. On our way back to the mission we saw more novelties: a Rivoli's hummer, a boat-billed flycatcher, a couple of white-winged tanagers in the treetops. We were becoming sated with novelty, exhausted by the heat, yet happy in this tropical dream world.

Next morning Bob promised us the cloud forest. If we started at dawn, he advised, we would avoid the worst of the heat. Our guide, Emidio Esquibel, called for us soon after sunup and we started up the mountain trail, accompanied by a horde of barefoot children. One boy was so keen to accompany the queer Americans that we eventually relented and let him come along; as it turned out we were glad to have anybody carry our gear. Even the lightest camera or tripod was a burden in that heat. The temperature soon climbed toward 100° F., and the breezes that met us round corners were like blasts from a giant hair drier, hot and solid. Now and then a level patch of the forest was cleared for cornfields, or had been cleared and was drifting back through scrub to secondary forest.

While resting by the trail, almost reduced to indifference by the heat and exertion, I was suddenly brought back again to my days of youth by another butterfly that I remembered in the school collection: a medium-sized butterfly, known as the 88 (because of the markings on its underwings). It had only recently emerged from its chrysalis, and I was able to take it in my hand.

A similar experience took Roger back to his own schooldays when a small gem of a bird, iridescent blue and violet, with coral-red legs, flashed into a bush near the path. It was a blue honey creeper, the same *Coereba* that had captured his imagination thirty years before when he discovered one in a glass case in the upper hallway of his high school.

Ahead the mountain path climbed into a dark forest of oaks and sweet gum. Here it seemed much cooler—refreshingly cool—for we were getting close to the threshold of mist and cloud that shrouded the upper slopes. A raven, soaring against the cloud edge, reminded us of the northern world. An Indian came quickly down the path, smiling shyly as he passed, trailing a great bundle of thick sticks fastened at one end by an ingenious head-harness. Later two more Indians passed us on the steep trail, with a huge log of mahogany slung between them by the same kind of harness. For carrying almost anything the Xilitla Mexican Indians use man power, and use their heads.

As we sat in the clearing, admiring a distant view of the village below, I ticked off some of the new birds we had encountered. And it began to dawn on me how rarely the ordinary bird watcher must see some of these species, for they are called one thing in the new Mexican check-list, something else in Blake's *Birds of Mexico,* and often a third name in George Sutton's *Mexican Birds.* Usage had not yet decreed standardized names for many of them. To name a random few: the brown-headed chlorospingus (or common bush tanager); LaFresnaye's (or flame-colored or Swainson's) tanager; Mexican (or yellow-faced) grassquit. Dear me, I hope they can do something about the instability of these vernacular names!

If I mentioned *all* the birds we saw in Mexico, this account would read too much like a list. Of the 135 species we saw during five days, 76 were new to me, 60 new to Roger, but not one was new to Bob. After all, he was our guide.

We plunged into the forest again, into the cool darkness from which the wood cutters had emerged. Beside the steep path, under the sweet gums, grew huge spreading tree ferns, twenty feet tall or more. This, indeed, was cloud forest. We could never have spotted the birds of the high jungle had it not been for Bob's experienced ear—two nightingale thrushes, for instance, the orange-billed and the rare black-headed. A loud series of descending whistles from the dark shadows was an ivory-billed woodhewer; and an explosive song in the undergrowth, a gray-breasted wood wren.

Somewhere between 3000 and 4000 feet above sea level, we reached the top of our hill and stepped out of the jungle into an open clearing at the edge of a huge bowl-shaped sink, perhaps 200 yards across. Beyond the sink the forest began again. From the depths of this forest came a queer gobbling *coo,* the voice of the mountain trogon.

We tried to get on close terms with the fabulous trogon, although we never did see it. But we were not disappointed. Hadn't we had our eyeful of bright birds of the tropics by now—parrots, parakeets, motmots, tanagers, hummingbirds, and all? As we started back down the trail, down through the tree ferns, we began to realize that we had only tasted of the cloud forest. There were more things here than at first met the eye. Unseen, a singing quail worked up to its clear liquid whistle. We saw the masked tityra, a pair of them—gray, staring-eyed, fat big-billed creatures that *grunted!* And the blue mockingbird, all gray-blue. But the climax came when Bob, by a most efficient bit of range and bearing drill, found for us, in the forest canopy, one of the most beautiful exotic creatures I had ever seen. Until it moved among the leaves, it was almost impossible to distinguish, because it was almost entirely green, undershaded with a lighter green. Its big bill was yellow above and black below. It was the emerald toucanet, the only toucan that normally gets as far north as San Luis Potosí.*

The small boy who helped carry our cameras urged us to try a different path back to Xilitla, a new route amid green canyons. We passed a little waterfall where a brown-backed solitaire was singing a mad jumble of flute and oboe music, as if all the other thrushes of the world were amateurs. We passed through banana groves, glancing into thatched cottages where the Indian women sat sunning and sewing by the threshold. Inside, nearly always, the cane walls were papered with religious pictures.

Back in town we drank pints of Coca-Cola and then more Coca-Cola while a crowd of half-naked children gathered round. When I crossed the square to photograph the church, I got an extremely black look from the lieutenant in charge of the army post, who thought I wanted to photograph his post. After locating Roger (temporarily lost), we piled into the car and glided away.

Some time after leaving Xilitla, with ten miles of mountain road still before us, we discovered that the fuel gauge registered empty. There was no gas pump between us and the Pan American Highway. To save gas we coasted downhill most of the distance, almost all the way to the Rio Axtla.

* In the 1950 Christmas Count, Irby Davis saw four keel-billed toucans near Xilitla.

Once we were over the ferry, Bob and Roger politely told me I perhaps hadn't searched hard enough for the valuable wallet, so they left me in charge of the car while they beat a mile or two cross-country to have another look. I said I'd plenty of notes to write up, but instead went to sleep. They woke me an hour later; by retracing our trail like a couple of bloodhounds, through the cane beds, across the maize fields, through the *Morpho* wood and along the riverbank, they succeeded in finding the wallet.

Now, if the car would only hold out till we got to Huichihuayan! We nursed it up slopes and coasted down, and we got there—only to find, when we filled her up, that we had plenty of gas right along and that the needle wasn't working.

WE COULD NOT HELP viewing the rest of our visit to Mexico as something of an anticlimax. We took a new way home, continuing north from Victoria along the Pan American Highway, traversing a magnificent desert, with the bold sierras a hazy blue curtain to the west. When we overtook a huge truck after darkness had fallen, not far from Monterrey, a stone thrown by its giant wheels smashed into our windshield and drew an opaque veil over the lower half of it. Bob woke up in the back. "Started shooting already," he murmured, and sank back into sleep.

We arrived at the International Bridge at Laredo early the next afternoon, and could not restrain James from trying the flying-saucer gag again, this time on U.S. Customs. But they had seen a parabolic reflector before. It didn't stop them from tearing us apart in an inquisitive way, admiring our photographic equipment as they did so, particularly the camera gun, which they all took turns aiming. What would they think, we wondered, if they lifted the hood of the engine and saw the five small skeletons? But we were through in an hour, and Bob Newman and his skeletons managed to catch the Greyhound bus home to Louisiana.

19

Sun on the Lost Land

"A STRAWBERRY ice-cream soda, please," ordered James. "Make it two," I said.

We had dreamed of this moment all morning, particularly during the last fifty burning miles on the desert, before recrossing the Rio Grande into Texas at Laredo. After we had downed a second tall frothy soda, James dashed over to the post office and found to his relief that there was a package from Luther Goldman. Luther had found the binoculars.

This part of Texas, the southwestern flank, looked desperately thirsty. There had been no rain for weeks. Along one dreary stretch of road even the thorny mesquite scrub seemed to be dying. As we passed a ranch house a pup-dog barked at us and I wondered whether it was old enough ever to have known the pleasure of muddy feet. Clearly, a dust bowl would again be in the making if the rains did not come soon. It has been said that in certain areas rain is so rare that Texans have been known to faint at the sight of it—and they are revived by having sand thrown in their faces!

There are some astounding facts and figures on the amount of Texas grassland that has been usurped by mesquite.* "Overgrazing" is blamed for it, but actually, any grazing will change things in this terrain where survival is so delicately balanced. When edible grass is repeatedly eaten and the thorny scrub is ignored, there is opportunity for the less desirable growth to spread and inherit the land. And the invading mesquite certainly has inherited a large slice of Texas—it has extended its domain by 35,000,000 acres, at least. We drove through it hour after long hour, mile after endless mile. Bird life seemed scant, except for scissor-tailed flycatchers. These "Texas birds of paradise," pale pearly gray with a touch of salmon pink, perched like kingbirds on the wires, several to the mile. Like king- birds they bickered and engaged in aerial battles, opening and closing their long tail-streamers.

It is this broad belt of mesquite that separates East from West, biologically. The landscape becomes drearier, stonier, more desert- like as the fast straight road approaches the Pecos, there to pause and wind down into the steep canyon like a cautious rattlesnake before climbing out on the other side. It was at this precise point that we felt that we had left the last of the eastern influences behind and that we were now truly in the West.

When Judge Roy Bean was "Law west of the Pecos," this country- side through which we were passing must not have been so dry. It was cattle country in those days, at least some of it was, but we saw neither cattle nor grass—just a waste of mesquite and gravel. The town of Langtry, where Roy Bean held court, is almost a ghost town today, but the dead tree from which the ruthless judge hanged those on whom he passed sentence still stands. It was high noon when we lurched past this stark reminder of frontier justice and walked into a small pub, as James called it, and ordered the man behind the counter to "set 'em up." This county, we were informed by the Mexican proprietor, was officially "dry," but we could have soft drinks, he said. James commented that things certainly had changed since Roy Bean's day—a pity—but he would be quite satisfied with a grape soda. A disgruntled cowpoke, one of three hard-looking

---

* The Soil Conservation Service estimates 55,008,000 acres of mesquite in Texas out of a total of 168,732,160 acres.

characters at a corner table who had brought their own drinks, took note of James's remarks and his Eton-Oxford accent and decided that somehow Langtry must be vindicated. He could not shoot up the place, of course. After mumbling to his companions and then brooding silently for a few moments, he let out a riproaring coyote-like *Ya-hooooo!,* a preface, we feared, to bigger and better things. Startled by this unexpected exhibition, James gulped down his grape soda and I my root beer; we hastily put down twenty cents on the counter and departed.

At Langtry we parted from the river and rolled through rolling desert country, gradually rising as we sped west. We stopped briefly at a small canyon where scaled quail—the "blue quail" or "cotton-tops"—called their quick sharp disyllables from the scant grass. We had left the eastern quail—the bob-white—behind. A red-tailed hawk soared overhead, looking for ground squirrels. Turkey vultures were still with us, rocking unsteadily on their rigid sails, gliding on the thermals generated by the hot, rocky terrain. We saw no black vultures (although we had seen many farther east), nor golden eagles, and I wondered how much the killing campaigns in Texas had to do with their absence. When Paul Parmelee questioned 66 Texas ranchers he learned that since 1940 they had trapped and killed (conservatively) 100,000 vultures. Some of this may have been necessary, because black vultures do eat newborn livestock at times. Turkey vultures are blameless, however, and neither species carries anthrax or hog cholera, as was formerly believed. These organisms do not survive passage through the digestive tracts of the scavengers.

As for the golden eagles, there is less evidence on which to condemn them. True, individuals are known to take lambs, but their normal diet is rodents and other non-domestic animals. Yet, *thousands* of eagles have been shot down by air pilots who are hired as executioners by the local sheep ranchers. One pilot alone boasts of shooting down 512 golden eagles (in 2800 "eagle-flying hours"), more eagles than exist in all of Scotland, where they are now zealously guarded. Another pilot claimed a score of 2000 eagles. Surely not an eagle will remain in the entire state of Texas—and the drain of migrants from the whole West is inevitable.

Even in the Big Bend country, which we reached late in the afternoon, we saw no golden eagles, although there used to be three pairs in the Park.

May 28

"Visitors should fill their gasoline tanks at Marathon before leaving U.S. No. 90," the Park pamphlet had warned us; we took its advice and then turned off the main highway onto a new dirt road to the left.

"Only eighty miles now," announced Roger, as we swept south into another endless desert, toward the distant Santiago Mountains, which crept toward us with agreeable rapidity as the big car parted the desert heat and hot drafts blew around the cockpit. We slowly dropped in altitude, the desert became unbelievably hot, and Santiago Peak to our right rose high. We crossed a dry creek bed where a tall post marked the depth of nonexistent water—6 ft.–7 ft.–8 ft.–9 ft.–10 ft.—enough to sweep over the top of our car and force us to swim for our lives should we be stalled here in a flash flood. At the moment the dry wash looked as though it had not known a drop of water in a thousand years. We sped up the hill shoulder and saw a new range before us—the Chisos Mountains—"like a medieval walled city," as Freeman Tilden has described them. We were entering America's loneliest National Park (if we except Alaska's Mount McKinley) and the sixth largest in area—1100 square miles. Before us the sanctuary of the Chisos, the old stronghold of the Mescalero Apaches, rose like a castle in a rolling garden of wild desert plants.

Stretches of mesquite and creosote-bush scrub, varied displays of yucca and prickly pear, then grass unrolled as we climbed the two thousand feet into the castellated mountains. Roger remarked on the way the grass was coming back. Some of the hills had been almost reduced to rock piles by sheep and goat grazing before the National Park took over. Now there is again a good growth of golden grass on some of the slopes and scaled quail are quite numerous. Antelope—pronghorns—have been reintroduced and two deer flourish: mule deer, the ones with the big ears, and white-tails, not much larger than the "toy" white-tails of the Florida Keys. Lack of water, apparently, stunts their size.

The canyons began to steepen, to close in. In the rocky clefts dark juniper began to replace dusty mesquite. On the spurs the xeric plants became more varied, queerer, taller, and more colorful. The spurs

Road-Runner

were altars, decorated with bouquets of flowers, and illuminated by
countless candles and candelabra; the tall candles were sotol, and
the candelabra, agaves, century plants. The stand of agaves in Big
Bend's basin, in the heart of the Chisos, is the finest garden of these
astonishing plants outside Mexico, and they were just coming into
flower. Some were still at the point of sending up their flower stalks,
which looked, Roger said, "like a stalk of asparagus stuck in an
artichoke," only the artichoke was large enough to cover the table
and the asparagus tip was six inches through and several feet tall and
growing at the incredible speed of nearly a foot a day. The century
plant (which lives a quarter of a century or so—not a full century)
pours everything into one final fantastic spurt, the climax of its
existence, for it flowers but once before it shrivels and dies. The
flowering stalks shoot up until they reach fifteen, twenty, even thirty
feet, and from these masts, from half their height to the top, grow
slender lateral, horizontal branches, which bear each a brilliant boss
of gold, like a gilded coral, dripping petals in an idle breeze, a
spluttering firework blazing in the sun.

Many of the agaves' flower clusters were now bursting. At these
blossoms broad-tailed hummingbirds were feeding, buzzing angrily
in Lilliputian air battles when one bird trespassed upon another. The
agave gardens of the Chisos are the best place in the U.S. to see

Lucifer's hummer, a rare amethyst-throated wanderer from Mexico; Roger had seen one here two years before. But the broad-tailed hummer, superficially very like the ruby-throat of the East, is the most noticeable of the several kinds here; it is *the* hummer of the Rockies, of the mountain West. The males, flashing their shrill-green backs and rose-red gorgets in the afternoon light, darted from agave to agave, making a queer tinny trill with their wings, a sound that no other U.S. hummingbird produces. We heard this high trill in canyon and in mountain forest. "We're in the West now, all right," said Roger.

There seemed no end to the fantastic forms taken by the desert plants on these rocky slopes. Hedgehog cactus nestled in clumps among the boulders, its blazing blossoms surrounded by murderous needlelike spines.

A massive yucca lifted a profusion of creamy white bells from clumps of wicked dark daggers, while another yucca-like plant with frayed leaves—the sotol—erected a tall pom-pom of tightly packed blossoms six or seven feet long that suggested tall candles—or the ramrods used in old cannons. A third yucca-like plant, lechuguilla, had narrow curved leaves, which apparently the deer found edible, for we saw many plants neatly nipped off to their bases.

Strangest of all the strange plants in this strange landscape was the ocotillo, or monkey-tail cactus. It is not really a cactus, in fact its nearest relative is the even stranger boogum tree of Baja California. The monkey-tails, also known as "wolf-candles," twice the height of a man or taller, are spindly stalks that spring in clumps from a common base and bear at their tips bright red blossoms—like the flame of a blowtorch. Tiny green leaves lined some of the stalks; these soon fall off and the stem of the leaf remains to form a sharp thorn. Everything in this inhospitable country seems to carry thorns, hooks, or needles, threatening and defying.

"The Basin" of the Chisos is a wonderful natural amphitheater surrounded by the great jagged, folded, basalt-invaded, erosion-shattered, talus-aproned peaks. The Park headquarters and cabins in this protected hollow are approached over a steep narrow lip called Green Gulch, where the road hairpins among high rock gardens. One of the rarest songbirds in the United States—the Colima warbler—lives on the oak-covered slopes above this gulch, where Roger once found a singing male. We did not turn up a Colima this time, but

nearly half of the birds we were seeing now were new—typical
western species: Cassin's kingbird, another "difficult" flycatcher to
add to my confusion (Roger got it by its voice); Say's phoebe, a
quiet rust-bellied flycatcher; Couch's jay, a subtly colored bluish
jay; black-headed grosbeak, a rather good singer; and brown towhee,
the plainest of plain birds.

Dominating the Basin the massive peak of Casa Grande caught the
full brilliance of the afternoon sun. As we scanned its perdendicular
cliffs with our glasses, a Swainson's hawk, the buzzard of the dry
country, sailed along the rock face. Higher up there were white-
throated swifts. These strikingly patterned swifts are reputed to be
the fastest of all North American birds. I could well believe this as
we watched them hurtle past the high crags.

After checking our cabin reservation, Roger insisted on running
down to Hot Springs (a mere 50 miles or so) to see his old friend
Peter Koch, brilliant photographer of Big Bend's desert beauty, who
lives somewhat of a hermit's life where the Tornillo Creek enters the
Rio Grande. Mule deer galloped across the road as we glided down
the Basin's outfall-canyon, and swung east and southeast to circle
the Chisos range. The road wound through arroyos, crossed mesquite-
bordered washes, even forded a trickle once or twice; in storm
weather it would have been impassable.

The Rio Grande flowed, brown and low, through gravel flats.
Across in Mexico lay the adobe town of Boquillas in the State of
Coahuila; a town cut off from the rest of Mexico by fifty miles of
roadless desert and so remote that letters from Mexico City go first
to Texas, where the postman picks them up at Marathon and drives
100 miles to Peter Koch's border store. The Mexicans ford the river
on their mules to pick up their mail in the U.S. Such is the frontier!

Peter Koch is one of those fabulous individualists one sometimes
meets at outposts such as this. Graceful in his stride as an Indian, and
tireless (Roger tells me), he knows these lonely desert mountains and
river canyons as does no one else. As we chatted with him
and listened to his tales the quick southern sunset caught us; the sun
dropped fast behind Emory Peak, the near-8000-foot crown of the
Chisos, and the desert shapes and colors changed with sensational
rapidity. The shadows of the mountains and rocks walked across the
blushing desert, then rushed, sweeping the last purples and reds and
blues out of it.

When we waved goodbye, Peter Koch told us to keep our eyes peeled when we crossed the Tornillo. In the middle of the wash there was a dead mule (we had seen white-necked ravens at it when we came in); after dark the coyotes would be feeding on it. But we saw none of these wily dogs of the desert; they had already stripped the last few scraps from the carcass and had gone.

Our headlights, on the drive back, illuminated a queer nether world of colorless foreground backed by impenetrable black mystery. Eyes glinted in the glare, and once or twice just before we dropped from Green Gulch into the Basin a white-tailed deer's tail-flash disappeared into the black.

May 29

This morning, down among the lowland scrub, the ocotillos, and creosote bushes, we turned west at Government Spring. Almost at once we lost touch with the desert vegetation, for we were in a painted desert, a terrible wilderness of erosion, of arroyos and gullies, waterless open canyons where a few scanty plants struggled. The alluvial earth, swept down by the ages from the rocks of the Chisos and the neighboring ranges, had been channeled and runneled by the sudden, violent desert storms and winds into a wilderness of miniature plateaus, hogbacks, hanging valleys, dunes, and draws; here the sand was white, here yellow, orange, red. Great piles, pyramids, and arêtes were mauve, almost purple, slabbed light, gullied dark.

All deserts, I thought, are painted. Naked soil and rocks have as much magic, as much color, as plants. I remembered Iceland's central desert, where two years before Peter Scott and his wife Phil and Finnur Gudhmundsson and I had ridden on horseback four days to the great goose grounds of the oasis of Thjórsarver. Four days through black, red, brown, gray, purple, orange, olive, yellow, through an ever surprising mosaic of colored rock. Finnur, who was to join Roger and me in a month's time near Seattle, would be amused to know how much the dry-desert West could evoke the wet-desert Iceland. Evoke to the eye, that is, for the desert of the West, I was beginning to find, teems with hidden life and supports an incredible community of plants and animals adapted to its exaggerated climate and sudden changes. It is, in fact, a living desert.

We looked for peccaries, the little wild pigs of the border country, but we saw none. There were plenty of ground squirrels and white-tailed antelope squirrels running among the mesquite. We also saw several jack rabbits rather like our big European hare, but longer of leg and longer of ear, fast animals that can leap fifteen feet and sprint up to forty-five miles per hour when pressed by a coyote.

Round a bend, under an aproned butte, we came to the remains of an adobe hut that was slowly returning to the desert. This had been the home of Gilberto Luna, an ancient, almost legendary Mexican who lived in this one spot all his long life—and he died at the age of 106! Mesquite from the desert was Gilberto's staple; its beans his food, and his cattle's food, the stems his house posts. His hut was long and low, cornered with desert stone, wattled with mesquite, and filled in with adobe. The sagging roof would soon collapse; the door was gone and it was black inside, for there were no windows. There had been a small corral, and by it an old buckboard whitened in the sun, its wheels now stilled, but its wood preserved by the dry air. We stepped from the desert's glare into the gaping black hole of the hut's interior, and when our eyes became accustomed to the darkness we could discern the remains of a bedstead and two or three orange crates which had been used as shelves. Nothing more. Behind the hut rose the naked rocks; in front stretched the vastness of Terlingua Flat, the hottest, most desolate place one could have chosen in all the Big Bend for a home. I was reminded again that no animal on earth is more adaptable than man.

In front of us a new mountain, the Sierra Poncè, faced us. Its long cliff (actually in Mexico) invited us, and at the foot of the red-brown wall flowed the Rio Grande again. We inserted the car as far as we could into a grove of cottonwoods and willows (for the heat was appalling) and on foot plunged through the grove to the water's edge.

How shallow was this great river! The drought, and the demands on its water upstream, had reduced it to an olive ribbon of slow mud water, yet there was more flow here than where it reached the sea. Terlingua Creek joined the Rio Grande where the willows grew, and in a moment we were across this creek bed dry-shod.

It was impossible to believe that this stream, the Rio Grande, could have parted the limestone cliff before us. But that is just what it has done. For ten miles the Rio Grande has cut, in a knight's move, across the great mountain, along the line of a huge fault in the limestone. We stood at the mouth of Terlingua Creek and looked up the Santa Elena Canyon. On our left, Mexico's Sierra Ponce; on our right the United States' Mesa de Anguila (Plateau of the Eel). Between them a dark slit through which the river flowed, zigzagging among fallen house-high blocks, hemmed in by sheer 1500-foot walls of purple, brown, gray, and white. A trail led us along the bank and up a rocky shoulder right into the canyon where the stony path hugged the walls. Dropping lower it wound between large boulders until we reached the water's edge. The canyon was as hot as a bake-house; the sun, which had not yet crossed the narrow gap above, blazed down and we found relief only by crouching in the cool shadows of the huge undercut boulders. At length we came to a point where we could go no farther. Here, with Texas under our feet, we could look up and see Chihuahua a thousand feet and more over our heads; so undercut is the great slab on the Mexican side. Adventurers in rubber boats have explored the full length of the canyon, one of three spectacular river canyons within the Park boundaries (Boquillas and Mariscal are the others) and lives have been lost when sudden floods from rains in the mountains have trapped them in the treacherous gorges.

Turkey vultures and ravens floated lazily against the high red-brown walls but small birds were few; several rough-winged swallows skimming back and forth; a painted bunting singing in the desert willows; Bell's vireo singing as if through clenched teeth; house finches and a black phoebe—the very same birds, Roger said, that he had found here two years before.

Finally we were driven from the canyon by thirst, as much as anything. As we were leaving, a falcon whipped by and glided along the mesa, giving us just time enough to make sure that it was a peregrine (and not, as we had hoped, the rare Aplomado falcon).

As James and I recrossed the dry bed of Terlingua Creek we paused to take a last look at the dark mouth of the canyon from which we had emerged. Who was the first to discover this "Grand Canyon of the Rio Grande," we wondered. Cabeza de Vaca, ship-wrecked in Florida, passed through the Big Bend in 1535 after eight years of wandering during which most of his companions died. Did he see Santa Elena? We knew that a party of U.S. soldiers came upon the canyon in July, 1860. Led down Terlingua Creek by Lieutenant Echols, they were ragged and thirsty (indeed, earlier in the month they had almost perished from thirst), when they saw the cool water of the river flowing from the great cleft.

The Big Bend had never before seen such a cavalcade, for with the soldiers and their pack mules were twenty camels, the first camels to set foot in west Texas since the end of the Pleistocene. It was Jefferson Davis, during his tenure of office as Secretary of War, who brought in these ships of the desert to be used as military transports. The Civil War and the coming of the railroads put an end to the experiment; and the remaining camels were turned loose in the arid lands where they managed to survive for many years, contributing much to the legends and folk tales of the desert.*

The camels are now gone, but a satellite remains, *Zizula gaika*— a small blue butterfly from Africa—which apparently came in with the camels in their fodder. *Gaika* has prospered and spread down the Rio Grande as far as Brownsville. We saw small blue butterflies this day which may have been *gaika*.

As we drove up the shimmering, eye-hurting road past the lifeless hut of the centenarian Luna, I noticed a rude wooden cross that had been propped up by a small pile of boulders, but now lay toppled on its side. What compelled Luna to live in this sere desolation all his long life? Did he have something on his conscience and was this his penance? On the other hand, if this was the only place he knew, perhaps he was content. But what about Peter Koch down at Hot Springs? He had known the world; he had once been a newspaper reporter in Cincinnati. What had driven him "ever to the sun on blistering rocks"? Perhaps he knew the whirl of the world too well; centrifugal force may have thrown him to this remote spot, finally to put down his roots. Deeply in love with the austere land, he is the only one who really knows every canyon and peak.

As for myself, I would be very uneasy here. The Chisos are magnificent, no doubt about it, and the park people live in a garden spot in the Basin. But as for the desert itself—there is too much history, or rather, prehistory etched in the eroded rocks. This is a has-been land, not a to-be land. There are fewer plants to clothe the half-naked hills than there have been; fewer big mammals. The bighorn sheep are gone, the mountain lion is rare, and the jaguar only a memory.

* One camel was reported as late as 1940.

Even the Montezuma (Mearns's) quail, the "fool quail" of harlequin colors, has not been seen lately. There is less moisture than there has been, and when the heavens do open up, the waters wash through in flash floods, doing little good, rushing in an unholy hurry to get back to the sea. No, I could not be comfortable here. Nor could I abide the ruthless attitude of some west Texans toward their wonderful state, as exemplified by the eagle killers and those who would eliminate every last cougar and coyote—the same men who would overgraze their own grassland until it is reduced to desert. The Big Bend is a dying land; the name *Los Chisos*—"the ghosts"—seems appropriate for the silent mountains that stand guard.

Such were my thoughts—a bit depressed—as we rounded Rattlesnake Mountain and took the left fork across the Park boundary to the ghost town of Terlingua.

Terlingua was dead. All that remained of the once busy town, where 1000 people had lived before the quicksilver mine ran out, were the rectangular flat-roofed adobe houses of the departed miners, the abandoned mine sheds and plant, and one store. We were to meet many such lost towns in the West. Only two families of Mexicans still lived here. But the store, run by an ancient couple, was still open to the occasional customer. For this we thanked heaven, as, hot and exhausted, we topped up with sodas and cokes.

The big Ford ate the hundred miles of new dirt road to Alpine like a greedy monster. I dozed as James swung it round countless bends, over arroyos, across washes, round canyons, across plateaus. The road, said James afterwards, was a masterpiece of desert engineering, and the car equal to any demand. For miles he cornered in middle gear, near-sliding the long station wagon on the grit surface of the hairpins, foot simultaneously on brake and accelerator for best control.

"Where are we?" I mumbled, when I finally woke from my long doze.

"Back from the back of beyond," James replied. "You've missed some fabulous country," he said, "but fabulous!" A month earlier he would have said "interesting," perhaps "very interesting." He was beginning to talk American.

20

Islands in the Sky

$\mathcal{T}$ HE CONTINENTAL DIVIDE came "not with a bang, but a whimper." No sensational Alpine pass through the high mountains; just a sign on a flat plain between Deming and Lordsburg in western New Mexico at an elevation of only 4584 feet. Beyond this point a drop of water, supposedly, would flow toward the Pacific. James marveled at the pioneers who had pushed west across this vast emptiness— "What faith they must have had!"

Only once had the Ford, our modern prairie schooner, complained —furiously complained. That was in west Texas, where we were forced to lay over for an overhauling. Nothing was seriously wrong —just a congenital difficulty; the car, bought in the East, had to have its thermostatic controls adjusted for high-altitude western driving. But this delay had cost us time; we had to write Carlsbad off our itinerary. We would not see the world's largest caverns, but we consoled ourselves with the thought that it was a bit early in the season anyway; the bulk of the Mexican free-tailed bats, reputed to be two or three million, had probably not yet arrived at their subterranean grotto.

Along the Rio Grande above El Paso, before we continued toward the Continental Divide, James had been struck by the contrast of the irrigated land, man-made oases, man-made green. But he was critical of the towns, or, rather, the approaches to the towns with their wirescapes and confusion of neon signs. But later he wrote in his journal:

> *In all the recreational areas of the United States, official or unofficial, I found no outrage to my sense of fitness. We British are supposed to be very sensitive to "blots on the landscape"; but have succeeded in blotting a lot of our own. Of course, ours is crowded—only the Scottish Highlands have empty spaces comparable with those of the States. But I would like to record here that, in my opinion, public taste in wilderness architecture is as good in U.S. as in any part of Europe, and better than most. The heights of the Appalachians, the Big Bend, Mount Lemmon, and places like them have no screaming neon or loud advertisements. These are kept in their place, in the cities and on the main journeyways. There are too many of them there, I suppose; but somehow they have become a language of communication, a natural, acceptable custom. Each town has its galaxy of discharge tubes, blazing messages of beds, meals, and gas at its outskirts. I had to like them, against a flickering will at first, and at last unreservedly; they warmed the night driver's heart.*

Certainly the neon-lighted tourist courts on the outskirts of Lordsburg warmed our hearts this evening; we were road weary. Although we had ample camping equipment with us we preferred the luxury of a cool air-conditioned motel after the day's heat. We could have slept for ten hours, at least, but we had to make do with six. Before the hours of night had passed I roused James and insisted that we start on our way again, so that we might cover the distance to the mountains while the desert was still cool.

Before us on the horizon, as we crossed the Arizona line, rose the big blue Chiricahuas, the mountain fortress of the Apache renegades and the outlaw gunmen of the old West, the sanctuary of Cochise and Geronimo and Massai; of Billy the Kid and Johnny Ringo and Sam Bass. There they were, in the crystal morning light, rising like a massive blue island from the sea of the desert. And an island it was, in truth, part of an archipelago composed of a dozen similar ranges. They are as much a true archipelago as the Azores or Hawaii, but no surf washes their talused bases; instead the desert, dry and shimmering, besieges their foothills and sweeps across the flats to the next range, twenty, thirty, or forty miles away.

And like islands, their climate, plants, their animals are as different from those of their surroundings as though they were isolated by the sea. The ranges that make up the southern Arizona archipelago have a family resemblance, many things in common, but like islands, each one also has its own personality, its specialties not shared with its neighbors; that is why mountaintops (and islands) capture the imagination of field biologists. The Chiricahuas, for example, are the only place in the United States where the Mexican chickadee, a gray-sided chickadee with a husky voice, lives; here also is the home of the twin-spotted rattlesnake and endemic flowers and insects which have probably been marooned on these sky islands since the end of the

Barrel Cactus

Pleistocene, fragments of populations that must have been more widespread when the climate of the Southwest was cooler.

A modest sign on the main highway pointed the way to Portal, eight miles up a gravel road that crossed the outwash plain. This frontier hamlet, well named, stood at the entrance to Cave Canyon, a dramatic canyon guarded by unscalable cliffs of heroic size, a painted canyon whose red sandstone walls were pockmarked with huge open caves and amphitheaters. Did the Apaches live in some of these caves? Probably not; they preferred the groves of sycamores along the stream bed. On previous trips I had camped in these benign groves and from my sleeping bag had listened to the melancholy hooting of spotted screech owls at night and to the hollow cooing of band-tailed pigeons at dawn. In 1947 I spent nearly a month in these brooding mountains, but could never feel that I really knew them. How, then, could I possibly show them to James in a single day and how could I expect him to sort out all the new birds, strange plants, life zones and niches?

"Life zones—" pondered James. "Why don't we ever use the life-zone concept in Europe?"

"Perhaps because Europe is so much older," I replied.

"I don't follow you."

I explained that it was in Arizona that Merriam first got his idea —at San Francisco Mountain. We would see this peak in another two days. When Dr. Merriam and his colleagues climbed the slopes back in 1890, they found, as they gained altitude, that the bird and mammal life changed. When they left the desert they no longer saw certain species. New ones appeared among the piñon pines. These were replaced by still others when the exploratory party reached the yellow pines and the firs. The birds and mammals seemed to be tied up in some way with the plants, an obvious fact that many naturalists had noticed long before; but Merriam wanted some order or system by which he could describe the situation—that's why the "life zones."*

* Dr. Clinton Hart Merriam separated the area around San Francisco Peak into seven major zones: (1) Alpine; (2) Subalpine (timberline); (3) Hudsonian (spruce); (4) Canadian (balsam fir); (5) Neutral (pine); (6) Piñon pine; (7) Desert. Merriam stated that "temperature and humidity are the most important causes governing distribution, and that temperature is more potent than humidity." Within the next several years, using temperature summations, he extended his system to include all of North America, until he had arrived at the revised zonal terminology with which American naturalists are so familiar.

"I know all that," interrupted James, "but you still haven't answered my question: Why haven't Europeans adopted this concept?"

"Because Europe is older," I repeated. By way of amplification I explained that the concept fits best in primeval country where vegetation has attained a climax and is in equilibrium. It is far less satisfactory in "disturbed" countryside where man has tilled the land or where the original forest has been cut away and the clock of plant succession has been turned back. There it seems to be the "plant form" or vegetational niche that influences the birds and other animals. If the niche—that is, low bushes, open spots, vegetation along streams —can be duplicated in more than one life zone, so, frequently, can the birds. It seemed quite logical, I concluded, that such an idea should have been conceived in wild western North America and not in western Europe.

"Actually," observed James, "there is very little of Europe that can be called undisturbed by man."

"Exactly." Not only have Europeans never embraced Merriam's idea, I thought, but few even have a clear idea of it. When describing bird distribution they often speak of "biotopes." I remembered how the Swedes always pronounced it "be-a-tops." Later I found it just meant *habitats*.

Even though the zones are an oversimplification, they are convenient pigeonholes, and as we climb the mountains they present a forceful sermon in ecology, the relation of living things to their environment.

This morning we had greeted the dawn in the Lower Sonoran Zone where the highway crossed the Ciénega of San Simon, and here vermilion flycatchers sky-larked above the watercourse willows. Now, as we entered Cave Canyon, we were in the Upper Sonoran Zone with a numerous array of new creatures. I doubt if James retained a very clear picture of many of them, except for two "Mexican" specialties—the sulphur-bellied flycatchers that sang from the sycamores in excited duet like unoiled wheelbarrows and the painted redstart, which he glimpsed as it postured among the oaks and flashed its broad white wing- and tail-patches.

"The most beautiful warbler of the whole, beautiful American lot," he commented.

The life zones are not simply a matter of altitude. Here in the mountains the micro-climates complicate the picture. Where cool drafts from the heights funnel down into the ravines, the Transition Zone sends down fingers of pine forest; at the same time the hot oak hillsides above can still be classified as Upper Sonoran. But except for this puzzling modification, the Transition Zone, which is the next cooler and wetter zone, is the one that lies higher up. Here pygmy nuthatches piped among the rough branches of the pines, painted redstarts became more numerous, and another beautiful parulid, the red-faced warbler, put in its appearance.

After we had zigzagged for miles up the rugged mountain flanks to the camp ground at Rustler Park we found ourselves at the edge of the Canadian Zone. Here on the cool north slopes pines gave way to Douglas fir and we were not too surprised when an evening grosbeak flew up from a spring where it had been drinking. Here also were crossbills, pine siskins, and red-breasted nuthatches, all birds of the northwood country, Canadian birds isolated on this sky island. We saw the first robins we had encountered in weeks and the first creepers since we left the eastern mountains.

We walked across a glorious meadow hemmed in by open pine park on one side, and by dense fir forest on the cooler slope. The shadow of a turkey vulture sped across a lawn of grass and irises, larkspur, and lupines. Broad-tailed hummingbirds fed and darted, darted and fed, chased each other like sunbeams across the glade. We climbed to the saddle of the ridge where during several evenings in May, 1947, Herbert Brandt and I had watched the wild turkeys go to bed high in the yellow pines. But we saw no turkeys today; we did not even hear a gobble. Arizona red-backed juncos flashed their white tail feathers in the dim shadows and big dark blue Steller's jays cried *shook shook shook,* reconfirming the fact that we were in the Canadian Zone. Only one more life zone lay above us, the Hudsonian Zone, which clothed the peaks above 9000 feet in a mantle of Engelmann spruce where few birds other than kinglets foraged. We had, in a few hours, touched five life zones.

As we plunged back down the steep slope James seemed deep in thought. "I gather that this is a National Forest," he finally said, "part of the Coronado National Forest. But aside from lumbering, just how does National Forest policy differ from that of the National Parks?"

The National Parks, I explained, are inviolate. Not only are their forests preserved, but all wildlife is protected and grazing is not allowed—in fact all commercial exploitation, including mining and damming of rivers for hydroelectric schemes is forbidden. They are set aside for the 40,000,000 people who visit our parks annually. The National Forests, on the other hand, are not only managed for timber, but can be hunted in and might be used for other purposes —under careful regulation.

I told James of the primitive areas—78 of them, some very large —within the National Forests, tracts where roads are taboo, where no buildings may be built, and where all wildlife, even the mountain lion, is safe. Such an area existed here in the Chiricahuas—18,000 acres of roadless wilderness.

"Do you mean the Chiricahua National Monument?" James asked.

"No, that is another sixteen thousand acres," I explained. "More like a National Park—the same rules apply." A National Park can be created only by an act of Congress. A National Monument, on the other hand, can be set aside by Presidential proclamation on lands already federally owned. What it amounts to is that cultural use supplants commercial use.

When I mentioned that the National Park Service administers about 21,000,000 acres James seemed astonished, but I pointed out that it was actually less than three-fourths of one per cent of the land area of the country.

"I hope you Americans will always hold on to these primitive areas," said James, thoughtfully. "We would give our souls to have some of them on our side of the Atlantic. You cannot realize until you are as crowded as we are how important wilderness values are."

Yes, I thought, as we reached the car; they are a spiritual necessity. The need for wilderness is in most men; there is a strong craving for naturalness in a high-pressure world. That is why our parks have the passionate backing of hundreds of thousands of organized and ardent conservationists, who, as Freeman Tilden puts it, "swarm forth like wasps when someone throws stones at the nest."

June 1

The sun was nearly overhead as we eased the car out of Rustler Park and coasted down the mountains. Roger and I had risen at dawn, and flogged ourselves silly among desert and canyons and life zones and crazy rock architecture and bizarre plants, exotic birds and new mammals. We climbed from the flat burning desert to cool fir forests at nearly ten thousand vertical feet, and rolled down again to the desert; two hundred and fifty horizontal miles at the end of the day. Dead towns, living towns; dead desert, living desert. Roger says that this corner of Arizona has a greater variety of nesting land birds than any comparable area in the United States, and Herbert Brandt in his *Arizona and Its Bird Life* lists no less than 166 species that nest in it. We wallowed in birds; yet these are not what I best remember of the desert border country of Arizona.

First impression: I have been here before, surely. Most English have been to Arizona before—at the movies. Arizona was strangely familiar, and familiarly strange. Across the plains, out of the canyons, around the buttes and mesas, half seriously I expected—almost anticipated—a sheriff's posse, an Apache war party. Little wooden towns like movie sets, with false-front hotels, swing-door saloons—these we found; but the hitching posts had no silent twitching horses; the gun belts, no guns.

This morning we traveled in five thousand vertical feet, from Mexico to Hudson Bay, the equivalent of two thousand horizontal miles and more.

When we left Rustler Park we drifted back down through the firs, and then the pines. We headed west at Onion Saddle down Pinery Canyon, down through the dry oak hillsides to high grassy desert. Down through three life zones we dropped: Canadian, Transition, Upper Sonoran. Turning east we entered the Chiricahua National Monument. "We mustn't miss this," said Roger. "Lots of geology." Here nature the earth-mover is spectacularly at work. The canyon entrance to the "Wonderland of Rocks" is forested by a magnificent stand of dark Arizona cypress and live oaks, indicators of the steeper, higher levels of the Upper Sonoran Zone; but the eye is seduced from these at once by the forest of rocks that dwarfs all vegetation, a mad maze of pillar architecture, a ruined town of a thousand roofless temples that have known no denizens but wild creatures; it teems with turrets and teeth; spires, steeples, and spindles stand in serried steps along, above the canyon sides, soaring sharply into the sky, or towering to titanic toadstool heads, terrifyingly balanced, tempting the traveler to topple them with a thrust. The rock from which erosion has carved Cathedral Rock, China Boy, Duck's Head, Mushroom

Rock, Duck on a Rock, the Big Balanced Rock, Punch and Judy, the Pinnacle Balanced Rock, Thor's Hammer, the Old Maid, and thousands of other geologic curiosities was lava, laid down, flow after flow, some millions of years ago. The flows had settled into layers of differing hardness, later to be gullied and undercut by erosion. Hard caps and blocks stood, umbrella-like on softer, narrower stems; sometimes lay shattered at the foot of stalks from which they had toppled; often perched menacingly over some canyon edge, even over the road. One part of the amphitheater south of Massai Point looked like an army of busbied soldiers charging into the green forest; another like a board of table bagatelle, its pins bent and twisted under some giant's foot. Skittles, cats, ducks, owls, men were carved by nature, the only sculptor who can afford to spend a thousand years at a sitting, and a million years at an assignment.

It is a paradox that the fondest memories of a trip, the lasting memories, are those of the more trying moments—such as the incident that took place after we left the Chiricahuas and headed out across the naked desert for the town of Tombstone. Miles from anywhere we ran out of gas. I put the car in neutral, while we calmly discussed which of us had forgotten to remind the other. It glided on and on and on, slowing down surprisingly slowly. "We've got a breeze," observed Roger, "behind us."

"We'll make it," said I, "if we open the doors."

So with all doors opened, like a square-rigged ship, we sailed four miles to a house, to a kind rancher with a can of gas!

By way of anticlimax, we ran out of gas again before we could fill the tank and hitchhiked for an hour before we found a lonely pump in a dead mining town at the only occupied house in that wrecked landscape of tattered boards and cracked stucco house fronts.

Then I vividly remembered the big pinkish-looking snake—a "red racer"—five feet long, at least, that slithered across the dusty road and stood its ground when we jumped out of the car to make its acquaintance. Never had I seen a more alert serpent as it held its triangular head high on its thin neck, facing us, waiting, weaving slowly, ready to counter any hostile move we might make. "Of course, you are going to take some movies," I said to Roger, but he showed little enthusiasm. He was anxious to get to Tombstone and a tall glass of beer.

Dust devils swirled across the flats; the dirt road seemed aimless, endless. The sense of space was almost frightening and yet, empty as it all was, one had the feeling that it hadn't always been this way. Abandoned settlements, abandoned mine diggings, and abandoned cattle range, where grass had given way to cracked desert pavement, told eloquently that man had been here and gone.

Tombstone was parked cars, arthritics searching for health, drugstores, root beer, and masses of books about Tombstone's gory past. Even Boot Hill Cemetery had been cleaned up since Roger had last been there; the white crosses were all of a pattern. There was the one with the pathetic inscription: "George Johnson—hanged by mistake." And the one that marked the grave of the Clanton boys, all new and tidy, quite out of keeping with the untidy and bloody days of Wyatt Earp. I suppose I should have remembered only the things we came to see, like the fantastic jumble of erosion forms in the Chiricahuas, or my first sight of the giant saguaros. But outstanding in my memories of this hot hazy day are the tombstones of Tombstone, bogus and newfangled though they were—and, also, our empty fuel tank.

In the distance, as we turned our backs on the dreary rock pile of Boot Hill, were the Huachucas and the Santa Ritas, blue-purple against the late afternoon light, like stage-set mountains, or cardboard cut-outs. We wound through hilly desert dominated by sparse gold grass and tall yuccas topped with creamy lily-bells; almost im-

Painted Redstart

perceptibly we dropped into Lower Sonoran Desert with its cactus gardens, and it was here, after crossing miles of flats studded with teddy bear cholla and prickly pear that we encountered the first saguaros. The low sun which flung long shadows across the sands made of each of these tall cacti a sun dial. The giant cactus, one of the most remarkable growths of the desert, is a Mexican plant; it is found within the U.S. only in southern Arizona and a small area of southeastern California. Each individual is a spiny-ribbed leafless cylinder, tapering gently up and down from greatest girth at about a third of its height; and its height is often thirty feet and occasionally fifty. These vegetable monoliths are most numerous on the stony slopes at the edge of the desert plain, which they adorn as obelisks adorn a graveyard, sometimes in clumps, but more often in a wide scatter of single pylons. Many of those we saw had crowns of a dozen or more big waxy white flowers with creamy centers. The bigger, older saguaros had branches which protruded from their waists, running horizontally at first but thence usually curving up—but sometimes down or sideways—and often bearing showy flower bouquets at their tips.

While I was admiring the saguaros, which I thought were the oddest plants I had ever seen, Roger gently reminded me that we had an appointment to keep with the evening owls at Madera Canyon. We paused once more on the plain before we entered this wooded gash which furrows the west flank of the 9400-foot Santa Ritas, as the evening sun shone an orange light. Lesser nighthawks skimmed low over the mesquite and palo verde. Black-tailed jack rabbits had come out for their evening feed and were bounding about wherever there was a patch of edible green. And feeding with the others, we met a great rangy, white-sided creature, bigger than the black-tails, with colossal eight-inch ears without black tips. This was the rare antelope jack rabbit of western Mexico—rare at least in the United States, for it enters the States for a few miles only in New Mexico, and around the Patagonia Mountains and the Santa Ritas in Arizona.

A soft deep hooting from the oak slopes announced that *Bubo* the horned owl was abroad. Rabbits are its quarry; but if the jack rabbits knew the sinister voice they seemed to pay no heed. It was some time before we realized that another owl of the oaks was hooting in the distance, hooting a quiet yet penetrating song, a sequence with a code of four: - - - -, - - - -, - - - -.

"Spotted screech owl," said Roger. "It's Mexican; just crosses the border in these mountain canyons. Nobody found its eggs till 1936—Herb Brandt, of course."

Roger apparently knew this canyon very well and it was here—almost at this precise spot—that in 1939 he had met his distinguished fellow bird artist, Allan Brooks. When Roger drew attention that night to a spotted screech owl calling on the steep mountain slope, Brooks took out after it without a light and was gone for an hour—a bold performance for a man past seventy.

The road in Madera Canyon peters out at about 7000 feet—in the Transition Zone—where fingers of pines reach down among the oaks. We had not stopped long when another hooter sounded off. This one yelped like a muffled puppy. Roger was excited. He listened carefully and then announced, "Mexican spotted owl!" He recognized it from tape recordings he had heard; this was a new one for him. The spotted owl, related to the barred owl of the East or the tawny owl of Europe somehow had always eluded him on other trips west.

Roger said that we should certainly hear the Mexican screech owl, whose call sounds like a bouncing rubber ball, but instead we picked up an unexpected voice. "Listen," he cautioned. He was tense and quick as he picked out the sound for me; a plaintive *boot,* or *boo-boot,* repeated at regular intervals.

"A rare one; that's good," he exclaimed. "Flammulated owl—I didn't expect to hear one below eight thousand feet," he explained. It was a rare event even for him to hear this retiring little owl. Its rhythm reminded me much of our little scops owl of southern Europe, which must be almost its counterpart.

The owl chorus was interrupted from somewhere uphill by the rolling accent of a whip-poor-will. "That's that," said Roger happily after a bit. "Come on, it's late." We suddenly realized we were tired and hungry. But the owls had not finished with us, for as we coasted under an overhanging oak, an excited chattering broke out. The car's lights spotlighted for an instant a couple of tiny forms fussing on a big lateral branch. "Stop!" yelled Roger, but he had no need to shout: I had stopped.

Two elf owls had their nest in a hole and tamely went about their business in the light of our beams. These tiny gnomes are no bigger than a sparrow, six inches long, midget insect eaters known in the U.S. only from the border country of the Southwest. They are certainly commonest in saguaro country, where they live in the wood-pecker holes, but our pair was nesting in an oak over 5000 feet up, beyond the saguaro limit. When Roger met Allan Brooks in 1939 they found an elf owl's nest at almost this identical spot. This tiny, round-headed bird is probably the smallest owl in the world, smaller even than the pygmy owls, a group of owls which live both in western North America and on the continent of Europe.

"Long hours of owling with relatively few adventures is the rule in the big canyon country," wrote Herbert Brandt from his long experience of skillful hunting. Even Roger, no sluggard owl finder, commented on our luck, for as we ended our day we had heard five owl species within half an hour.

"Eighty-four today, old boy," I announced to Roger later that night after totting up my list in a Tucson motel.

"Eighty-four. Thirty-three lifers. What a day!"

But Roger was fast asleep.

21

Desert Gardens

OUTSIDE OUR CABIN, while we slept, the night-blooming cereus, that flimsiest of cacti with the most breath-taking of blossoms, was unfolding its showy white petals to belittle the stars, and, dimly etched against the moonglow, the tall saguaros, also of the tribe of cereus, were opening up tomorrow's bouquets of waxy white blooms. Exhausted, we slept during these enchanted hours when we should have been out there with our jack-lights trying to spot some of the creatures we had traveled so many thousands of miles to see. Here on the desert the scorched wastes come alive when the sun goes down. The real time to see the four-footed ones—the timid ones—is when the moon and stars are out.

"Only mad dogs and Englishmen," I reminded James, when I woke him in the predawn, "go out in the noonday sun." But then, Englishmen (and Americans too) are, in reality, water-cooled engines, capable of sustained activity when other creatures must hide in the shade. Many of the desert animals would be killed by the midday sun in a matter of minutes; they cannot withstand the desiccating effect of the desert pavement, which often reaches 150 degrees, hot enough to blister the tough soles of a barefoot boy. But eighteen inches or two feet below the surface they are snug in their moist, air-conditioned burrows which stay at a temperature of about 60 degrees. It is only when the night air outside drops close to the temperature of their sleeping chambers that they venture abroad.

Everywhere, at midnight, the desert is hopping with rodents—white-footed mice, pocket mice, kangaroo rats, pack rats. The darkness holds a million dangers for these small ones, and a mouse must truly be one of the boldest of all creatures, not the most timid. The odds are stacked against it, but it must eat; it must take its chances while it sifts the dry seeds from the desert gravel. But like the innumerable seeds, the rodents themselves are numerous and form the food base for a legion of nocturnal predators that crawl, run, and fly. At dusk the Gila monster, the only poisonous lizard north of the border, drags its clumsy beaded body from its rocky den and the equally venomous rattlesnake slithers from the protection of the mesquite, or from under a deep ledge. Ring-tailed cats, bobcats, kit foxes, and coyotes compete for their agile prey, while screech owls and great horned owls swoop down silently from above.

A kangaroo rat never takes a drink in its life, but gets its moisture entirely from the dry seeds it eats, so efficient is its water-manufacturing mechanism. The bobcat that eats the rodent gets its moisture, in turn, from the flesh it devours. It will drink water when it can; so will many of the other desert creatures, but water is a luxury rather than a necessity. Only man, the water-cooled engine, who may lose through perspiration a pint or, under extreme conditions, a quart of liquid in an hour, must drink water frequently—or drink Coca-Colas, as James and I did.

Even so, a water hole is the best possible place to see the larger animals. How I wish I had known about the Arizona-Sonora Desert Museum at the time of our visit. There, twelve miles west of Tucson, we could have made our headquarters and there James would have seen some of the things I saw later in the year when I returned to Arizona. Near a small pool at the foot of a twisted saguaro, Lewis Wayne Walker had built a blind and there I spent three fascinating nights. Each night during the hours before midnight a procession of

Cactus Wren

mule deer came clattering over the loose cobble to take their turns at the water. They seemed not to mind the lights which we switched on while they drank, but they obviously did not like the sound of my Cine-Special. At the touch of the button they bolted into the blackness; I suppose it sounded too much like a rattlesnake. Occasionally a coyote on the ridge would set up a wail that triggered all the other coyotes within hearing into a weird paean to the moon. Once one of these dogs of the desert slyly approached the water and I could see it dimly moving back and forth behind the deer, but it could not screw up enough courage to face the bright lights. Once a band of collared peccaries came shuffling and snorting down the bajada slope and for the first time in my life I was able to watch these little wild pigs at a distance of not more than fifteen feet. Pocket mice (I think they were) scampered under my camp chair and a little spotted skunk entered the blind, walked over my feet, sniffed at my trouser legs and walked out again—much to my relief!

All of the struggles, the minor triumphs and tragedies of the eaters and the eaten, take place in the dark, unwitnessed by our eyes. But the dawn when the coyote and the bobcat go home from their hunting sees new life, the hustle and bustle of the birds, who must have their brief hours of activity before the rising sun forces them to retreat among the cactus and mesquite. Palmer thrashers, tan birds with sickle bills, call *whit-wheet!* from the chollas, strangely like a human whistling for attention; Gambel's quail, like small plump chickens with nodding topknots, scurry across the open stretches; phainopeplas, black and silky, sit in the mesquite tops. It was at this magic hour when the deep blue-purple of the night sky was rapidly fading to a green-gold glow above the Santa Catalinas that we started the day where the road north of town crosses the Rillito.

In his book *Arizona and Its Bird Life,* Herbert Brandt wrote: "Down amid the tree growth along Rillito Creek we would occasionally see evidence of stray house cats which evidently dwelled there in numbers and were as fierce as any wild creatures could be." I must have had these animals at the back of my mind when I said "house cat" as a black cat padded across bone-dry Pantano Wash, a bird in its mouth, and disappeared into the brush. The bird looked about the size of a Gambel's quail.

"Jolly big cat," James said. *"Jolly* big cat . . . long cat . . . long tail. I've never seen such a cat."

We looked questioningly at each other, but suggested nothing. About a couple of hours later we both had our "delayed take." Each of us meanwhile had had a quiet look at the mammal *Field Guide.**
"That cat," I ventured, as we were hairpinning up Mount Lemmon; but James cut me short, for he was too involved in heavy motoring to start an important conversation. He settled the car into the straight and said, "I know what you're thinking—"

"There's no doubt about it," I continued. "Twice the size of any house cat—jaguarundi—the black form of the jaguarundi."

We had the privilege of glimpsing this little-known cat in a part of its range where it is very rare. In only one other district north of the Mexican border is it known to occur—Brownsville, Texas. This feline, which ranges widely from Mexico to the Argentine, has a sandy phase, looking like a miniature mountain lion, but the one we saw was the black form—the eyra—once thought to be a separate species.

Zigzagging up Mount Lemmon, the master peak of the Santa Catalinas, we repeated the altitudinal experience of the day before. From Sabino Canyon at the mountain's foot, where white-winged doves cooed in cockerel accents from the flowered saguaro tops and the big green collared lizard sunned itself on the talus (and where

* W. H. Burt and R. P. Grossenheider, *A Field Guide to the Mammals* (Boston, 1952).

James spotted a new hummer with a coral bill, the broad-billed hummingbird), we traveled vertically from life zone to life zone until we
reached the firs, where Audubon's warbler sang and a new chickadee
with a white eyebrow—the mountain chickadee—appeared.

Here among the cool evergreens it was hard to realize that the
desert below was at this moment a furnace unendurable. The scudding clouds, born of the sea, are pulled to the peaks as by a magnet,
and are relieved of their moisture while the flatlands below stay hot
and thirsty. The top of Mount Lemmon, at 9185 feet, probably
averages twenty-five inches of rain a year, while Tucson at 2400
feet gets only eleven inches and sometimes as little as six.

Far below us the desert swept away to the hazy horizon. What an
immense landscape this was, where half a dozen massive mountain
ranges such as this could be encompassed at a glance, yet each one
separated by enormous vistas—great sloping bajadas, and miles and
miles of naked flats.

We took a logging road that wriggled down the other side of
Mount Lemmon, coasted the twenty twisty dusty miles to Oracle.
James seemed to relax in the sheer pleasure of maneuvering a big
car on a difficult little road that darted into canyons, nudged around
spurs, changed its mind and wriggled uphill, thought better and slid
down again. We had expected the saguaros to climb up to meet us
when we dropped to the 4000-foot level; but there were just oaks,
scrubby oaks, all the way down to the yucca flats. Had we left the

Collared Lizard

cactus forest behind? Later we met the saguaro again and the teddy bear cholla, the barrel cactus, and all the rest. We learned that the saguaro does not do well on the north-facing exposures, where the frosts of winter are more severe. It has its limitations, but each giant lifts its arms heavenward as if proclaiming the miracle by which it can survive at all under the relentless conditions imposed by its environment.

Consider how improbable is this creation of the vegetable world: living on the desert it is composed of at least 95 per cent water—ten tons of water are stored in the big ones. Like an animal, it has a sort of skeleton, a cylinder of ribs, somewhat like fishing poles, which enclose the white melon-like flesh. A tough green epidermis, studded with tufts of spines, covers these ribs closely, giving each pylon a fluted aspect, a Grecian column effect. The ribs are expandable; during long dry spells the saguaro becomes unmistakably gaunt, but when the rains come it may quickly suck up a ton of water through its shallow root system, which commands a circle of a hundred feet or more. Swelling out, it becomes a storage tank that can survive for three or four years without another drink. Not even a camel can match that!

James admitted he felt a bit self-conscious as we drove through the groves of giants. They seemed to be watching us, he mused. Most of them held their arms aloft as if in horror or surprise; others, with down-curved limbs, gave the appearance of standing arms akimbo, while one or two seemed to bow gallantly to offer us their bouquets of white blossoms now wilting in the midday heat.

In several places we noticed sick plants, afflicted plants, rotting, dying from a fetid black rot which sloughed off their green flanks and slipped to the ground in a horrid mess. Other giants, now dead, stood with their rodlike ribs exposed to the bleaching sun; the bones of their arms lay toppled like bundles of laths. The agent that introduces this dread necrosis is a tiny caterpillar, the larva of a small moth, *Cactobrosis fernaldialis,* which tunnels into the soft pulp and transmits a bacterium which it carries in its intestines. Conservationists have been very disturbed about all this; there have been some very serious outbreaks which threaten to eliminate these long-lived symbols of the desert from the Arizona scene. But the gilded flicker, and probably that other tree-surgeon of the saguaro, the Gila woodpecker, are fond of a fly that breeds in the decaying pulp; in digging out the flies from the pockets of rot they often clear up the lesion, making possible callousing and recovery—a remarkable bit of natural surgery and cure.

To the east of Tucson nearly a hundred square miles of cactus forest have been set aside as the Saguaro National Monument. Here grow the finest cacti of all, giants two hundred years old, many of them forty-five or fifty feet tall, with half a dozen arms or more. But conservationists again are alarmed, for they note that nowhere in the monument is there regeneration, no young saguaros. In fact, in all my wandering through the cactus forest, I do not suppose I have seen more than two or three really small saguaros. Usually what looks like one turns out to be a barrel cactus with its hooked spines. Although a saguaro spawns its seeds by countless thousands, almost every small rodent and many birds are eager to eat them. Only one in millions, protected by some thorny "mother tree," perhaps a palo verde, germinates and grows. At first it is a tiny twin-leaved dicotyle-don, so minute that the foot of a mouse could crush it; at two years it is a quarter of an inch tall; at ten, the size of an ostrich egg. Only after thirty or forty years, when it attains the height of a man, does its growth accelerate. Then it might slowly, mercilessly, kill off the foster parent that sheltered it. That is why we sometimes see two or three saguaros growing very close together, at quite a distance from their kin; they obviously were protected in their youth by the same mother tree, now gone.

From the air, the desert is a spatterwork of dark specks—polka dots, clusters. Each plant is well spaced, keeping a proper distance from its neighbors, drawing the precious moisture from whatever radius its root system can command. This comfortable, garden-like aspect is dispelled on closer examination, for everything that grows in this meager land seems to be armed to the teeth with spines and barbs. At first glance it would seem easy to avoid all these hostile growths, but unseen nubbins of cholla lie in the gravel, waiting to jump at the touch of a shoe to fasten their painful barbs in an ankle.

To man, the bitter struggle for water in the arid country has been resolved by drilling deeper and deeper wells, but the plants have solved their predicament by other adaptations—or should we say, by their ingenuity—in meeting the harsh terms imposed by this spartan environment. Whereas the saguaro stores its water above ground and has flimsy roots, its close relative, the night-blooming cereus, is frail

Gila Monster

and emaciated above ground but keeps its water tank below the surface, a huge turnip-shaped tuber which might weigh fifty pounds or more. These, and a host of other cacti, store up moisture against the dry spells, protect it from evaporation with a thick epidermis, and defend it with their armature. But they are not the only plants that have sacrificed their leaves; leaves, after all, transpire precious moisture all too freely. The palo verde, the "all-green tree," which stands naked like a big bundle of green switches, has its chlorophyll on its velvety branches and twigs; here photosynthesis is accomplished. But, as if in dim memory of some ancient habit, it does put forth leaves for a brief month in spring, tiny leaflets barely an eighth of an inch long, which are lost in the show of gaudy yellow blossoms. The witch-wands, or monkey-tails, of the ocotillo shed their inch-long green leaves and stand naked while their blossoms continue to burn flame-red. The brittle-bush, during prolonged dry spells, lets its branches die back while its roots sustain life.

In contrast to these austere long-lived growths of the devil's garden are the ephemerals. A few are always to be seen, lavender sand verbenas and other frail annuals, but the real show comes when a rare downpour stirs the spark of life in countless seeds that have long lain dormant in the sand and gravel. Then, in a matter of days, the wasteland is transformed into a flower garden, carpeted—or scatter-rugged—to the horizon with bright magic colors. In from two to six

weeks their gaudy show is over; the desert is again browned-off by
the searing sun, and the fragile ephemerals disappear, completely.
But, meanwhile, new seeds have been produced to lie in wait, perhaps
for another year, perhaps for five or ten, until another life-giving
downpour stimulates the vital germ.

James and I saw no such display; in fact, I have never been on
hand to see it. This year the desert was even drier than I had remembered it on other visits. Even the staghorn cacti did not seem to bear
as many of their waxy pink or orange blossoms as usual, nor did we
see as many of the broad yellow blossoms on the prickly pears, those
Opuntias which lift their beaver-tail segments "like a sort of hot water
bottle display." But, here and there among the rocks of the foothills,
we did see the deep orange-red blossoms of the hedgehog cactus and
other less common kinds.

Because of the slow driving on rough mountain roads James and I
changed places at the wheel every fifty miles. Our road twisted
through an endless series of outcrops, small ranges, and flats, some
sterile and lifeless, others repeating the desert's two main themes:
yucca, ocotillo, and grass, or cacti, mesquite, and palo verde. Pylons
of saguaro, like armies of gray-green telegraph poles marched by
thousands down the bajada slopes while great gardens of teddy bear
cholla, back-lighted by the sun wore countless silver halos.

Switchback, hairpin, curve, hairpin, switchback. Suddenly, as we
rounded a sharp bend I slammed on the brakes—just in time. The
other car slid to a halt only a few feet away.

James, his nerves frayed thin by the heat, nearly blew up. When
we were out of hearing of the other driver, he snapped, "If you
weren't doing fifty that wouldn't have happened."

"Fifty!" I remonstrated. "I was not doing thirty!"

"And what's the idea of hugging the middle of the road when you
should have been on the outside—there was room to pass."

"And go over the precipice? I once lost a friend in just that way—
forced over the edge."

"Well, have it your way," finalized James. "I think you're a bloody
bad driver."

I record this conversation exactly as I remember it, because it was
the only time in all the thousands of miles that tempers flared. But
I suspect James was not really too nervous* about my driving,

* No comment.—J.F.

because he often dozed peacefully for hours on end when I took the wheel.

It was late in the afternoon when we reached the north rim of the great rocky desert. We crossed the canyon of the Salt River, which would be regarded as one of Arizona's most spectacular wonders if it were not for the fact that the Grand Canyon itself was not many hours distant. Slowly, mile by mile, we labored up the Mogollon Rim, the great barrier beyond which the flora and fauna of the Sonoran desert do not pass. Here on the plateau we found ourselves in an endless forest of piñon pines—a green land, for a change, instead of a brown land. Beyond lay the Painted Desert and the Petrified Forest National Monument. Night dropped its curtain of blackness while we were still far short of our day's destination, and we flew on and on.

Somewhere in the endless miles between the Petrified Forest and the boundary of New Mexico, while I was doggedly piloting the car through the empty dark, James suddenly burst into laughter.

"What's so funny?" I asked.

"Look at it," he said, "way out here—miles from nowhere. Right in the middle of all this nothing—miles and miles of nothing. It's so American!"

"What's so American?" I asked, puzzled.

"That—down the road, *there."*

All by itself, out in the middle of this infinite void, flamed a huge neon sign. Dwarfing the building which supported it, it was one of the biggest, most dazzling, must lurid neon beacons either of us had ever seen; it could have shouted down any of those in Times Square or Piccadilly Circus.

All it said was:

BAR

22

Land of the Old People

June 2

LAST NIGHT, close to midnight, we stopped at Gallup in New Mexico. We would never have found the Thunderbird Ranch, our destination, had we pushed on in the dark. It was only the second —and very slight—break in Roger's incredible schedule on the whole of our journey. Apart from this we were sometimes late and occasionally early at our rendezvous, but we always made it.

As we drove back into Arizona this bright morning we found the plateau not as smooth as it had seemed; every now and then it was parted by some erosion-rift; we flew over little canyons and wriggled down big ones. We were in a new kind of desert, a sagebrush desert. Yesterday, in the late afternoon light, we had climbed up over the Mogollon Rim, a forest-clad ridge which forms a barrier between the cactus and creosote-bush Sonoran desert in the south, and the sagebrush desert in the north. The Painted Desert had slid past us in the blackness outside our headlight beams, but this morn-

ing we found it again. Bare, red, brown, blue, patched with an occasional purple or green oasis, the desert made us feel small and lost. Indeed, we *were* lost. Somewhere we had got our directions fouled, and after following an aimless track for miles across a sterile depression, a lifeless moonscape, we met an ancient Navajo with a face as furrowed as the eroded hills. We asked him how to get to Chin Lee, but he did not seem to understand. His watery, uncomprehending eyes searched the inside of our car and his several words were unintelligible. Uncomfortable and uninformed, we drove on. Forty miles from the desert's hilly pine-clad edge we hit a pavement which the desert winds had sandblasted into a pitted, pockmarked, rutted surface. We passed occasional hogans, Navajo houses, that looked like defensive pillboxes. To our surprise and relief we came to a marker that said "Chin Lee" and soon we crossed a green-bordered arroyo and pulled up to the little settlement at Thunderbird Ranch. Roger went directly to the trading post to apologize to Mrs. Cosey McSparron, who had kept dinner waiting for us last night. I sat in the sun and watched the Indians.

The whole of northeastern Arizona, as far west as the Grand Canyon, and also the neighboring corners of Utah, Colorado, and New Mexico, is a vast Indian Reservation, most of which belongs to the Navajos, the great sheepherders, weavers, and silver workers. The Navajos prosper in the desert, putting their hogans where corn can grow, and trading, riding, singing, dancing. They ride in cars or trucks now, these Indians of Arizona. As I lounged in the yard a truck dashed up, braked smartly, reversed into a narrow space between two other trucks; at the steering wheel a young Indian woman in slacks and sunglasses reached across, gathered up a swaddled infant on a papoose board, slung him (or her) over a shoulder, like a rucksack, picked up an empty basket and marched across to the store. In the back of the truck a man on a pile of sacks woke, pulled his sugar-loaf hat farther over his eyes, and went to sleep again. In the store half a dozen black-haired, bang-haired Navajo housewives in blouses with big silver buttons and flowing skirts were carefully, slowly shopping.

The Navajos, in their 25,000-square-mile Reservation (the size of Belgium and the Netherlands combined, or three times the size of Massachusetts), now number more than 60,000; yet a quarter of a millennium ago they had scarcely arrived. They came from the north, with their cousins, the Apaches, speaking an Athapaskawan language. It was not long before the birth of Christ that the Athapaskawans had entered North America across the Bering Strait, the last wave of Asian colonists to the new continent, if we except the Eskimos. In two thousand years they had reached Arizona and New Mexico, their vanguard the warlike Apaches and the Navajos. The Navajos settled in northern New Mexico; the Apaches pushed on to southeastern Arizona.

The Navajos have become the largest, and one of the most cohesive of the surviving Indian tribes because of their remarkable adaptability. Far more quickly than the Apaches they learned from others—from the Europeans, sheepraising; from the Pueblos, weaving; from the Comanches, those fierce Indians of the Plains who came through on their raids to Mexico, silver working; from bitter experience (and Kit Carson's punitive expedition of 1864), the benefits of pastoral peace over hunting and guerilla warfare. They have become better weavers than the Pueblos, from whom they learned; everybody wants a Navajo rug.

The first Spanish expedition to northwestern New Mexico was in 1540, and the first serious Spanish attempt at colonization was in 1598. Both Europeans and Athapaskawans, with their very different cultures, found themselves in conflict with the "Old People," the Pueblos. The triangular contest was over by the coming of the Anglo-

Americans in the nineteenth century; indeed it was over by 1700, when the Spaniards controlled the country, except for North Arizona's Hopi Pueblos, whom nobody has ever defeated, and who remain their own masters to this day.

The Pueblo Indians were the old apartment-house builders of the canyon walls and desert mesas. Before pueblo-builders, basket makers; before basket makers, Stone Age men; all the same people, "the Old People," at different stages of their evolution. Who were these, the first Americans, ancestors of Pueblo, Maya, Aztec, Inca, and whence did they come? We know little more than this: they were Americans ten thousand years ago. It is scarcely possible that they came from anywhere but Asia, and probably they came dry-shod across the Bering Strait's land bridge, as did several other wild animals. Their Old Stone Age life cannot have differed much from that of western Europe ten thousand years ago, save that the Old Stone Age Europeans were artists as great as any since, and there is no evidence (yet) that Old Stone Age Americans were artists at all. Perhaps one day the West may disclose an unexplored cave temple like Lascaux or Altamira, with a frieze of animals of the hunt. It is not impossible.

The entrance of the Canyon de Chelly, flat-floored, sheer-walled, lies not far from Thunderbird Ranch. For about twenty miles the main canyon eats back into the rising land; long side canyons zigzag from it. Not far from the entrance its walls are already nearly a thousand feet high, yet the hill it claws into is scarcely more than a plateau rather steeply tilted. Roger picked up trail directions and we set off at once along the rim. In less than half an hour we had reached a vantage point a thousand feet above the twisting, curving river bed, a broad dry wash of pink-white sand, the alluvium of ages, bordered by bright green strips of cottonwoods and willows. Far below us on a green lawn in a bay of the flat was a Navajo hogan. The great red-purple canyon walls were quite vertical, eighty, ninety degrees steep; even a hundred degrees here and there where overhangs shadowed the cliff face. Smooth, watersmooth, windsmooth was this rock face, stained, striped by storm waters. As we stood looking down, white-throated swifts came gliding along the rim and rocketed by at incredible speed.

We humped our gear down a zigzag trail, an artificial trail carved out of the living rock into tunnels and deep cuttings between the

natural staircases. After a scramble we soon trod the hot sand of the
canyon floor, where black phoebes flitted among the willows. We
felt like Lilliputians as we walked downstream between the Brob-
dingnagian walls. Rounding a corner, Roger saw the White House
first. I did not see it immediately, for I was looking in the wrong
place. It was up in the wall, in a great slot in the red sandstone, a
hundred feet from the canyon floor, and overhung by a smooth
water-stained slab that towered for another eight hundred feet. It
looked like what it was, the ruins of a medieval castle. Its form was
squat and rugged, with straight walls, sharp clean-cut corners, small
square embrasures, flat-topped ramparts. Doors and window holes
were crowned with flat slabs; there was not an arch in the place. Just
below the ledge, chipped into the rock, was a petroglyph that looked
like some kind of stylized bird. I wondered if it was from this figure
that Thunderbird Ranch had taken its name.

We walked through a grove of willows to the foot of the great slab, and there, almost hidden, we found the ruins of another cubist apartment house. This lower village dwelling was far more decayed than the fortress above, whose inhabitants had taken their ladders away and shut up house during the great drought of 1276–99, and never came back. The National Park Service, which looks after the Canyon de Chelly National Monument, does not replace the ladders —except for maintenance and research workers.

At the lower house, we soon found the kivas, the circular stone chambers which alone break the straight-line architecture of the pueblos. For these buildings were, indeed, ruins of some of the earliest buildings of the Old People, the Anasazi, who, about fifteen hundred years ago, started to change their circular cliff-foot pit houses into chambered castles of dressed stone. At first they added rectangular granaries; next they found that big rectangles made good living rooms; keeping the old round pits for ceremonial purposes they later improved them, even built new, huge ones, as sacred clubhouses. But there is no big kiva in the Canyon de Chelly as there is in New Mexico's Chaco Canyon.

The occupation of the Canyon de Chelly by the Anasazi dates back to the Second Basket Maker Time, between A.D. 300 and A.D. 500. About A.D. 900 (as the tree rings in the old house beams suggest)* the pueblos of White House, Antelope House, and Standing Cow were built. They were occupied for four hundred years, through the classic time of pueblo culture (called so, for their architecture was never as good again after the drought). This pueblo time was one of great advance. In A.D. 500 the Old People had their beautiful baskets, grew corn and squashes, kept dogs—although they lived in pit houses, had a throwing stick but no bow, and could not weave; but by the drought they had acquired, invented or evolved apartment houses, religious meeting places, beans, domestic turkeys, pottery, jewelry, bows and arrows, looms and cotton.

When Roger and Barbara first visited our old rectory in Northamptonshire I had pointed out of the window while we were having lunch. "That," I said, indicating our medieval church, "was built before you were discovered." To pile it on, I took them birding in

---

* The dating of the Four Corners civilization from tree rings, one of the great detective stories of archaeology, was the triumph of A. E. Douglass, the Arizona astronomer and archaeologist.

the county that afternoon—at least I told Roger it was birding; but we found ourselves under the Saxon tower of Earl's Barton, a thousand years old.

Now Roger got his own back. "These were good farmers here," he said, "when you were submitting to the Romans. That White House is older than Earl's Barton."

"Yes," I said, "point taken. But Earl's Barton is still used for the purpose for which it was designed."

"So are many kivas in the modern Pueblo country," countered Roger. "After the drought the Pueblo people of the San Juan River scattered far and wide. Some settled on the mesas between here and the Little Colorado—those are the Hopis. Some went south beyond Gallup to the Zuni country. Many went to the upper Rio Grande in New Mexico."

It must have been a great, a sad migration. Everywhere around the Four Corners where the modern states of Utah, Colorado, New Mexico, and Arizona come together the drought struck. It drove the Pueblos from their civilized townships; from Natural Bridges and Hovenweep in Utah; from the fantastic houses of Keet Seel, Betatakin, and Inscription House in Navajo National Monument, and from Canyon de Chelly in Arizona; from Mesa Verde, most wonderful of all the pueblos, with its Cliff Palace (with over 223 rooms and kivas), its extraordinary Spruce Tree House (with 114 rooms and eight kivas), its Fire and Sun Temples, and from Yucca House in Colorado; from the Aztec Ruins of northern New Mexico.

In their new homes the Pueblos continued their ways until some time after the Spanish came, in 1540. For years, in mutual tolerance, they took or bought from the Spaniards sheep, horses, wheat, peach trees, steel, and religious instruction, using the last sparingly. In 1680 they rose and drove out the Spanish from Sante Fé, which was not recaptured for thirteen years. At the reconquest the Pueblos became divided. Many merged with the Navajos; some in New Mexico resettled their old pueblos or established new ones and came to terms with the Europeans; others, in Arizona, fled west to the already occupied mesa-pueblos of the Hopi country, where they were safe from the Spaniards, or anybody else. Here they still pursue a simple agricultural life, and their own peculiar, practical, self-denying religion, and live to ripe old age. No warfare, military or psychological, has ever subdued the Hopis, and doubtless none ever will.

"This evening," said Roger, "we will visit *real* Indians. Real Americans. People who were probably settled Americans before any of your surviving British tribes were settled."

I didn't argue; we have no surviving British tribes. We are as mongrel, ethnically, racially, as are the ordinary inhabitants of any state in the Union—only we became mongrels earlier.

This afternoon we would leave the Canyon de Chelly, the ruined homes of the Old People, and strike cross-country to the mesas of their descendants, the unconquerable Hopis. In the sun-trap of the canyon our gear weighed a ton as we sweated up the cliff trail. As we reached the rim we looked back rather enviously, for humming along the dry floor far below was the sand buggy of the Thunderbird Ranch, returning from a trip to the Canyon del Muerto, the Canyon of Death, where in 1804 the Spaniards had massacred a Navajo settlement in revenge for raids. If we had kept our schedule we should have been on this trip, to see another dwelling of the Old People— Antelope House—and strange petroglyphs on the sandstone walls.

Drinks, glorious drinks, at the Thunderbird; soft drinks, unfortunately, not beer, for Indian Reservation rules reign at the ranch. Roger and I must each have replaced half a gallon of water when we felt restored. We bought rugs and Indian jewelry for our families and drove southwesterly into the desert down the old raiding route of the Navajos.

"The Connellys are expecting us for supper," Roger said, "but it's worth a short stop in this piñon pine country for a couple of things." Our stop was indeed short, but in a quarter of an hour we had found what Roger was looking for, a short-tailed, sharp-billed bird, the gray-blue piñon jay—the "little blue crow" of the piñon pines and junipers. Here we also made a much rarer find, the gray vireo, another juniper bird. I was gradually beginning to realize the planning and care and experience behind Roger's conducted tour of North America; scarcely a mile was wasted. Our apparently casual stop in these pinelands of northern Arizona had, I suspected, been contrived, quite deliberately, at Roger's desk in Maryland the previous winter.

The mountain plateau sloped slowly to the south until the pines and junipers came to an end at the rim of an escarpment; we were at the edge of the Black Mesa. Below us was the desert flat again, the heart of Hopi-land, the big Hopi enclave within the vast Navajo

Reservation. It was arid country. In the distance, far to the southwest, a snow-capped peak rose out of the desert haze. Here, at last, was famous San Francisco Peak, and for the next hundred miles this silvery mass would be on our left, to seduce our gaze toward the horizon. To field biologists it is more than a mere mountain; and even though they may be critical of Merriam's views, they admit there is at least a partial truth in them. Therefore I was pleased to see, even from a distance, the remote peak that inspired the life-zone concept.

Once we were down on the desert, and motoring west, the escarpment kept returning to us. We would cross a flat wash, motor up a gentle slope among the sage, and find the scarp to our right hand again, sometimes five or six hundred feet high, with its flat-topped cliffs rising vertically from a deep apron of broken talus full of shadows.

Perhaps the sun was in my eyes when Roger said, "Hopi village."

I looked around at the cluster of houses and commented, "Bit of an anticlimax, isn't it?"

"I don't mean this," said Roger. "This is Polacca . . . almost new. New houses—new school. But look up there."

I looked up. The mesa was turreted, castellated, a confusion of gray rock. Gradually my unaccustomed eyes sorted out the hilltop into living rock—and pueblos. Hopi houses so subtly added to the rockscape that only their rectangular architecture distinguished them from the natural boulders and ramparts of the cliffs. The Black Mesa here had stretched a long narrow finger between two wide washes, and upon this impregnable natural fortress—First Mesa—were built three villages. Farthest east was Hano, a village that was established about 1720 by Tewa Pueblo people from the Rio Grande after the Spanish-Pueblo war; people who to this day speak a language rather different from that of the other Hopis. Next, and almost continuous with Hano was Sichomovi, dating from about 1750; and on the southwest tip of the promontory, separated by a knife-edge neck, was the oldest pueblo, Walpi, founded about 1700.

Across the Wepo Wash, Second Mesa hove in sight—two more pueblos, Mishongnovi and Shipaulovi atop. Before we reached these, another arm of this Mesa protruded, at its top Shungopavi, and at its foot a collection of modern buildings, the Hopi Day School where our hosts, John and Carlotta Connelly awaited us.

The Connellys teach at one of the Hopis' four schools; they are the servants of these ancient, proud people—servants, and students, for service and study are what the federal government, through its Indian Service, now gives to its most ancient aboriginal stock. To them it also gives roads, fine hospital care, other essential services. It is sparing with unsolicited advice. Religious teaching is not provided; this is the job of the private missions, and ever since the first Spanish priests, four centuries ago, tried to bring Christianity to the Hopis, they have found the fundamental beliefs and customs of these great conservatives almost impossible to erode. Missionaries and laymen alike cannot fail to regard the mores of the Hopis with respect.*

This respect we encountered at once, for the kind and wise Connellys had an almost dedicated attitude toward their masters; they lived for the Hopis. Their job, to teach their children English, reading, writing, arithmetic, and all the other keys to the wide white world without. They had themselves adopted two little Hopi boys, the younger not much older than their own jolly infant. They were helped by Hopi women assistant teachers and a Hopi housekeeper.

"You see," said John that evening after supper, "these people *want* to be Hopis. The young men went to the war, saw it all, and did what they had to do, and did it very well, and when it was over, came back to Hopi life because it was the most natural thing in the world. Many people cannot understand how 'primitives' *want* to be primitives."

"But *are* they primitive?" asked Roger.

"Of course not," said John. "The word is meaningless, applied to a Hopi. You heard me put it in quotes. From no point of view are they primitive. Their material needs are small, because skillfully, easily, they can grow what they want. They're not farmers so much as magical gardeners. If they *really* need something the whites only can make, like a motor truck, they earn the money and buy it. They don't particularly want household appliances, radio, modern plumbing. If they wanted them they would have them. They don't want white entertainment, white food, white drink, white wives or hus-

---

* It would be quite out of place for us, visitors of a moment, here to give an account of Hopi beliefs. The best contemporary accounts are those of Walter Collins O'Kane, the entomologist (and ethnologist) who has devoted much of his life to Hopi study. Published by the University of Oklahoma Press, they are: *Sun in the Sky* (1950) and *The Hopis: Portrait of a Desert People* (1953).

Walpi

bands. They've got something nobody else in America has got—an ineradicable tradition, a tradition of European length, and a tradition guarded, kept safe, partly by isolation, but really because it *works*. They are too individualistic to be truly democratic, and too respectful of personal rights to be oligarchic. They are the only true conservatives in America if [and he turned to me] I can use the word in your European sense."

"Yes," added Carlotta, "and they're just about the only Americans who've got enough *time*. Time means little to them. Seasons—yes; hours—no. Few of them know their own age, but many live to ninety or even a hundred. They have a calm poise that carries them through their lives."

"You'll lose your calm poise," I told Roger, "if you ever try again to average three hundred miles a day on a trip like this."

We talked long that night; of the Hopi doctors who, through long years of experience and much handed-on common sense, have become fine intuitive psychologists; of the new developments in Hopi art, associated with Shungopavi's own Fred Kabotie, the greatest liv-

Hopi Kachina Doll

ing Indian painter, and the recently founded Hopi Silvercraft Guild at Oraibi.

June 3

In the morning Carlotta took us to Old Shungopavi on the crest of Second Mesa. The road to the mesa crest slanted up among the cliffs and reached the top some way from the village. Backtracking along the promontory, we parked the car among the houses. "Don't take your cameras," warned Carlotta. "They don't like their pueblos to be photographed."

We left them in the car. Cameras have been barred from the mesas ever since 1914, when the Hopis began to realize that what was sacred to them—their way of life, their ceremonies—could be to the outside whites "quaint Indian customs."* The proud Hopis are not

* The famous snake dance, the Hopis' prayer for rain, was photographed (at Walpi by E. G. Scott) for almost the first and last time in 1913.

quaint; and nowadays film is politely but firmly extracted from cameras by the watchful guards and dropped over the mesa edge if anybody is obstinate enough to expose it. The snake dance and the Kachina dances (dances in which supernatural beings are represented by wonderfully masked figures) are Hopi mysteries, ancient ceremonies born of the deepest emotion. They differ not at all today from what the Spaniards first saw more than four hundred years ago.

The Old Pueblo of Shungopavi was a queer jumble of block houses at all levels. Here and there curved walls showed the presence of kivas, the secret religious meeting places. Some houses were partly demolished, some building. Some had been built on top of others; the village had no order, no apparent plan; its streets (if we can call them that) twisted and turned around blocks of one, two, or even three stories. Most of the people were away at the fields, or at the summer houses that had been built below the mesa. We sat awhile on a wide patio at the mesa's edge (a dance space, Carlotta told us) and watched an old man, wearing the Hopi's wide hair band, humping a sack up a steep zigzag on the talus slope. A screaming gang of happy little Hopi boys in jeans poured past him down the steep, on some purposeful childish errand.

From Second Mesa the road ran along the plateau for a distance, dropped down to cross a wash, and climbed again to run along the rim to the Hopis' oldest village, Oraibi. Below, on the flat, was New Oraibi, with its modern high school, home of the new renaissance of Pueblo Art. Old Oraibi, at its finger-end of mesa, is a dying village —but not yet dead, though it looked deserted. Most of the young people are moving to the more modern village below. But the older Hopis who remain must take pride in their inheritance of the village, and in some cases the very houses and rooms, that have been inhabited for the longest time of any in America—at least since 1150.

From a respectful, and permitted, distance (on a rock outcrop an eighth of a mile away) Roger and I photographed the oldest village in America through his telephoto lens before returning to Shungopavi.

23

"Something Has Happened Here"

June 3

At BREAKFAST this morning at Shungopavi, John Connelly quietly said, "You English have climbed Everest. It was on the radio, with the news of the Coronation—a beekeeper, they said he was. New Zealander. Name was Hillary, I believe, with a native Sherpa."

"Must be Sherpa Tenzing," I said, and added, "yes, Hillary, English. The New Zealanders are more English than the English."

It was some time before I realized fully what had happened. Hunt's expedition had got to the top; climbed the world's highest mountain ("on the shoulders of nearly a dozen previous expeditions," as I heard Sir John Hunt later put it).

Less than a year before, Roger and I had been with Jack Longland, an old Everest climber of the 1933 expedition. We were on an abortive sea trip to reach and climb Rockall, the North Atlantic's loneliest rock. In the course of never getting there, we had plenty of time for talk. "Will they make Everest?" we asked Longland.

"Yes, I think so," said Jack, "they're taking New Zealanders. New Zealanders have to walk fifty miles to start climbing their mountains; they're the strongest and toughest, the most experienced in carrying enormous weights."

When, a few days later, frustrated in our plans to get to Rockall, we reached that haven in Wester Ross, Scotland, Tom Longstaff's house at Achiltibuie, in sight of the Summer Isles, we put the same question to that great pioneer Himalayan explorer, who had been on the first serious attempt to climb the mountain in 1922. He also said, "Yes, I think so." Thoughtfully, he added, "If they get their final assault camp high enough."

The predictions of Longstaff and Longland had come true. A New Zealander had led an Asiatic to the top, from a camp at 27,900 feet, the highest place on the world's surface that any man has ever slept on.

It was with some emotion, therefore, that I took the wheel of Roger's car across the Painted Desert late this morning. "All this and Everest, too," I murmured, thinking of yesterday's Coronation, and unconsciously repeating the headlines in London's papers that wet but happy day. My mind was therefore, to a large extent, on other things as we waved goodbye to blond Carlotta Connelly and the two little Hopi boys and took the wind-roughened road through the Hopi Reservation, and through Tuba City and the Navajo Reservation, and over the gorge of the Little Colorado and onto the limestone pavement of the Kaibab with its open pine forest. Finally Roger announced: "Here we are."

"Oh?" I said. "Interesting forest. . . . Where are the sandwiches?"

"Let's wait a bit with the sandwiches," suggested Roger.

"Wasn't it marvelous about Everest," I said. "What's this place?"

"Navajo Point, or Desert View, it's usually called. It's just beyond that screen of pines; we have to go down here a few yards."

I went down there a few yards.

The world ended; began again eight miles away. Between the ends of the world was a chasm.

The chasm was awful.

Awe. Time brings awe to the traveler less often, no doubt, as time goes on; for time gives him, too, the accumulated, stored, recorded experience of those who have been before him. With all of these I had prepared myself—words, music, paintings, photographs, three-dimensional color movies, even. Yet all of these were, at that first moment of shock, reduced to a whisper, whispering, "Yes, this is true; this is real; this is it; this is the greatest abyss on the face of the earth; this is the Grand Canyon of the Colorado River." The loud voice (I have never heard it louder) was the overwhelming voice of awe. I had heard this voice before, in many places, some unexpected: on the precipices of Pillar in England or Lliwedd in Wales; on Spitsbergen's icecap and sea-flowing glaciers; among Iceland's volcanoes, lava beds, and geysers; in the flamingo lagoons of the Camargue of France; in the Alps; from the top of the Empire State Building in New York; loudest of all at St. Kilda's incomparable stacks and sea cliffs; even at tiny, lonely Rockall. But never had my awful friend, awe, stood so long at my elbow, so close, as by the rim of the Grand Canyon. Never will it come so close again.

Roger, who knows that I talk too much, says that I was silent for ten minutes. So was he. The first thing I said was, "I shan't want the big lens; I wish I had a wide-angle," drying my eyes under cover of my handkerchief while pretending to dry my forehead.

We had arrived at that time of day, late afternoon, when the sea of silent colors—reds, yellow, grays, and lavenders—was most vivid; when shadows were slowly creeping up the walls, throwing into relief each mesa, plateau, and rocky temple. The scene flattens out at midday. But to describe the beauty of the staggering panorama risks triteness. No painter, even on a giant canvas, has ever been able to give more than an impression. But artists such as Moran somehow have succeeded a bit more than the color camera; for color film is more limited than the eye in detecting the full range of color, particularly in the shadows. Words are not adequate either; one can be duped by the dictionary.

This, the greatest natural wonder of the world, can be reduced to statistics; to geology; to geomorphology; to art, poetry, drama, anthropology, natural history, history. Yet it is far, far more than the sum of these parts. In some ways the most incredible thing about it is the concatenation of circumstances that produced it. The Grand Canyon is a marvelous piece of luck.

Length, 217 miles; width 4 to 18, with an average of over 8 miles; depth from the South Rim a mile, from the North Rim a mile and a quarter. Colorado River at the very bottom, fluctuating between 2½ and 10 miles an hour and even 20 (after storms); normally 18 feet deep, sometimes down to 12 or up to 45 feet deep; 300 feet wide. Bare statistics, these, but fantastic statistics. Something like a thousand cubic miles or more have been taken out of the Canyon by erosive action during the ages, down the river toward the Gulf of California. For the Grand Canyon has been formed entirely by erosion.

At present the river carries half a million tons of silt past the end of the canyon every day; sometimes over a million. Only a relatively very small (though not inconsiderable) part of this silt comes from the canyon itself. Most of it comes from half of Utah, about half of Colorado, and large parts of Wyoming and New Mexico! In the canyon the silt from upriver is one of the chief agents of the erosion, scouring and abrading the rock walls.

Let us consider the luck of the canyon. First, there had to be a big river, with a drop along its course and a plentiful waterhead: the Colorado, the second longest river in the United States (about 2000 miles) drains an enormous area, a high wide tableland on the western side of the highest mountain mass in the United States.

Second, through the ages there had to be a gradual uplift of the land, just not too fast to outstrip the cutting power of the river and deflect it somewhere else.

Third, arid, semidesert conditions in the region of the canyon: arid conditions prevent—indeed forbid—the dense vegetation carpet which in a moister climate would slow down the erosion almost as completely as it would cover the rocks. Farther upstream, of course, the opposite conditions are necessary to produce the waterhead.

All these circumstances seem to have conspired but once in the history of the present world, and the result of the conspiracy was the Grand Canyon, the most humbling of all the wonders of nature to man's pride of power.

No rock in the Grand Canyon is younger than Permian, the period that ended about 190 million years ago, to which belongs the Kaibab limestone of the tilted plateau through which the canyon was cut. But once, six or seven thousand feet of younger sediments lay on top of Kaibab. These were probably removed entirely by erosion from the neighborhood of the canyon before it began—in relatively recent times—to be cut. The rise of the dome, by gradual elevation, was part of the great mountain-building movements in the Tertiary Era, or Age of Mammals, which produced, in addition to the Rockies, the

Himalayas, Alps, and other great mountain chains of the world.

What were the feelings, we wonder, of the Canyon's discoverer, Don López de Cárdenas when he looked out over the colossal abyss in 1540? He had been sent by Coronado to look for the "Seven Cities of Cíbola," where the streets were paved with gold, only to be blocked by this chasm which his men could not cross. In the Canyon, he reported, there were rocks "taller than the great tower of Seville." But his main reaction was one of frustration, not wonder. Cursing his luck, he turned his face toward Mexico; and it was another 236 years before the Canyon was again visited by a Spaniard.

Although the Grand Canyon of the Colorado has been called "probably the greatest visual shock ever experienced by man," there are those who, seeing it for the first time, are left singularly unimpressed. They cannot comprehend what they see until they have taken a mule down the long rocky trail, down through five life zones, to the great brawling river at the bottom.

Quite different was the reaction of a Texas cowboy whom they tell of, who had taken a job in Arizona. One day, searching for stray stock, he suddenly found himself on the South Rim. No one had told him about the canyon. He looked into the awful chasm, bug-eyed, and was shaken by what he saw. Wiping his forehead he exclaimed: "My Gawd! . . . Something has happened here!"

That afternoon on the South Rim, Roger and I went from viewpoint to viewpoint: Lipan, Zuni, Moran, Grandview, Yaki, Yavapai, El Tovar, Hopi. Each point discovered for us a new personality of the canyon, a new range of colors, mosaic of shadows. As we watched from each, the gradual swing of the sun made new shapes and shadows. New capes, buttresses, stacks, and towers emerged from the mad wilderness of rock. At Yavapai, perhaps the grandest viewpoint of all, we felt that the whole of geology lay before us (actually, there *was* more than half of it; more than half of the history of the earth's crust). Here an observation station and demonstration museum had been most cleverly constructed, and a Park naturalist was giving to an interested crowd one of the most lucid outlines of the history of the rocks I had ever heard. He certainly had magnificent material handy! We stood at just a little over seven thousand feet above the sea; and below us were exposed in every detail:

First, the sedimentary rocks of the Permian period, occupying about 1900 feet, or nearly the top half of the canyon, laid down in the 30 million years that ended about 190 million years ago. The deposits of the last 190 million years, as we have seen, are now absent.

Second (with an interruption in time, or unconformity, between them and the Permian rocks above), 500 feet of the sediments of the Carboniferous period, laid down early in the previous 60 million years.

Third, below that, but in some places only, some shallow deposits of the Devonian period, which ended 280 million years ago.

Fourth, nearly 1000 feet of Cambrian rocks, laid down between 500 and 400 million years ago. Between these and the Carboniferous (or Devonian) rocks above was another unconformity, a missing 100 million years (and more) of history.

Fifth, a chaos of faulted and tilted sedimentary rocks of vast antiquity, separated from those above by another unconformity. These are much intruded and metamorphosed by bosses and fingers of granite pushed up, liquid, from undercrust volcanic sources, slowly to cool and crystallize below or within the heavy old sediments. The younger parts of these ancient sediments lie, in places, 900 feet thick, and belong to the Proterozoic Era, for they contain traces of extinct life—the wavy markings made by algae, among the most primitive of plants. Proterozoic means "of the first life," and no known sign of life is earlier than these alga markings. The schist below them has no fossil or clue of life and is placed in the Archeozoic Era; the mud from which it was formed was eroded from lifeless rock by lifeless water, in an era which was probably closer in time to the birth of our planet than to the present.

Here, in a 1000-foot inner gorge, walled by granite and gneiss and these sediments laid down more than 500 million years ago, the Colorado River swirls and roars on its way toward the sea.

Not until the beginning of the Pleistocene epoch, which began not much more than a million years ago—or possibly at the end of the Pliocene epoch, at most two million years ago—did the erosion of the actual canyon begin.

The river has kept pace with the smooth rise of the land, and has had to cut down about six inches in a hundred years—on an average—to do so. The rise has been consistently greater to the north, so that the north rim of the Canyon is now a quarter of a mile higher than the south.

We listened with rapt attention while the ranger-naturalist pointed out the various bands of color and layers of rock, giving their names, and explaining how the steepness of their cliffs reflected their varying hardness. Once an old lady, after listening to the ranger's careful explanation of the erosive action it took to cut the canyon, concluded: "Well, young man, that sounds all right, but you can't make me believe this canyon was dug without human help." Occasionally indignant fundamentalists point out to the ranger that the Book of Genesis states that the world is only 6000 years old and was made in six days.

The evening came quickly at El Tovar, where the hotels and administrative headquarters overlooked one of the boldest, ever changing views. Here the Bright Angel Trail zigzags down to the Tonto platform below. Far down across the inner gorge was the famous Kaibab suspension bridge, the only crossing of the river within the canyon. The bridge (122 tons) was packed down on mules and by humans in 1928, down the Kaibab Trail, a masterpiece of engineering. From the cliffs Roger and I watched the last mule parties on the last zigzags before Phantom Ranch, the guest house in the bottom of the canyon. As the sun set the canyon filled with shadows; each butte and temple and buttress had its last moment of bright illumination and contrasting definition before being quickly engulfed.

Roger's eyes strayed to the canyon edge. "Just the place for a poor-will," he said. "We should get one."

We never did, actually, but Roger's remark reminded me that we were back to normal; neither of us had given a thought to birds for three or four hours. We had been looking at something much bigger.

But next morning we were back on our field routine, for Harold Bryant, the superintendent of the Park, had promised us the morning with the wild animals of the South Rim. What a dynamo was this remarkable man! It was hard to realize that he would soon be retiring from the service. His influence on park policy has insured him a sort of immortality; a trained biologist, he began the training program for ranger-naturalists, and perhaps more than any other living man has molded the National Park Service's attitude toward nature presentation. Roger is firmly convinced that the most effective single contribution to conservation education in America is made by the

National Park Service and its ranger-naturalists—dedicated men who do their work on a surprisingly slim budget.

In the sunny forest we met a party of band-tailed pigeons, big *Columba* pigeons, which flew up from a place where the deer came to drink. We heard their hollow cooing, more owl-like than that of other pigeons. Bryant was proud of these heavy, gentle birds, and of a rare warbler that we encountered at the same time, Grace's warbler, a gray-backed, yellow-throated, trill-songed bird that is restricted, in the U.S., to the pine-clad mountaintops of the Southwest.

The most distinguished resident of these tall open pines is not a bird but the Beau Brummel of all American squirrels—*Sciurus aberti* —the tassel-eared squirrel, a large gray animal with a red back and marvelously tufted ears, which give it a look of Britain's perky native red squirrel. It lives in just a few mountain areas of the Southwest, the most continuous of which is the dome through which the Colorado River has cut. Sometime in the distant past, when the river gorge became too broad to cross, part of the population of tassel-ears became prisoners on the North Rim. Separated, they became different;

the northern form, known as the Kaibab tassel-ear, has a black belly and a stunning pure-white tail; the animal of the South Rim, Abert's tassel-ear, is white below with a tail black on top. We finally discovered one of these aristocratic squirrels crouched on a broken-off branch of a towering pine. From its high perch it could undoubtedly look out over the canyon to the North Rim among whose pines its relatives live. Only fifteen miles separate them, but it might as well be a thousand; they are separated for ever.

The thirteen Spaniards under Cárdenas, who were the first white men to see the Grand Canyon in 1540, were not alone in their failure to get across. The canyon is no great barrier for birds, though some, like Grace's warbler, reach the limit of their range on one side of it. But the Colorado River is an impassable barrier to many mammals, as many naturalists have noted, particularly the great collector, Edward A. Goldman.* During his lifetime Goldman described over 300 North American mammals, mostly geographical races—more than had anybody else then living. There was nobody better qualified to analyze the position of the great gash of the Colorado River as a faunal barrier.

The Grand Canyon National Park's sixty species of mammals are distributed in zones; the rodents of the canyon bottom (where the climate closely resembles that of central Mexico!) are quite different from those of the rims. Mammals that fly and swim, naturally, are not found to be racially divided by the great river. And some sedentary forms evidently crossed it somehow. But it is most interesting to consider the large number that *are* separated by the staggering gulches.

The Colorado River is the western and northern barrier, for instance, of the Yuma antelope squirrel; of three forms of pocket gopher; of four species of pocket mice; three woodrats; and of a field vole.

Species to which the Colorado River forms an eastern and southern barrier are the rare dwarf shrew, the least chipmunk; three pocket mice, the Great Basin kangaroo rat; and a field vole. Of the pocket mice Goldman wrote, "The upland species thus confronting one another across the river are all widely divergent, and the time measure of their separation must be enormously long."

* "The Colorado River As a Barrier in Mammalian Distribution," *Journal of Mammalogy,* 18 (1937):427–35.

Many sedentary ground mammals are represented on the two sides of the Colorado River by forms that amount to geographical races rather than full replacement species. Species having such separated forms are the kit fox, the cougar, the white-tailed antelope squirrel, the cliff chipmunk, the Colorado chipmunk, the valley pocket gopher, the little pocket mouse, the Merriam and Ord kangaroo rats, the grasshopper mice, the canyon mouse, and the desert and bushy-tailed woodrats.

But the most vivid example of all these "divided mammals" is the handsome squirrel we had seen this morning in the pines.

It can be seen that to an evolutionary zoologist the Grand Canyon and the rest of the Colorado River's gorges form the apparatus of a great natural experiment in geographical isolation. Below the canyon, where the barrier narrows, the replacement forms may be divided by only a few hundred feet of space, but by a million years or more of history.

Grand Canyon is a perfect park, not only in its setting, but in its administration. Railhead, roadhead, camp ground, cabins, and hotels saw nearly 750,000 visitors in 1952, who left the Park satisfied, refreshed, emotionally stirred, and with another stake in America. And the attitude of the visitors, since the Park was established in 1919 (it had been a National Monument since 1908), has been such that wild creatures walk and run and fly within its boundaries with no fear of man. "Extreme caution should be taken when driving along the park roads," writes the Park Service guide. "Squirrels are tame," it adds, "and their existence is imperilled by fast driving. Many deer range the forest and sometimes the highways, and care should be taken not to hit them." The mule deer are almost domestic; for a long time we watched a doe wandering along the East Rim Drive, making friends with the visitors. In a clearing in the pines a pygmy nuthatch perched to eat peanuts first on Harold Bryant's finger, then on Roger's, then on mine.

One of the differences between the comparatively old National Parks of the United States of America and those of Great Britain, which are all very new, is that the great North American parks have had time to become nature reserves. In Great Britain many naturalists still talk as if there was a fundamental incompatibility between the national park and the nature reserve. "Keep them separate," has been the cry. "You can't have one within the other. People and sensitive, rare wild animals and plants will never mix."

But they *do* mix. All over the States the National Parks are thronged each year with thousands—millions of visitors.* They pour in by automobile, by bus, and on foot. And when they come—whether they come from country or town—they behave in a special way. Many know nothing of animals or plants or geology, and have decidedly queer ideas about scenery. But the great American public, the most powerful and individualistic public the world has known, becomes in the National Parks deeply respectful, orderly, extraordinarily tidy, obedient to instruction and trustful of advice. Nobody dragoons them, shouts at them. There is a minimum of regulation and warning. Yet, with few exceptions, this public assumes, on crossing the Park boundaries, a new code of behavior—almost a new tone of voice.

In the Parks a visiting lumberman may scan the great standing trees with thought of cubic feet; seeing a deer cross the road, a hunter may reach for a nonexistent gun; a housewife stretches as if to pick a flower. But all these urges are quickly inhibited by the special feeling of the special place, are swept away by pride and wonder. And why? Because of the presentation, and education by the National Park Service. Because of the formal entrances to the Parks, imposing without undue magnificence, with controlling rangers ready with leaflets and information. Because of the Park naturalists who lead field trips and give movies and evening lectures at the hotels and camp grounds. Because of the museums, exhibits, pamphlets, and books. Because of the careful control of the concessions, with most adequate feeding, sleeping, and shopping facilities that serve the customers without bringing any indignity to the Park. Because of the excellent roads and parking lots, engineered so as not to mar the landscape. Because of inviolate wilderness areas where no roads shall be built. Because of the well-laid-out picnic and camping grounds. Because of well-marked trails. Because of the things, in fact, that are almost or entirely lacking in our own national parks at present. Sometimes in Britain, these seem parks in name only, their boundaries unknown to the public, their dedication still flaunted and their use abused by schemes for hydroelectric power and exploitation which they were supposed to be created to prevent. Perhaps we in Britain think it's

* 46,000,000 in 1953.

vulgar, or something, to make a park act as a park, but until we do, they won't *be* parks. A park is not nature wrapped in a plastic bag and filed away in the freezer, but nature served up, to nature's best customer. A customer does not defile or waste the goods he saves and works to buy.

24

From Inferno to Valley of Torture

N<small>EARLY</small> a hundred years ago, when Brigham Young proposed to bind the Mormon empire more closely, he called upon some of the outlying colonies to pull up stakes and join him in Utah. Heeding the summons, a devout group of Latter-Day Saints set out from San Bernardino, California. Leaving their fertile valley they crossed Cajon Pass into the Mojave, as weird a desert as one will find anywhere, a desert in which the dominant plant is a sort of tree, yet not a tree, a giant yucca twenty to forty feet tall. They named it the Joshuatree. An earlier traveler, Captain John Frémont, pronounced it "the most repulsive tree in the vegetable kingdom." But to the Mormons, who frequently encountered it as they progressed northeastward toward their promised land, it became a symbol, a prophetic figure whose wildly gesticulating limbs seemed sometimes to point the way, sometimes to lift heavenward in a gesture of hosanna.

Some hours after leaving the Grand Canyon, before James and I

crossed the turbid torrent of the Colorado into California, we passed a few scattered Joshuatrees. In one or two places we even saw the Southwest's two strangest "trees," the saguaro and the Joshuatree, growing together. In the post-Pleistocene days of the giant ground sloth, *Nototherium,* the Joshuatree apparently grew over a much wider area. We have, as evidence, its leaves in the fossilized dung of this extinct beast found in Gypsum Cave, Nevada. Most of the modern groves are probably relics. To see a great forest of the big yuccas one must invade the Joshua Tree National Monument, a 1344-square-mile section of the Mojave which has been set aside for the preservation of the largest existing stand.

To think of yuccas as lilies is not easy, yet they are bona fide members of *Liliaceae*. But instead of symbols of purity or peace, they are arsenals of defiance. Each arm of a Joshuatree, for example, clutches a handful of daggers. Other yuccas go by the appropriate name of Spanish bayonet.

As we drove into the gathering dusk I told James about the *Pronuba* moth and the yucca, one of the most perfect examples of mutual symbiosis—mutually advantageous partnership—known to biologists. Each of more than twenty species of yucca in the Southwest has its own specific *Pronuba* (or *Tegeticula,* as some systematists now call it). Yucca pollen is too heavy to be wind-carried, so the moth performs the vital role. Collecting a pellet of pollen, it carries it on its head to another blossom and crams it onto the stigma, the organ of fertilization. Then, crawling down the outside of the blossom, it punctures the funnel-shaped ovary and lays its egg. Without the moth no fruit would develop and without the fruit no larvae would survive. Countless insects pollinate flowers, but the *Pronubas* are the only ones which seem to do so deliberately, almost as though they understood the process.

We wondered whether some of the moths streaking before our headlights could be *Pronubas.* The bright channel of light probing the roadside ahead not only spotlighted the night insects but also picked up the eyeshine of small mammals. But we spotted far more shiny beer cans than animals, mementos left by the great traveling litterbug. Once a kit fox, small and huge-eared, darted from the brightly illuminated highway into the wall of blackness. We saw no kangaroo rats, but later these queer rodents, like miniature kangaroos with ruby-red eyeshine, would be abroad. They would emerge when the temperature of the night air dropped to approximately that of their air-conditioned burrows where temperature and humidity are fairly constant.

The best way, I thought, to see these noctural creatures would be to spend the night on the desert, to camp somewhere in the yucca forest. If we were lucky we might even see *Xantusia,* the desert night lizard. An attendant at a gasoline station where we stopped advised us against this. We would never find our way over the mountains to the Joshuatrees in the dark. We decided to wait until morning. James seemed relieved. He much preferred to spend the night in one of the air-conditioned motels at Indio.

The proper way, I knew, to enter the Joshua Tree National Monument was to the north by way of the town of Twenty-nine Palms. But it meant a drive of many extra miles. The map showed one or two questionable roads entering from the south, but if we took one of these we must climb formidable canyons. Mountains, the most sterile lifeless rock piles imaginable, stood like a jagged wall between us and the Mojave where the Joshuatrees were. The Ford took things very well at first, but the old mining road which we elected to follow soon became so rough and broken that I turned the wheel over to James. A better driver than I, he enjoys the challenge of tricky roads; hadn't he maneuvered the toughest roads in the Scottish Highlands? But the Highlands were never like the San Bernardinos. The sun beat down upon us unmercifully; there was no shade anywhere. We were not surprised to learn later that in these scorched hills that rim the Salton Sink, Hollywood had chosen its locale for a filming of Dante's Inferno. It was, we agreed, a searing hell hole. The road became rougher at every switchback. Rocks banged and scraped the bottom of the car; we feared the fuel tank might be punctured. When we came to a place where flash floods had swept the roadbed completely away even James gave up. We turned back, down the canyon, into the dreary greasewood plains. The morning was now too far advanced to make the long swing around by way of Twenty-nine Palms and also go to the Salton Sea on the same day. To James the great Joshuatree forest was to remain somewhat of a myth.

An hour later and thirty miles to the south, as we rolled down Highway 99, we first glimpsed Salton Sea; blue and shimmering it lay in the desert on our left. Thirty miles long, and covering approximately 300 square miles, it is about the size of the Dead Sea. This salt lake, whose shoreline is 237 feet below sea level, arrived—yes, arrived—fantastically, dramatically, and violently, in 1905-6.

The intense noonday heat was too much for James, who dozed while I drove. He insisted he is a Viking by nature, attuned to the subarctic, not to this godawful climate. When we stopped at a wayside stand for a glass of cool orange juice we were told that the summer's heat had not really started. Temperatures often reached 120 degrees.

Little wonder the first Spanish explorers under Melchior Díaz had called the Salton Sink the "Valley of Torture." Sent from Mexico by Coronado in 1540 to search for the Seven Cities of Cíbola, they found instead, a dreadful desert, so hot and dehydrating that few of the soldiers survived. Scalding water bubbled forth where they had hoped for cool springs. Great brown mud bubbles belched and popped their foul gases.

In those days there was no water in the sink. There had been none, it is believed, for at least 100 years prior to that date. Nor was there water for the next three centuries, not until 1900, when canals were built to divert irrigation water from the Colorado River into the lower end of the desert. This area, rechristened the Imperial Valley, soon became one of the richest agricultural regions on earth, where successive crops could be harvested throughout the twelve months. But in 1905, the capricious Colorado widened its entrance into the irrigation canal. Makeshift dams were built, but the river swept them aside. By June half of the river was pouring in and a great sheet of water which rose several inches a day was collecting in the lowest part of the Salton Sink. The settlers soon realized that they would have to stop it at all costs before their homes and farms were submerged. They struggled to close the gap with steel, concrete, and boulders. A huge bucket dredge was ordered from San Francisco, but before it could be delivered the great earthquake and fire of April, 1906, leveled San Francisco and destroyed the dredge. Meanwhile 100,000 cubic feet of water per second were pouring into a sea already 400 square miles in extent. Gorges, some of them 1000 feet across, quickly cut their way into the highly erodible desert. Four times as much earth as was dug from the Panama Canal, it is estimated, was washed from these cutbacks into Salton Sea. President Theodore Roosevelt declared a national emergency. Stubbornly, day by day, month by month, men fought to divert the Colorado with dynamite and thousands of carloads of rocks. Just as the battle seemed won, a flash flood pushed everything aside and the Colorado again poured in—this time through a gap 1100 feet wide. But eventually even this breach was brought under control.

By 1920 the sea had subsided to nearly its present size. Engineers called it their "tamed" sea, one which they could control by floodgates.

Like all bodies of water in arid country where water is precious it soon became a bird paradise. Ducks, geese, pelicans, and other water birds flocked in by hundreds of thousands. During the early twenties, unsuspected by ornithologists, a phenomenon was taking place. Gull-billed terns, which had never before been recorded from the West, somehow found Salton Sea. It was a magnet—an ecological magnet. The saline waters, bordered (at the south end) by broad fertile fields where they could hawk for insects, exactly suited their needs. When ornithologists discovered them in 1927 there was a thriving colony of five hundred pairs.

Shortly after we had stopped for the orange juice, several miles north of the town of Brawley, I spotted a signpost with the familiar symbol of the flying goose. It pointed the way down a dirt road to the federal waterfowl refuge at the southern end of Salton Sea. James, who had dozed off again, was jolted into consciousness when we left the smooth concrete.

June 5

It was midday when we reached the refuge. Lord! How hot it was! Roger's friend at the headquarters, a capable young man, Edward O'Neill, seemed to be quite accustomed to this sweatbox. But he complained that to manage a refuge nowadays one has to be not only a biologist and a public relations man but also an engineer and a dirt farmer. We had noticed the tractors and other heavy equipment on our way in. The big corner of Salton Sea occupied by the refuge was largely covered with salty water until the present network of dykes, sluices, and control blocks was established; hundreds of acres have been planted to barley, vetch, and wild millet to divert the hordes of hungry ducks from descending on the surrounding farmlands.

The refuge, covering nearly 60 square miles, was established in 1930 for the benefit of wintering waterfowl, of which hundreds of thousands (if not millions) visit the Salton Sea, attracting hunters from most of southern California and beyond. There is no doubt that refuges and food are vitally necessary on the western flyway. The human pressure on the duck population is very great. In California, where some duck hunters have old habits (many wrongly think there are still as many ducks as there used to be), where farming is on the move, and the human population is furiously increasing (millions have poured into the Golden State since the war), the problems of game management are becoming really acute.

O'Neill and his assistant, Eugene Kridler, took us in the pickup truck, with a boat on its back, to a broad earthen causeway separating the island-dotted arms of the Sea from a reclaimed marsh. In a

Avocets

shallow lagoon a large tame herd of avocets and stilts were feeding; the birds were hurrying about in short noisy flights, sweeping, dipping. We had not seen so many herons since we left the coast of Texas— six species were present. There were also a few white-faced glossy ibises. Among the reeds were moorhens (sorry—Florida gallinules I must call them here, even though this is California. Roger points out that the name "moorhen" is no better because, even in England, they don't live on moors. Why not some compromise like "red-billed mud hen," or—can't somebody make up our minds?). In the deeper coves there were a few eared grebes, but nothing like the numbers to be found in winter. O'Neill told us that an aerial survey in January had revealed at least 500,000 of these little divers peppered over the open lake.

A novelty was my first western grebe—a counterpart, perhaps, of the European great crested grebe—a very large black and white bird with the slenderest and longest neck of all the grebes. Roger spotted a group of fulvous tree-ducks, long-legged, almost goose-like ducks, which fled with whistling cries. Even though winter is the season for ducks here, we saw mallard, gadwall, shoveller, redhead, buffle-head, and ruddy duck. The buffle-head, a male with big white head patches, was weeks late in his trip north—perhaps a bird "pricked" by shot.

We launched the boat and the outboard into a channel which took us through the fringe of marshes to the wide water. We were amazed to see clusters of barnacles attached to the partly submerged stalks of bushes, as much at home as though they were on pilings in the Pacific. Barnacles in the desert! How did they get here? O'Neill said they had apparently come in during the war—about 1942—on the pontoons of navy P-BY flying boats which used the lake as a base. Now barnacles are everywhere and can even be found attached to such un-nautical supports as sagebrush, a desert shrub which is some-times inundated by the Sea's gradually rising waters. In fact, because of enforced changes of diet, the barnacles have already developed definite physical changes, leading one authority to bestow on them the subspecific name, *saltonensis*. Well—it seems just a bit hasty! Mullet, anchovies, and several other introduced salt-water fish are flourishing in water which now has a salinity of 3^1_3 per cent—near that of sea water. We might predict that in the long years ahead, when the lake stabilizes and evaporation concentrates the salts still further, as has happened in Great Salt Lake, these inhabitants of the Sea will die out. Roger tells me that the water of Great Salt Lake supports only brine shrimps and brine flies.

O'Neill piloted our boat to what must be a secret island—a muddy island close to the west shore of the Sea. This is one of the most curious bird islands in North America. The Salton Sea has been in existence for only half a century, yet the white pelican, gull-billed tern, and the laughing gull, crossing extensive deserts, have all found it! There is no other nesting place of any of these species within hundreds of miles. The white pelicans arrived in 1907, the year after the Sea was formed; their nearest known breeding colony at that time was 200 miles northwest, and is now much farther away. Probably the gull-billed tern nests on islands in the Gulf of Cali-fornia, otherwise its nearest breeding place is in Texas, a thousand miles away. And the nearest breeding place of the laughing gull (which was first noticed here in 1928) is also on the Texas coast, across vast deserts and mountain ranges!

These curious outpost breeding populations were all together on the same small island. In earlier years the pelicans had nested farther out in the lake on a small barren island, seemingly secure. But there is no security today, even in the wilderness. Atomic-energy testing

installations (of all things!) forced the pelicans to move from their island to this less desirable island, closer inshore.

When we ran our boat's nose up on the mud and flopped ashore, the place was singularly quiet. Where were the pelicans? There were a few gull-billed terns around. The laughing gulls were at home too, though we never saw more than eight individuals, and found only one nest, with two eggs.

Warden O'Neill told us that earlier in the season there were 25 to 30 pelican nests on the islet. But these had been washed out by high water; and we saw only the remains of a dozen eggs or so. Our eyes soon told us plainly that there had been another, more recent, tragedy. Broken eggs, much smaller than those of the pelicans, lay scattered about. In dismay we went from nest to nest, only to find smashed eggs in most of them. What had happened? Had raccoons raided the colony? We looked for their handlike footprints but could find none at first. We picked up seven dead gull-bills; each had been neatly decapitated. Had the big Caspian terns attacked their neighbors? Of their nine nests only one contained broken eggs. Very puzzling. Finally O'Neill pointed out the unmistakable foot-prints of a raccoon; and we could only deduce that these animals, attracted by the pelican eggs, had raided the island after the storm and caught the gull-billed tern colony in full occupation. We counted no less than 207 gull-billed tern nests, with one, two, or three eggs. No less than 157 of the nests—three-fourths of the lot—contained at least one broken egg. In some, all three eggs were smashed. There was no means of telling how many eggs had been taken from the other 50 nests that contained unbroken eggs. A few of these were still being incubated; and one single lonely nest contained one live young.

A raccoon raid, like a wolf- or rat-raid, or a man-raid, of course, can result in the destruction of far more life than the raider can eat. These animals seem exceptions to the general run of predators, which kill only what they need and have a more adjusted relationship with their prey. How vulnerable were these rare birds on their special place! The only other birds besides the terns and laughing gulls breeding on the island were three pairs of stilts. Their clutches of three, four, and five eggs were untouched.

The gull-billed tern colony of the Salton Sea, when discovered in 1927, had about 500 nests. In 1937 it had less than 200; in 1940 up to 250 pairs were about; and in 1942 about 75. So the population of 1953, with 207 nests, was about "normal"—but how vulnerable!

THIS RATHER SINISTER little episode of the terns which James describes seems very much in keeping with Salton Sea. It is a rather violent place, just a bit terrifying—and a bit reassuring. A place of abundant life in the midst of barren desert; a place of regeneration and rebirth, but also a place of bitter uncompromising struggle and competition. The fabulous green fields, producing crop yields second to none on earth, have been wrested from the wasteland by prodigious human effort, but in the attempt to exploit nature there have been penalties. Ducks by the thousands (at times, hundreds of thousands) —mostly American wigeon which are more addicted to grazing than any other ducks—sometimes flock in by night and strip entire alfalfa fields before dawn. In the files of the Fish and Wildlife Service in Washington, D.C., I have examined reports such as these: "along the west road ducks stripped 70% of a 160-acre field"; "about 200 acres damaged by puddling"; "150-acre plot about 80% stripped." Little wonder there has been so much pressure in California to liberalize the bag limits of waterfowl—some would even have the refuge abolished. A few duck hunters, thinking only of this season's ducks, go along with these pressure groups, but others who want their sport to continue back up the Fish and Wildlife Service in its efforts to reclaim submarginal land upon which diversionary foods (buckwheat, etc.) can be grown. In California the Fish and Wildlife Service not only plants great acreages of these buffer crops for the waterfowl but actually employs "goose cowboys," who, using helicopters, herd the geese from agricultural fields onto the refuges.

Since 1948, and particularly since 1951, a puzzling thing has been happening to Salton Sea. The waters are rising again—at the rate of a foot and a half a year. The waterfowl refuge has already lost 12,000 acres, nearly a third of its original area. The runways, piers, and docks of the 3,000,000-dollar atomic energy test station on the lakeshore have had to be rebuilt at great cost, but inasmuch as it is the invisible taxpayer who pays, we have not heard a howl such as has gone up from the embattled farmers who are losing their land. Some have sued the irrigation authorities, insisting that they are responsible by not regulating the flow of waste water properly. As a matter of fact, no one really knows for certain what is happening. The more wide-eyed ones believe that the Gulf of California—the whole ocean—is seeping in through subterranean channels. The most likely explanation is that after years of irrigation the spongy subsoil has reached saturation, resulting in a slowly rising water table.

25

The Cliffs of Coronado

Darkness caught up with us in the Laguna Escarpment after we left the low depression of Salton Sea. These arid mountains were the final barrier we must cross before reaching America's western ocean.

We arrived at La Jolla so late that we did not get our first sight of the Pacific until next morning; there it was, from the bedroom, as large as life and twice as natural. James commented that it might have been the Atlantic, with western gulls giving a careful imitation of black-backs along the shore. Our host, Dr. Carl Hubbs, informed us that the big launch of the Scripps Institute of Oceanography was to depart shortly for Guadalupe Island on a seal survey. Therefore we would take a smaller boat for our trip to the Coronados.

After an early breakfast we drove to the naval dockyard, where the launch was waiting. Lewis Wayne Walker was already aboard. While we set sail from the harbor he brought us up to date on his recent activities—the new desert museum that he was helping Bill Carr develop at Tucson, Arizona, and the condors he was trying to capture for Belle Benchley, who hoped to insure their survival through avicultural methods at the San Diego zoo. But the bird islands of Baja California were his favorite theme; he certainly knew more about them than anyone else. He had landed on the Coronados many times. Standing in the bow, with his hair streaming in the fresh breeze, he pointed out a procession of Heerman's gulls flying low over the waves. These pretty gulls, slate-gray with whitish heads and red bills, were on their annual pilgrimage from the Mexican islands far to the south where they had nested; some would travel northward the full length of the Pacific Coast of the United States to Puget Sound. We kept a sharp lookout for albatrosses, but saw none of these saber-winged mariners from the central Pacific. However, there were many sooty shearwaters, small dark relatives of the albatrosses, which had come a long way from their natal home in the neighborhood of Cape Horn or perhaps New Zealand.

James was excited, because the mounds that loomed on the sea horizon to the south of us were his first Pacific islands.

June 6

At one time or another I have seen all the islands of England, Wales, and Scotland, and many of Sweden, Norway, Spitsbergen, Bear Island, and Iceland. Many's the time I've seen a new rock, looming up across a new sea, above the bows of a boat. But the thrill never lessens; here were Mexican islands, in a new ocean, above the bows of a U.S. boat. Around me the natives (U.S. natives) chattered excitedly: Lorna Hubbs checking our stores and equipment, Carl, the icthyologist, talking to Roger about fellow scientists and fellow science. Lewis Walker and I watched the sea, and the great Coronado rocks creeping near.

There are four islands of the Coronados, whose northern point is three miles within the Mexican border; they are about seven miles offshore and twenty-five from San Diego. We visited South Island first; it is the largest, about two miles long and 672 feet high, and on its seaward side, half enclosed by a sweep of shattered, slabby cliffs is a beach. Skillfully the ship's crew landed us from a whaleboat where the rocks formed a steep staircase at the edge of the heaving water. We scrambled up, crossed a shoulder of rock, and found ourselves within a few yards of a herd of several hundred California sea lions. This was not our first sight of the herd—we had watched it from afar, when they looked like maggots on the beach, and above the growl of the breakers that well-known circus voice had asserted itself. The California sea lion is, of course, the great circus seal. Adaptable, rather amenable, and very intelligent, it quickly learns the balancing tricks for which its marine, fish-hunting life prepares it. The Coronado herd has increased lately under a certain amount of protection—the Mexican and U.S. governments co-operating.

As we advanced into the rookery the bulls—the large ones with the high foreheads—and then the cows, took to the water, where they swam, frisking and back-pedaling and barking while we made friends with their pups. We did not keep the cows long away from their offspring, but before we left we made close acquaintance with three other magnificent sea animals that had hauled out in the rookery. These were young male northern elephant seals.

Elephant seals are true seals. Unlike sea lions, they cannot turn their hind flippers forward to shuffle. So on land they are very slow—which explains why our big friends had not joined the sea lions in the surf. They just lay there on the gravel and looked mournfully at

us with their large watery eyes. We walked around them, touched them, and Lewis Walker even deftly patted the big one on its ugly wrinkled snout without receiving more than a threat display. It laid its head back on its rubbery neck, erected its nose bladder and yawned wide, exposing its teeth, and uttered a sound like a groan or a long belch. Unable to intimidate us it undulated off, between the slippery rocks and into the surf, moving quite unlike the sea lions, great muscular ripplings flowing down its sluglike form.

These young elephant seals were small in comparison to the size attained by full-grown bulls. There were about twenty at the island. The largest of the three animals we saw closely—all males—was about nine and one-half to ten feet long, the other two about eight. The adult bulls run to eighteen feet, and probably reach three-ton weight; cows reach nine feet.* One of our young bulls was probably in its fourth year (on the verge of sexual maturity) and the other two in their third.

These animals had come from the suboceanic island of Guadalupe, about 160 miles off the Lower California coast, 240 miles to the south, or possibly from the San Benito Islands farther south. They were thought to be almost extinct when a small group was rediscovered on Guadalupe in 1892. Probably the world population had been brought below a hundred, by uncontrolled commercial exploitation. Under protection by the Mexican government they recovered, slowly at first, but fairly quickly from 1910 to 1930, and since 1930 in geometrical progression; early in 1952 George A. Bartholomew, Jr., and Carl Hubbs found 4548 on Guadalupe and 908 on the San Benitos. Our young males were the overspill from this rising population, and perhaps the vanguard of a new colonization of the Coronados.

As we picked our way back to the landing place we looked over our shoulders at the barking sea lions. Riding the swell and holding their heads high out of the water, they all faced the beach and their bleating pups. They slid gracefully back through the surf, and scampered ashore, their bodies wet-black in contrast to the dry-brown they had worn when we met them. Quickly the colony settled down to

---

* *Mirounga angustirostris.* The Antarctic and subantarctic southern elephant seal, *M. leonina,* a very close relation, is the largest of all the seals: its bulls run to twenty feet and certainly three tons (possibly four or five); its cows to twelve feet and a ton.

normal life as we rowed out to the launch, embarked, up-anchored, and sailed for North Island.

North Island is about a mile long, a quarter of a mile wide and 467 feet high. Near its middle is a jutting rock platform furnishing a clean-to landing place. Here, assailed by a cloud of complaining western gulls, we landed stores for a night's picnic and camp and sorted out our photographic gear. Nearby at the bottom of the steep hillside was a small hut used by Mexican fishermen; it seemed to be untenanted except for two abandoned half-grown kittens. Here we found a trail which led up by long zigzags to the top of the ridge.

Big, spectacular brown pelicans, with their white nuptial head plumes and enormous flat bills, were nesting all over the heights of North Island—a colony that has been known for at least sixty-five years (a long time in western American ornithology) and is probably very ancient. Mexican fishermen, perhaps the owners of the hut, had recently been ashore for bait, and the pathetic remains of a score or more young pelicans were strewn above the landing place. But their depredations had touched little more than the edge of the colony;

vast numbers of pelicans were tending their young on the high slopes. The newborn babies were naked and rubbery. Most were in the pudgy stage, covered with white woolly fuzz, and the larger ones carried dark hearts on their backs where the tracts of dark feathers were emerging. On big ledges the larger young herded up into crèches, and noisily solicited their parents as they came gliding in from the sea to land gymnastically among them. The brown pelican is much less clumsy than it looks.

Busy among the pelican nests, looking for fish scraps, were members of North Island's vast western gull colony. We photographed a western gull and an adult pelican sitting on a great boulder near the summit, looking at each other as if they were ornaments at each end of a chimney piece. Several times we saw gulls swooping sharply at the heads of young pelicans as if to make them disgorge the fish their parents had just fed to them. The gulls were busy round the other colonies, too, among the Brandt's cormorants on a big stack at the end of the island; and earlier in the day we had seen them among the sea lions on South Island, scavenging, quarreling. They quarreled in a different, more querulous, voice than that of our Atlantic blackbacks.

The Brandt's cormorants, dark birds with metallic-blue throat pouches, were new to me. Not new was the double-crested cormorant, present in much smaller numbers. This was a Pacific race of the cormorant that lives on both sides of North America. The third cormorant of the West Coast, the little Baird's cormorant, most pelagic of the three, used to nest on the Coronados, but we never saw it.

From North Island's ridge we saw a tall, long-legged bird, standing at the edge of a bed of thick kelp that trailed in the sea current from the cormorant rock. Had I seen it in England I would have called it a common heron. This was the California race of the great blue heron, which in some places nests on sea cliffs. A substantial population along the coast seems to earn its living on the kelp beds that trail and float offshore.

From our high vantage point we swept the open sea to the west through Roger's telescope, but even its sixty-power ocular failed to spot an albatross over the sun-silvered waves. At sundown we were still up the hill; we had stayed to take what advantage we could of the waning light for photography. A rock wren, one of the Coronados' three resident passerines, trilled away among the boulders (the house finches and song sparrows had fallen silent). Roger and I watched a lesser nighthawk quartering erratically along the steep cliffside. Then another nighthawk came, and then another. But the last one seemed a bit odd; we could see no white patch in the wing and it seemed small. It was a poor-will, a sort of miniature nightjar.* Later in the evening Roger heard it calling the lonesome notes that give it its name. I will never forget this little night bird, busy hawking for insects on those Coronado steeps in the June evening.

We stumbled down the hill, clattering among the stone slides, crunching ice plant underfoot and trying to avoid the cactus. Lorna Hubbs had a fine supper waiting for us, round a campfire on the rock flat by the landing place. After coffee and much cheerful talk and transatlantic badinage, we prepared our sleeping bags. This done we drew our torches from our kit to welcome an expected evening visitor. The Coronado Islands are the only breeding place of the black petrel within sight of the United States. This purely Pacific seabird is like a big Leach's petrel but blacker, without the white rump, and at sea has a slower, more ternlike flight. After dark it would come in from its oceanic wanderings to its crevice burrows in the talus.

All was quiet, except for an occasional gull cry far up the slope, as we brewed our second large pot of coffee, until suddenly—"Did you hear?" *Puck-apoo—puck-puck-a-poo,* in the dark air, up the hill, round the rocks, over the landing bay, here, there—but where? Dark moth-shapes appeared from nowhere, and disappeared to another nowhere. What queer ghostly birds they were! We crawled up to the undercliffs and for long we sought their burrows. Then suddenly a sharp musical trill began from the zigzag path and then another from the broken bottom of a rock buttress above our picnic rocks, and then another, ventriloquial, which we never tracked down. For a time we heard ground-song and air-song at once. Carl and Roger, luckier than I, found a sounding burrow near the hut, and caught in their torch beams a bird in the air. It was as crazy and batlike as Leach's—as all the storm petrels seem to be in their arrival flights at their colonies. Within an hour Roger succeeded in catching five birds at the mouths

* The poor-will, a small western relative of the whip-poor-will, is the extraordinary bird that was recently discovered actually hibernating among the rocks of a California canyon. Kept under observation by Edmund Jaeger through three successive winters, its temperature dropped from the normal 106° to 64°, a drop of no less than 42°. A stethoscope detected no heartbeat; a mirror caught no mist of breath. One winter it slept 88 days without food.

of their nesting crevices.

This night flight of burrowing petrels is compelled, it must be supposed, by the danger of gull predation. Entirely defenseless for a long
moment are these sprites of the sea, when they turn from agile air-
gymnasts to awkward ground-shufflers, pitching among the rocks and
pushing themselves with their weak legs, breast to ground, into their
holes.

While the black petrels were still coming in, it began to drizzle,
then it rained. It was little comfort to be told that such a thing was
exremely rare on the Coronados. Bedded down on air mattresses, we
lay in our sleeping bags and basked (or was it bathed?) in the rain.
Sleep was fitful for me, and impossible for Roger, who had punctured
his mattress on a rock.

As I lay there listening to the soft lapping of the waves and the
elfin sounds of the petrels, I reflected that after the two thousand
miles of sandbeach coast of the eastern states this memorable day
on the Coronados had been like a play of home, but with our native
seabirds impersonated by a different cast. It reminded me so much
of journeys to Scotland's great rocks, like St. Kilda or Foula, or
Wales's Skokholm, or England's Farnes, journeys I shall make again,
but without the magic of novelty.

AFTER THE SHARP ROCK had punctured my inflated rubber mattress I
could soon feel every one of the hundred or more other small rocks
on which I had made my bed. I couldn't sleep, but the drizzle kept me
in my sleeping bag for a while. Fearing that I too would soon be punctured as my mattress had been, I got up and joined Lewis, who was
still listening to the petrels. I had brought my portable tape recorder
to the island for the express purpose of recording these night voices,
but I did not want to risk its delicate mechanism in the rain. Or was
it inertia that kept me from hauling it up the rocks in the dark?

Earlier in the evening, just before the petrels came in, we had
heard a high twittering note over the water; it sounded vaguely gold-
finch-like. Lewis suspected it was made by the incoming petrels, but
we never heard this note from the petrels after they reached the land
—either in the air or in their burrows. Now these puzzling sounds

seemed closer. Taking our flashlights, we threw their bright beams over the water. The fine drizzle slanted silkily across the light, and about a hundred feet away we could discern a shape bobbing dimly on the now calm sea. The shape turned into a little bird, black above, white below, which got brighter as it swam toward us like a contrasting print in a developer bath. Dazed by the light it swam our way as fast as it could; it dived and continued its course just under the surface, bobbed up again when it reached the rock, and clambered ashore right into my waiting hands! It was a Scripps's murrelet, the other nocturnal visitor to North Island. I hurried over to show it to James, who had got up to warm himself at the remnants of our fire. This bird, which looks something like an over-sized dovekie, is a race of Xantus's murrelet, the most southern of all the auk family. Like the black petrel, it breeds in crevices and holes in the talus. Unlike most other auks, it usually lays two eggs.

After midnight I smoothed my rock bed as best I could, blew some more air into the deflated rubber mattress and crawled into my rain-soaked sleeping bag. Slumber was impossible, so I turned my thoughts to the sea lions. What a curious freak of terminology it was that the male "lions" (which are really seagoing bears of a sort) should be called bulls, the females cows, the babies pups, and their colonies rookeries. And what is more, the bulls bark and the pups bleat! Amused, and confused, I drifted into a coma that could not have been called sleep.

Some time later, in the predawn I was aroused to consciousness by the sound of murrelets in the air. The eerie cries came from all around—the murrelets and the petrels, like the tortured demons and lost souls on Bald Mountain, were fleeing from their citadel of rocks with the first light of dawn. Then, in the increasing half light, another sound arose—the awakening chorus of the gulls, a most remarkable reveille. For some minutes every voice in the great colony seemed synchronized, beating out their yelping cries in perfect unison. I had never heard anything like it in any other gull colony—but then, I had never before been in a gull colony at daybreak.

Soaked through as we were, it took even more than Lorna Hubbs's excellent breakfast to bring us back to life. What we needed was some good warm sun. The sky was still murky, though the sea was relatively calm. In the clear deep water where the boat was moored, we saw a number of bright orange fish—"garibaldis"—idly swimming, and nearby floated several huge jellyfish, with umbrellas two feet across and long furbelows that trailed in the current. I believe I heard Carl Hubbs tell Lew Walker that these medusae were probably of an undescribed form.

Before turning our bow homeward toward San Diego we took the boat to one of two islets between North and South Islands. We landed and James, still stiff and cold, was attacked by a bad cramp in his legs on what would ordinarily have been an easy rockclimb. A wandering tattler, an off-season migrant, flew from the water's edge and we saw a pair of black oystercatchers. But the treasure we were seeking was Leach's petrel; Lew Walker had found it here several years before. The forms of petrels from the western coast of North America and from Guadalupe Island which used to be known as Beal's (white-rumped) and the Socorro (black-rumped) petrels, respectively, are really well-marked races of Leach's petrel. The birds of the Coronados are interesting because they are intermediate; in measurements they are nearer the Beal's, though only about half the birds have the white rump patch. We discovered a few petrel burrows on a turfy slope and after sniffing each one hopefully, and almost dislocating our shoulders by reaching in, we located two or three incubating birds. But they turned out to be black petrels. We could not find any of the odd, dimorphic, race of Leach's petrel. Had they disappeared?

We had an appointment to keep in San Diego; Belle Benchley expected us at the zoological gardens at lunchtime. Leaving the petrel matter unsolved we up-anchored and followed our compass needle to the north.

That afternoon after a tour of the gardens, one of the most attractively landscaped zoos in the world, we were introduced to its most prized acquisition—three koala bears from Australia. James, an old zoo man himself, was allowed to climb a ladder into a eucalyptus tree to pay his respects to these teddy bears from down under. At a distance of three feet the visitor from England gazed in admiration at the visitors from Australia. But they returned his interested scrutiny with a blank stare. Already the Coronados seemed far away.

26

Pleistocene Giants

WHEN A CALIFORNIAN boasts that his state has the highest mountain in the country, the lowest and hottest desert, the highest waterfall, the greatest bird, the most extensive vineyard, the biggest oranges, the tallest and oldest trees, he is stating simple fact. California has infinite variety. Hollywood directors claim they can duplicate the Alps, the African veld, the Sahara, and the shores of the South Seas or the Mediterranean without leaving the state. And California also has contrast. No seacoast in the New World is more heartbreakingly beautiful than certain stretches of the California coast and—let's face it—none is more of a hodge-podge than other sections along its 800-mile length. It was through one of these cluttered stretches that we approached the sprawling city of Los Angeles.

Had I mentioned the La Brea tarpits, that repository of Pleistocene bones within the city limits, James would have demanded unequivocally that we go there. As a matter of fact, neither of us thought of

La Brea as we neared the film capital. Instead, the English novice in America, haunted by the celluloid specter of Hollywood, wanted to lay the ghost.

June 7

I HAD INSISTED that Roger navigate us into the heart of Los Angeles, and thence out along Sunset Boulevard. Roger did not mind; it was the only place, he said, where we could be sure of picking up an established alien, the Chinese spotted dove.

We hummed along the coastal road, through town after town, all new and shiny. "It looks," I told Roger, "as if California has just been discovered, and everybody's rushing in."

"It has," he replied, "and they are. A thousand a day."

No wonder, I thought, that this area looks like a stage lot imitating the worst parts of Sussex. Aloud, I said, "Magnificent wirescape."

"They haven't had time to put the wire underground," answered Roger, "and I don't suppose they ever will."

"Anyway, if they can't enjoy the scenery they can all call each other up."

"You wait until you see Los Angeles."

We didn't have to wait long. Before we saw the fabulous city we could smell it; it stank of oil. We approached it from Newport Beach through a grove of oil derricks, pumps seesawing and clanking, breathing sweet-sour vapor all around. Casual fences of clapboard, ends of wire, weedy road shoulders, pools of black water marbled by the rainbow films of oil. I had expected almost any scene at the portals of the movie capital, but not this ghastly grove of gas-trees, greedily grabbing gain from the alkali flats. Roger was less moved—he had seen it before. It was, according to him, just the place for Belding's sparrow. Sure enough, among the *Salicornia* and *Atriplex* that were fighting the oil seeps for their place on the soil, we found this dingy race of the savannah sparrow.

From Wilmington we burrowed the straight nineteen miles to up-town Los Angeles through a planner's nightmare. Long live enterprise, I thought; build what you like, how you like, where you like. Garnish the result with wire and neon and rubbish, flavor with crude gasoline, and serve hot. But don't serve me!

We reached the end of Figueroa Street, ticked off Roger's Chinese spotted dove in a tree-shaded square, and swung west into Hollywood along Sunset Boulevard. My inward disgust at Los Angeles' southern approaches I had already begun to find a bore; I had been getting on fine with the American way of life and did not like being shaken. The depth of my reaction surprised me. A guest in a house, I suggested to myself, should not call at the back.

The front garden was quite different. I had expected ostentation and vulgarity; there was little of either along Sunset Boulevard. Ranch houses, patios, the new style, the old style, the houses of the movie stars, neat and prosperous in a blaze of flowers, their swimming pools as blue as the Mediterranean, looked extremely agreeable, oddly respectable. "Done up, regardless," I said to Roger, "but done up proper. They've made themselves very cozy—I wonder if they ever have time to be cozy."

"If they took time off to *be* cozy," said Roger, as we slipped the car between a Jaguar and a Mercedes, "they'd never be able to afford to *look* cozy, far less buy fast European cars."

Perched on a height of Beverly Hills, we looked back to the sea, across twenty miles of roofs, avenues, traffic. Sunset on Sunset Boulevard brought a thousand electric stars a minute winking, blinking into a landscape over which, within living memory, golden eagles, bald eagles, condors hunted, and naturalists could write, by way of explanation, in their notes and papers, "Hollywood—a suburb of Los Angeles."

ACTUALLY, I reminded James, the golden eagles and the last handful of condors, flying high over the Sespe range, can still see Los Angeles from their station in the sky, at least on days when the smog does not blot out the great city, which lies only thirty miles away.

Next morning, as we climbed the steep mountain grade in low gear, I remembered past visits to the condor country. America's third-rarest bird (and its largest), is no longer as accessible as it was in 1936, when I stepped to the station platform in Los Angeles with six hours between trains. Five Junior Audubon members from the Eagle Rock High School, discovering I was in town, took me to

Sespe Canyon, showed me my first condors—tiny specks in the blue —and hurried me back to the station with only minutes to spare.

Four years later I saw condors to better advantage by abandoning the canyon floor and climbing to the ridges where the great birds glide on the deflected air currents. As they floated past, with primary tips spread like fingers, they seemed prehistoric birds and, in a sense, they are, if we accept Loye Miller's opinion that they are a "senile species, far past its prime."

Alexander Sprunt, less lucky on his first condor quest, was discovered by a group of bird watchers, we are told, lying beside the road at Sespe, trying to look like a cadaver. But the wily cathartids are not so easily duped.

In the opinion of some there are probably no fewer condors today than there were fifteen years ago. That is the belief of Carl Koford, the recipient of an Audubon Fellowship, who spent three years living in caves and camps in the back country while studying the habits and population dynamics of the condor. He believes the present population of sixty has been stable for a decade. Others insist there has been a further decline. But the reason the condors are no longer as accessible as they were in 1936 is because the Sespe country has been declared forbidden ground, even to the field-glass fraternity.

The Rancho La Brea tarpits in nearby metropolitan Los Angeles have yielded bones which prove that *Gymnogyps,* or a bird very similar, has been around a long time; during the Pleistocene it was frequently mired in the tar with the now extinct dire wolf and the saber-toothed tiger. In fact it was Loye Miller, the author of the debatable statement quoted above, who exhumed many of these bones from their sticky casing of asphalt. He found, however, that *Gymnogyps* with its wingspan of nine and one-half feet, was not the largest vulture in those dim days of big carnivores and big herbivores. There was also *Teratornis,* with a spread of about twelve feet. If you descend into the circular observation pit at La Brea you can actually see a wing bone of *Teratornis merriami* lying *in situ* in the black asphalt, alongside the skull of a mastodon and the scattered bones of the giant ground sloth. Recently an even larger *Teratornis* was discovered in the deposits of Smith Creek Cave thirty-four miles north of Baker, Nevada. This monster, known from a single wing bone, has been given the apt name of *Teratornis incredibilis*. Its wingspan is computed to have been between sixteen and twenty feet!

California condors once ranged completely across the continent, if we are to accept the evidence of bones in Pleistocene deposits at Sarasota and Seminole Field in Florida. Even as recently as 2000 years ago they soared the blue skies of the Big Bend. But by the time the West was invaded by the first white pioneers they were already restricted to the Pacific slope. Lewis and Clark at the end of their history-making trek found condors at the mouth of the Columbia River, where they observed one feeding on fit fare for a behemoth—a dead whale. Later Meriwether Lewis, in his journal of February 17, 1806, wrote a careful description of a living condor and made a drawing of its head. Within the next forty years the condor disappeared from Oregon. The small population there apparently withdrew to California, where vast sheep and cattle ranchos operated by the Spanish missions were enjoying their heyday. With the gradual breakup of the ranchos and the switch from millions of sheep to a lesser number of cattle, the big scavengers disappeared from one California county after another (and from northwestern Mexico) until they were concentrated in their present mountain fortress north of Los Angeles. Sheep, Koford points out, provided in the old days eight to ten times as many carcasses as an equivalent pasturage of cattle. When modern methods of ranching came into vogue the food supply was further reduced. Livestock were inoculated against disease. Those few animals which now die from one cause or another are usually buried or burned. Lately, the condors have been forced to subsist at times on such marginal fare as poisoned ground squirrels.

No other American bird has a lower reproductive potential. Of the sixty living condors, about a third are immature birds which take at least five years to mature. The forty adults—twenty pairs—do not nest every year, but lay their single egg every second year. These eggs, ten each year at most, require six weeks to hatch into babies that take five months to fledge. After leaving the nest they are dependent upon their parents for several months more. With such a long period of dependency—the most protracted period of helplessness of any North American bird—it is not likely that more than five young condors augment the clan in an average year, about enough to balance the losses.

Just as the wingspan of the California condor has been often exaggerated (some authors stating twelve feet—and even fourteen!), so has the collectors' value of its eggs. Although in 1910 a single egg did go for $300—to a man who already owned seven—there is no truth in the newspaper stories that a condor's egg is "worth up to $1000." If one were filched, no one would dare or care to buy it, even at "fence" prices. But, at the turn of the century, things were different. One unscrupulous collector even tried to sell the Smithsonian Institution swans' eggs as eggs of the condor; but microscopic examination of the eggshell exposed the fraud. Koford, who has knowledge of 130 skins and at least 60 eggs in the collections of the world, is convinced that commercial collecting must have had a very definite effect on the dwindling condor population forty or fifty years ago.

Although oölogists are no longer a menace (deterred by a possible $500 fine), irresponsible deer hunters, who come from a distance, and know nothing about the condor situation and perhaps care less, are to be reckoned with. So, believe it or not, are photographers, whose presence might impose hardships on nesting birds. It therefore was deemed best to exclude everyone from the Sespe except a few authorized guards and other persons. Fifty-five square miles of the Los Padres National Forest are included in the closure, which is now known as the Sespe Wildlife Preserve. The condor itself was decreed a "Nature Monument."

When all seemed well, the question of oil leases came up. Because of oil discoveries nearby, there was pressure to prospect in the Sespe; it looked as though derricks might displace the last condors. But after a public hearing, oilmen versus conservationists, a compromise was reached. In the sixteen square miles where most of the nests are located no drilling is to be permitted, unless it is done by "directional drilling" (at a slant)—from outside the area. Nor may any drilling be undertaken in the remaining area "within one half mile of a condor's nest active within three years." However, no drilling has yet taken place; it seems unfeasible because of the rugged terrain.

Even bird watchers are excluded from the preserve, but it is possible to see condors from any number of peaks in Ventura County, if one is patient enough to wait for the wide-foraging birds to fly over. It was on this chance that we accompanied Sydney Peyton, who knows condors and the country well. He had keys to the gates of several ranches in the hills, and James became one of that select company who had seen a living condor. But let him tell about it.

June 8

Leaving the citrus groves behind, we piloted the car into the foot-hills. The Sespe ridge is not high, but it is rugged, and quite soon we were hairpinning and spur-cutting up a road that quickly became a track. Every now and then Sydney Peyton got out to unlock a gate. The grass on the steep south slopes was golden-brown, not green; and the canyons which cut through the Sespe sandstone echoed to no sound of rushing water; yet this mountain drive reminded me, in a spasm of almost violent nostalgia, of a mountain drive in Wales. Perhaps it was the steep hillsides bearded with hanging oak woods— or perhaps it was the pursuit of a rare raptor, that brought memories of wild hilly Wales. The last time I visited a Welsh oak-hanger I was looking for the kite. In all Britain the red kite survives only in Wales, and its numbers there—its history, too—parallel remarkably those of the California condor.

After about an hour of skillful maneuvering, Sydney Peyton's son at the wheel, we reached the summit ridge. Below us, and around us, was chaparral—shrubby, scrubby growth dominated by scattered oak and ilex clumps, sagebrush, manzanita. Above us was cloud, too much cloud; wisps of vapor stroked the hilltops, settled like fog upon us and blotted out our view. When the clouds lifted we saw a deserted, scrubby maze of canyons wriggling down to the Sespe Creek, four thousand feet below. It was hard to realize that one of the larg-est cities in the world was not forty miles away.

Somewhere in the scrub a strange bird was calling, a fruity *wook?* in an interrogative voice; this was the mountain quail of the Pacific ranges, a boldly patterned bird with a long blade-like head plume. Frequently we heard another voice in the brush, a sharp pinging that accelerated to a trill. After poking around we found the singer, the wren-tit, a seldom seen, often heard bird that frequently intrudes its voice onto the sound track of Hollywood films. In contrast to this drab skulker was my first lazuli bunting, a small bright bird that flashed a brilliant green-blue as it darted to its song perch in the *Artemisia* and chirped a loud, tweety song. Several times we heard the sweet musical *tink-oo* of another finch with a gray head and a black face, Lawrence's goldfinch, a bird found only from central California to northern Lower California, and nowhere else in the world.

"But we aren't after dickeybirds," Roger reminded me. "I'm worried about the cloud. Even if we could see, it's bad soaring weather."

Peyton led us along the ridge. We passed several big-cone spruce trees where condors often sunned themselves, but this morning they were not there. California jays fussed around crying *kwesh-kwesh-kwesh,* and a black-headed grosbeak sang a passable imitation of a robin song from the oaks below the crest. At an overlook we sat down to wait. Like a conjurer, Peyton produced from a paper bag the most wonderful oranges in California (he grows them). The cloud flowed around the deep, broad canyon below us; then suddenly it lifted like a curtain. Quickly we put down our big oranges and swept the amphitheater of rocks with our field glasses. A dark semicircular cave on a flat sandstone face held our attention.

"That's the cave in Hopper Canyon," said Peyton; "one of the best places—a roosting place." And as he spoke two specks floated across the rock wall, half circled, slid out of sight, but not before we had got a quick focus on them with telescopes.

"So small," I said. "Can they be?"

"Oh, yes, they're condors," said Peyton. "How far away do you think that cave is?"

"Mile, or so?"

"Four. Seven miles by trail. But the birds don't like the weather. I hope they'll soar, but I'm very much afraid they won't."

Big raptors are sailplanes. California condors often operate up to a hundred miles from base, but not on their own power. Buzzards, and other broad-winged hawks, though much lighter, are sailplanes too. All these sailing raptors must use the air, must find up-currents to exploit, or remain almost home-bound. Mountain breezes, deflected upward by the ridges, give them such currents; but the slow clouds, scarcely moving, showed us that our day had no wind for slope-soaring. Thermals give lift, too. We looked for the sun. Would it break through the cloud-veil enough to warm the canyon basins, start columns of hot, light air to bring the raptors up? Certainly the cloud was lifting, breaking. We waited in an aroma of orange peel, and waited.

At about noon Roger called, "There's a *Buteo* up. Red-tail." The bird came sweeping over the ridge, saw us, side-slipped, circled up again, then glided down a canyon. It was a start; one raptor at least had found a thermal. But no more; we waited, scanned often the great wall in Hopper Canyon, and ate more oranges from Peyton's inexhaustible bag. We finally had to give up. Disappointed, we walked back along the ridge to the car, packed up our gear, and slid and lurched down the steep dirt road.

We could say we had seen the great rare bird, but we had really only half seen it. Late though it was, we entertained a lingering hope and, stopping on the last and lowest of the foothills, paused for just a minute more. To mock us, a turkey vulture came gliding over, its dihedral so marked that we recognized it at once. The thermals were working, but the wrong raptors were using them. Regretfully, we turned to the car.

"Why the hurry?" said Sydney Peyton, quietly, from behind his binoculars. We followed the slant of them, to a speck in the sky. The speck was a California condor, and it was coming our way.

It came right over. I could not estimate its height (I'd made a bad enough mistake in distance-judging already), but we had a perfect view. It was like a bomber, its flat-winged posture quite unlike the glider-dihedral of the turkey vulture. It was huge, black, pale-headed, and as it came over the big white bands forward on its underwing showed it be to an adult. For five minutes we watched its monstrous ten-foot span, its primaries spread like fingers. It made a couple of slow flaps, as if it had all the time in the world, caught a new thermal, and soared away to the southeast until it became a tiny speck and disappeared.

"Tally most incredibly ho!" I said as I ticked it off on my checklist.

"Quite a bird," commented Roger. "Exhibit A."

"Worth seeing, actually."

It had been worth seeing, actually, worth traveling ten thousand miles to see.

AFTER THE GIANT BIRD passed beyond our vision James and I wondered what the future would hold. Would putting out carcasses help the condors? Perhaps not, if we are to be guided by the testimony of photographers who have tried to bait them. John Pemberton tried thirty times before he finally had a group feeding before his blind. Other photographers have waited patiently a day or two, then have given up, only to return and find the birds devouring their bait. I once had a similar experience with turkey vultures in New York state. Upon finding the carcass of a white-tailed deer that had collided with a car, I hauled it to an open slope, put up my burlap blind, camouflaged it with wild grape vines. For two long days I stewed in my own sweat while the carcass, thirty feet away, ripened, and flies swarmed. The vultures, at a discreet distance, sat hunched in a tall dead hemlock like undertakers waiting to officiate at a burial. On the third day I dismantled my blind. Less than three hours later a friend chanced by; as he approached, a cloud of vultures flew up. All that remained of the deer were a few scattered bones. Had they detected my presence, or do they demand in their carrion a certain stage of putrefaction?

On another occasion, trying for griffon vultures in Spain, Guy Mountfort and I waited an entire day in two expertly concealed blinds. We placed the body of a deer in an open place at the foot of a gnarled dead cork oak. It was a perfect setting—one that Gustave Doré would have chosen for vultures. But not even a kite came to investigate. The Spanish horsemen and *guardas* who had helped us construct the hides seemed disappointed in the *Inglés* and the eccentric *Americano* when we returned to the *coto* at sundown and reported our lack of success.

At the time of our visit to the condor country, a last-ditch attempt was being made by a group of conservationists who believe that when a bird is so desperately down, any straw—even artificial propagation —is worth grasping. Belle Benchley, director of the San Diego zoo (who introduced James to the koalas), had demonstrated that she could successfully hand raise Andean condors from the egg. In fact, by removing and incubator-hatching the first egg, a second fertile egg could be procured in a short time. Then, by removing the half-grown young, a double breeding could be induced the following year. This resulted in four hand-reared young in the period in which it would take wild birds to raise a single youngster. In the belief that this could be duplicated with California condors a permit was issued by the California Fish and Game Commission, over the protests of the opposing faction of conservationists. Two birds were to be trapped alive for the project. Although Lew Walker tried for several months to accomplish his mission of trapping the birds (outside the reservation) he failed, and the permit ran out.

Perhaps we are sentimental in going to such lengths for a creature that we probably cannot hold. How long will it be, we wonder, before it joins *Teratornis,* the La Brea condor, the Grinnell eagle, the La Brea stork, the La Brea owl, and the California turkey? In the slow flow of time many more species have lost their grip on existence than grace this terrestrial sphere today. The California condor has seen a lot of history: it was here long before man became man. Today the last pathetic individuals, big and unwanted, still patrol the Sespe; while above, at a height of 30,000 feet, jet planes from California's mushrooming airfields trace their ribbons of frozen vapor through the blue.

27

Golden Coast

$\mathcal{T}$HE BLUE SEA and the gold hills gave a Mediterranean savor to our journey; so did the Spanish names. The chain of old red-tiled adobe missions—San Buenaventura, Santa Barbara, Santa Ynez, La Purísima Concepción, San Luis Obispo—reminded us that Spain held these valleys and the coast before the Americans pushed west to the Pacific; in fact, before there was a United States of America.

Clumps of California poppies, Eschscholtzia—the state flower of California—blazed orange-gold beside the road, but we saw no flaming hillsides of these poppies such as the early Spanish explorers described. They called this the "Land of Fire." Today the hills are tawny with grass where tawny cattle feed; the great natural flower gardens are almost a thing of the past. Road shoulders, protected from grazing cattle by wire fences, are now the best places to find some of the flowers of the grass country. Here we saw many showy composites, lupines and other flowers, yellow, white, and pink. To

James's English eyes most of them were unfamiliar, for the western roadside, unlike the eastern road shoulder, is not dominated by adventive plants from the Old World. But even though the poppies were orange instead of scarlet, the plant life had the same xeric look as that of the Mediterranean.

The Santa Ynez Mountains drove us inland, among golden hills of grass, so unlike the fields of England, or of New England, so like the Mediterranean slopes. We dropped down to the picturesque harbor at Morro Bay and skirted the sea northward, hugging the precipitous flanks of the Santa Lucias, blue sky steep above and blue sea sheer below. We settled down to a hundred miles or more of gentle motoring along a magnificent unspoiled coast, which made our memories of the cluttered sea edge below Los Angeles seem like a bad dream.

"Last year, at this time," James said, "I was motoring along just such a coast at this—the Côte d'Azur. Only, instead of the chaparral there were cistus and olive groves. Aromatic Mediterranean scrub, wormwood scrub—like this. Instead of live oaks, cork oaks. I keep looking for Sardinian warblers here, and I keep expecting Monte Carlo around the next corner."

"Orange-crowned warblers in the same niche," I commented, "and Monterey instead of Monte Carlo at the end of today's journey. And sea otters in between. You don't get *those* in the Mediterranean."

I did not mention redwood trees; in fact, I had not given them a thought until we entered a shady cleft in the hills where a cool stream cut through to the sea. A sign read "Los Padres National Forest." Here trees, giant evergreens, lined the sides of the ravine, and then I remembered that the redwood has a southern outpost here in the gullies of the Santa Lucias.

"*Wellingtonia,*" said James.

I raised my eyebrows.

"It seems to grow well here," he went on. "Replanting, I suppose, with exotics."

I said nothing.

"*Wellingt—*" The penny dropped. "Oh dear—and you won't have the name *Wellingtonia,* will you?"

"Or *Washingtonia,* either," I replied. I remembered the many sequoias and redwoods I had seen in England, particularly the long avenue of them near Virginia Water, where they had been planted about a hundred years ago; and I recalled how my British friends insisted on calling them Wellingtonias.

Actually, when the coast redwood was first named by the English botanists, it was regarded as a sort of cypress, a *Taxodium*. This view was held for some years, until a German, Stephen Endlicher, decided that it represented a wholly new genus. A student of things American, he gave it the name of a famous chief of the Cherokees, Sequoya, who had devised the Cherokee alphabet. (Or was there some hidden pride, on Endlicher's part, in things Germanic? This chief had a German father and an Indian mother.)

When a tree even larger than the coast redwood was found in the Sierras, a visiting English horticulturist, William Lobb, was told of the discovery. A man of initiative, he set out to see the trees for himself, took specimens, and without a word of his plans to his American friends secured passage on the first boat home. There the material was put in the hands of the botanist John Lindley, who published on it immediately. This tree, the mightiest, most nearly immortal of all living things, was described as a new genus, *Wellingtonia,* honoring the Duke of Wellington, who had died only the year before.

Loud was the howl from the American botanists, who had been scooped. Some, with chauvinistic fervor, proposed the name *Washingtonia*. (Actually this name was given later to another California tree, the desert palm.) Then a Frenchman, Decaisne, stepped into the picture. He demonstrated beyond a doubt that the big tree of the Sierras belonged to the same genus as the coast redwood, *Sequoia sempervirens;* and therefore he proposed the name *Sequoia gigantea*. And *Sequoia* it is today.

But to my English friends it is still *Wellingtonia*. They suggest that Decaisne had the defeat at Waterloo in the back of his mind.

This confusion of names is, after all, academic, I thought, as I looked up at the towering trees and was again captured by their magic. These groves in the Santa Lucias are only a detached province of the redwood empire, the main part of which stretches from the Golden Gate to the Oregon line in a belt about three hundred miles long and averaging only fifteen in width. These, and the big trees in the Sierras, are the last remnants of a genus of trees that were widespread over a large part of the world a hundred million years ago, fit contemporaries of dinosaurs and huge flying reptiles. England once had its own redwoods; now it has them again, borrowed—or on permanent loan—from California. Someday Britons can hope to see in their own country redwoods as towering as those James and I saw in the Santa Lucias, trees 200 feet tall, for in spite of their long life, a thousand years or more, they grow fast. The century-old trees in England are already 125 to 150 feet high.

The king of the redwoods—the tallest tree in the world—is the Founder's Tree, a colossus of 364 feet, near Dyerville in Humboldt County; living proof that a certain Englishman was wrong when he calculated mathematically that a 300-foot tree could not stand, but would collapse under its own weight. He was as much in error as the aerodynamics expert who proved conclusively, with faultless logic, that a bumblebee could not possibly fly.

No one knows the age of the Founder's Tree, but it might well have sprouted in the second century after the birth of Christ. Such a tree, cut down, will often sprout from its stump, to grow for perhaps another thousand years. If any living things approach immortality, these trees do.

When a huge diesel-powered truck roars by bearing away the body of one of these slain giants, no one with a conscience can help but wonder whether we have the right to take the life of a thousand-year-old tree for our ephemeral uses. Already, about half of the original stand of coast redwood, estimated at 1,600,000 acres, has come to earth; another forty years will see all of the primeval trees cut except for those which the Save-the-Redwoods League has been able to buy up. True, second growth will replace the first, but nothing can bring back the serenity of a virgin grove that has remained at peace and laid down its thick humus over the ages. We need wood; we must cut trees; but what bitter resentment coming generations would feel if our generation dissipated their entire inheritance and left none of the old trees standing!

This is not likely to happen. About 55,000 acres of virgin redwood are now in the California state park system. The famous Redwood Highway in northern California, one of the world's most spectacular drives, runs for a hundred miles through memorial groves. There are more than a hundred of these: the Pioneer's Grove, the Stephen Mather Grove, the Native Daughters of the Golden West Grove, the National Tribute Grove, the California Federation of Women's Clubs Grove, the Garden Club of America Grove; also many others, given by individual men of wealth. The 18,000 members of the

Save-the-Redwoods League, who deplore the passing of the giants, have chipped in $6,000,000, which has been matched, dollar for dollar, by the State of California.

James and I would not see this "Avenue of the Giants," for our itinerary had not been planned that way, but there were plenty of redwoods here in the Santa Lucias. In the park at the Big Sur, where we stopped in the afternoon, the trees were not really large by redwood standards, but they were, nevertheless, the largest trees James had ever seen. Great boles in their ponderous armor lifted straight up a hundred feet or more before the first limbs broke their symmetry. Through the canopy motes of sunlight filtered down between wraiths of mist, for the redwood, growing as it does in the valleys of the Coast Range, is constantly moistened by the sea's breath, which gives a smoky light to the forest openings. Deep moss and clover-like oxalis carpeted the floor, ferns decorated the buttresses. Most of the flowers of the giant forest are modest, easily overlooked, and so are most of the birds, except the Steller's jay, but here even its jarring *shook shook shook* is muted. One gains the impression that there are few birds among the redwoods; actually there is little for them to eat, because these indestructible evergreens are almost completely free of insects.

June 9

Leaving the cloistered shade of the redwoods we found ourselves again on the steep open slopes which tumbled abruptly down to the sea. We had an appointment, Roger reminded me; he had promised Laidlaw Williams we would meet him at four.

At exactly four o'clock we found ourselves on a rocky, lonely part of the coast. Offshore stacks and islets, ruffled by short white breakers, swam in calm kelp-stranded blue sea. All along the coast this kelp band floated, an apron of long seaweed tresses. On a natural lookout, where the road broadened to the edge of a rock-rampart, a car was parked, and a rangy figure with baggy trousers was sitting on the running board, a battered hat shading the eye-piece of a tripod telescope.

Laidlaw Williams looked up. "Hullo, there," he smiled. "At four, punctual. What time did you start?"

"Sixty days ago," said Roger.

Laidlaw seemed excited, but not, I felt, entirely about the supreme accuracy of Roger's schedule. He seemed anxious to get back to his telescope. "They're here," he said, "two lots."

Pacific kelpweeds, with their long fronds and dark stems and large black float bladders rolling in the swell, simulate mobile animals most confusingly. A pack of diving ducks they could be, one moment, and the next a sea serpent. It was quite some time before I could focus on, and recognize, the sea otters among the kelp. Then I found one; after five minutes I was on to a dozen.

The sea otters lead idle lives, on calm days basking on their backs among the kelp, their noses pointing to the sky, arms folded over their brown breasts, paddle-feet gently waving like turning weed, short tails awash. Four or five slept while we watched, anchored by kelp tucked under their arms. We saw others disappear below the surface, reappear; none brought up its shellfish and pebble, to bash the clam or abalone open on the table of its breast as Miss Edna Fisher* has recorded in words and pictures. But one of them was hugging something, clutched to its breast by an encircling left arm, as it slept. Once or twice the object moved a little, and then I realized it was a little baby, lying midst sleep and suckling on the safe cradle of its mother's belly. After the baby sea otter is two days old, Miss Fisher found, its mother can let it hold on to a kelp mooring while she hunts clams down below.

These peaceful, beautiful creatures, basking in the gently rocking kelp along the Riviera coast of California, are living proof of the new climate of opinion in America. Nobody thinks of them any more as thousand-dollar pelts, but as rare native sons of the California coast, whom the state has the duty and privilege to preserve. The

---

* *Journal of Mammalogy,* 20 (1939): 21–36, writes: "The red abalone is the mollusk most commonly eaten . . . the shell is laid on the chest or abdomen until the otter is ready for the next mouthful. I have never seen an abalone shell roll off the body even when the water was rough and the body nearly awash.

"It is not an uncommon thing to hear a sharp clicking sound . . . This sound is always made by an otter that is trying to crack open something with a very hard stone-like shell . . . The object is held with both paws and with full arm action from well over the head it is brought down hard on a piece of rock that rests on the otter's chest."

sea otter once lived along a great arc of seacoast that extended for
five thousand miles from northern Japan, along the Aleutians, and
down the west coast to California. But so prized was its fur by the
Russian aristocracy and the courts of the Manchus that these animals,
which once must have numbered hundreds of thousands, were brought
close to extinction. Tartars, Cossacks, and Slavs left a trail of
plunder and even murder across the north Pacific until, pressing
their operations southward to California, they were met by the
Spaniards working northward. The sea otter all but disappeared; for
a while it was actually regarded as extinct on the California coast,
when to the jubilation of naturalists a herd of 94 was discovered in
1935 very near this point where we were watching them now. The
protection of *Enhydra lutris,* the most specialized of all the weasel
family, has been a great success; since the return of the species, at
least three bands have built up their numbers, and for thirty miles
or more, from south of the Big Sur to north of Carmel they live in
peace.*

* When Laidlaw Williams joined us in Europe for the International Ornithological Congress a year after our meeting at the Big Sur he told us that a new
band had appeared off Point Lobos.

June 10

Laidlaw's home is in the Carmel Woods, back of the Monterey Peninsula. Monterey pines, where hermit thrushes sing, crowd about his door and march down toward the shore. This rocky strip of coast from Point Lobos to Monterey, with its wind-sculptured cypress and pine, is the most picturesque coastline in the United States. Here the transition from dry southern coast to humid northern coast finds its point of balance. At Point Lobos, which we visited this morning, plants and animals of both climates grow. Here is the most southerly substantial outpost of Canadian birds and other animals along the Pacific Coast. Here guillemots and Baird's cormorants meet the brown pelicans of warmer seas, and northern sea lions share the rocks with California sea lions. The 354 acres of this picturesque peninsula have been dedicated as a state park; it is the finest surviving example of the near-pristine, unspoiled community of plants and animals once characteristic of the California coast. Flowers grow in the profusion that the first Spanish settlers saw. With its stands of pine, live oak, and cypress, its meadows and lupine gardens, its sagebrush and wormwood, its granite rocks and little beaches, its birds and sea lions, it is held inviolate as an ecological study area. Not a plant is to be picked, a branch broken, or a stone removed. Twenty years ago (in 1934) the late Joseph Grinnell and Jean Linsdale made a survey of the vertebrate animals here and established a yardstick by which changes can be measured.

This policy of leaving things alone undoubtedly saved a little bird, a parula warbler, and its two wives when it chose to nest here in 1952, 1500 miles from its normal range, the most fantastic example of a songbird nesting where it shouldn't. Wind-drifted, as birds sometimes are during spring migration, these three individuals by an extraordinary coincidence managed to wind up at this spot, found each other, and, what is equally important, found the niche they require: not Spanish moss, nor usnea, but *Ramalina,* or lace lichen, which festoons the pines and cypresses with gray beards. To the parula, apparently, the important thing is not the botanist's classification, but the purely visual similarity (Spanish moss is a bromeliad, usnea a lichen; and Roger has even known a parula to tuck its nest under a flood-stranded strip of burlap). Here *Ramalina* filled the bill. The birds built two nests, which kept the little bigamist busy.

Tradition among California museum men demands that a first state record such as this be substantiated by a specimen. (They wanted to know, was the bird an ordinary parula, or a related Mexican form?) Finally, it was decided more important not to collect the bird, for to do so would violate the purpose of the study area.

It is probable, through the hit-and-miss pioneering of occasional birds such as these, that ranges are sometimes extended. But this year no parulas had returned. We listened for the up-scale buzz among the festooned evergreens, and heard only the Steller's jays, Oregon juncos, chestnut-backed chickadees, hermit thrushes, olive-sided flycatchers, and the other usual "Canadian" birds of the pines.

The pines that threw their shade across our path were the same Monterey pines we so often see in England. No tree in the world is more widely planted (often under other names), but here in its native woods it is rather restricted, confined to the Monterey area and only two or three other spots within the fog belt of the central California coast. Even rarer is the Monterey cypress, which has been crowded by the pines into two groves at the edge of the sea, one at Cypress Point and one at the tip of Point Lobos. From these two groves, embracing only a few thousand trees, have descended the hundreds of thousands of Monterey cypresses in cultivation throughout the world. In cultivation they lack the character of these wild trees sculptured by the sea winds. Here at the tip of Lobos they assume the tortured tight-twigged shapes of trees at timberline, each one as decorative as a tree in a Japanese print.

On the seaward side of the grove we came to a cleft in the granitic rocks where the white foam and green water sloshed back and forth. Here pigeon guillemots (really a race of the black guillemot) flew in and out, their big vermilion feet straddling the air. *Tystie, tystie,* they wheezed in their gentle voices, calling the Norse name of their Atlantic brothers.

As we walked through the sage and *Ceanothus,* where Nuttall's white-crowned sparrows wheezed their dreamy *chee chee, chidi-chidi, chee,* so expressive of this fog-drenched coast, we could hear the dog-barking of California sea lions. Presently, we saw them on their island offshore, a rocky skerry topped by a cormorant-whitened castle. These were all bulls, and not half a dozen of them. Mixed with the barking was a curious lowing, mooing noise, and at once we saw the owners of this bovine voice. With faces like benevolent

bears, and vast humped bodies like giant slugs, were some Steller's sea lion bulls. These big phlegmatic animals of the North were twice the weight, and more, of the California sea lions. Roger has heard them bark when they are agitated, with a voice not unlike that of their southern cousin of the circuses. But these sounded like a herd of sick cattle.

There was much to see at Lobos; Roger commented that it was like watching a three-ring circus. Not only were there sea lions on the big rock but also a busy colony of Brandt's cormorants. On an islet off the point, Baird's pelagic cormorants, iridescent black birds, built their untidy nests on ledges against the walls, after the fashion of European shags. Brown pelicans traded to and from their island at the south end of the reserve. A trio of black oystercatchers came shrieking by, pitched and scuttled along the rock pools colorful with weeds and anemones. Sedums, ice plants, and other succulents decorated the lichen-painted rocks. The tide pools at our feet were teeming aquaria, crowded with spiny sea urchins, flower-like anemones, chitons, and what appeared to be abalones, those unique shellfish with iridescent linings which have no counterpart in the Atlantic. While examining these pools we discovered a sea duck, black with white head patches, swimming off the rocks. It was a drake surf scoter, a new bird for me, for though it is known in European waters, I had never met it. For some exciting minutes too, we stalked a queer whitish gull among a pack of western gulls and photographed it. It proved to be a glaucous gull—a straggler from some part of the arctic North.

Later in the day, near Cypress Point we found more northern sea lions—the Steller's—still in company with a few Californias. This is the part of the coast where their ranges meet and overlap. One old bull was obviously the loser of a recent fight—great bleeding tears in his back skin yawned as he hauled slowly ashore, groaning and retching. A great chunk of flesh was torn from his chest and his mournful face reflected his agony.

Our hour on the rocks at this coastal lookout was a productive one. To see a new animal that weighs a ton is enough for a day; but no sooner had we focused our telescopes to infinity and explored the waves beyond, than we found the sea to be alive with shearwaters, gliding in strings and packs across the gentle rollers as far as we could see. There were thousands of them out there, mostly sooty shearwaters, the same wanderers from southern seas as sometimes travel to English waters. Several times among the dark birds we saw one with a white belly. Roger identified these as pink-footed shearwaters, another wanderer from the Southern Hemisphere. We watched the sailing shearwaters for some time, until a much bigger, dark seafarer came gliding through their ranks, tilting on stiff, thin, seven-foot wings, outgliding, outflying every shearwater in sight.

"Ah!" said Roger. "Black-footed albatross."

We were lucky to see it from shore. Later we saw two or three more. These great birds seen through our telescope were a mile or two offshore, at least. Roger had once taken a boat out there; and albatrosses had come almost within arm's length when he tossed pieces of suet to them. He assured me we would see these mariners at closer range off the coast of Washington. But I shall never forget my first view, my first albatross. It is a moment in a marine ornithologist's life when he first sees a member of the most highly adapted family of flying oceanic birds. The black-foot, which comes to California from islands in the central Pacific, is a small albatross (the great wandering albatross has a wingspan of eleven feet); but it's a Great Bird, all right, a master of the ocean, a bird of the windy waves not from choice but from necessity—an example of nature's exaggeration, a living sailplane.

28

Big Trees and the Big Ice

"IT'S JUST what I expected," said James. "It's a hell of a place!"

He was deliberately paraphrasing the words of James Savage, who 102 years before was probably the first white man to see Yosemite. Major Savage was trying, in 1851, to round up Indians, not looking for scenery. He scarcely noticed the scenery. But his young companion Lafayette Bunnell was wide-eyed at the natural grandeur. He doubted if such cliffs and waterfalls existed elsewhere. Indeed, they do not.

Below us, as we stood on Glacier Point, was the incomparable valley; and plunging over its sheer walls were several of the highest free-falling waterfalls in the world.

Yesterday afternoon James had slept his way across the hot golden sweep of the San Joaquin Valley, and it was not until we started to climb the foothills of the Sierras, where the shadeless digger pines grow, that he showed signs of life. Daylight had faded among shadowy avenues of ponderosa pines and incense cedars by the tumbling Merced River before we entered the valley.

This morning we woke to the muffled roar of Yosemite Falls in the pleasant home of Donald McHenry, the Park naturalist, who devoted this day to giving us a personally conducted tour of the "valley of the grizzly bear"—*Yosemite*. That is what Lafayette Bunnell christened it a century ago. He took the name from the acorn-eating Indians, two or three hundred of which lived a Stone Age life on the valley floor at the time. The grizzly bears have gone these sixty years from their valley, but the black bears and about seventy-five other mammals remain. James, in spite of his irreverent remarks, was bright-eyed and bushy-tailed as we explored this improbable never-never land. He was pleased to learn that James Hutchings, the first pioneer to take up permanent residence in this garden spot, was originally from Northamptonshire, his home in England.

June 12

Today we saw the most beautiful valley in all North America— perhaps in the world—and some of the world's highest waterfalls, the biggest monoliths, and the world's largest and oldest living things —all in one day. It was, to say the least, exhausting.

We oriented ourselves at the museum at Park headquarters, admiring the first pictures ever sketched in Yosemite, the work of Thomas A. Ayres, who was a member of the first "tourist party" to enter the valley in 1855. Reconstructions—models in relief—of the valley at its different stages of glaciation had been inspired by the work of François Matthes of the U.S. Geological Survey. Donald McHenry, whose work as Park naturalist is combined with the directorship of the museum, explained the exhibits with an infectious enthusiasm.

Outside the museum we were back among the sounds and sights and smells of Yosemite: the not-so-distant roar of Yosemite Falls, the granite walls changing pattern under moving sun-shafts and cloud shadows, the aromatic smell of pines.

At the service station Roger parked the car by a rustic shelter while an attendant filled the tank. The shelter was supported by thick pine pillars, and in one of these a pair of white-headed wood-

(opposite) Grizzly Giant

peckers had excavated a nest. The birds came to and fro, quite unconcerned with the busy people, automobiles, and gasoline pipes that fussed continually about their home. They were indeed striking, with jet-black bodies and white heads, accented in the male by a red cockade. In the time it took to gas and oil the car and polish the windshield we had photographed both birds at the nest hole—the quickest windfall our cameras had achieved in the whole trip.

The view of Yosemite from Inspiration Point, where we made our first stop, is in everybody's snapshot album, in every guide to the beauties of America. There is nothing subtle about it; its symmetry and grandeur slam the eye. "A movie editor," I told Roger, "would build up suspense music before he cut that shot in."

"We don't need the music," mumbled Roger, into his viewfinder.

Guarding each side of the valley were great granite towers, perhaps the biggest exposed monoliths in the world. Dominating the valley on our left soared El Capitan, its top 7564 feet above the sea and 3604 feet from the valley floor. Its buttress-precipice falls a sheer 3000 feet, straying from the perpendicular no more than a tree does as it broadens to its roots. Half Dome, as neatly cleft as though it had been sliced by some huge stone-cutting instrument, oversoared the valley's head. Its quarter-spherical mass is 8852 feet above the sea and 4892 feet above the valley; its very top overhangs by 80 feet the clean perpendicular slab of its upper 2000 feet.* As we watched the cloud shadows chasing each other across the gray granite of El Capitan and over the dark carpet of conifers of the valley floor, suddenly a beam of morning sun caught the lip of Bridalveil Fall where it leaped over the Cathedral Rocks into the shadows. It shone like a magnesium flare.

But to see more clearly how the valley was formed, to see the master plan, one must view things from the rim at Glacier Point, 3250 vertical feet above the valley floor. To reach this high lookout we followed the winding road into the Canadian Zone with its lodgepole pines and red firs. What would John Muir—who explored every inch of Yosemite on foot—have thought of this new motor road, which takes the traveler in his air-conditioned automobile from the Park headquarters to the dizzy rim in less than an hour and a

---

* Half Dome's precipice is taller than the height above sea level of Britain's highest mountain, Ben Nevis, 4406 feet. El Capitan is higher than Snowdon, the highest mountain in Wales, 3560 feet.

White-headed Woodpecker

half? But, in a sense, it was John Muir who brought the motor cars to Yosemite, by acting as its understanding, "untiring, articulate press agent," as Freeman Tilden puts it.

From our Olympian lookout the valley below looked like a terrain model landscape. The Merced wound like a silver ribbon through green meadows and dark groves. Across the horizon, above the Hudsonian conifer belt, the snowy peaks of Clark, Florence, and Dana (11,000 to 13,000 feet) rose high above the wind-swept roof of the Sierra. Under some of these snowfields was John Muir's permanent ice, and from them the melt-water surged down the old ice roads to leap in eight fantastic rim-falls (not all visible from where we stood) to the vast canyon below us. There was Nevada Fall, plunging over its granite rim nearly 600 feet to lose itself in clouds of spray. Rushing and roaring for a mile the river leaped another 300 feet over Vernal Fall to the wild cascades that tumbled to the valley. Across the valley was the greatest fall of all, Yosemite, still heavy enough in mid-June to pile a fog of spray that could hide a battleship. The Upper Fall billowed like a shining ribbon across a sunlit granite wall; Lower Yosemite fell through shadow, blue-white, to the wooded valley bottom. As we watched, a golden eagle, the first I had seen in America, soared by on some updraft deflected by the valley's sheer walls. It shone red in the light, circled right over us before disappearing up Tenaya Canyon.

Such wonders of the world as Niagara (167 feet) come nowhere near the first twenty of the world's highest waterfalls. Ribbon, in Yosemite, is nearly ten times the height of Niagara; very probably it is second only to Angel Falls in Venezuela as the highest free-falling waterfall in the world, for it drops 1612 feet.* Yosemite Falls are higher, but not as a free fall; the Upper Fall drops free 1430 feet to the Middle Cascade (675 feet), from which the Lower Fall drops free another 320 feet. Its total of 2425 feet is eclipsed by Sentinel's water steps (3000 feet), of which the greatest free drop is 900 feet. Perhaps a third of the free waterfalls *in the world* over 300 feet are in Yosemite.

Below us as we stood on Glacier Point was the great example, which lives in all the textbooks, of the work of the Pleistocene ice. In Yosemite it seems that it had finished its work but yesterday—the plant carpet on the valley floor just quick weeds sprung overnight, the granite slabs smoothed into shiny new panels, the rolling upland with its pavements newly bulldozed. They should have left a notice, I thought: "Pleistocene Incorporated, Scenic Contractors and Landscape Artists. Gone to Lunch. Head Office now Alaska." Perhaps they would be back after lunch; it was impossible to believe they had gone forever. John Muir had that feeling of immediacy and impermanence back in 1871 when he was the first to find a surviving glacier in the High Sierra, under Merced Peak. Eventually he discovered sixty-five of them, two-thirds of which were in or near the Yosemite Sierra.

The natural wonders of the world seem to have this in common: each is a climax of some process of nature that has worked alone, or nearly so—worked without the confusion of other processes. Fujiyama, in Japan, is not only the most beautiful volcano in the world, but the best textbook example of pure volcanic action. The Grand Canyon's overwhelming splendor derives entirely from the erosive power of running water. St. Kilda's breath-taking gabbro and granite precipices and stacks are wholly the work of one agent, the sea. The agent of Yosemite was the Pleistocene ice.

Starting with a narrow, deep V-valley which had been cut by

* The recently discovered Angel Falls in Venezuela drop 3212 feet—2648 in one leap.

the Merced River while the Sierras were being tilted up during the Pliocene, the ice deepened it another thousand feet or more and gouged it into a broad U-shaped valley. There was no hurry about all this; for the Ice Age lasted nearly two million years. Three successive glaciations came and went and now Yosemite Valley is half a mile deep and a mile and a half across. It has been planed, or rather filed, through solid granite. Loose rock in the firm grip of the ice acted as the stone-cutting tool. At times during the Ice Age the massive ice-river overflowed the whole valley and spread over the surrounding plateau, so that only the tops of some of the heights that now dominate the valley (Sentinel Dome, Half Dome, El Capitan, Eagle Peak) stood out.

It is about 150 million years since the granite was intruded, molten, under folded Jurassic sediments (most of which have long since disappeared); as it cooled it crystallized into rock as hard as any. It formed great monolithic blocks and slabs, mile-sided crystals (we can quite legitimately call them that) with flat facets; and the immense monoliths that hem Yosemite Valley's floor have, by the stroke of geological luck that creates great scenery, facets that are nearly vertical. Away from these facets the glaciers (with their emery-paper files of rock debris) quarried the smaller blocks and slabs, carried the dross away from them and swept them clean, so that they soar naked from the flat valley floor, with but the smallest apron of talus at their foot.

The last dying glacier filled the bottom of the valley with its dirt, and blocked the mile-wide entrance between El Capitan and the Cathedral Spires with its terminal moraine, behind which a five-mile lake formed. Long ago this burst through the moraine and flowed away down the cascades of the Merced, but it left behind a flat alluvium that has become a lovely fertile meadow, about 4000 feet above the sea. Upon this meadow, on each side of the Merced River, the fine roads of Yosemite National Park run, and a well-contrived scatter of administrative buildings hides among the ponderosa pines and Douglas firs and black oaks. Seen from the valley floor the great canyon of Yosemite has a box shape: flat-bottomed, vertical sides —the tops serrated, dissected into monstrous pinnacles—cut back (but only cut back a little) by side canyons. The side canyons end above a granite wall 2000 feet up. They are hanging valleys of a classical textbook type, valleys past whose mouths the great Pleistocene ice scraper has swept, as a six-lane highway sweeps past the tracks to little farms. Down all these hanging valleys flow streams in spring (a few flow throughout the year), and when the streams reach the granite precipices they plunge over in the incredible waterfalls.

Here in Yosemite *everything* is big. A conspiracy of climate, geology, and history has made the western side of the Sierras, between 5000 and 8000 feet above the sea, the theater of organic size.

Ponderosa pines, white firs, Douglas firs, and incense cedars tower 160, 170, even 180 feet above the road. Topping all are the colossal purple-barked sugar pines, six to eight feet through their massive trunks, branchless for a hundred feet, dangling huge cones from the tips of their upper branches. Nearly 200 feet above us, these cones did not look big; it was not until I stepped off the road and picked one from the ground that I realized how much nature's proportions in Yosemite had outrun my imagination. The pine cone reached from my fingertips to my elbow—eighteen inches—and Roger said that it was not a particularly large one. What would one of these do if it fell on one's head from a height of 200 feet, I wondered.

I had been conditioned to big trees by the time we approached the Mariposa Grove; therefore I did not see anything unnatural in the first sequoias—"The Sentinels"—that met us by the roadside. Not monstrosity, I thought, not exaggeration, but size. There was nothing outlandish about these first sequoias; they were growing in the great California hillside in a garden where everything is gigantic, and everything belongs. Life must have its climax somewhere, and has it in the Mariposa Grove, in the seventy other sequoia groves in the Sierra. But at the climax, life is still just life. So I thought, when suddenly the Grizzly Giant confronted us. Then I knew what Muir meant when he said that a mastodon or megatherium would not be out of keeping with such trees. It made me think, as I paced around the hundred-foot perimeter of the fire-scarred bole. This great buttress would block traffic from curb to curb on Brook Street; that first great limb would clear Selfridge's store. The limb itself was much, much larger than the big sycamore tree in the garden at home.

The Grizzly Giant is not the tallest tree on earth. It measures only 209 feet; but its diameter at the base is more than 34 feet—twice the length of Roger's big car. Its weight has been estimated as 3700 tons. Only four other trees in all the world can claim to be larger in volume.* Its crowning distinction is that it is probably older than the other four, although no one can definitely prove the point. That would make it the oldest living thing on earth; its age is probably near 4000 years. This tree was nearly 2000 years old when Caesar's legions were landing in Britain!

Fires had consumed over 80 per cent of the bark and sapwood at the base of the ancient tree, and had eaten a great hollow many feet into its heart, but still it lived, for big sequoias are practically indestructible. Lightning had riven its top, accounting for its stocky proportions. In fact, during a single storm the Grizzly Giant was struck five times with shattering effect to its hoary crown—but still it lives. A single bolt of lightning has been known to kill sequoias outright, virtually exploding them, but most will survive a hundred thunderbolts and a hundred fires before life is finally extinguished.

Deer browsed in the sunny glades and came to us inquisitively. It was then, as we watched these graceful animals walking through the corridors of the trees, that we began to get some idea of scale. The sequoia groves were not dark forests like those of the coast redwoods; they were much more open, much drier, for though the snow often lies thirty feet deep here in the winter, the summers are exceedingly dry. Redwoods grow taller, but sequoias are far more massive, tapering relatively little from buttress to crown.

We visited nearly all of the two hundred giants in Mariposa Grove (most of them have names and pedigrees). The tree most tourists want to see is the Wawona Tree, through which a tunnel was cut— back in 1881, when Americans were more ebullient about their natural wonders. While Roger drove through the tree I photographed the station wagon underneath more than a quarter of a million board feet of timber. "There's enough stuff here, according to the lumbermen," said Roger, "to build thirty six-room houses."

"All right," I said. "Why don't they build 'em?" I knew that the real reason the sequoias enjoy a sort of security, even outside the Parks, is because their wood is far inferior to that of the redwood and shatters hopelessly when the thousand-ton trees crash to earth.

* The other four are:
General Sherman Tree (Sequoia Natl. Park), 267 ft.; 32 ft. diam. at base.
General Grant Tree (Sequoia Natl. Park), 271 ft.; 34 ft. at base.
Hart Tree (Sequoia Natl. Park), 281 ft.; 27 ft. at base.
Boole Tree (Converse Basin), 261 ft.; 35 ft. at base.

Roger and I looked up the statistics, of course—height, diameter, circumference. They are a lot of fun; but they cannot measure the serene immensity of the gigantic plant community of Mariposa, or convey its living spirit. One day ecologists will assemble all the facts about the sequoias' environment, and we will learn that what has made them grow is not magic, nor Wells's Food of the Gods.

"You know, what impressed me most," I said to Roger later, "was not the sequoias, but the sugar pines. Those clean, stalwart, straight trees, growing among the sequoias, showing that all life can be big."

We got back late to the McHenrys' house in the valley. "It's been a big day," said Roger.

"Yes," I said. "Big."

STAYING with Donald and Bona Mae McHenry gave James a nostalgia for home. Perhaps it was because their hospitality and table conversation so closely resembled that of so many like-thinking protectors of Britain's wilderness. "They remind me of Ken and Esther Williamson of Fair Isle," said James, "or Ronald and Jill Lockley in Pembrokeshire, or Eric and Dorothy Ennion in Northumberland. When you're in their house you don't remember that you're anything but a naturalist."

Our party in the morning was typical of the assorted slaves of the lamp of Natural History. Don McHenry in his smart uniform, professional Park naturalist with an amateur twinkle in his eye (I use the word amateur in its proper sense—one who is fond of something); Bona Mae, and her friend Ruth Cordner, with slung binoculars and quick eyes; Dr. Arnold Small of the Department of Life Science at Taft Junior College; and W. J. FitzPatrick ("Fitz," the valley postmaster), who seemed to know every tree and glade and bird place in the Park.

Fitz called attention to a minute knob on the very tip of a 150-foot cedar. Our glasses resolved it into a tiny bee of a bird, less than three inches long, a calliope hummingbird, its throat a sunburst of metallic red rays. In a valley where almost everything is big, it comes as a surprise to find America's smallest bird. I suppose the littlest bird may sometimes perch on the tip of the biggest sequoia.

Over the green meadows bordering the placid Merced cruised half a dozen black swifts. Their appearance reminded James of the big dark swifts at home, but there the similarity ended. The black swift of the West is one of the rarest of birds; shunning towns, it nests in the wildest of wild spots—either on sea cliffs above the surf, or behind waterfalls. Indeed, very few nests have ever been found. The third known nest was found here in Yosemite by my friend Charles Michael, who has since passed on to whatever experiences are beyond the horizon.

Of the 200 bird species in Yosemite, which assort themselves through four life zones, there are several, such as the black swift, which are specialties. One is the pygmy owl, a tiny day-hunting owl that we had found perched high in a pine near snowline the previous day. We were put onto it by the mountain chickadees, Audubon's warblers, red-breasted nuthatches, kinglets, and Cassin's purple finches, who were creating a fuss. And agitating with the others was that ethereal singer, Townsend's solitaire, a gray unthrushlike thrush with white eye-ring and white outer tail feathers.

We were looking for the pygmy owl's big brother, the great gray owl that has a southern outpost here in the high Sierra. In Europe this same owl lives in arctic Sweden, but does not venture south of Scandinavia. These western mountains, I reminded myself again, pull the northern birds much farther south than do those of Europe. This is because the mountains of America run north and south and not mostly east and west as they do in Europe.

For some hours we wandered among lodgepole pines and red firs where banks of snow remained unmelted. We never did find the great gray, though we searched its favorite meadow among the lodgepoles, where it often sits at the wood edge. A goshawk flew over and, spreading its rounded wings to their fullest, towered on a thermal. Lincoln's sparrow sang from the willow scrub and crossbills reminded us of the altitude. In the open underwood from which the snow had recently melted, snow plants were in bloom, big blood-red saprophites that thrust their fleshy foot-high fists from the mat of pine needles.

At the far end of a boggy glade, quietly watching us, was a large cinnamon-colored bear. Presently a cub, then two, then three walked out and stood looking at us. James and I fought for the Kilfitt lens and stalked the watchful mother and her playful charges, keeping the trunks of pine trees between us and them. Earlier, we had seen one of the Park's 300 bears beside the road, a tame two-year-old, begging for a handout; but this mother bear, Fitz said, was really wild. "Don't fool with a bear that has cubs," he warned. "She might run for it; she might charge. When you see those shoulders weave, like a boxer getting ready to throw a punch, she's getting ready to charge." I once had a mother bear rush me and I did not care to repeat the experience. Fortunately, this bruin favored discretion. With some secret sign she sent the three youngsters scampering for the timber while she brought up the rear.

At the mirror of Tenaya Lake, where we searched for arctic three-toed woodpeckers among the pines, we had a picnic lunch before parting from our kind friends. From here our road took us across the snowfields of Tuolumne and over Tioga Pass at nearly 10,000 feet (one of the highest highways in the United States) before dropping violently by hair-raising switchbacks to the hot dry sage-lands of Mono.

29

Goose Country

"TRY TO get there for the changing of the guard," said Ruth Hopson. "When the marsh hawk makes its last flight, and the short-eared owl takes over."

"We will be there," I promised. "Fifteenth of June at the Lava Beds—at dusk." We had arranged this rendezvous three thousand miles away in Boston during the Christmas holidays, at the time of the annual meeting of the American Nature Study Society. Dr. Hopson was soon to succeed me as president of this society whose membership is made up mostly of teachers, and others who are concerned with the teaching of nature study.

James and I had hurried down out of the Cascades, from snow-capped Shasta, and found ourselves with hours to spare when we reached the prairie country of Klamath and Tule. I had heard much about the great duck nurseries here; of their fabulous concentrations of birds at the beginning of the century; of the drainage schemes that

Ruddy Ducks

had turned this waterfowl paradise into a parched plain where dust-devils swirled; and of the recent restoration of the water table—and the birds.

Our road took us across sagebrush country into a broad intermontane plain. The symbol of the flying goose on an enameled metal sign indicated that we were in the Lower Klamath Refuge of the Fish and Wildlife Service. A dirt road angling off to our right took us onto a broad dyke, where construction work had recently been finished. Thousands of ducks were already using the impounded water areas and the new canals. At one point a golden eagle, a young bird with much white on its tail, flew up from the canal's edge and crossed the road only a few feet from us.

A pickup truck met us on one of the dykes, and its driver, a rangy good-looking man with the look of the outdoors, stepped out. He introduced himself as Thomas Horne, manager of the Refuge. Four refuges in one, really: Lower Klamath, Tule Lake, and Clear Lake in northern California, and Upper Klamath just over the line in Oregon—over 100,000 acres, of which more than half are water and marsh. These lakes are not dry blots, acres of cracked mud-pan, as are so many other lakes in the arid country; they are shimmering waters, calm and broad among a checkerboard of canals and dykes. They have but lately returned to the glory of a half-century ago. For many years, as Reclamation Service areas, their management was torn between the conflicting functions of irrigation and wildlife conservation and only recently, by dint of ingenuity and much struggle has the way been found to serve both masters.

If you were to read the notes of William Lovell Finley* in the early years of the century and then visit the refuges today and watch the thousands of western grebes, you might conclude that affairs have scarcely changed. Actually, they could not have changed more, for betweentimes Lower Klamath Lake disappeared and Tule Lake was reduced to a puddle. Now they are again filled with water, the stopping place of millions of ducks, geese, and swans. Consider these figures, jotted down from the official reports of the 1953 season:

Pintail	5,200,000
Mallard	275,000
Baldpate	200,000
Shoveller	49,000
Redhead	29,400
White-fronted goose	340,000
Snow goose	93,600
Cackling goose	71,500
Canada goose	10,200
Whistling swan	5,700
Coot	555,000

These were the peak numbers, the birds present *at one time* on Tule and Lower Klamath in the fall of 1953, not *all* the birds that stopped while on their way southward to their winter homes in the California valleys and elsewhere; that number might be closer to 12,000,000. This region is a bottleneck where birds *must* stop on their way south; for it is hemmed in on all sides by mountains and forests and deserts. A waterfowl must fly at least 150 miles in any direction before it can put down again. One eminent biologist stated that "As goes the Klamath-Tule, so goes the Pacific Flyway." Little wonder that western sportsmen have vigorously (but not always successfully) opposed schemes that would whittle down the acreage of the refuges.

These lakes are at their best in late October, when the vast num-

* *The Condor,* 9 (1907):97, and *Bird-lore,* 13 (1911):348.

bers of birds almost blot out the sun, but they also are no mean pro-
ducers of young birds; here thousands of young ducks first see the
light of day. Present this mid-June were 2500 pairs of mallards, 5000
pairs of gadwall, 1000 pairs of cinnamon teal, 3000 pairs of redheads, 1000 pairs of ruddies, and lesser numbers of pintails, blue-
winged teal, shovellers, canvasbacks, and Canada geese. Of the 200
federal waterfowl refuges, covering an acreage of 3,240,000 acres,
none gives a better picture of the work and problems of the Fish and
Wildlife Service than Klamath-Tule. Inasmuch as James could not
visit all 200 of them, this area was as good as any.

June 15

Mount Shasta, which we had left nearly a hundred miles behind
us, could still be seen in the distance, white against the blue sky, when
we ran into Thomas Horne and his assistant, Henry Christensen,
somewhere on one of the dykes that control the water level of Lower
Klamath.

Little groups of mallards, gadwall, pintails, and shovellers flew up
from the canals and ponds as we drove along. Redheads were diving
on the open pools and there were many cinnamon teal, deep russet
with blue wing patches, lovely western teal that I had never seen
wild before. Drake ruddies, tails cocked like wrens, bobbed and
trembled in their odd display and thumped their big cobalt-blue bills
on their chests. All these were breeders; some ducks were already
convoying flotillas of downy young through the reeds. A few canvasbacks, lesser scaup, and buffle-heads were still about, en route to
their northern homes. I thought we had been seeing a great many
ducks, but Horne told us that Lower Klamath was just beginning to
produce birds. "Wait until you see Tule Lake," he said.

On one of the dykes we met a little gaggle of snow geese. "Every
year," said Horne, "we have a few late ones. Not at all unusual.
Pricked birds, possibly—but not certainly."

There were at least eighteen snow geese still on the refuge; they
should have been on the arctic tundra by now. Roger had not prepared me for this windfall for our list. I ticked it off, as the little pack
—perhaps a couple of family parties—beat up into a rising, warm

wind, caught the sun on their white wings and flashed it off their snowy feathers. Across the blue sky their wing-ends beat a black rhythm against their dazzle-white.

Honkers, big Canada geese with black neck "stockings" and white cheeks, were everywhere at Tule Lake. A few were non-breeders or lonely ganders, off duty while their mates incubated in the marsh, but most were full family parties, waddling over the dykes, goose first, well-grown goslings next, gander last; or swimming from us across the lake, goose in the flat posture with neck on the water, gander trailing the family with head erect. These Canadas, near the south of their breeding range, nest early. Already Horne and Christensen, in an airboat, had rounded up nearly a thousand goslings and their molting parents into pens on dry land, and had banded and released them.

As the day wore on I began to realize that here was a concentration of inland-nesting water birds such as I had seen before only in Iceland, at the wonderful fly-lake Mývatn, densely dotted with ducks through the short summer season, and at the oasis in Iceland's center, Thjórsarver, where the pink-footed goose has its world headquarters.

A pack of white pelicans floated on a bay like paper boats. Double-crested cormorants dried their black scarecrow wings on the rocky piles of rip-rap that has been dumped to act as loafing bars for the ducks. A few Bonaparte's gulls, small gulls with black heads, were late passengers to the northern muskeg, but the California gulls, like small green-legged herring gulls, were residents. The Forster's terns and the abundant black terns were nesting here, but the big red-billed Caspian terns had probably come over from their colonies on Clear Lake. Herons were all over the place. The men on the refuge estimated the Tule Lake population this year to be 2000 American egrets, 270 snowies, 650 night herons, 30 great blues, and 900 bitterns.

To me, the most exciting water birds of Tule Lake were the grebes —*thousands* of grebes. Eared grebes (we call them black-necked grebes in Britain) were nesting among the tules and reeds so densely that in places they were in colonies, peeping and whickering. Floating outside the reed beds were the off-duty birds, thorn-billed, dark, high-crested, their golden ear tufts flowing like helmet plumes from their eyes to the back of their necks. But as numerous as the eared grebes were, they were outclassed by the big western grebes—"swan grebes"—with a wonderfully slender neck and thin yellow bills shaped like steel paper cutters. They were black and white, the black curving in a band from the modestly crested crown down the back of the neck to the black back; the face, throat, and breast a snowy white. They had eyes that were blood-red, and a voice like a broken ratchet. Facing the rising wind and slickly breasting the short surface-chop, hundreds of western grebes sat on the bays and lagoons, bodies low in the water, heads on thin necks like the masts of waterlogged boats. Hundreds and hundreds of them. Roger and I had counted a thousand when we came round an embankment corner and found a bay with hundreds more. We gave up counting. Near us, one swam with a tiny gray baby on its back and, as we watched, slid under water with scarcely any ripple, baby and all.

Later at the Refuge headquarters they told us that their census of nesting grebes on Tule Lake this year showed 3500 pied-bills, 5200 eareds, and 4300 westerns. It seemed incredible that this had been brought about entirely by water manipulation and marsh management on land that had been once reduced almost to desert—13,000 grebes where there had been virtually none! Although these federal refuges are primarily duck nurseries—or to put it bluntly, duck factories—financed largely by the sale of the two-dollar duck stamp to sportsmen, all marsh birds benefit, not just the waterfowl.

All around Tule Lake were fields of crops. "We have to be farmers," Horne said. "See that field?" He pointed to a sea of barley, fresh and green. "There are 800 acres there. All for the ducks."

He went on to explain the system of sharecropping. The Refuge contracts with the local farmers to plant a certain acreage of barley on the refuge lands. Part is harvested by the farmer; the government's share is left standing for the ducks, to keep them from descending on the surrounding farms. This year at Tule and Klamath, 6640 acres (360,000 bushels) of barley would be left standing. By the end of October, when the big mob of waterfowl had departed for points south, these control crops would all be eaten. Depredations are not a serious problem in the basin. "It creates a lot of talk," said Horne, "but you don't hear about the good the birds do. Mechanical potato-pickers leave a lot of small spuds going to waste in the fields. The geese like to eat these, and they leave behind tons of high-grade fertilizer."

Near the headquarters building was a duck hospital. "It's not large," said Horne. "We don't have the problem with botulism that

they have at Bear River." Duck botulism, or western duck sickness, is caused by a bacillus that belongs to the same genus as one of the agents of human food poisoning. It is twenty years since the bacillus was identified, and since then the Fish and Wildlife Service has learned to control it on the crowded refuges, where epidemics may strike hundreds of thousands of ducks. Nowadays the disease can be checked by careful water control (or, rather, mud control, for the bacillus thrives in shallow mud). To solve the problem of gathering the stricken ducks the famous airboat was developed at Bear River Refuge in Utah. An airplane propeller, placed aft, and above water, makes it possible to skim a flat-bottomed boat over mud covered by only six inches of water. When a sick duck is approached, a spaniel jumps overside and gently retrieves the bird, which is put into a receiving pen. After it is inoculated with antitoxin it is given fresh water, and unless too far gone recovers in a few days.*

Not far from the laboratory a basalt hill rose sharply from the plain in red tumble-footed cliffs. Great blocks of rock hid the entrance of low caves where Indians once lived. A team of researchers from the University of California were planning to spend the summer here investigating these ancient homes and the pictographs on their smoke-blackened walls. Hundreds of cliff swallows with buffy rumps twittered overhead and flew about the rock face where their jug-shaped nests lined the overhanging ledges. Stumbling about the caves at the cliff-foot, Roger and I put up a covey of chukar partridges—a new game bird successfully introduced into California within the last twenty years. The population at Tule now numbers about 450 birds. It was odd to meet in this outlandish spot a bird whose close cousin, the red-legged partridge, I had last seen from my bedroom window in England, skulking among the brussels sprouts in a snow spell.

From the entrance to one cave we flushed a horned owl. As the big dark bird jumped it dropped something large from its talons, and, pitching on a rock a hundred yards away, stood blinking at us while a thousand cliff swallows swirled in panic overhead. We soon found why it was hanging around; a fresh-killed young night heron lay sprawled where the owl had dropped it. We left *Bubo* to return to

---

* Because of the near-perfect regulation of water on Tule Lake in 1953, fewer than 200 ducks were afflicted by botulism. Western grebes are subject to another sickness, not botulism; 700 western grebes, mostly young of the year, succumbed to this mysterious malady at Tule in 1953.

his meal, for the hour was late and Horne had promised to show us a colony of tri-colored red-wings.

If one were to pick the most widespread songbird in the United States it would undoubtedly be the ordinary red-wing, the black bird with red epaulettes that swings on the reeds in every swamp of every state in the Union (and perhaps in every county where a reed patch exists). Like most other songbirds, it is territorial, each male keeping his neighbors the proper distance at nesting time. But the tri-colored red-wing, which looks almost exactly like it (except that the border on its red shoulder is white instead of yellow) is colonial, perhaps the most colonial of all passerine birds; as many as 5000 to 10,000 nests are sometimes crowded into an acre of reeds. I wanted to see this phenomenon. So, as the sun dropped toward the horizon, we made a last run out on one of the causeways until we reached a tule-bordered lagoon. Deserted nests dotted the tules, and we thought for a moment that the colony was gone. Then we heard a murmuration in a big bed of tules beyond, and saw a quiver of busy black birds, fussing in their evening roost-place, flashing their red and white shoulder shields. Some tricolor colonies run to a quarter of a million birds, so ours was a small one—a few hundreds only.

Funny, I thought, when you compare them to the common red-wing. How did they get like that, I wondered. California distribution. Different voice. Just the white instead of yellow on the shoulder shield. And *social*. Aloud I asked, "How do you suppose this isolated, queer species evolved?"

"Ask me another," said Roger, as we zigzagged back to the main road.

JAMES AND I had not forgotten our rendezvous with Ruth Hopson. The sun had dropped behind Sheepy Ridge as we crossed the south boundary of the Refuge into Lava Beds National Monument, where Ruth was to fill the post of ranger-naturalist this summer. In the fading light the marsh hawk still tilted over the meadows, but no short-eared owl appeared. The night shift had taken over, however, for when we reached the Devil's Homestead, our meeting place, a great horned owl sat silhouetted in the top of a juniper at the edge of the flow of black lava, a sinister bird against a sinister background. We wondered if it was the same horned owl that we had seen an hour earlier.

We never did see the short-ear. Ruth thought we might still find it somewhere in the moorlike country between the Lava Beds and Tule Lake. Nighthawks with their yellow-green eyeshine flipped up from the roadbed, and once we thought we glimpsed an owl as we passed the gloomy stronghold of "Captain Jack." Here, eighty years ago, was fought the Modoc Indian War, said to be the most costly war—in relation to objectives attained—ever engaged in by United States forces. Fifteen hundred troops spent a year trying to round up fifty ragged Modocs under the leadership of a renegade by the name of Captain Jack, who hid in the caves and catacombs of the lava beds and skillfully picked off the soldiers one by one. At the cost of $500,000 (when a dollar was worth a dollar) and 167 U.S. casualties (the Modocs had five) Captain Jack was finally caught and brought to the gallows.

Our aimlessly wandering road through the sage brought us to the foot of a sheer wall—Petroglyph Point. The ghostly forms of half a dozen barn owls scattered from the cliff face and faded into the dark, while high up in a crevice we could hear the rasping plaint of hungry owlets. Ruth cautioned us to watch our step, for rattlesnakes lived in these crevices and went forth on their hunting in the dark of the evening. James half hoped we would stumble on one, half hoped we would not. The bright beams of our flashlights picked up the petroglyphs on the walls, strange symbols and designs scratched on the rocks by Indians of long ago. "No one knows what these markings mean," said Ruth.

"Perhaps they don't mean anything," suggested James. "Just some Indian boys doodling on a Sunday afternoon. . . . Probably they got a beating from their parents for marking up the wall."

James was getting silly. In fact, we were all pretty tired. It was well after midnight when we found our way back into town and had a late supper, at the only place open at this hour—the local night club. After all, I reminded James, as he wearily eyed the reveling night owls at the nearby tables, this too was a facet of Wild America.

30

Deep Blue Lake

$\mathcal{F}$OR FOUR HUNDRED miles and more, as we flanked the Cascades, the pine-clad mountains that form the roof-tree of the Northwest, one snow-capped cone after another rose majestically, to tower above the surrounding peaks and ridges: Lassen, Shasta, Hood, St. Helens, and divine Rainier. It took no acute knowledge of geology to see that these lofty peaks were of volcanic origin; in times past the fires under the earth had found outlets through which they erupted their molten rock and ashes. In such manner were these cones built up. But of this string of peaks, one was missing; one had, not so long ago as geologic time is measured, destroyed itself, and in its deep caldera now lies the bluest lake in all the world.

Ruth Hopson had been a ranger-naturalist at Crater Lake National Park the summer before, so when she came to call for us this morning she was wearing her olive-green National Park uniform; she said that the old hands at Crater probably wouldn't recognize her if she wore other attire. Women ranger-naturalists are few in the Park Service. Ruth was one of the first.

The prairie, flat and shimmering, dropped behind; we skirted Upper Klamath Lake, where western grebes floated like mirages on the glassy surface, and another thirty miles farther on we found our-selves in a greener landscape. Short grass gave way to aspen groves as we slowly climbed, and soon we were among the yellow pines.

The sugar pines, a few of them at least, were still with us; their eighteen-inch cones dangling from the extreme tips of the wide branches made a distinctive silhouette against the sky. It was about seventy-five miles west of here, near Roseburg, Oregon, that David Douglas, the redoubtable young Scotsman sent forth by the London Horticultural Society, discovered this monarch of the world's eighty pine species. On the Columbia he had been shown cones so large that he could scarcely credit his eyes. Setting out alone into un-mapped, savage-haunted, grizzly-haunted wilderness, he finally found the tree he sought. That night, the 26th of September, 1825, he wrote in his journal:

> *About an hour's walk from my camp I was met by an Indian, who on discovering me strung his bow and placed on his left arm a sleeve of raccoon skin and stood ready on the defense. As I was well convinced this was prompted through fear, he never before having seen such a being, I laid my gun at my feet on the ground and waved my hand for him to come to me, which he did with great caution. I made him place his bow and quiver beside my gun and then struck a light and gave him to smoke and a few beads. With a pencil I made a rough sketch of the cone and pine I wanted and showed him it, when he instantly pointed to the hills about 15 or 20 miles to the south. As I wanted to go in that direction, he seemingly with much good will went with me. At midday I reached my long wished Pinus (called by the Umpqua tribe Natele), and lost no time in ex-amining and endeavoring to collect specimens and seeds.*

After measuring a fallen tree 215 feet long and 57 feet in circum-ference three feet from its base (larger than any now known to exist), Douglas tried to find a way to secure some of the fresh cones, which he said hung from the tips of the branches "like sugar loaves in a grocer's shop." He describes his difficulties:

Being unable to climb or hew down any, I took my gun and was busy clipping them from the branches with ball when eight Indians came at the report of my gun. They were all painted with red earth, armed with bows, arrows, spears of bones, and flint knives, and seemed to be anything but friendly. I endeavored to explain to them what I wanted and they seemed satisfied and sat down to smoke, but had no sooner done so than I perceived one string his bow and another sharpen his flint knife with a pair of wooden pincers and hang it on the wrist of the right hand, which gave me ample testimony of their inclination. To save myself I could not do by flight, and without any hesitation I went backwards six paces and cocked my gun, and then pulled from my belt one of my pistols, which I held in my left hand. I was determined to fight for life. As I as much as possible endeavored to preserve my coolness and perhaps did so, I stood eight or ten minutes looking at them and they at me without a word passing, till one at last, who seemed to be the leader, made a sign for tobacco, which I said they should get on condition of going and fetching me some cones. They went, and as soon as out of sight I picked up my three cones and a few twigs, and made a quick retreat to my camp, which I gained at dusk.

How things have changed in a century and a quarter! This lake to which we were climbing by means of a well-engineered road was unknown in Douglas' time—except, perhaps, to a very few Indians.

As we gained altitude, dense stands of lodgepole pine closed in upon us; our road snaked through forests of millions of these spindly conifers. Many were dead or near dead, for this highly competitive tree usually sends up far more seedlings than an acre of earth can support. They were countless. All reached straight up for the light and wasted little on branches. Toppled trees were scattered about like jackstraws; many were propped up by their neighbors, for there was little room to fall in their crowded ranks. Some tracts of trees seemed all of a size, and almost certainly they were of the same age, germinated simultaneously after some forest holocaust, for their dormant cones, sealed by resin, pop their seeds only after baptism by fire. The lodgepole is, as Donald Culross Peattie puts it: "the archetype of the fire forest, which is as distinctive a formation as the coniferous rain forest of the Olympic peninsula."* Mr. Peattie uses

* *A Natural History of Western Trees* (Boston, 1953).

the word "formation" advisedly, for a million square miles of western North America are cloaked in a mantle of this forest, an area twenty times that of England.

How odd that the lodgepole, I thought, the straightest of all the pines, should bear the scientific name *Pinus contorta!* On investigation, I learned that the reason for this apparent misnomer was that the first ones described to the world were found growing along the seacoast—where they are, indeed, contorted trees, squat and wind-sculptured. Little would one guess that the scrubby beach pine and the lance-like lodgepole, most regimented of all trees, are sisters under the skin, or rather, under the bark.

Patches of unmelted snow appeared in the shady sheltered spots as we climbed; dirty snow at first, then deeper drifts, hard-packed and clean, giving a wintry aspect that belied the fact that this was mid-June. But certain bird voices confirmed the calendar date, for as we listened in the crisp air we heard not only the expected woods-foragers of the Canadian cold, the chickadees and the kinglets, but also their summer associates who perhaps only a month before had been in the cloud forests of Costa Rica or Colombia. The burry phrases of the western tanager sounded in the snow-carpeted pine-wood and, even more out-of-place in this snowscape, the *hip-three-cheers* of the olive-sided flycatcher. These travelers had outstripped the advancing season. Like the summer rangers of the Park staff, they were on hand to greet the first of the season's tourists.

For yesterday was the first day of the Park's official summer season, even though the drifts were all of eight feet deep outside the administrative building. We stopped briefly to meet the young men who would spend the summer here interpreting Crater Lake and its wildlife to the thousands of tourists soon to pour in.

As we drove the last three miles to the rim, the snow became even deeper, ten, fifteen, even twenty feet deep where the snowplows had carved their way through the hard-packed drifts. As we pulled into the parking area the sheer walls of snow completely cut off our view of what we had come to see—the lake. On one side of the road were the permanent comfort facilities, reached by a long boarded tunnel through the drifts. On the other side a snow gauge that indicated a maximum depth of thirty feet. Would it all melt, we wondered, before the summer was over? Over that wall of snow we climbed, the three of us, James, the true Viking, in the lead.

June 16

Roger parked the car under the wall of a sliced drift, and we scrambled up the snow among hemlocks and whitebark pines, and looked into the crater. It was exactly a hundred years (and four days) since the prospector John Wesley Hillman had been the first white man to see what we saw. "Deep Blue Lake" he called it.

It was a still day when we looked down into the crater. Not a bird or boat ruffled the dark mirror. "It's not a place for waterfowl," said Roger.

Not even the Swan of Tuonela, I thought, which floats on the black river of death. It's a plot, another geological plot, this place. Western North America has these staggering examples of luck. Arizona's Grand Canyon, California's Yosemite Valley, and now Oregon's magic lake. All that geology can do, paraded in the pages of a living textbook. Grand Canyon, the world's water wonder;

Yosemite, the world's ice wonder; Crater Lake, the world's fire wonder.

Once a 12,000-foot volcano, Mount Mazama, stood here—a rival to Rainier. Less than five thousand years ago it blew. There were men in America then, and some must have seen it go. For the next several years sunsets around the world may have been exceptionally beautiful—as they were after the explosion of Krakatoa in the Pacific. Its eruption was of ash, pumice, and lava, and of tremendous violence; it spread at least ten cubic miles of the mountain over distances of up to eighty miles from its heart. Rivers of molten lava bled from great cracks that opened in the sides of the torn mountain, so that when the eruption died down it left a heartless empty shell.

Into this chasm the whole roof of the mountain collapsed. Nobody knows how deep the heart pit was when the roof fell; it was still four thousand feet deep afterwards, and six miles across. The highest peak on Crater Lake's rim, Mount Scott, 8938 feet above the sea, was only part of the shoulder of the great mountain. The seventeen cubic miles of the upper part of the ancient mountain had totally disappeared. From the floor at least one crater was subsequently thrust for nearly 3000 feet—its cinder top, Wizard Island, projects above the lake for 780 feet.

Crater Lake is the deepest lake in North America; its greatest measured depth is 1983 feet. Fed by snow and rain and drained by sun and wind alone, the elements conspire in a nice balance to raise and lower its surface but one to three feet in a year. In this water of great depth and clearness, the blue rays of sunlight are reflected, while the rays of other colors are absorbed, making it the bluest blue lake in the world.

Sharp steep walls, red and black under the snowfields and drifts, ring the lake in an almost perfect circle, five hundred to two thousand feet above its ultramarine surface. Only the regular cone of Wizard Island and the jagged pinnacles of the islet known as the Phantom Ship break its near-symmetry.

As I looked into the crater I felt like a boxer coming up for the last round. "Makes you think," I said to Roger. But it hurt to think. The intolerable blue of the lake, which infected every snow slope, swamped with emotion my flickering power of analysis. Analysis, I thought. Why, it's all here on the guide sheet: clear, deadpan stuff

—tells you how it all happened. List of trees, birds, and other animals —all that. Aloud I said, "Roger, we'd better not go to any more National Parks. I can't stand the pace."

I've learned several things about Roger in the course of our acquaintance, and one of them is this: that Roger talks most of the time about birds. When the subject switches, a faraway look comes into his eye. He just waits for a lull and steps in where he left off. Now this leads you at first to the conclusion that Roger *thinks* of nothing else. This is, of course, untrue. He thinks about almost everything, and even has intense emotions about almost everything. Ornithologists would describe his way of showing them as a "displacement activity." For when Roger is overcome with emotion he continues to talk about birds, but with twice the speed. At Crater Lake's edge I noticed a crisis of this sort. Roger was fumbling feverishly with the turret of his movie camera. He nearly dropped the big lens in the snow. And he was talking birds nineteen to the dozen— of all the birds we were going to see up here among the whitebarks of the Hudsonian Zone: of Hammond's flycatcher, of solitaires, juncos, kinglets, crossbills, siskins, and leucostictes—talking with a glazed look and tense intensity. Roger was finding the blue lake, on which no swan sits, hard to take, too.

"If you've finished contemplating the absolute," I rudely told him, "that lens screws on right-handed. And it's lunch time; let's go." Not knowing what else to say, I added, not for the first time, "This is a hell of a place!"

A fatuous expression: a hell of a place—the easy throwaway line of any tourist bewildered by beauty and worried for words. It occurred to me, later, that rough old James Savage, who made this classic expression when he first saw Yosemite, must have been just doing his best.

But Roger did not want to go just yet. He was trying to photograph the Clark's nutcrackers. The rim of Crater Lake is a great place for them; they were hopping about the snow under the whitebark pines, as tame as house sparrows, taking peanuts from the visitors and almost stealing the show from the blue lake itself.

Sanctuary tameness, I thought. Nutcrackers are shy things in their natural home, but around these mountaintop lodges like Crater Lake, Mount Hood, and Mount Rainier they become cheeky beggars. Several birds carried color bands; they were under individual observation by the Park naturalists.

"A new species of woodpecker" Clark called his new bird. When Lewis and Clark made their famous trip west over the Rockies and down the Columbia, they discovered a woodpecker that looked like a corvid (or crowlike bird) and a corvid that looked like a woodpecker. The first was named after Lewis, the second after Clark. Now we call the latter bird Clark's nutcracker (or Clark's crow) for it is a true nutcracker, but it certainly flies like a woodpecker, as many bird watchers have recorded.

While Roger and I were having our usual struggle for the big lens, and as we photographed the nutcrackers at point-blank range, another gray bird flew down from an overhanging branch of a mountain hemlock. "Camp robber," said Roger. "Whiskey-jack. Canada jay. They call it the Oregon jay here—one of these local names. The next edition of the A.O.U. *Check-List* will settle things once and for all by calling it the gray jay."

Gray, black, and white are the house colors of these two boreal birds that range south even to Arizona on the mountaintops. Only one bird ranges higher than these two Hudsonian Zone corvids—the rosy finch, which alone of all the birds makes the Arctic-Alpine Zone of Mount Scott its home. We were lucky to discover two of these brown and rosy birds with gray hoods feeding on a sun-warmed patch of bare earth near the lodge. The size of house sparrows, and with the voices of house sparrows, they hopped about the edges of the drift. This habit of searching for chilled insects at the drift's edge has earned them the nickname of "refrigerator birds." We shall see more of them in Alaska.

Among the snows of Crater Lake, with the desert now far behind us, and the torrid heat of Mexico a memory, it is possible for me to see Alaska coming, and believe that familiar travel, arctic travel, is part of our journey.

Not for another month will the snow be cleared from the rim road, so we left Crater Lake by the southeasterly Pinnacles Road. Here the lava flows of Mount Mazama's great eruption had become differentially hardened by the escape of gas imprisoned below their cooled mass. The hard parts, some of which still show the old gas vents as hollow vertical cores, have resisted the erosion which has swept away the softer pumice around, and now stand in the gorge of Wheeler Creek as ranks of thin, upright pointed obelisks—the Pinnacles. Park naturalist Donald Farner has found violet-green swallows, mountain bluebirds, and mountain chickadees nesting in cavities of these strange stone pillars. As we stopped to take some documentary shots Roger, who always pulls my leg about my note system, said, "Where are you going to file that one—nest site or geology?"

"I'll be lucky," I said, "if I get my notes into any sort of sequence, far less break them down under subject headings. I'm not sure whether I won't just chuck everything into a box when I get home, and thumb through it when I want something.* Another day like this and I'm done for."

"You just wait," said Roger, "till you get to Alaska!"

Alaska! It is, indeed, only six days away. But what days: Mount Hood, the Columbia River, the Tillamook Burn, Destruction Island, the Olympic forest! We have had our first real taste of the snowy North; but we are not finished with the States yet, not by a long chalk. Not by several long chalks.

---

* This is roughly what I did. It invariably takes longer to "write up" an incident than to experience it. Every naturalist who writes needs ten days to sort out one really productive day in the field.

31

Ghost Forest and Rain Forest

THERE IS no place like home! And because this is a universal truth, most visiting Europeans judge North America—and particularly its various climates—by comparison with their beloved homeland. Thus a Spanish acquaintance wrote his mother: "I have, at last, found a part of America that is like Spain." He was writing from southern California. The sweeping grainfields of the San Joaquin Valley and the vineyards reminded him of Andalusia, while the golden hills with their scattering of live oaks were reminiscent of Spanish hills with their cork oaks. On the other hand, Finnur Gudhmundsson, our Icelandic friend, on his tour of this continent was most favorably impressed when he stepped from the plane at the small airfield at Cold Bay on Alaska Peninsula. He looked about, at the gray overcast sky, the grim snow-capped mountains, the treeless moors, and the foggy sea beyond. "This," he exclaimed enthusiastically, "is just like Iceland!"

James was no exception. Unconsciously he was looking for a reflection of England in our sprawling continent. Newfoundland had suggested Scotland, just a little, but was really more like northern Sweden. Some New England towns such as Concord, Lexington, and parts of Cambridge seemed almost too like England to be true—with their museum pieces of eighteenth-century Georgian architecture. The thread of the past could easily be traced to the mother country. But as we traveled around North America's perimeter, the divergence became greater. There was very little in the sultry Southeast or the arid Southwest to suggest Britain. But on this sixty-eighth day of our travels, when we dropped from the high Cascades into the valley of the Columbia River just above Bonneville Dam, we saw growing beside the road clumps of magenta foxglove—*Digitalis*. It was not in someone's old-fashioned garden, but was growing wild as it does in its native England and Scotland. Less than sixty feet away grew a flamboyant patch of fireweed, *Epilobium angustifolium,* a native American which now flames throughout the British Isles. James cited this swapping of plants as an example of reciprocal trade relations— or reverse lend lease. Actually, we have contributed few wildflowers to the European scene compared to the hundreds—yes, hundreds— of Old World plants which have crossed the sea as stowaways to find a foothold in our fields, roadsides, and vacant lots.

Bonneville was a dam of concrete slammed across the Columbia by giant beavers. Like a beaver dam it had method in its sprawling, asymmetrical design. We threaded our way through its intricacies of platform, bridge, sluice, round its towers and machinery blocks, to a concrete flat through which the fish ladder climbed. We watched big salmon in the green water running the steps; each tank was tiered above the tank below by a salmon's leap. Without this ladder the chinooks would be unable to travel the thousand miles or so to the upper reaches of the Columbia, to the Snake, Spokane, Clearwater, and the other great tributaries that pour down from the west side of the Rockies.

Lewis and Clark, I told James, came down here in canoes. But they were stopped by the Cascades above here—sixty feet of drop in two miles was too much for them. They had to portage, and somewhere near here they put their canoes back in the water again.

"They wouldn't recognize the old place now," said James.

"Oh, I think they would," I replied. "We're only big beavers.

We've felled the forest, and built a dam. And we've built Portland and Seattle and Tacoma. But there's wilderness left; you'll see."

As we drove down the Columbia, we saw more and more foxglove; this importation from the Old World is now very widespread throughout western Oregon and Washington. The fact that it will thrive on its own here, but not in the East or in the Midwest, is an indication of a rather English climate—moist, cool, with a relatively mild winter. The Columbia is, unquestionably, America's most beautiful river. In a distance of a few miles, as our road skirted the basaltic palisades that hem the valley, we passed nine breath-taking waterfalls, one of them, Multnomah, plunging more than 700 feet to send a veil of spray across the highway. As we approached the city of Portland the benign climate expressed itself in attractive farms, lush green fields, orderly orchards. The countryside had indeed an English freshness, and James admitted that he could really feel at home here.

In the Northwest, timber is king. The farms which clustered around the Columbia thinned out as we continued westward toward the coast. Each lonely farmhouse with its green clearing seemed to be there on sufferance, surrounded by luxuriant dripping wilderness on all sides. It was some miles beyond Portland that we noticed all the trees silhouetted against the skyline were dead. Swinging around a wide curve on a hill, we suddenly left the living forest; we found ourselves in a ghost forest, where great tree skeletons, charred black, gestured in agony with their stubs of branches. Groves of smaller trees—where the fire had rushed through without consuming the heartwood—had slipped their scorched bark and now stood bleached and naked, like forests of weather-beaten sticks. We were in the great Tillamook Burn. In 1933, when the fire struck, most of the Tillamook was virgin wilderness. Sitka spruce and Douglas fir towered straight and clean for two hundred feet or more. But they are all dead now, although their lifeless boles still stand.

Although the Pacific slope of the Northwest is "rain forest," drenched in fog and rain much of the year, it also knows its dry season—when air humidity might drop to the aridity of the desert, sucking all the stored moisture from the mossy humus and leaving it as inflammable as a tinderbox. When this danger point is reached, all lumbering, indeed every activity in the forest, is stopped. Trout fishermen and campers are excluded. There is too much danger from campfires.

The summer of 1933 was following the usual pattern, when in August the humidity fell to the danger point. Warnings went out. A logger, about to quit, had one more log to pull. The ground cable to which it was attached fell across a punky cedar windfall. Friction set the dry stuff ablaze and before the handful of men could put it out a heap of slash caught fire. From that point on, control was impossible. The fire "exploded" and ran away. More than 300,000 acres were burned, nearly 500 square miles—or, to put it differently, 12,500,000,000 board feet of timber, roughly equivalent to the amount of lumber which the United States used in that year of 1933. An army of firefighters tried unsuccessfully to stop the conflagration and then, as if the Creator had decided that the lesson was severe enough, the fog and rain blew in from the Pacific and put it out.

In twenty years regeneration has taken place over parts of the Tillamook; there is a healthy green second growth under the tall snags. Other, more reluctant, parts of the burn have been a costly problem to foresters, who have attempted wholesale reseeding by airplane. The old stubs are a hazard, harboring smoldering embers after bracken burns and thereby causing new fires. In places the Tillamook seems so sterile that one wonders whether trees will ever take root again.

There have been larger fires than the Tillamook, but not in recent years. Although nine out of ten fires today can be traced to human carelessness, lightning and other natural causes must have started fires since time immemorial. The scars at the bases of still-living sequoias record fires that swept through the groves 1700 years ago. Similarly, Engelmann spruces on Colorado mountain slopes bear witness to fires in 1676, 1707, and 1781.

Great fires rank with floods and earthquakes as catastrophes. Every schoolboy knows how Mrs. O'Leary's cow kicked over the stable lantern one night in 1871 and set Chicago ablaze. Yet few seem to know as much about the great woods fire that started *on the very same night* in Wisconsin, wiping out Peshtigo and other lumber towns. Over 1,280,000 acres went up in flames. At least 1152 lives were lost, six times as many as were lost in Chicago. Even fewer know that on that same fiery day, another inferno was laying waste to 2,000,000 acres of land in northern Michigan.

It was the 3,000,000-acre fire of 1910 in the Bitterroots of Idaho that brought things to a head. The Weeks Law was passed, which made available $200,000 of federal funds to states that would co-operate in protecting the forested watersheds of navigable rivers. Today the yearly outlay by the various states and by private owners exceeds $17,000,000. The federal government furnishes an equal amount. Costly, perhaps, but it is paying off. Compared to the zero year of 1910 (a zero year in many fields of conservation), when 5,000,000 acres burned on national forest land alone (a fraction of the fires on all forest lands), the average yearly burn in national forests is now less than 300,000 acres. Tall fire towers, strategically placed on heights of land, guard the wilderness. We often saw these towers as we traveled through the mountains. Fires are spotted and fought while they are still small. "Smoke jumpers" parachute from planes to fires in the roadless back country. Formerly it took as much as two days to pack in by foot or muleback to some of the more inaccessible fires.

Depressed by the ghost forest, the miles and miles of dead trees, James and I were relieved when we entered green wilderness again. Turning northward we crossed the Columbia River. It was here, near the mouth of the Columbia, that David Douglas in 1825 first glimpsed the giant trees which were to bear his name. Standing at the rail of the *William and Ann,* which had taken eight and one-half months to make the journey around Cape Horn, he at first imagined them to be some sort of pine. Later he measured many fallen logs, one of them 227 feet long and 40 feet in circumference. Seeds which he dispatched to London were later planted in English soil. In fact the tallest tree in the British Isles today is probably a Douglas fir at Powis Castle. Standing 180 feet, it might well be the tallest tree in Europe.

What a remarkable pioneer was this man Douglas! His travels in the Northwest make our own later-day odyssey seem, by contrast, a two-penny half-penny adventure. After a particularly trying day he wrote in his journal: "How irksome a night is to such a one as me under my circumstances! Cannot speak a word to my guide, not a book to read, constantly in expectation of an attack [by Indians], and the position I am now in is lying on the grass with my gun beside me, writing by the light of my Columbian candle—namely, a piece of wood containing rosin!"

What a rebuke to James and myself, who so often failed to keep up our journals at night.

We had been seeing Douglas fir, from time to time, ever since we had been in the high mountains near the Mexican border, for it is a widespread tree; indeed, one-fourth of all the standing "saw timber" in the United States is Douglas fir. But here on the Olympic Peninsula this noble tree attains proportions almost as titanic as those of the sequoias. The tallest Douglas fir, one near Ryderwood, is 324 feet high, loftier than all but the most towering of the coast redwoods.

The forest on the Olympic Peninsula, covering an area the size of Connecticut, is the largest tract of unbroken forest in the United States. As we sped along the single highway that loops this sea-girt peninsula we had the same feeling we have often experienced when crossing the desert, or the sea. Here trees were an elemental thing like the waters of the ocean. We both fell silent as the thin ribbon of concrete took us through seas of Douglas fir, Sitka spruce, western hemlock and cedar. Trees, trees, trees—an endless green treescape seldom relieved by a house, a field, or a village.

Great trucks came rumbling by, carrying their forty-foot sections from fallen firs; sometimes one great log, sometimes three, piled in a ponderous pyramid. Later they returned minus their loads, strangely telescoped, for the logs themselves had formed the long body of the vehicle and the rear set of wheels, detachable, now rode up behind the driver's cab.

How long will this big timber last, I wondered, as truck after truck rolled by. Statistics show that Sitka spruce is being felled at ten times its growth rate and more than half of the virgin Douglas fir in the Northwest has gone in the last thirty years. In the years that had elapsed since my first visit, the primeval forest had all but vanished along this roadside. But so rapid is the reproduction here that only the most recently cutover areas were eyesores. The new green growth formed an agreeable jungle of vegetation on the denuded slopes.

Except for a few avenues of giants towering over the highway, one must now go up the side roads that lead into the heart of the peninsula to see the great primeval stands—to Olympic National Park, a virgin area of 850,000 acres established by congressional action in 1938.

How fortunate for the people of America that this park was dedicated to their recreational use before the axe, the saw, the donkey engine, and the cat-tractor had made of the place a shambles. But there still are lumber operators—particularly the "gypos," who would like to pawn these crown jewels. As Freeman Tilden describes it, they gaze at the standing timber "with all the avidity shown by a herd of cattle looking at a cornfield through a barbed wire fence." They speak of "wastage" and "locked-up resources" and "trees rotting from old age." Their appreciation is measured in board feet—yet, where does a lumberman often spend his holidays? In the National Parks, believe it or not!

We must cut and we must build, for man is a consuming animal. But, actually, less than 1 per cent of our forest resources lie within our National Parks; and there are other destinies for a tree besides houses and artifacts. It would be criminal if we allowed the saw the freedom of the Olympic park; the Park belongs to all Americans, and not to a few to make a profit from. Lumber operators can no longer "cut out and get out," always moving west. Their backs are now to the sea. They must face the facts of life and think in terms of sustained yields, as Weyerhauser and some of the other more progressive companies apparently are doing: a cycle of harvest, balanced against regrowth, on their present lands.

Not all of the 1300 square miles of the Park are forest-covered. In its center rises a jumbled mass of open peaks, crowned by Mount Olympus, the home of Jupiter—*Jupiter Pluvius,* the rain bringer. Seven glaciers flow down the slopes of Mount Olympus, some blue, some white, for this peak gets the greatest precipitation of any spot in the United States—perhaps 250 inches, most of it in the form of snow (the annual snowfall must be close to 250 feet—*feet,* that is, not inches). The average rainfall of the whole western slope of the Park is about 140 inches a year, which, James tells me, is the same as that of the four wettest places in Britain—all on the tops of the highest mountains (Scafell Pike in England; Snowdon in Wales; Ben Nevis and Sgurr na Ciche in Scotland).

From these Olympian heights the water cycle can be appreciated as clearly as on a demonstration model. To the west stretches the Pacific, from which the moisture rises, to be condensed and pulled as clouds to the peaks. There the precipitation falls, and some of it is detained awhile by the hundred glaciers, before returning through the rushing rivers to the sea. The hundreds of thousands of giant trees on the slopes below are themselves wondrous waterworks, as Florence Jaques suggests in *As Far As the Yukon,* each one "pulling a column of water from deep in the earth, lifting it to the far tree tips and spraying it out into the air (by transpiration)—hidden fountains, far higher than the Yellowstone geysers, the most stupendous array of fountains in the world."

What trees these are! On the Queets River stands the largest Douglas fir—17 feet, 8 inches in diameter. Here within the Park boundaries are also other record trees: the largest red cedar, 20 feet in diameter; the largest western hemlock and the largest Alaska cedar. Sometimes whole troops of little trees germinate and grow on the bodies of prostrate giants. I have counted a row of fourteen young hemlocks straddling one fallen log. When the log finally disintegrates they will seem to be standing on stilts. There are few rain forests outside the tropics, and the Olympic forest is by far the largest and densest of them. It is so lush that it may contain the greatest weight of living matter, per acre, in the world.

The greenest woods are those of the valley bottom along the Quinault, where the big-leaved maples grow. Here the upholstery of moss is deeper and the pendent streamers hang like ancient frayed battle flags. But the lordly Sitka spruce, the most impressive of all the Park's trees, are at their best along the Hoh, that stony river swollen with milky glacial water where harlequin ducks play. Many of these emperors stand 200 feet tall, even 250, with a diameter of 10 feet or more, trees that took root in pre-Columbian times. The rough columns soar from the deep green moss and the sword ferns until they disappear in the intricate canopy above. Here the varied thrush breathes its haunting harmonics, a long windy whistle with the quality of escaping steam, followed, after a pause, by one on another pitch —an eerie song, the true voice of the rain forest.

The time to visit the rain forest is when it is raining—or at least, when the light is diffused, the sky overcast. Then it is a much greener green, a fresher green, as though everything has had its face washed. A sunny day, rare in the Olympics except during the brief summer, is not the best time for photography. Color film, less sensitive than the eye, turns in a disappointing, overcontrasted performance—deep shadows with holes and highlights of green-gold and old ivory. On a cloudy day, the light is more diffused; the eye does not have to adjust quickly from bright spots to ink-black shadows.

James, who had never been in a rain forest before, was deeply moved by the quality of the light. He wrote the following in his journal.

WHEREVER we took the trail we stepped into a strange soft world of silent moss. We walked as if shod with felt slippers; our knees slid through clumps of ferns. Sometimes the ferns rioted over the pile carpet and up the tree trunks. But the carpet climbed the tree trunks, too, as far as the eye could see; a green, gray, bluish-yellow moss carpet—from which sword ferns and lady ferns sprayed like garlands. The forest was a carpeted hall of pillars, pillars ten feet across, pillars in close ranks which soared, smooth and round, as big as the pillars of any medieval nave, and disappeared through a canopy of green filmy banners. They were as round and solid as the pillars of Durham, as close and tall as those of Peterborough, and had the stately lift of those of Bourges. And on the carpet between these towering pillars, along its narrow corridors, shone a cathedral light. The open windows of the clerestory of the trees admitted this light irregularly; and by the time it reached the carpet it was diffused and sunspotted. Innumerable leaf-spaces projected pinhole images of the sun on the forest floor, dappling the green moss with hundreds of circular yellow spots. This yellow-green underlight of the great rain forest has been commented on by every visitor. It is a queer light that gives the corridors a magical quality. This is the forest, I thought, which leads to the giant's castle. Indeed, it does; the rugged mosaic of peaks of the mountains is a great castle beyond, above the wood, moated by a hundred blue glaciers.

I thought of cathedrals because of this light. Cathedrals have their special light. The blue of Chartres shines through hundreds of little panes, whose artists skied them where God alone could read their story—until the days of binoculars. One should always take binoculars into French medieval cathedrals and churches.*

* A year after this I had an evening rendezvous with Roger in a small town in the hills of central France. Conversation at dinner was the usual exchange of rival reminiscences. Our party had birded their way through France with cathedral diversions. Roger's party had just birded. When I spoke of Chartres, Roger looked distant (his faraway ornithological look, Arnold Boyd calls it), so I grabbed the nearest subject, quickly. "Did you ever go back," I asked, "and film that light in the Olympic rain forest?"

32

Cave Dwellers of Destruction

Not far from the mouth of the Hoh, where its glacial water from Mount Olympus pours into the sea, the road skirts the shore. There we had our first glimpse of Destruction Island. Four miles out in the gray sea, it is not like most of the Olympiades, those picturesque rocks that lie just offshore; it is not a stubborn fragment of a former headland. It is, instead, a relic of an ancient valley floor, protected from the eroding surf by a series of outlying reefs. On one end of the island was the lighthouse, dimly visible in the drizzle. That was where we would be tomorrow. Setting up the telescope we could make out a constant procession of seabirds moving past, a mile or two out, but their identification was hopeless. They were alcids—auks—all right, but were they rhinoceros auklets? "Rhinos" were the birds we wanted to see, the reason for our trip to the island.

William Leon Dawson, who visited Destruction nearly fifty years ago, wrote:

About this island of sixty acres gather a few memories of the human, a tragedy of discovery, a shipwreck or two, and latterly the brave, lonesome life of lightkeepers. But these are matters of two centuries, a mere yesterday. Drop down behind the seawall out of sight of the friendly lighthouse and you could forget man ever lived. Nor would you suspect what is the real interest, the historically continuous interest of this post—by day. It is the home of ten thousand Horned-billed Puffins (Rhinos). They are the cave-dwellers of Destruction.

Late in April the Puffins, stirred by a common impulse, muster from the wild seas and move upon Destruction by night. If there has been any scouting or premature development work, it has been carried on by night only and has escaped observation. In fact, it is a point of honor among the Rhinos never to appear in the vicinity of the great rookery—or puffinery—by day.

At the tribal home-coming, the keepers tell us, there is a great hub-bub. If the location be a brushy hillside, the birds upon arrival crash into the bushes like meteors and take chances of a braining. Upon the ground, they first argue with old neighbors about boundaries. If growls and barks and parrot-like shrieks mean anything, there are some differences of opinion discovered. Perhaps also the details of matrimony have not all been arranged and there is much screaming avowal.

Although the island is only four miles offshore it is no small project to get out there. The local Indians on the Hoh reservation are not anxious to risk their small boats crossing the treacherous stretch of sea, when they can make far more in a day by catching salmon in safer waters. To my knowledge, no ornithologist had been out there in recent years, not even Garrett Eddy, whom we would meet that evening. Eddy had arranged for a 125-foot Coast Guard cutter to transport us from the base at Neah Bay sixty miles up the coast. We would take aboard the tape recorder and the big parabola, for if Dawson was right about the hubbub we would be the first to record it on tape.

That evening at our rendezvous in the Indian village of Neah Bay we were joined by Barbara, whom I had not seen in two months, not since James and I had stopped at our home in Maryland, and Bill Cottrell, whom we had last seen in Boston. Garrett Eddy was with

"Rhino"

them, and Dr. Gordon Alcorn and Finnur Gudhmundsson, director of the Icelandic museum. James had camped with Dr. Gudhmundsson two summers before on the Hofsjökull in Iceland, where with Peter Scott they trapped and banded over 1100 pink-footed geese. There was much to talk about over the coffee. After receiving our sailing orders from the captain we turned in for a few hours of sleep, if sleep was possible on the eve of such an exciting sea trip.

We left the mooring at daybreak and headed out into the Strait of Juan de Fuca toward Cape Flattery. Three small dumpy brown birds skittered like skipping stones over the wavelets of the sheltered bay and, finally airborne, buzzed off into the gray mist. Our glasses showed them to be marbled murrelets. James was agog, for this was the mystery auk, the last North American bird whose nesting remained unknown. (The much publicized bristle-thighed curlew was not really the last.) It seems incredible that a seabird, one that is quite common along two thousand miles of coast, from the Aleutians to California, should withhold its secret so long. There is one bona fide egg of a marbled murrelet at the U.S. National Museum. It was taken from the oviduct of a female shot by a Haida Indian boy in the Prince of Wales archipelago. There are also two or three other *alleged* eggs in collections, but the actual nesting place of the bird is still a mystery.

The Indians say that they heard this bird, the *Tichaahlukchtih,* "at night passing high over the mountains." According to Dawson, who himself had heard marbled murrelets at night over the coastal mountains:

> *The Quileute Indians claim that they do not nest like the other sea-fowl, upon the rocky islets, the Olympiades, but colonize*

upon some of the higher slopes of the Olympic Mountains, where they lay their eggs in burrows; and one of their number claims to have come upon such a colony several years ago while hunting in company with a white man. I have toured the Olympiades three different seasons in Indian canoes and I found my Indian guides infallible in the identification of sea-birds. The marbled murrelet certainly does not nest on any of these islands, where birds of thirteen other species are known to breed. Obviously, if it nested on islands or coastal cliffs as do all others of the Auk tribe, its nest would have been found long ago.

Circumstantial evidence indicates that these brown-barred gnomes fly at night to forested mountain slopes, perhaps as much as 25 miles from the sea, where burrows in the mossy ground or under logs and rocks may be used for their nests. Why then, a well-known European ornithologist recently asked me, can't you locate them? I should like to turn him loose in the high rain forest for a week—or a month. He would understand why.

Our boat, the cutter *McClane,* rounded Cape Flattery, crossed the tide rips, and headed almost due south. We were on the open Pacific, which this morning was not quite living up to its name. However, it was not really rough (otherwise the coastal command would not have OK'd our landing on Destruction), but just rough enough to send at least one of our party below deck. There is no better antidote for *mal de mer* than bird watching. It is only when things slack off and become dull that one has time to ask himself whether he is feeling as he should. But things were not dull. Birds were constantly passing: California murres, pigeon guillemots, scoters, tufted puffins, shearwaters. Three or four black-footed albatrosses crossed and recrossed our wake, giving us some close looks. These saber-winged birds had come all the way from Midway, Laysan, or one of the other central Pacific islands, thousands of miles away. With this ability to glide almost effortlessly over such great distances, albatrosses, one would think, should turn up more often in the North Atlantic. James offers a simple explanation: the doldrums near the equator act as a block to birds such as these, which *depend* on sea winds for their transport.

While we drank coffee below deck the patches of chilling mist completely disappeared from the surface of the sea. On returning topside we found the sun full out, while far to port the Olympics, which had sucked the sea moisture to their crests, were heaped with

huge dramatic cumuli. Destruction Island, dead ahead, looked fresh
and green against the sparkling blue of the water. James, who knows
a thousand islands, wondered what this one would be like.

June 19

Here we were in boats again, making a landing on a rocky sea
island. It might have been the Hebrides, any one of a hundred land-
ings I have made at one time or another—at least, until the birds
reminded me I was thousands of miles from the Hebrides.

I have seen every sea island in the British Isles except those off
western Ireland—thousands of islands; and I've seen quite a few like
Destruction, standing rather low, alone, off a wet misty mountainous
coast. From all sides Destruction looked flat, steep-sided, and as we
neared it its top showed abundantly green. It was covered with a
thicker scrub than any small island in the Hebrides. Its black cliffs,
twisted into countless gullies, buttresses, and peninsulas, embraced
little inlets and bays where the sea swell surged in an oily rise and
roll. At the west end of the island's plateau stood the lighthouse, and
below was the landing bay, with its built-up concrete jetty. We made
a wide swing around reefs where the white water broke, and came in
from the south, into a deep cove. It looked a pretty routine landing
to me, but the ship's captain, who was, after all, responsible for us,
made us put on kapok life jackets. Finnur Gudhmundsson, who
stands a head taller than most men, looked like a giant from Mars.
Roger watched anxiously as the crew swung his precious optical
gear into the whale boat. In two or three journeys from ship to jetty
we were all ashore.

There were very few breaches in the sixty-foot wall of dark sandstone that ringed Destruction Island's tangled green plateau. We
climbed by means of a steep ramp with cleats to the top of the island.
"Just the place for a wren," I said, and sure enough, just then a
troglodyte sang from the cliff top. The vegetation was rank and practically impenetrable. Fortunately the Coast Guard Service had driven
concrete paths through it, or it would have been practically impossible to get about. The thicket was salal, mostly, and salal six feet
high. Only Finnur could see over the top of it. And besides salal there

were salmonberry bushes—with yellow berries and red berries, hanging from them. They looked delicious. We tried some but found them disappointing, tasteless.

"I can't get over these wrens," I told Roger. Europe, Britain, even St. Kilda, all the little Scottish islands except some very remote ones like Rona, everywhere these northern sea-cliff coasts have the wren. And Alaska too, through the Aleutians, even the Pribilofs. What an extraordinary, ubiquitous, successful, hardy little bird is *Troglodytes troglodytes,* the winter wren.

The wrens are a New World family, of course. There are many kinds, each with its place in the sun: some live in marshes, some prefer gardens, some canyons, some cactus. The winter wren, being the marginal one, the one that lives farthest north, Roger pointed out, naturally was the one to reach the Old World via the Bering Strait or the Aleutian steppingstones. Once on the other side it swept across to Britain, where, relieved of competition with other wrens, it even lives in gardens (which in America are inhabited by house wrens and others). Even in Iceland there are winter wrens; their stubby wings and the wind have taken them seven-eighths of the way around the world. Of the principal northern lands, only Greenland lacks wrens.*

Here on Destruction, I thought, the little birds sang a weak song—buzzy and almost insect-like. They were not at all like the strong explosive singers back home or the sweetly musical ones of the American Northeast. Here would be a virgin field for the tape recorder—the song dialects of the winter wren. Barbara tried the portable tape recorder on the wrens near our camping spot, but the combination of wind through the salal and the wave noise soon discouraged her.

Round the lighthouse buildings there were house sparrows, and barn swallows too, hawking for flies. We saw ravens, which gave us a further reminder of the Old World element; but the rest of the land birds here belonged to the New World and nowhere else. Rufous hummingbirds, bright rusty with fiery throats, buzzed about the flowering shrubs, and violet-green swallows sat on the clothesline by the buildings. Russet-backed thrushes and fox sparrows sang their

---

* According to E. A. Armstrong, the leading authority on the wren, there are 49 recognizable races in the world. Like steppingstones, no less than 11 subspecies bridge the Bering Sea.

fine songs and orange-crowned warblers their colorless trills. American robins, yellow-throats, purple finches, and goldfinches were in residence. So, on the island top, I could not dream myself at home for very long.

Seldom does Destruction Island see a more sunny day. We spent most of the afternoon scrambling about in search of nests of the tufted puffin and the rhinoceros auklet. It was a frustrating search, for nowhere was it possible to climb down to the puffinery from the top: impenetrable thickets barred the way to the arêtes and buttresses in which they had their burrows. Fortunately, when the tide was low, we could step down from the landing place and walk along the tide-exposed erosion shelf, and climb up from below. It was fairly easy climbing until we got among the caps of thick turf.

There were hundreds of these bizarre puffins, so unlike the puffins of the Atlantic. They were bulky black-bodied birds with staring white faces and the biggest triangular orange-red bills that any sea-birds ever carried. Curling back behind their eyes were bright buff-yellow ear tufts, a glorious flaxen hair-do. These trailed straight back as the birds flew, and shook down in a graceful swirl when they landed. In places their burrows honeycombed the turf like those of the Atlantic puffin on its islands. On Carroll Islet the tufted puffins sometimes nest among the roots and stems of the thick mat of salal bush, not in burrows at all. But we didn't find this on Destruction. Never did we hear the tufted puffins utter a sound, as they pitched to a landing at their nesting burrows and waddled in.

After a time Garrett Eddy and Gordon Alcorn, who had been pursuing their own search, shouted us over and we scrambled to see what they had found. They had dug out a rhinoceros auklet. It seized our gloved fingers savagely as we examined the carunculation, or rhinoceros horn, on its thick brown-yellow bill. It also had two plumes on its black head, neither of which had the magnificence of the ear plume of the tufted puffin, but were startling ornaments, nonetheless. The plumes were white—one ran back from above its eye, the other back from the corner of its mouth, rather like a white mustache. I could not agree more with William Leon Dawson, who long ago insisted on calling it a puffin and not an auklet. But, unlike the puffins that were constantly flying overhead, this bird comes in only at night.

Try as we might, we could not find a second auklet; the burrows

Tufted Puffins

went back too far and we nearly dislocated our shoulders reaching into them. Hot and sweaty, we soon became filthy with the damp sandy earth. We were eventually forced by the rising tide to retreat to the landing, where we found the Coast Guard boys, bored with life on their island, amusing themselves by feeding bits of shellfish to the sea anemones.

While Barbara was preparing a picnic supper the rest of us climbed the winding stairs in the lighthouse to the platform that surrounded the big lenses. The sun was going down in a burst of gold, on a calm sea where wisps of mist were beginning to gather. Small flocks of rhinoceros auklets had gathered on the water a quarter of a mile offshore, but they would not be coming into their burrows in the turf and under the boulders until blackness concealed their arrival.

As we marched back along the path a shadowy figure detached itself from a clump of salal and barred our way. "It's only Bambi," said one of the lighthouse boys who was with us. "Bambi, our tame doe!" Somebody had brought her over to the island as a fawn several years ago. Bambi was certainly tame, too tame. She came trotting up with a somewhat sycophantic look (if deer can have such looks). She nuzzled us for food and idled round the picnic in a hinting manner. The lighthouse boys stood aside and laughed. "Now you see the sort of nonsense we have to put up with!" During the rest of that night, as we blundered about the island top, we kept encountering dear Bambi.

The five young coastguards who ran the lighthouse invited us in for coffee. One of them had baked the most colossal cake in America. Each of us had two pieces but declined a third. We signed our names in the old guest book, and idly flipping the pages came upon the name of William Leon Dawson (of *Birds of California* fame), who had paid this island a visit in 1907 and came again several years later. Ralph Hoffmann, who wrote the handbook of the *Birds of the Pacific States,* had also been here, not long before he fell to his death from a bird cliff on the California coast. Destruction had not been entirely ignored by the famous naturalists of the past.

It was night-dark when we rounded up our flashlamps to watch the rhinos arrive. We scattered, occasionally shouting or flashing our positions to each other. Roger and Barbara set up the parabolic reflector and tape recorder on the slope near the landing place, but not a sound did the incoming rhinos make, just a sudden *whir-r-r* and a flutter as they crashed into the bushes and sought the entrance to their nesting crevices. I cautiously felt my way along the foot of the cliffs to the cove where we had worked in the afternoon. Often I was able to follow an incoming bird through the air with my torch beam until it made a landing. One dazzled bird looked dazedly around, walked down the smooth rock to a sea pool, and swam up and down. I caught several quite easily at the entrance to their ledges. It was a queer place in the light of our torches—buttresses of rock, fractured and split by erosion, full of eerie wet caves, grottoes out of some elf story, with the queer rhino gnomes fluttering and flapping about. Not one uttered a sound. There was no vocal hubbub, as Dawson had described. Nor were there 10,000 birds—hundreds certainly, but not 10,000. I wondered how even a trained oölogist like Dawson could arrive at such a definite round figure in such impossible terrain.

Before we were through with the cliffs and with the fluttering auks of the night, the stars had become obscured by a mist moving in. Drops of moisture glistened on the salmonberry bushes as we returned along the concrete path to our camping place. Bambi lurched into our torch beams, her coat glistening. We tried to settle down for the night as best we could. Caught again, I thought, remembering the wet night on the Coronados. "Oh, it's all right," Roger had said. "Everybody sleeps out without a tent in the West in summer." But I wasn't so sure. I rolled up in my bag under a rubberized cover and decided to make the best of it. I woke two or three times in the night and rolled over. The bedding felt strangely heavy, but it wasn't till dawn that I found it was completely sodden.

In the grayish dawn there were still a few flashings and flutterings about the cliff, and bangings in the bushes. Perhaps there were some tufted puffins or rhinos nesting under the salal after all. I rolled over for another forty winks while Finnur, hardy Icelander, had a bathe before breakfast, after which we re-embarked for the cold run back to Neah Bay.

Guillemots

33

Tundra of the Emperors

WILD ALASKAN peaks, deep under snow and glacial ice slid beneath our big airliner. Had anyone ever set foot on these mountaintops, we wondered? Except for parts of arctic Canada, Alaska is certainly the wildest remaining part of wild North America.

We would reach Anchorage in an hour, so we dug out our notebooks and brought the bird list up to date. Vaux's swift on the Olympic Peninsula had been our last new bird—Number 497. Our running total now equaled Guy Emerson's record. We had, in just over ten weeks, seen as many species north of the Mexican border as anybody had ever previously seen in a year. Anything from now on would be a new record.

The crucial bird—Number 498—came shortly after we reached Anchorage. Flying overhead near the airport was a short-billed gull.

We sent Guy Emerson a telegram informing him that he had lost his throne as champ of the bird-listers.*

Our stop at Anchorage was just long enough to get oriented before taking one of the Alaskan airways to the outpost town of Bethel on the Kuskokwim. Here we bought provisions for a week's stay on the tundra. Coca-Colas, we noted, were still with us at this Arctic outpost. This enterprising beverage quenches the thirst of a continent; but whereas the Mexican Indians at Xilitla pay three or four cents a bottle and drink it warm, the Eskimos stick a quarter in the slot and get theirs ice-cold from the big red refrigeration machine.

The small plane that we chartered at Bethel would safely carry only 1000 pounds, including the four of us and our equipment—no more. We did some quick figuring: Finnur Gudhmundsson weighed 280 pounds; James Fisher, 230; I weighed 200, and Bill Cottrell is a good-sized man. The four of us weighed nearly 900 pounds—and my camera equipment weighed 50. This posed a problem. We had our camping gear—and the two big boxes of food. Jimmy Hoffmann, our pilot, figured we could make it if we took fuel only for the outward trip; he would take a chance on picking up gas from the Eskimos at New Chevak after he had dropped us. It was an uncertain moment when our small float plane, heavily laden, faced the fresh breeze on the Kuskokwim and took off for the abandoned village of Old Chevak.

We had been unable to find Old Chevak on any of our maps. In fact, we couldn't even find New Chevak, but Hoffmann, who had been making this run for eight years, knew exactly where they were. As we flew over the tundra we could see why this country was still inadequately mapped. Rivers looped back upon themselves like tortured snakes, complicated, braided rivers that meandered among a million potholes, ponds, and lakes. Finnur Gudhmundsson said it was the most exciting-looking terrain he had ever seen. Here one could

* James pulled a fast one in Anchorage. While I stayed in the hotel to work on a drawing he went into the mountains with Ed Châtelaine of the Fish and Wildlife Service and came back with five new birds on his list. He retained this margin until he returned to England; and so, for a month, an Englishman held the record list of birds seen in one year in North America. It was not until I returned across the continent in August that I caught up.

Incidental information: my year's list at the end of 1953 was 572 species (not counting an additional 65 Mexican birds). R.T.P.

Mine was 536, plus the 65 Mexican species, plus 117 others seen in Europe, a total of 718.—J.F.

still have a lake or a small stream named after him. Niall Rankin, the British bird photographer, came here on a goose chase in 1951; now a stream in the heart of the black brant grounds is known as "Rankin's Slough."

As our plane sped along we tried to spot birds below. They seemed few at first, but with each mile as we approached the coastal marshes the frequency of ducks, geese, swans, and cranes increased. An hour later, when we came in for a landing, James pointed excitedly to a Sabine's gull as it swept past our windows. Soon we felt the broad pontoons hit the water and we taxied up to a slight rise on the tundra where stood a one-room wooden building. This was Old Chevak, or what was left of it; for the Eskimos now had a new town, a few miles distant. This forlorn building, which had been the old Russian church, was to be our headquarters for a memorable week.

June 24–July 1

When the Cessna lifted from the water and roared off, the four of us—Finnur, Bill, Roger, and I—gazed after it rather soberly. Jimmy Hoffmann promised to be back on July 1, but we knew that if the fogs rolled in from Bering Sea we might be stranded for two or even three weeks, with food for only a week.

Our home was to be the old church, which at the time of our visit was inhabited by Matt Peterson and his young assistant, Jack Paniyak, trained Eskimos employed by the Fish and Wildlife Service on goose counts and goose marking. In the old days the Chevak Eskimos used to drive the geese across the tundra—when they had big goslings and were in their flightless molt—and net them in thousands for food, a method of wildfowling known also to natives in northern Canada and Siberia, and in Iceland, where it became a great art in the Saga Age.*

These tundras between Chevak and the Bering Sea have been called the greatest goose nursery in North America. Influential conservation organizations have made representations to the U.S. Department of the Interior, urging that this area be set aside as a federal

* See Peter Scott and James Fisher, *A Thousand Geese* (London and Boston, 1953).

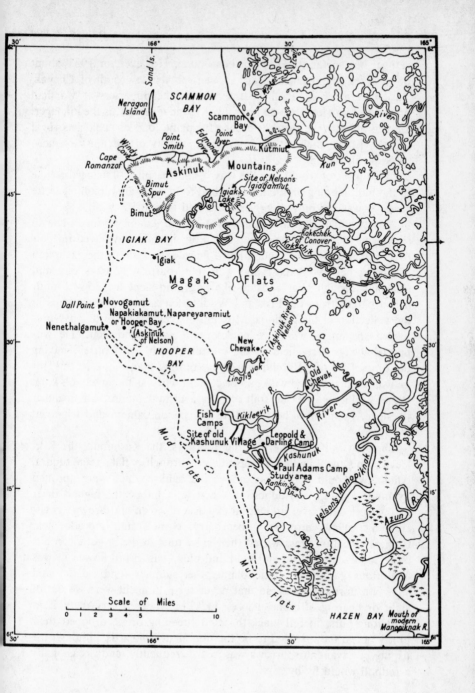

Scale of Miles

0 1 2 3 4 5   10

refuge, but so far this has not been done. However, in 1937 about 6800 acres round Hazen Bay, about twenty miles south of Chevak, was made a refuge. Paul Adams, with his headquarters at Marshall on the Yukon (less than an hour away by float plane), is the manager. During our stay he brought a cheerful plane load of ecologists for a night's visit on their return from an air survey of the musk ox herd of Nunivak Island.

"Had a bit of trouble on the way," said the pilot. "Snagged a hole in the hull, landing on a lake. Paul had to lose his aluminum cigarette case—it was the only thing we could find to patch it with."

"Matty and Jack will look after you," Paul Adams told us. "They'll show you the geese." And they did. For eight days we lived in their two outboard dinghies, and enjoyed fine weather (with the exception of one rather awful day) and were out fourteen hours a day and splashed through bogs and ate like hogs and slept like logs. Finnur had a permit from the Fish and Wildlife Service to fill some gaps in the collection of his National Museum of Iceland, and was busy preparing specimens while we cooked and wrote and slept. He was nearly always first afield in the morning, with Bill Cottrell, having the time of his life. Bill did more pure birding than the rest of us, for he was unencumbered with gun or camera. He was the notebook king. Roger's silhouette, as he stalked over a distant tundra, was a queer five-legged animal as he trailed his big movie camera and tripod at the ready.

The slow winding rivers of our journeys, the Kashunuk, the Kik-leevik, and the Lingliguak, meandered through a flat green tundra. Afloat, we could seldom see above the banks, which were aproned by mud—quaggy and adhesive. When we climbed the higher, drier banks we looked over an eternal expanse of green and brown: grass, creeping willow, crowberry, bearberry, cornel, and Labrador tea. Clumps of cotton grass waved their silky tufts in the bright clean air, and Jacob's ladder, big and bold and blue, was in full flower. It was a glorious garden of arctic plants, this summer tundra-delta, and stiff with northern birds, so that never for a moment were we out of sight or hearing of crane, goose, duck, or wader. Everywhere Lapland longspurs, in full black-throated breeding dress, dropped their pretty notes; they seemed to be the dominant songbirds, although the lisping of savannah sparrows was heard frequently, and occasionally a redpoll would fly by.

The great permafrost maze of grassy marshes, moors, tarns, lakes, sloughs, and rivers is a paradise for wildfowl and waders such as exists in few other places in the world. In sheer variety and numbers it beats anything in the glorious tundras under the central icecaps of Iceland. Its only rivals are the alluvial deltas of the Athabaska and Mackenzie in Canada's northwest, or the great northward flowing-rivers of Siberia.*

Just back of the old church, on a dry hummock raised a few feet above the surrounding countryside, was the cemetery of the dead Eskimo village. Here on the tundra the permafrost forbids any digging and the Eskimos bury their dead above the ground. Wooden crosses at their heads, the coffins sprawled about the top of the hummock. Some had disintegrated and a whitened skull or femur or humerus marked the grave spot. The newer coffins were covered with canvas painted white, which caught the eye even farther off than the church.

Near the cemetery a hen willow ptarmigan tried frantically to distract us from her brood. We frequently came upon these white-winged arctic grouse as we explored the creeping willow swards and the bearberry moors. A short-eared owl, which haunted the cemetery in its search for voles, also had a family nearby, a half-dozen golliwogs in a grass-lined nest. Short-ears we saw quite often, but never a snowy owl. This was not a lemming year.

Waders of a dozen sorts were nesting, singing, scolding wherever we went. The air resounded to the whickering of godwits—the Pacific race of the bar-tailed godwit, an Old World bird that invades the New only in western Alaska. Excitable, and inquisitive, these cinnamon-colored birds with long, slightly upcurved bills followed our movements across the tundra like village dogs inspecting a stranger. The air was full of the lovely rippling trill of the dunlin, reminding

---

* Herbert Brandt in one season listed 86 species in the Hooper Bay area, not far from Chevak. Our own week's list of 52 included neither the sea nor the mountains. Other Alaska lists are: Cape Prince of Wales, 79 (A. M. Bailey); Point Barrow, 60 (McIlhenny). Few Greenland tundras can raise more than 36 species, seabirds included. A few other tundra samples are: Perry River, Canada, 44 (Peter Scott); central Iceland, 29 (Fisher, Gudhmundsson, Scott); Baffin Island, 30 (Soper); Spitsbergen, 28 (Fisher); Novaya Zemlya, South Island, 33, North Island, 25; Franz Josef Land, 21. Siberian deltas would run between 30 and 40. So we were privileged. Our tundra at Chevak was a super-tundra.

me of certain summer moors in north England; and Finnur thought of Iceland. Roger picked up a sky-larking male in the bull's-eye of his camera gun and followed it in slow motion across the sky, closer and closer until it nearly filled the picture, at which point it was joined by its mate. Quivering on parachute wings, the pair sank gently back to the marsh a few yards away, their mutual display imperishably recorded.

Along the edges of the tarns the little western sandpipers fluttered and twittered, running, raising their wings as banners, then flying up into quivering dunlin-like display flights with their high bubbling notes. Pectoral sandpipers, like large streaked stints, and black-bellied plovers in full nuptial dress, pale above and black below, we found only on the drier ground. Ruddy turnstones on the drier tundra inland gave way to black turnstones downriver. These dusky turnstones, new to me, were among the most numerous waders. Several times we saw curlews that we suspected might be the rare bristle-thighed curlew (which Arthur A. Allen found nesting less than 100 miles northeast of here), but we listened in vain for the plover-like notes that distinguish it from the ordinary Hudsonian whimbrel. Unexpected were a flock of four Hudsonian godwits—obviously wanderers, for this rare wader is not known to breed in this part of Alaska.

Spinning on the dark mirror of every pool were northern phalaropes, slight swimming waders, subtle in their breeding dress. They were whirling about, dabbing nervously for tiny unseen prey, whickering musically, and pursuing each other in endless courtship chases. The phalaropes are waders in which the role of the sexes is largely reversed, for when the larger, more richly-colored female has laid her eggs, the modest male has all the duties of incubation. Only on the tundra do the phalaropes have much to do with the land; most of their year is spent on the sea, on the oceans south of the equator.

Young Western Sandpiper

Occasionally we found a red phalarope, in full deep-russet dress, so unlike the gray phalarope we sometimes see in passage in England, and which is the same species in winter feather.

Down the Kashunuk River, Matty and Jack, the Eskimo boys, had established a field camp under the guidance of Paul Adams, with a decent big tent stretched over a wooden framework—comfortable quarters from which to do their job of assessing the goose population. On our way downriver to this camp we ran a gantlet of waterfowl such as I had encountered but once before in my life. Only at Mývatn in north Iceland had I seen as many species of nesting waterfowl in one day. We scored 16 species of Anatidae in the Chevak tundras all together, and more than once saw 13 or 14 in a day.

This was the week of the big hatching. Everywhere geese were convoying their fuzzy goslings to the water. There must be survival value in this simultaneous hatch; the predators—particularly the glaucous gulls—cannot make the inroads that they would if hatching took place over a longer period. Once the young have grown a little they are fairly safe. Often as we went downriver we would slow up to avoid disturbing a family of cackling geese caught in midstream. These diminutive Canada geese, hardly larger than mallards, would sort themselves out: the goose leader in the crouched position, neck stretched forward, the goslings, sometimes as many as seven, wobbling behind her, the gander bringing up the rear, neck erect, head aggressive. On reaching the muddy banks they would scuttle up with some difficulty, flapping their wings to keep balance. These cacklers were very courageous in defense of their young, and allowed us to come within easy photographic distance. To repay them we tried to get the photography over as quickly as possible, and we always saw to it that the family was totally united, with the glaucous gulls out of reach, before we left. The big gulls were always overhead seeking what they might devour, waiting their chance to snap up goslings separated from their parents.

It was on the Kashunuk River that we met the noble goose we had come so far to see—the emperor goose. You must go to western Alaska to see this white-headed, scaly-backed bird. Seldom does it winter outside the Aleutian chain, and its summer grounds are confined to the deltas of the Bering Sea. It may be one of the few species of wild geese that Peter Scott has never seen wild, but he finds little difficulty in breeding it in semicaptivity in the fine collection of the Wildfowl Trust in Gloucestershire.

In nature the emperor does not look quite as neat and shiny as it does on the Severn Grounds, because, like many swans and geese in the North, it picks up iron stains from the soil. We saw lots of emperors, and all of them had their white heads stained orange or rusty. We met them on the river, and often beside the boggy tundra pools, walking with their new broods in the rushes with their feet awash. Their goslings were gray, almost greenish-gray in general tone, much more like the goslings of the black brant than the brown goslings of the cackler. We could usually spot emperors some distance away by voice before we could see them. Their rather hoarse, far-carrying, two-syllabled calls (like a very deep pink-foot) kept finding them for us.

While we were still among the cacklers and emperors we came upon our first black brant, leading parties of greenish goslings on the rippling waters of the gray river. They growled as we approached. Only once did we hear the ordinary winter voice of the brant, the *cronk cronk*. Mostly they talked to each other with this guttural voice. A large population of black brant breeds between Hooper Bay and the south entrance to Baird Inlet—that is, in a smallish area of coastal tundra centered on Hazen Bay and the Chevak marshes. Downriver from the camp we were in the heart of their nesting grounds.

In 1950 David Spencer, Urban Nelson and Winston Elkins, making counts by plane, found that the tundras between Chevak and the coast supported about 130 nesting waterfowl to the square mile, of which 60 per cent were cacklers, 20 per cent black brant, 10 per cent emperors, 5 per cent white-fronts, and 5 per cent pintails. Inland from Chevak the density goes right down to 17 waterfowl to the square mile, and these marshes are dominated by ducks: American scoters (30 per cent), scaup (17 per cent), pintails (15 per cent), lesser Canada and cackling geese (14 per cent), white-fronted geese (6 per cent), old-squaws (5 per cent), and lesser numbers of swans, mallards, baldpate, teal, and others.

All our way down to Matty's camp we kept on landing, staggering through the prehensile mud, to gain some green marshside with its families of cacklers and emperors, with the clanging of cranes in the background, and the distant bleating of Wilson's snipe, and the

Emperor Geese

laughs and scolds and complaints of little colonies of Sabine's gulls, and the lovely aerial songs of the waders. We often cut off the motor, to drift down upon a Pacific loon fishing in the middle of the channel, or to listen to the bubbling quacking of a red-throated loon going downriver on its way to more marine feeding grounds.

Female Pacific eider ducks waddled across the mud flats with their peeping ducklings hard at their heels. We never saw the king eider; it passes this coast only on migration. But the rare Steller's eider, with its white head and red breast, was about in small numbers. Finnur marched over acres of boggy tundra not far from the sea until he had found a duck incubating her eggs. It was a little bird compared with the big dark Pacific eiders that were nesting all around. Farther inland we occasionally saw female spectacled eiders, with a curious ghost of the bright "spectacles" of the male, but nowhere could we find a drake. They were probably all down at the club, having done their duty for the season; for drake eiders take no part whatsoever in the management of the family. On a little pond near Matty's camp we found a female with two tiny dark babies clinging to her apronstrings. We tried to herd the little family into camera range, Roger on one side of the pond, Finnur and I on the other. Jack Paniyak, with his strong Eskimo sense of humor, doubled up with laughter at the sight of the three large forms (certainly the three largest ornithologists in Alaska at the time) that were gesticulating like wind-blown scarecrows, all because of one little duck and her brood. But this was no ordinary duck. None of us had ever seen a spectacled eider before we came to Chevak.

Wherever we went we found those curious anomalous sea predators, the jaegers, which we in England call skuas. On pointed falcon-
like wings they hunted over the tundra. Scarcely ever did we look
up without seeing a parasitic jaeger with its three-inch tail-points,
or a long-tailed jaeger with ten-inch tail-streamers. There was no
evidence that either of them did any harm to the ducklings or goslings,
but once while we were watching a leggy young western sandpiper
only a few feet away, a long-tail swooped from the sky and carried
it off.

To me, Sabine's gull was the real surprise; this pretty little gull with
its forked tail and bold triangular wing pattern was one of the commonest birds. I had always thought of Sabine's gull as one of the
most northerly of all high arctic species—and one that nested in
single pairs or small numbers, often taking the protection of an
arctic tern colony. But here it was a dominant bird, breeding in
scattered colonies, without much sociability and with communal dis-
play-grounds of a rather desultory kind round the muddy edges of
the pools. Here the gulls quacked and laughed and pattered about
in their hunched displays, made agitated choruses with their mates,
took off, circled round, strafed and dive-bombed us—behaved almost
exactly like the black-headed gulls back home in England.

On the 27th of June we ran the fifteen or twenty miles down to
Hooper Bay and eight or ten miles up from the bay to New Chevak.
At a bend in the river before we reached Hooper Bay we stopped
at an Eskimo fish camp. All the men were away in their kayaks,
except for a deaf mute. He couldn't speak, but was eloquent, nonetheless, as he showed us in graphic mime how to hunt a seal in
winter. The women were running the camp, splitting dog-salmon
for wind-drying, sewing clothes for their children. They came out
of their store-bought canvas tents and paraded their children for
us when they saw Roger's movie camera. They were smiling and
jolly and, sure enough, put on a dance. It was a pretty good one,
but not nearly as good as the comic dance two of the girls did when
we were offshore on our departure—a priceless imitation in dance
mime of Roger's business with the movie camera.

The wind was whipping over Hooper Bay as we sliced into the
open water and cut across to the mud flats of the Lingliguak, a river
of interminable bends. The village of New Chevak was on a hill and
in full view during the last long miles of our voyage, but time and

again, as we headed straight upriver toward it, we would find ourselves swept by yet one more long meander, in the opposite direction.
The motor blew a gasket when we had two miles to go, and it was
quite late in the afternoon when we eventually stepped ashore in
the modern Eskimo village.

New Chevak is built on a modest escarpment of nearly a hundred
feet, which gives the village a wide view over the tundra, and on
clear days, even a sight of the Bering Sea. Chissicking along the
steep bluff was a reminder of home, a yellow wagtail, one of the
handful of Old World songbirds that spills over the Bering Strait into
Alaska. We saw an arctic redpoll in the low willow scrub, and there
was even a little tree by a lake where we found pectoral sandpipers
nesting—a tree with bushes beside it big enough to support a tree-
sparrow territory.

Matt's brother, Charlie Peterson, was the village chief and store-
keeper. With the utmost cheerfulness he offered us a roof for the
night, for our outboard motor had given up the ghost. He gave us
the liberty of the village store and as many new store blankets as we
wanted. We slept through a comfortable night, bought some thick
flannel shirts from Charlie in the morning, and enjoyed a terrific
breakfast of bacon and eggs out of the refrigerator, and airborne
bread toasted in an electric pop-up toaster. Such was Eskimo civilization, Alaska, 1953!

How different things were for the great pioneer birdman E. W.
Nelson when he first explored this area in 1878. He sledged in when
the geese were gone, though he learned from the Eskimos the first
news of the greatest goose ground of North America. He left St.

New Chevak

Michael, nearly 200 straight miles to the north, with the Yukon fur trader Charles Peterson, an ancestor of the Charlie Peterson who was now chief of New Chevak. On his way, below the Askinuk Mountains, Nelson stayed the night in an earth-covered hut, less than four feet high in the center, and sloping on every side. "The floor was covered with a deep layer of garbage, giving rise to a horrible stench, while about the low platforms on the sides crouched a number of pasty-faced children and sickly-looking elders, a litter of puppies were snuffing about among the wooden dishes in the farther end of the place. A large cake of ice served as a window in the roof, and everything bespoke of the most abject filth and poverty."

We did not stop long enough at New Chevak to learn much about Eskimo life today. Many of them were still living in barabaras, the primitive half-underground turf houses, but a number of wooden houses had gone up and a warehouse and a new school were being built. Some of these Eskimos, I thought, are more American, now, perhaps than Eskimo—with the very American idea that they can do it better than Father did.

The home of the affable Charlie could not be called typical. Obviously he was a very successful businessman. He even possessed a two-way radio and a Burroughs adding machine. He was the owner of three or four boats, including one shallow-draught cabin boat and half a dozen outboard motors. We looked rather enviously at his new outboards, for we knew there was little chance of getting our big motor going again, and that we would have to rely on the tiny spare one-horsepower motor to see the big dinghy back.

On our interminable journey back to Old Chevak, which took us close to 15 hours, we were chilled to the marrow by the damp and cold. The temperature was around 40 degrees. Two kayakers on their way to their salmon nets paced us for the first three miles. Their

kayaks were of traditional design, but whereas one of the Eskimos was in skin dress, with hooded parka, the other wore store clothes. The picturesque Eskimo is rapidly losing his cultural identity.

An arctic weasel started out of a hole in the riverbank as we slowly passed by, and slipped along the bank and over the rim. A little flight of whistling swans came overhead. We never found a whistler's nest, but many small parties were flying round the tundra. Incidentally, whistlers don't whistle with their wings as do the big mute swans. At the end of Hooper Bay a tern flew over the boat, giving us just enough time to confirm it as the rare Aleutian tern and not the arctic tern, which lives up and down the tundra rivers.

Except for this one miserable day, we had many long, happy hours in the field. Finnur, who was busy preparing specimens, was excused meal duties, and somehow Roger never came in for more than the tail end of washing up. Bill and I did most of the catering. Once we pulled Finnur's leg, for Finnur, though a great tea drinker, likes his weak. "Is this all right?" I said, as I added water from the kettle. "Too strong," said Finnur. "Still too strong." "Well, this then?" "Still too strong." Eventually I got it right. "Ah," he said, "that's just how I like it." It was not until after the meal that I broke it to him that the brown color of the fluid derived from a natural infusion of fresh-water plankton, mainly copepods, and that there were not any tea leaves in it at all.

On the last morning, Roger and I spent hours with the old-squaw ducks on the pool back of the church. It was extremely difficult to count the newly hatched ducklings; they kept diving, bobbing up, diving again, scuttling down to the other end of the tarn, hiding in the reeds. But eventually the mother got used to us, and disclosed fifteen youngsters. There are records of old-squaws having laid fifteen eggs or even more, but these are rare. When we showed Peter Scott

the movies afterwards he said, "Oh, it's pretty certain, though of course unprovable, that you've got two broods there; it's a very common thing among the sea-ducks—the pooling of broods, under one joint mother-cum-fostermother."

We were still watching the old-squaws when a humming in the sky announced the return of our plane. We were ready, all packed up, gear rolled up on the bank, goodbyes said to Matty and Jack. Jimmy Hoffmann waddled the machine onto the mud like a swan. It was with real regret that we carefully stepped through the mud to the ladder and climbed into the Cessna's cabin. We took off down a straight stretch of river, cleared the bend by a smallish margin, and roared off to Bethel, across the fantastic mosaic of unmapped land and uncharted water that forms what we are now quite prepared to believe is the most bird-rich tundra in all the arctic world. It had been a wonderful week. We had learned a great deal about birds, quite a bit about mud, and not enough about outboard motors.

Snow Bunting

34

The Islands of the Seals

THE MORNING PAPERS at Anchorage predicted Olympian fireworks. Spurr, the 11,000-foot volcanic peak at the head of the Aleutian Range, had been spitting smoke and ashes for the last day or two. An eruption seemed imminent. It would be well timed if it came today, for this was the Fourth of July.

As our plane took us down toward the Alaska Peninsula we peered out of the small windows, hoping for a glimpse of Spurr, but cloud masses hid the restless mountain (it did not erupt for several days). Farther on we passed Katmai, the volcano that like Mazama and Krakatoa had blown itself to bits (in 1912). With its Valley of Ten Thousand Smokes, it now stands as a National Nature Monument. Climbing through the cloud-ceiling into the sun, we cruised above a billowy sea of clouds, unbroken except for an occasional volcanic cone that rose white and glistening into the blue sky.

As we approached Cold Bay the plane slipped down through the clouds again and flew over treeless moors at an altitude of only a few hundred feet. Bob Reeve had instructed our pilot to show us an Alaskan brown bear; and sure enough, from the water's edge a brown form retreated along one of the well-worn bear trails that led inland across the moors. Our plane banked and circled low while all twenty passengers pressed their noses against the windows.

At Cold Bay, where the Aleutian chain of islands starts, our DC-3 made its last fuel stop before striking out over the Bering Sea, across 250 miles of water to the Pribilofs, the islands of the seals. Once a large whale broke water below; otherwise we saw nothing but the cold sea, now blue under the blue sky, now gray under scudding clouds. Usually fog blankets the Pribilofs, and the pilots who make this run for the Reeve Aleutian Airlines must slip under the overcast at low elevation to land the plane on the field at St. Paul. But today the sun was shining. We could see the swarms of seals on their hauling beaches as we came in, and the neat white houses of the town of St. Paul. After our plane taxied to a stop we stepped out into a garden of bloom such as I had never seen before—anywhere. Millions of yellow poppies lifted their faces toward the sun, and fields of tall blue lupines stretched to the horizon.

There had been ten successive days of sun, a thing almost unheard of in the Pribilofs. "This much sun is not good for people," com-

plained the resident Aleuts. They pointed out with alarm that the last time they had this much sun was in 1919, when influenza struck them down. We, of course, desired the sun for our photography, and all records were broken when fair weather prevailed during most of our stay. Other photographers have spent as much as six weeks on St. Paul with never a glimpse of blue sky.

All of us—Finnur Gudhmundsson, Bill Cottrell, James, and I— had read and reread Rudyard Kipling's "The White Seal" in *The Jungle Book;* and we also knew that famous old Smithsonian report, *The Seal Islands of Alaska,* written back in the seventies by an assistant agent of the United States Treasury, Henry W. Elliott. It was Elliott's report with its topographical detail and place, animal, and man names, and the numerous aquatint drawings by Elliott himself, that inspired Kipling's classic tale. To James, who had read everything he could find about the seal islands, these days at the terminus of our American journey were the fulfillment of a lifelong dream.

July 4–12

From the window of the DC-3 as we banked in a cloudless sky, our eyes for a moment embraced thirteen miles of seal coast, and about a million and a half seals.

Last time I saw a seal colony from the air was in Scotland—North Rona, the greatest nursery of the Atlantic gray seal. I remember comparing its mile triangle to a bone assailed by maggots. But the remote isle of Rona held only three thousand (a great number, indeed, of this particular seal). Here were five hundred times as many, something to dream about (in fact, I dreamed about this scene many times before seeing it, and many more times after).

Contrast our arrival in the Pribilofs in a comfortable airliner under a blue sky with that of the first men who saw the great fur-seal nurseries. Through almost perpetual fog Gerassim Pribilof, a ship's mate in the service of a Russian swan-hunting company at Unalaska, searching the sea of his countryman Bering for the breeding place of the fur seals, discovered it in July, 1786. The isolated, flower-covered, triangular basalt island that he found he named St. George, after his little ship. Out of the mist, he nosed her shoreward under the northeast cliffs. The place is called Tolstoi Mees, or Tolstoi Point; and here Yefim Popof, leader of the seal hunters, took his men ashore.

They probably landed in the middle of the sea lion rookery, and knowing the cowardice of the great northern sea lions, calmly dodged the sea-hurtling masses of flesh and scrambled to the foot of the irregular terraced cliffs, lush with vegetation and noisy with chittering auks, dithering kittiwakes and stuttering fulmars. The sea lion bulls, their ton of muscle, bone, and blubber now buoyant, reared their brown-bear heads up in the water to watch the men, while their quarter-ton cows swam around preoccupied with their bleating pups ashore. Soon the boats returned light to the schooner, and the shore party disappeared over the top of the 350-foot cliff. Groaning and belching, the sea lions began to haul ashore again.

The men made for a green hill, stumbling through vegetation-covered lava blocks to a sward blue with lupines. Glaucous-winged gulls laughed and stooped at them, jealous in protection of their young. Popof led to the top of the hill, and they looked west, along the north shore of the island. The fog had withdrawn a few miles to sea, and they could see the whole of the cliffy coast. Something seemed queer about it. In a few places there were breaks in the cliffs, valleys, and hillsides tilting down to the sea, and round these to quite some distance inland and uphill the green and yellow and blue of the summer vegetation was replaced by brown, a lively brown growth that appeared to have its own motion. For a moment shafts of rare sunlight and cloud shadow chased each other, and the Russians thought that the brown movement was an illusion of light; but soon they knew it was real—a herd of animals such as they had never seen in all their sealers' lives. In the course of the next hour or two, as they walked almost in a daze of triumph and amazement, they probably saw at least a quarter of a million fur seals on St. George's crowded northside rookeries. These culminated in a hillside that steeply rose from a little stream-fed beach to a thousand feet above the sea. Up this slope the great seal rookery extended, the seals at the north edge overlooking a sheer precipice.

It was by the stream that Popof decided to build the sealers' huts, and today that hillside rookery is known as Staraya Artil, the old settlement, though the village has long since moved. Leaving the sealers ashore for a summer's sealing and a winter's stay, Pribilof returned to Unalaska, for there is no harbor at St. George. Next year he was trailed back to the island by others, and Popof and his party welcomed quite a little armada, and welcomed them with some interesting news. From the bluff above the settlement, when looking for the returning ship on July 10, 1787, a rare fogless day, they had seen another island to the northwest, thirty or forty miles away.

Quickly the ship crossed over to the new land, which we now know as St. Paul. They found a bigger island, and five times as many seals! They found, too, burnt grass, an old pipe, the handle of an old knife. Nobody has ever discovered who had been there before them; but many people have been there since—business people, for as Kipling puts it in his famous story, "Nobody comes to Novastoshnah except on business." Novastoshnah, which means "the new growth" (newly sanded up from island to peninsula), is the northeast point of St. Paul. More than one serious mammalogist has pointed out that from Hutchinson Hill, overlooking Novastoshnah, more large wild mammals can be seen at once than from any other point on the earth's surface. The number is never exactly determinable, but according to Victor Scheffer and Karl Kenyon it is well over 100,000. In some years the number of harems in Reef Point's rookeries at the southern end of St. Paul may exceed those of Novastoshnah. Between these two great aggregations are the beaches of Lukanin (named after a sea otter hunter) and Polovina ("half way"). From the window of the airplane we saw them all on July 4, all those, and Kitovi and Tolstoi and Zapadni, all the fifteen rookeries of St. Paul.

All four of our party were nourished on Elliott's great report, as well as Kipling's great story. Each of us had a mental image of Sea Catch, the fur-seal bull, and Matkah his wife, and Kotick his son, the White Seal himself, and Limmershin the winter wren, and Sea Vitch the walrus; and the Chickies (big gulls), Gooverooskies (kittiwakes), and Epatkas (horned puffins). The reality, when all these creatures came to life, showed that Elliott was faithful to and Kipling no stranger than the truth; for the truth was far, far more extraordinary than either of them wrote—a climax to our American journey that will live with us for all the rest of our days.

The central character in the perpetual drama of the Pribilofs is *Callorhinus ursinus,** the northern fur seal. It was at Polovina that we had our curtain-raising performance—our first close-up of harem life. "Don't panic the idle bulls at the edge of the rookery," Clarence Olson, the manager, had warned us. "If they make a run for it they disrupt every harem along the way." We could go up on the elevated catwalk, he said, if we were careful. Here, eight or ten feet above the ground, we would be safe from any of the more bellicose bulls, for they can be very dangerous, as I learned later.

Our first impression was one of wild confusion. Thousands of big animals lay sprawled about, waving their rear flippers as if to keep themselves cool. Here and there a blubber-fat bull rushed violently about, now trying to keep a cow in check, now bellowing and fighting with a neighboring bull that had crossed the invisible walls of his private territory. The cows, much smaller, jostled each other, and crèches of little black pups sprawled and crawled and bawled. Incessantly, idle bulls at the edges of the beach caused trouble. Sometimes one sought the surf by a dash through the harems; running the gantlet it was rushed and mauled by every great bull along the way. One, split and gashed in gaping wounds across its back, made no attempt to lick them, paid them no evident attention, quietly went to sleep on a boulder by the shore. We thought it had died from exhaustion, but an hour later it swam into the surf and played away. On rocks at the edge of the surf the holluschickie—

---

* Translated freely, this means "bearlike with beautiful snout." This animal has three groups. *C. u. curilensis* breeds on Robben Island off Sakhalin in the Sea of Okhotsk, and the herd is now a Russian possession. *C. u. ursinus,* the typical race, lives on the Russian Commander Islands, between Kamchatka and the end of the Aleutian chain. The Commander Islands were discovered by Vitus Bering in 1741. His ship, *St. Peter,* was wrecked there, and during the winter of 1741–42 (in which Bering died) the famous German naturalist Georg Wilhelm Steller (who took charge of the party and brought it safely to Kamchatka in spring) discovered the great Poludinnoy seal rookery at the south end of Bering Island. It was from Steller's description that the animal was named in 1758 by Linnaeus. Later fur seals were discovered breeding on neighboring Copper Island. In 1941 the Commander Islands herd was about 40,000, though in the eighteen-seventies it probably numbered 1,000,000. *C. u. alascanus,* confined to the Pribilofs, has a broader head and thicker neck than the others, and the cows and young bulls are of a warmer brown, with less contrast between sides and belly; the pups are more silvery. Dealers, handling skins, can without fail distinguish those of the three races.

young bulls, two and three years old—played games that seemed good-natured enough now but would become deadly serious as they grew older. Farther out to sea we could discern other seals porpoising out of the water. The cows, at the peak of their arrival, were converging on their home beaches. Gradually, as we watched, a sort of pattern emerged from the seeming disorder.

An adult harem bull, or beachmaster, that comes ashore in May or June is seven years old at least, weighs from 350 to 600 pounds, is six feet or more from nose to the tip of its short tail. On the back of his neck, stretching between his shoulder blades, he has a big hump of fat (all he has to live on for two or three months), and this is covered by a "wig" of dense hair, which extends onto his crown. Facially he has a mean expression, accentuated by big lower-jaw canine teeth, which flash when he opens his mouth. He can raise himself on his fore-flippers to a height of four feet, and because his flippers turn forward like those of the sea lion, he can shuffle at quite unexpected speed when in a rage. In fighting he keeps low, shooting out his head in a vicious snake-like biting dart against his opponent's chest. At the end of each head-dart comes a violent expulsion of breath, often with a cloud of vapor and spit. The challenge sound itself, never absent from the beaches, is a cross between a roar and

a belch, an acrid, rough sound that just suits the acrid, rough smell of the rookeries. The rookeries could smell worse: no bulls defecate during their tenancy of the harems, and the cows and young bulls do so at sea. Only the pups foul the beaches. The chief odor is a sharp smell of decay—dead pup, dead bull, occasional dead cow. Afterbirths are swept up fairly quickly by the glaucous-winged gulls.

The adult cow is a meek creature, 100 to 130 pounds in weight before her 10- to 12-pound black pup is born. She is four to five feet long and has a placid, big-eyed face, more pointed than that of the bull. She has no hump, for she does not have to live ashore on stored food. She is quite free to fish at sea during her breeding time, for unlike her bull she has no territory to lose. She has no "wig"; neither do young males until they reach their fourth or fifth year.

The cows swim ashore on the breeding beaches at any time between mid-June and early August. Probably the old cows come first and the virgins last. Within a day or two of its arrival the cow has its youngster. Black and puppy-like, it has its eyes and ears open at birth and quickly gets the imprint of its mother, whom it can recognize by sight and sound across some distance of beach. The cow bleats almost like a sheep, and the pup exactly like a lamb.

When sheep were introduced on St. Paul many years ago they were often found wandering among the harems, dodging the infuriated bulls, while vainly looking for their sisters and nieces and nephews. Or their cousins, their uncles, and their aunts.

Five or six days after giving birth, the cow takes the bull; her gestation period is thus about 360 days. When she comes in heat she often solicits the bull by shuffling in front of him and nibbling at his chest fur; after one act of mating the cow's sole interest is her pup. When it is ten days old this active little animal has put on a lot of weight, and is playing with other pups at the edge of the harem. The cow then deserts it for the first time. Like a petrel, it leaves the pup for a three- or four-day foraging excursion at sea. As the pup grows older its mother's foraging trips may get longer.

The pups have an almost exact 50–50 sex ratio. They start paddling in the pools when they are about a month old, but it is three months before they are really free-swimming little masters of the element that washes their beaches. Fur seals, like albatrosses, have little use for land except to breed on. Other seals and sea lions may come ashore on almost any rocks to bask and rest, but the fur seal hauls out only at its breeding grounds. Here it comes ashore every summer after that in which it was born, though only desultorily in the first (even though cows are not impregnated until the end of their third or fourth year, and bulls do not have harems until their seventh).

In August the harems break up and the pups' fathers (or stepfathers), scarred and thin, go to sea for their long-awaited bathe and feed. Many virgins and bachelors and some yearlings in September

then invade the breeding grounds to play; the cows with pups continue their routine. By September the pups can swim well and often stray around the island in little swimming bands. This is when killer whales catch some of them. By November, about four and a half months after they are born, they are weaned and go to sea, as do their mothers. A few bachelors stay ashore through Christmas.

Such is the life of the northern fur seals of Pribilof's islands. Let us examine (with the kind help of the Fish and Wildlife Service biologists) the composition of the present Pribilof herd. Including the pups of the year and the yearlings at sea, and all the young bulls (holluschickie) due for skinning that summer, a modern season's population is between 1,500,000 and 1,750,000.

The pup population—sexes equal—is 500,000. Some of these die on the beaches on which they were born, lose their mothers, get squashed by their fathers, die of hookworm. Others are eaten by killer whales not long after they first take to the sea. When the first birthday comes round slightly more than half of the pups are gone, are dead. About 115,000 of each sex survive. They may come back to the neighborhood of the islands and play swimming games, but few come ashore—just some at the end of the season.

Perhaps 90,000 of each sex reach their second birthday. All go ashore at some time or another during this season, the females, which remain virgins, to the edges of the harem beaches; the males to the special loafing grounds of young bachelors. These lie adjacent to or between the main rookeries, and here young humpless, wigless males can go back and forth without running the gantlet of harem bulls. This tradition of freeway for bachelors is nicely rationalized by Kipling as "the Rules of the Beach."

Usually two-year-old bachelors are distinguishable by their size from those a year older and are rejected from the killing drives. The limits, which are shrewdly guessed by the skinning gangs, are between 41 and 45 inches in length. Bachelors within these measurements are supposed to be three-year-olds, though the biologists of the Fish and Wildlife Service have found (by studying teeth) that these size limits may embrace some two-year-olds, many four-year-olds, and a few five-year-olds. About five or six hundred of the 90,000 two-year-old males measure at least 41 inches, and get included in the killing pods. The vast majority, spared, return to sea.

About 75,000 survivors of each sex reach their third birthday.

About half the males of this age are included in the killing drives and become seventy-dollar pelts. They are at their commercial prime. When the females of this age haul ashore quite a number seek harem bulls and become impregnated, but others join the two-year-olds and wait another season.

The number of the original half-million pups that reach their fourth birthday embraces about 30,000 males and 65,000 females. Females (with very few exceptions) go to the harem bulls; those that went the year before bear their first pups. The males are included, as before, in the killing drives, and three-quarters of them are between the limits and become skins.

Next year only 6000 or 7000 of the original males survive. There are perhaps 55,000 females, nearly all of which arrive pregnant. A few hundred males, around their fifth birthday, are still under 45 inches and get picked up by the early-morning killing gangs. The rest play and mock-fight about the beaches; some have little humps and little wigs. Most survive until next year, as so few are killed ashore, and at sea they have had five years' experience. By their sixth birthday, they begin to fight in earnest, and though most are unemployed some become beachmasters with wives. Most have to wait, however, until they are seven years old, or more.

Once a cow is adult, she can breed every year. Very little is known, however, about how long the bulls and cows continue to reproduce themselves. The maximum age of both sexes may be about twenty-five years. Old bulls are cast out by younger, fitter animals, often go to lonely beaches to recover from their wounds or die. In fights some die, not so much from wounds as from exhaustion.

The *average* size of a harem is over forty. Harems of over a hundred are not unusual, and sultanates of over two hundred have been recorded. Each bull must come ashore early in the season, before the cows. The more powerful the bull, the earlier he comes. The better the place he gets, the bigger the harem—and the longer he has to fight and mate on the reserves of food and drink in his hump. Only in exceptionally hot weather have harem bulls been observed to desert their pitch and take the water. Early in the season they fight almost continuously. Sometimes it is only noise and bluff, but if that does not work they resort to the savage rush and darting tooth rip. As their cows arrive, the bulls spend much time preventing them from wandering to neighbors.

As it now stands, the annual Pribilof crop of sealskins averages 65,000 and turns over five or six million dollars. About $1,000,000 of this is profit for the American people. Over the years the seals alone have brought back to the treasury several times the purchase price of $7,200,000 paid to the Russians for all Alaska. In the first decade of this country, sealing at sea, mostly by the Japanese, reduced the herds to less than 125,000 and threatened the fur seal with speedy extermination. But on July 7, 1911, the envoys of Great Britain (representing Canada), Russia, Japan, and the United States gathered in Washington to sign a treaty that outlawed pelagic sealing and ushered in a new era for a great natural resource.

It may be that the herds have now reached their peak; that they can increase no further unless some means is found to control the hookworm that in recent years has killed off an increasing percentage of the pups. Between 50,000 and 100,000 pups may die in a single season from this scourge. Dr. O. Wilford Olsen, of the Colorado Agricultural and Mechanical College at Fort Collins, had given his summers for the last three years to research on this serious parasite, and we were privileged to accompany him and watch him work at Polovina and Novastoshnah. He had already discovered that the hookworm overwinters, dormant, in the soil of the rookeries and that control may rest in the chemical treatment of these beaches. With a gadget that looked like an oversized hypodermic needle he injected reagents into the hookworm-infested sands.

To treat the sands it was, of course, necessary to steal space from some of the athletic harem bulls that were bellowing at us and spoiling for a fight. When I offered to help, Dr. Olsen said, "Just take this pole and rattle the two tin cans on the end." Feeling somewhat like a toreador, I took the pole and rattled the tin cans right in the face of a 600-pound bull. I shouldn't have been facing the bull uphill when I did it; a quick dart of his head pushed the pole back at me and I lost balance and fell. This, I thought, was the end, or at least the end of part of me, for fur seals have been known to bite big chunks out of people. But out of the corner of my eye, as I lay, I saw the bull turn, belch with an air of triumph, look aggressively at a neighboring beachmaster, and shuffle back to an errant cow. Of course, I thought, I've done what he wanted: expressed submissiveness. I'm a fair cow! If he can't see me off, to see me down will do—and then, who's next? So, all that this experiment in animal behavior cost, was some inches of skin, left behind on the stones. But, I must confess, I've never been more terrified in my life!

The killing of the bachelor seals is done by the method traditional on the islands, started by the Russians when they first brought Aleuts to St. Paul and St. George to exploit the herds. It is as humane and expeditious as can be devised. The bachelor hauling grounds attached to each rookery are driven six or more times a season (June to mid-August). I wanted to see one of these drives before I left St. Paul, so at 2 A.M. when the alarm rang on Friday, I reluctantly quit my warm blankets. Roger mumbled something about not liking scenes of carnage and went to sleep again.

I had coffee and pancakes with the gang before we climbed into big red trucks full of Aleuts, clubs, and knives. It was cold and clammy, somewhere near 40 degrees, as we rumbled off in the dim half-light. A quarter of a mile from the rookery the procession stopped. The foreman shouted his instructions and the Aleuts set off through the wet grass to the beach downwind of the hauling ground. The bachelor seals were still asleep when the men slipped between them and the water. In a panic they awoke, but the men, waving their arms and shouting, turned them toward the meadow. Only a few broke through to gain the surf. It took a half hour to drive a thousand seals a quarter of a mile (sometimes the killing field is a mile away). The early morning is chosen because it is cool, and the herd is often rested to cool off; hot seals produce poor skins. A few young cows and oversize bulls were quickly spotted and left behind. The rest were moved along with shouts and gesticulations, until they reached the grass sward of the killing grounds. Here the boys penned up the main herd while pods of about twenty were driven to the clubmen. Undersize and oversize animals were weeded out. Then deftly the rest were stunned with single blows of hickory clubs that looked like six-foot baseball bats.

Immediately other men dragged the stunned animals to a strip of lawn and laid them on their backs in rows of ten. The gauge man came round, checked the measurement of each seal and the tally-man marked it off. Seconds later the sticker followed, quickly making a belly incision from chin to tail and plunging his knife into the animal's heart. The skinner, a highly skilled man, followed to make his quick accurate cuts round the base of each flipper. He skinned back the head to the neck and turned the dead seal over. Another man jabbed a two-pronged fork over the animal's skinned neck, pinning it to the ground, and two men at once attached a curious pair of tongs to the skin near the animal's shoulders. Seizing a rope tackle attached to the tongs they pulled backward and the whole skin jerked free of the seal, blubber attached. Trucks drove up the line and men forked the carcasses aboard. Within an hour they were on the slabs outside St. Paul's by-products plant, where they are converted into chicken feed and soap oil. The skins were left a little longer to cool. They were then trucked to the Fouke Fur Company's blubbering plant at the village, counted out by the Fish and Wildlife Service superintendent, and counted in by the fur company. Scarcely a skin has been miscounted in fifty years. One-fifth of the skins go to Canada in compliance with the treaty of 1911. Whereas the killing and skinning is done almost entirely by Aleuts, the blubbering is done mostly by young men working their way through college. They are brought up by the fur company specially for the three-month season. Colin Bertram of the Scott Polar Research Institute calls the management of the fur seal herds the "finest example of the rational exploitation of any wild stock of animals."

35

Birds of the Seal Islands

ST. PAUL was playing against the Fouke Fur Company in its annual Fourth of July baseball game when we first arrived in town on the airport bus. An Aleut boy stood at bat against a pitcher from St. Louis who worked at the blubbering plant. The Aleuts seemed to be in the lead. Father Baranoff, who had once been an officer in the czar's army and now, as a priest of the Russian Orthodox Church, acted as spiritual adviser to the St. Paul Aleuts, beamed approvingly and stroked his silver-gray Vandyke.

Later, we met two of the Fouke employees out for a stroll at the edge of town. They were restive, bored as men marooned on a desert island are bored. They were counting the days when they could return to the glories of St. Louis. When James told them that his visit to St. Paul was the fulfillment of a dream of thirty years, they looked at him as though he must be mad. "I'll be damned!" said one. "There is no accounting for tastes!"

July 4–12

If I am a madman, I am not alone: there are four of us. The days—long subarctic days—are still not long enough for us. Each morning the cook fixes a picnic lunch and Bill, Finnur, Roger, and I start off to explore the island, not to return until evening.

Bill Cottrell spent much of his time on the flowers and soon found and identified nearly 100 of the 170 species of plants known from these treeless islands. Many of the plants here—about 100 of them—are found on both shores of the Bering Sea and quite a few are circumpolar. The deep blue lupines and the bright yellow poppies dominate the show, taking the spotlight from the primulas, monkshood, and other attractive flowers. All but hidden by the rank growth is a black lily, just coming into bloom. More eye-catching is a bright pink *Pedicularia,* larger and more flamboyant than any lousewort we had ever seen before. At the cliff edges are little bosses of moss campion, and patches of little yellow saxifrages and potentillas; and up on the hill those ubiquitous plants of the North—cloudberry, crowberry, and creeping willow; in the corners of the ledges are old friends of the alpine rockeries of the world's other side—scurvy grass, cuckoo flower, saxifrages, knotgrass, sorrel, *Lloydia;* and on the grassy flats other world-wide northern flowers—silverweed, yarrow, speedwell, bistort, sheep's fescue. Finnur and I agreed that the rare sun, shining on the pretty flowers, illuminated the best alpine plant carpet we had seen since that of the Hofsjökull of Iceland. Perhaps it is a better carpet, we thought, for it has about half again as much variety, and the bold beauty of the lupines and poppies is overwhelming.

It was with this lovely background of flowering plants that we applied ourselves to the seabirds of the cliffs. Every nook, every ledge along miles of rock wall was occupied by murres, auklets, puffins, kittiwakes. The murres stood erect, facing the rocks, their dark backs to the sea. Each attended its single big greenish egg. These eggs are shaped like pears. This suggests an adaptation against rolling off the ledge, but maybe their shape simply fits well their owners' incubation-patch. As we approached their ledges the birds faced about,

(opposite) Walrus Island

presenting their white waistcoats, and, after much nodding of heads, exploded in a roar of wings. Some stayed behind. When we slowly edged round the clifftop corners, we found that we could get within a few feet of them. These acted as decoys for the others, and within a few minutes of awkward landings, pushings and shovings, pebble-stealing, bowing, and little gurgling cries, community life returned to normal. Roger tried to count the birds that stood shoulder to shoulder on a hundred yards of cliff, and using this sample estimated that a minimum in number of a million murres were on the ledges of St. Paul. Another group, not much smaller in number (for pairs spend rather little time together on the ledge) were away fishing, or floating in rafts of hundreds on the sea below the cliffs; sometimes they strung out in long lines—perhaps a fishing tactic. From our vantage point they looked like long-necked turtles below the surface as they dived into the deep blue water.

Both species of murres were present: the arctic bird, which is here called the Pallas's murre, and the common, or California murre—the same birds we had watched from the cliffs of Cape St. Mary in Newfoundland, only different races. There were hundreds of thousands of both, but we noticed that the Pallas's murre, the one with the short bill and white bill mark, hugged rocks that offered little more than a foothold, while the common murre, the one with the longer profile, seemed to command the broader ledges. The evidence seems to show that the southern species gets to the cliffs earlier in the season and bags the best places.

The tufted puffins were less shy than they were at Destruction Island; at Zapadni Point there was a high jutting rock past which

Tufted Puffin

Horned Puffin

they flew against the wind, and Roger was able to get good slow-motion flight shots. Several times we were able to creep close to unsuspecting "tawpawkies" standing at the cliff edge. While we peered through the range finder they would turn their huge orange beaks from side to side as they tried to make sense out of the apparition peeking at them from the tall rye grass. At close range they were even more bizarre than Atlantic puffins, comical, solemn, their long snowy locks slightly tinged with yellow, their outsize feet orange.

We had expected the other puffin of the Pribilofs, the horned puffin, to be quite like the familiar species of the Atlantic. But it laid its egg far back in the rocky crevices, as does our Atlantic razor-bill, so that nothing short of a blasting charge could dislodge it, whereas the tufted puffin usually nested in holes in the turf in the orthodox Atlantic puffin manner. The horned puffin has much more yellow on its bill than the Atlantic puffin and, of course, has its special slender "horn" above each eye. These horns are not really horny, but are soft papillae full of living tissue that the bird can erect when it is alert (which was most of the time while we were prowling about). Years ago H. W. Elliott noted, as we did, that "the *epatka* is the only bird on these islands which seems to quarrel forever and ever with its mate. The hollow reverberations of its anger, scolding and vituperation from the nuptial chamber are the most characteristic sounds. No sympathy need be expended on the female. She is just as big and just as violent as her lord and master."

Sitting by themselves in pairs or small groups were smaller white-breasted birds, with stubby, upturned red bills. These were the paroquet auklets, or *baillie brushkies,* that nested deep in the cliff crevices, from which we heard their high, musical, short trill. They were not as numerous as the murres or the puffins. Seldom did

Crested Auklets

we see more than six or eight together. When Roger eased up to the cliff edge above them with his fearsome camera, its turret head bristling with lenses, they stood their ground, staring at him with one white eye, then the other. In 1911 A. C. Bent's party found their way to St. Paul by following the paroquet auklets. So dense was the fog that they thought they had missed the island. When auklets began to fly past in increasing numbers they turned their course to follow them and soon heard the bellowing of the fur seals on the beaches near the village.

Flying over the water in little bands were birds about the size of paroquet auklets, but without their white breasts. By their slaty color we knew them to be crested auklets, but during the first week we seldom saw them on the cliffs. The compact flocks, as well drilled as starlings, would fly in from the sea, almost brush the cliff face, fly along it, and swing out over the water again. They seemed to be scouting, and we had reason to believe that they had just arrived, for it was not until the second week that they landed on the ledges in numbers. At close range, with their forward-curling head plumes and grotesque smiles on their waxy orange bills, they looked too absurd to be real. When first we heard their odd honking, yapping sounds under the ledges, we thought we were hearing foxes. *Canooskie*—"little captain"—is the Aleut name for this queer, noisy little auk.

It seems pretty certain that the chief evolution of the auk family (to which the puffins, murres, and auklets belong) took place in and around the Bering Sea, for of the 21 living species, all but three live in the North Pacific. Nearly half—eight—nest on the Pribilofs although only once did we see a pigeon guillemot. On the 5th of July, off the southwest cliffs of St. Paul, we spotted a recently fledged young bird which had probably been reared nearby.

Tiniest of the lot were the least auklets—*choochkies,* as the Aleuts called them. No larger than a starling without a tail, they perched and chirped in busy little bands on the piles of beach drift and boulders above high-tide mark. A few sat with the paroquet auklets on the cliffs. They buzzed in from the sea, like swarms of big bees, and pitched onto the rocks; stubby little birds with mottled whitish shirtfronts and a few whitish bristles in front of their eyes. They stood upright and solemnly watched while Finnur rolled many large boulders aside, hoping to find an egg, but the little birds had hidden their treasure too well. The Aleuts used to go to a lot of trouble to get their eggs for food, and still take some of the birds when they arrive in the spring, stopping them in full flight with long-handled nets in the same manner that the Greenland Eskimos catch dovekies. But the Aleut prefers his auklets cooked, not raw. The choochkies even invaded the seal rookeries. The big animals paid them no attention as they popped into crevices or sat chittering on nearby boulders, with a sound not unlike the food-call of young starlings.

As we watched the teeming cliffs and beaches we were forced to think of the vast amounts of food that must be eaten daily by these millions of birds and by the fur seals and the sea lions. All these seabirds of the rocks get their living from the sea; they eat either fish, mollusks, crustaceans, or other sea fare. We wondered why it should be, then, that some, such as the fish-eating murres and the shrimp-eating choochkies, should exist by millions, while the beautiful red-faced cormorants count their world population only in the low thousands. Besides the Pribilof archipelago, where they nest in small scattered groups, these slick, two-crested shags provedly

"Choochkies"

nest only on Bogoslof, the volcanic islet north of Umnak in the Aleutians, and on the Russian Commander Islands.* We found them nesting on the bracket ledges; they did not seem to mind if these were within a few yards—or even feet—of the roaring life of a fur seal harem. With their bright red faces set off by a touch of blue at the base of their bills, they seemed designed for Kodachrome and we never tired of throwing yards of film at them. So tame were they that even in the closest of close-ups none of us put one off the nest.

Why should this species be so local? It seems to have no cormorant competitors. Past voyagers have reported the pelagic cormorant on the Pribilofs but we saw none that we could be sure of (although we thought we saw one the first day). The red-faced cormorant seems to be the only cormorant of Bogoslof. What the situation is in the Russian colonies we do not know. The little foxes seemed to ignore the cormorants (few predators adversely affect their prey anyway) and man has never exploited this handsome seabird as far as we know—certainly not on the Pribilofs. Its scarcity must remain a mystery; perhaps a further study of its food may one day give the clue.

Such study might also throw light on the *goverooskie,* the red-legged kittiwake. This charming gull, a bit smaller than the ordinary black-legged kittiwake (which lives by millions in the northern seas around the world), has a distribution very similar to that of the red-faced cormorant. There is no evidence that it nests anywhere but in the Pribilofs, the Near Islands at the west end of the Aleutian chain, and the Commander Islands. The first *published* description of the bird was that of Bruch in 1853, from the "north part of the west coast of North America." So we are celebrating the scientific centenary of *Rissa brevirostris* when we watch it now in 1953 with its congener *R. tridactyla,* the common kittiwake, on the southwest cliffs of St. Paul and the south cliffs of St. George. In one place I photographed both species together, sitting on their nest pedestals and facing each other just like pottery ducks on a chimney piece. On their nests, their legs tucked under them, the red-legged kittiwakes were quite hard to tell from the black-legged birds. Their bills, as

---

* It has been recently reported by the Russian ornithologist Gizenko on Shikotan, at the very south end of the Kurile chain, 1200 miles southwest of the Commanders.

their scientific name implies, were shorter. Their heads were rounder. The gray on their mantles showed a little darker, but their voices were nearly the same! This was really most extraordinary. I spent an hour under the south cliff of St. George comparing the two. Both had the same *taterat,* the same rather plaintive, cry-baby *meeeuw,* the same sharp *quop,* on alighting on their nests. There *must* be some difference, I thought, but could find little, unless the red-leg's excited *kaeeah-kaaehah-yak-yak-yak* was higher and squeakier than the corresponding cry of the black-leg. Bill Cottrell did find a new field mark: the red-leg shows a darkish-gray underwing quite distinct from the whitish underwing of the black-leg. This was really very clear when the birds were all flying in a flock, uttering similar cries, hiding their legs, and otherwise confusing the observer.

Why and how can these two close species enjoy the same breeding grounds, have identical nest sites, apparently identical voices? The differences in their beaks suggest a difference in food. But nobody knows what this is—simply because the fair sample of red-leg stomachs (McAtee examined fifteen) is not balanced by a satisfactory black-leg sample from the Pribilofs.

We were tempted to stay on the cliffs and ignore the relatively birdless interior of the island. The first time Roger went exploring inland along the edge of the lava flow that ended in a dusty crumble near the road, a sandpiper ran like a rodent from his feet and, fluttering about, feigned injury. He knew that the four handsomely spotted eggs at his feet belonged to the Pribilof sandpiper and were rare in the museums of the world; only a few sets have ever been taken. This nest proved to be the only one we would find, although the birds seemed common enough in the middle of the island, where they perched on the big chunks of lava and fed and preened among the poppies. Roger could not quite get over the idea that they were dunlins of a sort. They had rusty backs and dark belly patches, rather like summer dunlins, but everything else about them—their notes, their manners—indicated that they were purple sandpipers, basically. I am of the opinion that they are just a race of the purple sandpiper and should not be regarded as a distinct species, but certainly, in their summer dress they do suggest dunlins. In winter plumage they are almost indistinguishable from purple sandpipers.

Only four small land birds live on the foggy Pribilofs. No sooner had we walked down the ladder of Reeve's DC-3 on the 4th of July, onto the red lava sand, than we saw snow buntings flitting over the blue lupines and yellow poppies. "Snow finches," Bishop Innocent Veniaminof called them in his account, the first, of the islands. They belong to the more inland parts of St. Paul, leaving the edge and the human habitations to the rosy finches. To hear them sing we sought the heights on the west end of the island. The black and white cocks were fluttering up into the air with fanned wings and tail, uttering a twiddling, tweedling song. Search as we might, we could not find a nest, although we saw their stub-tailed youngsters, already on the wing, among the blocks of the lava flow. If there had been no rosy finches, the snow buntings probably would have become the village sparrows as they are in Iceland, and in the Spitsbergen mining settlements, where there is no other bird for that niche.

The Aleutian rosy finches were handsome in their loose-feathered plumage of gray, brown, and rose-pink. We found several of their bulky nests among the derelict remains of the wartime watch-garrison at the southwest point. They overflowed the crannies in which they were built and were not hard to find. All the nests in the second week of July had young just about to leave; and the parents were anxiously fussing round with chirping voices that were very like those of house sparrows. Although they nested in the basalt cliffs on both St. Paul and St. George, the rosy finches were most common in St. George village. They were, in truth, the sparrows of the Pribilofs.

The pretty singer of the small birds is the longspur (Lapland bunting), even more numerous here than it had been on the Chevak tundra. Everywhere the males poured their skylark snatches into the air as they flew in display flight over the meadows—*tirraleeo-traleeo-tirralee*—a sweet song, all too short.

More than once we heard a wren from the broken cliffs of Zapadni on St. Paul—a snatch of bubbling song somewhat thinner than that of the ebullient winter wren of eastern North America, or the explosive wren of Europe. I cannot help contrasting the voice of these Alaska wrens with the voice of those on St. Kilda, the lonely Scottish island. Both have to sing against the surf of a stormy ocean. Having known and listened to the St. Kilda wren for a number of years, I am convinced that its robust trill has a special quality that makes it heard through continuous surf noise. The wren of the Pribilofs has no such quality; it is a weak singer.

Often, as we picked our way along the clifftop, our eyes would meet others, peering from among the lupines, watching us. We could never get very close to the arctic foxes; before the long lens was focused the little animals would be gone. Occasionally we found their burrows, the entrances littered with the wings of murres, auklets, and broken eggshells. Once I saw a white one, but all the others were in the "blue" phase, smoky gray with tawny tails, mangy-looking creatures, almost more catlike than doglike, with a curious, mirthless hollow cry that could hardly have been called a bark. Recently their pelts have been almost worthless—the market for their fur has collapsed and foxes have not been harvested for several years, yet we saw relatively few on St. Paul and these were quite wild. Later, we were told that a control program had been carried on and wondered why it was necessary. True, foxes live off the birds; but that is part of the normal economy of the Arctic.

Naturally, my first thoughts on the bird-cliffs were for the fulmar, a bird for which I have had something of an obsession. In my monograph on the fulmar I had described the Pacific fulmar from skins and from the literature. I was relieved, when I saw it for the first time in my life, off the southwest cliffs of St. Paul on the 5th of July, that I had got the idea of it right. The silver-gray, kittiwake-sized, day-flying little albatross (it is practically that) is the greatest master of sail-planing of all the breeding birds of Bering Sea, just as it is in the North Atlantic. The Pacific bird has a more slender bill than has the Atlantic fulmar, and the light birds are lighter, the dark birds darker. I was slightly surprised to find how much lighter and patchier many of these Pacific birds were than the lightest of the Atlantic fulmars. In Britain they would have been put down as freaks or partial albinos. I studied many of them on their cliffside nests at the southwest point of St. Paul, but never did I see a dark bird until we sailed to St. George.

Every two weeks or so, the *Penguin* makes the crossing between the two islands. On July 7 we went along on a routine trip, stayed over, and returned to St. Paul the following evening. This stretch of ocean can be rough indeed, but that afternoon, as we followed the compass needle south-southeast over the forty miles of water, the sea was relatively calm and we had no trouble using our binoculars. The auks thinned out as we put St. Paul behind us, so I went below for a cup of coffee. Bill Cottrell and Roger soon called me on deck to see some slender-billed shearwaters. We had been expecting this dark tubenose, which regularly wanders to the Bering Sea from its nesting islands around New Zealand. Putting my elbows on the ship's rail, and gently tilting to correct the *Penguin's* slight roll, I picked up the dark sail-planing birds through my binoculars and saw immediately that they were dark fulmars. Twenty years of fulmar watching had made it impossible to fool me on these. I couldn't resist the temptation to wipe Roger's eye with this one and suggested that he look it up in Peterson's *Field Guide.*

These birds were much darker than the "blue" fulmars of the Atlantic. Oddly, we had not seen a single dark bird on the cliffs of St. Paul, nor were we to see any on St. George; all were light. Yet, as we sailed between the two islands, the majority of the birds that flew by or settled in the sea were of this dark phase. They probably had come from one of the Aleutians, 300 miles to the south, perhaps from Chagulak. In the Atlantic, the dark fulmars are only present in real numbers in colonies in the high Arctic, where the sea surface is near the freezing point even in July. But in the Pacific the distribution is the opposite. In the north (Pribilofs and St. Matthew) the birds are light. Only toward the south (through the Aleutians and Kuriles) do the dark birds build up. On Chagulak, according to Gabrielson, they outnumber the light birds. Were the bunch we saw from Chagulak? They showed not the slightest interest in the Pribilof cliffs. Three hundred miles could just be within operational range of a nesting fulmar, for both members of the pair share incubation, and relieve each other at intervals, which may be four days or more—time to fly 300 miles and back, if the weather be stormy enough to give them a wind-lift, for these sailplanes fly best when the sea is at its worst.

The exaggerated darkness of the Aleutian-Pacific fulmars apart, there was something else funny about them. Not one of the many hundreds we saw, dark or light, took the faintest interest in the ship. If we had been in the Atlantic, nearly every fulmar within sight would have glided up to look at us, fallen into the stern breezes, hung about for ten minutes or so, and settled in the wash, if anything trailed astern from the galley or the bilges. It is the Atlantic fulmar's exploitation of man-produced fatty offal (which means that it learned to follow ships) that has been a primary cause of its incredible spread on the European side of the North Atlantic, I believe. It is true that Pacific fulmars follow fishing boats on their winter grounds off California, but *in their breeding area the Pacific birds do not appear to follow ships*. There are not many ships to follow, come to that.

The Pacific bird has not undergone any revolution like that in the North Atlantic, but if there had been trawling in the Bering Sea and in the Aleutians things might have been very different. The most important sea fishery in Alaska is for cod, and the boats operate mostly from Kodiak, the Shumagin and Sanak Islands. The fish are not gutted at sea, so the fulmars have had to stick to squids, plankton, and other natural food. I regard this as corroborative evidence for the offal-theory of the spread of the Atlantic fulmar.

As St. George loomed ahead the numbers of other seabirds increased. Murres skittered and bounced from wave to wave until they were airborne, or, failing this, dived beneath our advancing bow. First there were dozens, then hundreds, then thousands. Puffins flew by, singly or in small groups; crested auklets and choochkies buzzed about in compact little flocks. With our binoculars we swept the water in the direction of Staraya Artil and were staggered by the traffic pouring out to sea from the big cliff. It is not an exaggeration to say that at one time a million birds were within sight.

When we dropped anchor the bidarrah put out from the town landing. In the old days bidarrahs (pronounced *bydars*) were made of sealskin, today of oilskin and canvas, but their design is the same —a long double-ended boat, rowed by a dozen Aleuts, who stand up like gondoliers as they man the long oars.* As the boat lifted and dropped on the swell, experienced Aleut hands assisted us down

* There are five of these traditional Aleut boats on St. George (where they are the only means of freight-handling) and three on St. Paul. One can carry a big dynamo, up to 5 American tons of machinery or 7 to 8 of cement or coal. Two lashed together can fetch a truck or pickup ashore.

from the deck of the *Penguin*. The light was fading when we got our gear ashore, paid our respects to the resident manager, and were assigned our beds.

We were invited next door for coffee and cakes, but Bill Cottrell begged to be excused; he needed sleep. On our return he said, "You won't have any trouble photographing the *foxes* on this island!" After he had undressed and crawled into bed a fox walked in the half-open door, came into the room, and brazenly tried to make off with one of his shoes. Here on St. George they had not been controlled; they had almost become a nuisance. We frequently saw them, next day. One seemed to be playing a game of tag with a six-year-old Aleut tot. When she tried to make friends the animal would wait until she was about five feet away and then run a few feet, keeping ever out of reach.

On St. George the foxes probably ate the seal carcasses that lay in livid, putrid rows in the fields, for this island, with only one-fifth the seal population of St. Paul, does not have a by-products plant. The carcasses lay where they were stripped, generating a prodigious stench and breeding swarms of big black flies. These carrion flies are absent on St. Paul; in fact, we saw few insects of any sort. Pribilof Islanders boast that they have no biting insects—no gnats, flies or mosquitoes—which make life at times almost intolerable elsewhere in the summer Arctic.

There seemed to be far more seabirds on St. George than on St. Paul. It was debatable which were more numerous, the murres or the choochkies; both probably ran into millions. On St. Paul the choochkies nest only under the loose boulders on the beaches, but here on St. George the biggest colonies were nearly a mile from the water on the broken rocky hillsides behind the town. Here they flew up from the volcanic rubble in dense clouds, like flocks of starlings. One of the men stationed at St. George once tried to estimate the number of choochkies in this great hillside colony and after sitting out there for several days, watching them come and go, decided that there were about 36,000,000. This is probably an exaggeration, but Ira Gabrielson vouches for the fact that there are millions. We did not get the impression of quite such numbers, although the murres on the northside cliffs certainly ran into millions. We spent most of our day on the south side of the island, where the birds though less numerous were more accessible. When we returned in the afternoon we heard a wren below the town. It was too late to go to the high northwest cliffs where the red-legged kittiwakes have their largest colonies and where a few "blue" fulmars are said to nest.

THE JUNE DAY in 1950 when I first met James, we visited a murre colony. That was at Stora Karlsö, an island off Gotland in the Baltic Sea. Here in the Pribilofs, more than halfway around the world, we found ourselves again among the murres. James would soon be flying home, and it occurred to me that if his plane were to head north over the pole and down the other side, his journey would be cut in half (4500 miles instead of 9000) and his flying time would be reduced to 18 hours or less, providing he did not talk the pilot into landing somewhere on the icecap for a look round.

The murres, ranging across both the North Atlantic and the North Pacific in their populous colonies might well be the most numerous water birds in the northern hemisphere (although Darwin—wrongly—nominated the fulmar and others have suggested the dovekie). Finnur, who had visited countless murre colonies, was very eager to get out to Walrus Island, a flat island of 75 or 80 acres, seven miles due east of St. Paul. Here, he said, was a murre colony unique in the world; whereas other colonies (except a few on the flat tops of stacks) were on cliff faces and steep rocks, the huge colony on Walrus was horizontal.

James boarded the plane on the 12th for the long flight back to England. Bill, Finnur, and I stayed another week. It was only a day or two after James's departure that Mr. Olson announced the *Penguin* would make a run to Walrus for a count of the sea lion herd. No one had been out there for about four years. Usually thick fog and heavy surf prevented landing, but today conditions seemed ideal. An hour's run took the *Penguin* to the lee side of the low island, where the captain dropped anchor while we scrambled into the large dory that was to take us ashore. A welcoming committee of sea lions came out to meet us; a pack of fifty paced the boat, and with heads high out of the water barked and protested. Like porpoises they leaped about us, surfacing now and then in groups of a dozen or more to look us over. "We might have to shoot our way in," the boatman quipped; and for a long moment it seemed no joke as the big animals churned the water to a boil. The big bulls on shore added to the confusion when they plunged off the rocks, close to our boat, their ton of blubber hitting the water with a great splash. Although these big northern sea lions are two to three times the weight of the fur seal bulls, they have a more benign temperament. There was no need to fear them as we walked along the shore and examined their pups. Ford Wilke counted nearly 4000 adults and pups in his walk around the island. Walruses no longer live on this island; to find these old men of the sea with the long tusks one must now go farther north.

Top billing in the great show on Walrus Island goes to the murres. As we advanced, a solid mass of birds, acres of them, receded reluctantly and closed in again after we had passed. Each bird stood erect, penguin-like, or squatted over its pyriform green egg or jostled with its neighbors for a few square inches of space. The air above was a blizzard of buzzing birds, bewildering, countless.

The Pribilof Islands lie in the belt of overlap of the two murres; and, so well documented are the islands during the last century, that we know there have been great fluctuations in the relative numbers of the two species. Maybe Finnur is right in thinking that in normal seasons the common murres tend to arrive on the ledges before the arctic murres, and take the best places, the great, broad, flat platforms—leaving the arctic birds to secure what is left, the smaller ledges at the edge of the cliffs. Perhaps in some seasons the arrival of the common murres may be delayed, and the arctic murres get to the big ledges first. But does this explain the extraordinary changes, that are nowhere better shown than on Walrus Island? These must surely reflect some ebb and flow more profound than that of the seasons. The pendulum has swung from nearly all arctic murres in 1872 and 1874 to perhaps midway in 1890; to nearly all arctic in 1901; to nearly all common in 1911 and 1914; to all, or nearly all, arctic in 1940; to nearly all common in 1953.

Consider the history: 1872 was the first year in which H. W. Elliott visited Walrus Island—on the 5th of July. He was ashore there again in July, 1874. In the archipelago generally he found the common murre "in comparatively no number whatever, not one being seen where a thousand of the [arctic murres] are visible at once."

And of the arctic murre he also wrote, "Walrus islet is fairly covered by them."

Next came William Palmer. He was ashore on Walrus twice in 1890. On the 13th of June he visited the western and northern parts of the island; he saw no common murres at all—all were arctics. Yet on the 7th of August, when he landed on the southeastern part, he found there all commons and no arctics.

"No such striking pecularity of distribution was noticed by our party," wrote F. A. Lucas after his visit in July, 1900, "nor were the California [common] murres much in evidence."

On the 7th of July, 1911, the late A. C. Bent went ashore. The situation was evidently reversed. "Among the many thousands of California murres with which the island was mainly populated," he wrote, "we noticed a few of the thick-billed Pallas's [arctic] murres." Similarly, on the 16th of July, 1914, E. A. Preble "noted that the breeding colonies on the higher central part of the island were principally of the [common] species."

When Dr. Ira Gabrielson visited Walrus on the 7th of July, 1940, he found the arctic murre to be in the majority. "There may have been some Californias [commons] present," he wrote, "but I did not detect more than one individual that could be surely identified as this species. I tried to make an estimate of the number of murres but finally gave it up after I found that even the most conservative estimate ran into the millions." We, on the other hand on the 15th of July, 1953, found the colony to be almost entirely common murres; we have the movies to prove it. In fact, I did not see a single arctic murre, although Bill Cottrell saw a few at the edge of the colony. As for numbers, Bill, after a quick appraisal, said he did not think there were more than 2,000,000 birds. That, admittedly, was a "guestimate." Finnur and I made a few sample density counts, then took the detailed ship charts of the island, plotted the occupied acreage, and by means of simple mathematics arrived at a figure of about 1,000,000. At any rate, there were a lot of birds.

A few tufted puffins nested under the boulders and faced us with a cold white eye and a razor-sharp beak when we investigated. There were also some crested auklets and choochkies. A small colony of glaucous-winged gulls seemed to be waxing fat on unguarded murre eggs. Completely surrounded by murres, a male red-faced cormorant brandished a bit of seaweed, like a sprig of parsley in his bill. He waved it about, bowed gallantly, went through his entire bag of tricks—for the benefit of the foolish murres, or me, I thought—until I noticed a female sitting among the boulders a few feet away. He was directing his attentions to her, but I'm afraid it was a lost cause; murres by the dozen constantly got in the way. There simply was not space enough on crowded Walrus Island for even one pair of cormorants to nest in peace.

As I watched the show I was reminded of a sketch that H. W. Elliott had made when he first visited Walrus, eighty-one Julys earlier. His drawing was a galaxy of oreels (red-faced cormorants), chikies (glaucous-winged gulls), baillie brushkies (paroquet auklets), canooskies (crested auklets), choochkies (least auklets), and arries (murres). All these had come alive in the seal islands, the climax of our odyssey; and this day at Walrus (alas, without James) was the high point.

Returning from Walrus, we stopped at Otter Island, a volcanic cinder cone with a perfect crater in its top. Unhappily, I had but one roll of color film left for what proved to be the best island of all from the photographer's point of view. Although only five miles south of St. Paul, it was rarely visited by the Aleuts, and the birds were far tamer than on either of the larger islands. Hair seals swam in the lagoons between the submerged ledges. We watched one mother playing delightfully with her small pup. Wrens were more numerous here; we heard at least half a dozen, and one almost sat on Finnur's shoe when he investigated a nest. The little foxes were even more fearless than they were on St. George. One followed Finnur about and patiently sat only a short distance away while Iceland's big but agile ornithologist clambered down among the rocks. Finnur selected a well-marked murre egg for the museum at Reykjavík and, carefully putting it at the top of the cliff, went down again for another. When he returned the egg was gone and so was the fox.

As we boarded the *Penguin* again, we were reminded of another famous sketch of Elliott's entitled "Seal's Breath Fog," for off the end of St. Paul Island the murky mist was beginning to close in. Our luck had held until we had seen all the Pribilofs at their sunny best. The unprecedented weather had run its course; but it didn't matter now.

36

Back Home

WE HAD WAVED GOODBYE to James as the Reeve airliner blew spurts of red lava dust among the yellow poppies of St. Paul's airfield. Within four days he was home, whisked halfway round the world on the magic carpet of the modern flying machine. Bill Cottrell, Finnur, and I caught next Sunday's flight out of St. Paul.

After we parted, James made two or three brief stops before taking final leave of America—he spent a day with Barbara on snow-capped Mount Rainier and a day on the hot July sands of Martha's Vineyard, where Eddie Chalif found him his six-hundredth bird (upland plover) and another for good measure (roseate tern). But his capacity to react had finally been exhausted. Barbara, who had grown up within sight of Rainier, reported to me later that the great mountain had never been more dramatic, filling her with emotion as the clouds finally parted from its summit. To James it was one more mountain; he had seen so much during the past few weeks

that he had grown weary. I could understand, for the letdown had
hit me too. Only twice on the long way home in August did my
pulse rate quicken: once when thousands of marbled godwits rose
in a cloud over the Bear River marshes, and once when David Con-
don, the Park naturalist of Yellowstone, showed me forty grizzly
bears one night at a secret place where they gather.

As I recrossed the continent by way of Great Salt Lake, the
Snake River, the Grand Tetons, the geyser basins of the Yellowstone,
the Black Hills, the Dakota Badlands and the wheat fields of the
plains, now in harvest, I repeatedly wished that James could have
had another month or two. He had skirted the perimeter of the continent; he had not seen the heart country—the breadth of Canada,
the northern Rockies, the Great Plains, the Great Lakes. Perhaps
there would be another time.*

In due time, his batteries recharged, James was able to turn his
thoughts again to Wild America.

NEW YORK sweltered in a temperature over ninety while I waited
four extra hours for the transatlantic airliner. My last seventeen cents
in my pocket clinked against an English half crown, which was now
meaningful after a hundred days. This was my last of America—for
the time being.

The children were bigger and browner. England was greener. My
desks at the office and at home were white with work. I unloaded
Wild America out of my bags—and began on something else. I
suspect Roger did just the same thing when he got home; piled his
notes in a drawer and forgot about them for several months. The
marathon trip had sunk us. It was not until late in the year that we
simultaneously surfaced and began airmailing thousands of words
to each other across the ocean. And here they are—some of them.

It is more than eighteen months now since I saw Wild America.
I have had time to think about it; to sort it out a bit; to let the
marvels settle down, as far as they can (not far). A copy of Roger's
movie keeps the journey alive. I have run it many times now, this
color film. It has interested millions on television, and twice packed

* Goodness me, I hope so.—J.F.

London's great Festival Hall. I still enjoy it as much as anybody else.

What did I bring home from America—what was the most important thing?

Was it the four hundred and one new birds, which more than doubled my life-list? For one glorious three-week period or so, before Roger could catch up, I had held the North American year-list record. It was wonderful fun. But it was not the most important thing brought home.

Was it the searing vision of the Grand Canyon—the world's end, humbling, awful, serene? Or was it the other climaxes of scenic possibility: Yosemite, Crater Lake? Or the biggest and oldest living things—forests that shrank me to a tiny monkey in an endless corridor of dim green light, mountains that lifted white snow to white cloud, blue ice to blue sky; or a child's dream of a million seals come true, among a million seabirds; the great American desert, with its mountain-islands and strange life; torrid Mexican heat; the California sun; coral islands; goose-tundra? I brought these home, too, in notes and photographs and memories; but they were not the most important things either. Not quite.

Was it North America's oldest human inhabitants, living their long quiet lives, away from the world, on the mesas of Arizona? Very nearly, but not quite.

Was it, then, North America's more recent human inhabitants? Yes. The New North Americans; and what they have done to North America, in a few hundred years, and what they have *not* done.

We Europeans who have not visited North Americans in their homes, read of them and see what the movies show us. Many of us get half a light on half a life—the dollar half: Rugged Individualism, Private Enterprise, Showmanship, Power Politics. We do not see so well the rugged altruism, the public spirit, the guardianship, the fair dealing of the American at home. Why should they talk of what they take for granted? They talk to us of their doubts and difficulties, of their troubles and quarrels, old and new. We see them (forgive us) more as brave warriors, daring fliers, successful sportsmen, gunmen, lovers, than as builders, scientists, husbandmen, husbands.

They show us too little of their earthly paradise, and publicize too little their determination to share it with wild nature. Perhaps they have forgotten that they had dedicated National Parks before we in England had even one little, local, private nature-protection society. Or perhaps they think that to tell of these things would arouse again our not-so-secret resentment at the boast that all that the Americans have is bigger and better, and all that they do is swifter and surer. But do we resent it? Maybe. "If you feel the way you say you do about what you've seen," said Roger, "you tell them, not me."

And this is what I have tried to do—to tell of Wild America, and say that never have I seen such wonders or met landlords so worthy of their land. They have had, and still have, the power to ravage it; and instead have made it a garden.

The Savile Club in London was an hour or less, through the traffic, from London airport; its bar was on the way home. I was taking my first drink in England, when Evarts Scudder, one of our many U.S. members, walked in. "What did you think of America?" he said.

I put on my most English voice, slapped him on the back, and said, "Actually, old boy, 's an incredible thing, you're just like *us.*"

Now I come to think of it, that was not much of a joke. It was no joke. I hope—I believe—that it is true, for both our sakes. We have so much to learn and so little time to learn it in.

Sometime later Herbert Agar brought a distinguished visitor into our club—one who was relaxing, after a strenuous campaign, with a tour of the world that made Roger's and mine look like a picnic. I was introduced to the great man. Proudly, and not to be out-traveled, I told him I had just been twenty or thirty thousand miles in his country.

"Good heavens," said Adlai Stevenson, "what were *you* running for?"

APPENDIX

AND

INDEX

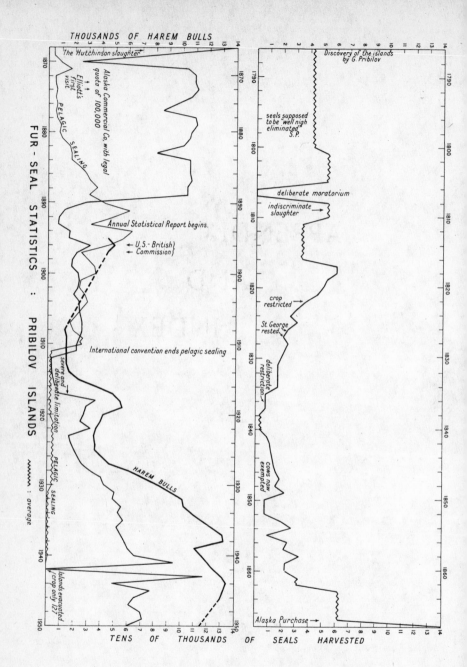

THOUSANDS OF HAREM BULLS

FUR - SEAL STATISTICS : PRIBILOV ISLANDS

~~~~~ : average

The "Hutchinson slaughter"

Elliott's first visit

Alaska Commercial Co., with legal quota of 100,000

PELAGIC SEALING

Annual Statistical Report begins.

← U.S.- British} Commission}

International convention ends pelagic sealing

severe and deliberate limitation

PELAGIC SEALING

HAREM BULLS

Islands evacuated, crop only 127

TENS OF THOUSANDS OF SEALS HARVESTED

Discovery of the islands by G. Pribilov

seals supposed to be "well nigh eliminated" S.P.

deliberate moratorium

indiscriminate slaughter

crop restricted

St George rested

deliberate restriction

cows now exempted

Alaska Purchase →

Appendix

History of the Fur Seal Herds

EVER SINCE the islands were discovered by the Russians, statistics on the fur seal herds have been available. Naturally these have varied in accuracy, and some can never be checked. Most important are the records of the annual commercial kill; and of the actual size of the herd on the two islands, or parts of them (e.g., certain rookeries), or elements of them (harem bulls, idle bulls, cows, pups, etc.). The most reliable figures are those of the kill. Since the purchase of Alaska by the United States from Russia in July, 1867, these have been fairly reliable, and since about 1906 completely reliable. Ever since the islands were discovered there have been guesses of the total population on the beaches, or of breeding seals and young, or of breeding seals. These have ranged from about 4000 (an exaggeratedly low and incorrect estimate in what was certainly a low year, 1836) to about 5,000,000 (one of the guesses in 1867). Serious efforts were made to estimate the total population scientifically by Elliott in

1873–74 (3,193,420), and 1890 (959,393), and by the United States–British Commission in 1897 (402,850). In 1904–6 and from 1909 onwards, the resident officials of the U.S. Fish Commission and its successor, the U.S. Fish and Wildlife Service, have published an annual computation, giving a figure for the total population on both islands, broken down into all its elements (pups, cows, harem bulls, idle bulls, surplus bulls, and nonbreeding females and males of each age group). These attempts at computation were certainly most successful when the total population was low. In the early years of the present century, the total population (including pups) was at its lowest during the American administration. It was probably below 200,000 from 1906 through 1911; in this last year it was computed at only 123,600, with but 1356 harem bulls, 232 idle bulls, and 41,420 pups. The only statistics based on direct observation were those figures of harem bulls, idle bulls, and pups, but since about 1922, when the pup population exceeded 150,000 annually, direct counts of these became no longer possible. Dr. Colin Bertram, Director of the Scott Polar Research Institute at Cambridge, England, and a world expert on seals, stated after his visit to the Pribilofs in 1949 that "the annually published computation, despite small textual disclaimers, has suggested to the world a knowledge of the composition of the herd which goes far beyond what is proven. The fact is that successful management has produced a herd so large that it cannot be counted by any method so far devised."

Certainly the figures for the total population published in the 1930's and 1940's, which reached a peak of 3,386,008 in 1946, were based on assumptions, which were unjustified, of the continued rate of increase of elements in the herd. The revised and very careful estimate of Karl W. Kenyon, Victor B. Scheffer, and Douglas Chapman for the total population in 1950, including pups, must be nearer the truth than any made in years. They gauged approximately 1,700,-000. This included about 12,000 harem bulls, 4000 idle bulls, 500,000 adult cows, 500,000 pups. The rest consisted of virgin females and immature males, including the 59,921 holluschickie that were killed on their hauling grounds in 1950. The half-million pups were less than half the figure computed by the previous method, which took no account of the possibility of "saturation" of the beaches and a difference in mortality on crowded beaches. By the previous method of computation the population was thought to have doubled in the past twenty years; in fact, it probably reached a peak in the mid-thirties and since then has remained fairly constant. Since nearing this peak the incidence of hookworm among the pups has become more serious, so much so that some of the advisers to the Fish and Wildlife Service believe that no further substantial increase will be possible until a method of controlling it is found.

It is worth plotting on a graph the annual harvest of these seals from the islands, and from the seas, as far as we know them (see graph). Pelagic sealing was prohibited by international convention in 1911. Since 1895 figures for harem numbers have been available, and these have been added, too.

Probably the Russian sealers in the first three decades of their work took too many, too indiscriminately, in their greed and hurry, though they do not appear to have averaged much more than 40,000 skins a year. Their governor, General Resanof, arrived in Alaska in 1805 and stopped sealing altogether for the next two years, and on St. Paul for two more years after that. But the sealers went back to indiscriminate slaughter, and a decline began in the 1820's from which the herd scarcely recovered, for forty years or more, in spite of restrictions and regulations in the 1820's and 1830's, and the total exemption of cows in 1847. After reaching bottom in the late 1830's, when only between 6000 and 7000 were annually taken, the average annual crop crept up from about 13,000 in the 1840's to about 19,000 in the 1850's. The Russians seem to have looked after the herd very intelligently, and the Aleut islanders still use today the methods of driving and killing devised by their Russian masters a hundred and fifty years ago. But they killed too many.

There are three different versions of the size of the harvest of seals in 1868, the first season after the Alaska Purchase. Before any sort of a planning organization could take charge, a group of entrepreneurs, of whom the most important was H. M. Hutchinson, took a crop variously recorded as 140,000, 242,000, and 365,000. The first of these, which is the only one that appears to be within the bounds of possibility, is the largest total ever recorded from the islands; the next largest was the 117,164 taken in 1943, by a secret party put ashore when the islands were within bombing range of the Japanese base on Kiska (in 1942 the islands were evacuated on military order on June 16, when only 127 skins had been taken).

The big crop of 1868 was followed by smaller ones in the next two years; but in the next two decades, the 1870's and 1880's, the Alaska Commercial Company (headed by Hutchinson), who gained the concession, took just about what was then the legal limit of 100,000 every year. In the second of these decades commercial pelagic sealing increased fivefold to 40,000 skins a year or more. The resultant collapse, when it came in the 1890's, pulled the island crop down for a time to under 8000 a year, and the total population, by estimate of the United States–British Commission, to under the half million. The great herd was at its lowest ebb. Pelagic sealing went on; indeed at least 61,838 Pribilof fur seals were taken at sea in 1894, about four times as many as on the islands.

International discussions, no doubt aided by the fact that at that time the Russian and Japanese herds were also decreasing, resulted in the International Convention of 1911. In exchange for a skin royalty for the other countries from the Pribilofs, the United States had the pelagic killing stopped. Cows and young bulls had been slaughtered alike in this wasteful killing. Many sank when shot; only those that floated became statistics!

The recovery of the herd dates from the 1911 Convention; it is as fine a proof as one could wish of human power to protect and cherish animals by national control. The harem count on the islands in the middle 1890's, the worst years of pelagic sealing, was about 4500. By 1908 it was down to 1303, the lowest on record since harems were counted. From the date of the Convention (1911) the recovery (see graph) was continuous, with one lapse. From 1912 to 1917 there was severe and deliberate limitation of the crop to what was needed by the islanders for food (only 2045, 2406, 2735, 3947, 6466, 8169 in these successive years). In 1918 the crop was allowed to be 34,890, and until 1922 was not less than 23,685. This was a mistake; the Commission had relaxed too soon. The mistake was corrected. The graph shows well the overreaching of 1918–22, and its consequent effect (after a short delay) on the number of harems. The Commission did not make the same mistake again. By 1932 the harems were over 10,000 and the crop back to 50,000, and neither has fallen below since, except for the wobble in the crop take due to the evacuation of 1942 and the especially big harvest of 1943.

The figures strongly suggest that the islands carry an optimum population of 11,000 or 12,000 harems, and can produce a crop of 60,000 to 70,000 skins. Maybe the Russians held the islands at their optimum for some years after they discovered them; and apparently the Alaska Commercial Company did so between the Alaska Purchase in 1867 and 1889, though the figures suggest that the crash at the turn of the century may have been due to overcropping on the islands as well as at sea. The island herd took five decades to recover from the Russian crash of the 1820's, and four decades to recover from the American crash of the 1890's. There is no reason why there should ever be another crash, and some hope that a new optimum population may be reached if the hookworm is overcome. Presumably if this disease is conquered, and no other takes its place, the food supply within the cows' swimming range of the islands will control the population. There is certainly room for more seals on the beaches, for many old rookery sites are not now inhabited.

INDEX